Modern Newspaper Editing

4TH
EDITION

4TH
EDITION

Modern Newspaper Editing

GENE GILMORE

IOWA STATE UNIVERSITY PRESS / AMES

GENE GILMORE has worked as an editor on papers ranging from the *Alma* (Michigan) *Record* (circulation 3,600) to the *Los Angeles Times* (circulation 1,043,000). He also has worked for the *Rochester* (New York) *Times-Union,* the *Portland* (Maine) *Press-Herald,* the *Syracuse Post-Standard,* the *Champaign-Urbana* (Illinois) *Courier,* the *Riverside* (California) *Press-Enterprise,* the *San Diego Evening Tribune,* the *Philadelphia Bulletin,* the *Washington Post* and Reuters. For seven years he was wire editor of the prize-winning *Gazette & Daily* in York, Pennsylvania. He started teaching in 1957 at Syracuse University and was on the journalism faculty at the Urbana campus of the University of Illinois from 1963 to 1986. His degrees are from the University of Michigan and Syracuse.

© 1971 The Glendessary Press, Inc., Berkeley, California, first edition through five printings

© 1976, 1983 Boyd and Fraser Publishing Co., San Francisco, California, second and third editions

© 1990 Iowa State University Press, Ames, Iowa 50010
All rights reserved

Manufactured in the United States of America.

∞ This book is printed on acid-free paper.

Fourth edition, 1990

TO VIRGINIA

Library of Congress Cataloging-in-Publication Data

Gilmore, Gene.
    Modern newspaper editing / Gene Gilmore.—4th ed.
      p. cm.
    Includes bibliographical references.
    ISBN 0-8138-0174-5
    1. Journalism—Editing. I. Title.
  PN4778.G5   1990
  070.4′1—dc20
                                        89-24728
                                            CIP

CONTENTS

Foreword   vii
Preface   ix

1. News Editing Today and Tomorrow   3
2. Editing the Copy   18
3. Word Watching   33
4. The Basics of Printing   44
5. Writing Headlines   54
6. Designing the Pages   75
7. The Editor and Journalistic Writing   105
8. Evaluating the News   120
9. Editing Wire News   136
10. The Subeditors   149
11. Picture Editing: The Art Show   162
12. Imagination in News Editing   180
13. News Crises and Edition Changes   196
14. The Law and the Copy Editor   205
15. Ethics for Journalists   223
16. Problems of Policy   236
17. Editorial Management   248
18. Newspaper Research   258
19. The Future of Editing   271

Glossary   281
Bibliography   299
Index   303

FOREWORD

IF YOU WANT TO BE A GREAT EDITOR, you're already late.

You'll have to hustle to learn all you can about everything from IBM and ICBMs to SMSAs and SEATO. Think fast, if you want to reflect on the "brave new world" of artificial hearts, fresh-frozen human embryos, and the effort to short-circuit the gene that makes you fat.

The pace really picks up in the newsroom, where there's never enough time to double-check the facts in a story, assure its balance, streamline the lead, sharpen the language, review it for libel, slap on a snappy headline, and squeeze it into a too-small hole with only minutes to go before deadline.

That's why today's editor, even before taking that first newsroom job, must be well informed on the widest variety of subjects and highly skilled in the fundamentals of the craft.

Knowing the basics is not enough. A sensitive and sensible journalist is the product of on-the-job seasoning—a sometimes treacherous rite that tests stamina, self-discipline, dedication, and judgment.

There are no shortcuts in the making of a journalist, but this book comes close, in a brisk and concise style that conveys the skills working editors call upon every day.

But this is more than a how-to book. By emphasizing such issues as fairness, impartiality, public service, and good taste, Gene Gilmore sets a standard that will serve anyone from a junior reporter at a county-seat weekly to the occupant of a network anchor chair.

Though he acknowledges candidly that the realities of the business often put editors on a collision course with compromise, he observes that "the realistic goal for the ethical journalist is to compromise as little as possible, for being pragmatic is not the same as being venal or cowardly."

But compromise, says Gilmore, doesn't apply to the pursuit of excellence: "The best editors aim high, and therefore hit higher than those who aim low."

That's what he taught my classmates and me nearly two decades ago at the University of Illinois. So far, his advice has worked fine.

Alan D. Mutter
Former assistant managing editor of the *San Francisco Chronicle*

PREFACE

ALL PEOPLE AT ONE TIME OR ANOTHER work as editors. They edit their letters, their reports, and what they say. News reporters, of course, edit their own stories glowing on VDT screens. Many of those reporters eventually will spend a good part of their careers as editors, for increasingly newsrooms for print or broadcast require large numbers of people skilled in selecting stories and graphic material, tightening language, assigning reporters, and developing story ideas.

Newspaper design once required little time. Now editors work hours to get the right pictures, the proper color, and a pleasing variety of type blocks onto the pages. Television editors long ago only spliced film and a reporter read the news, not much of a change from radio. Now TV editors must collect tape from a dozen places, including files, to piece together a 60- or 90-second story. Sometimes the reporter is not even seen. These changes have brought increased job opportunities for young journalists.

The shifts in journalism have occurred so gradually that few have detected them. A look at radio, television, and newspapers twenty years ago would show that often news is presented more thoroughly now, with better explanation and with more intelligent selection than ever. Much of the public responds to this quality, for the best newspapers have been among the most successful financially. Topflight radio news programs are available, and television network news usually gives a good digest of a day's news. All is not glorious, certainly. Many readers want frivolous publications or broadcasts, filled with forgettable snippets about TV and rock stars, gossip, and oddities.

Despite the dispiriting quality of some journalism, students should know that there is a large demand for enterprising and resourceful writers and editors. Much of the public requires facts and careful analysis of events to function in their work. Journalism needs people with skeptical attitudes and reflective minds who can provide that kind of analysis.

Students preparing for satisfying journalism careers will strive to develop writing and editing skills, to learn much about their world, to note society's changes, and to ponder how they may use their talents to help inform the public.

A sad personal note must be added. The first edition of this book was written by Robert Root of Eisenhower College and me. Root died before that edition could be printed. Fortunately, many of his ideas and insights remain in this fourth edition.

Acknowledgments

Preparation of a book like this requires the assistance of many people and many publications. The help includes little tips, reviews of chapters, and solid information. I am grateful for the advice.

Most of the help came from University of Illinois colleagues: Richard L. Hildwein, Kevin Barnhurst, Michael Smeltzer, Louis Liebovich, Brian Johnson, and Steven Helle. Former colleagues John Schacht and Lynn Slovonsky helped with previous editions.

My thanks also go to Ralph Otwell, former editor of the *Chicago Sun-Times;* Lee Hughes of the Chicago bureau of the Associated Press; William Kelly, chief photographer, and William Parker, photo editor, of the *Chicago Tribune;* Jane Peppard, research director of the *St. Petersburg Times;* Ronald Kuzoian, research director of the *Boston Globe;* John Timberlake, former research director of the *Chicago Tribune;* and Perry Williams, research director of the *Dallas Morning News;* John Lemmon, managing editor of the *Baltimore Evening Sun;* and Curt Beamer and John Dixon of the *Champaign-Urbana* (Illinois) *News-Gazette.*

Articles in *Columbia Journalism Review, Editor & Publisher, Quill,* and *Journalism Quarterly* provided information on news judgment, technology, legal issues, ethics, photography, and research. The *St. Louis Post-Dispatch* offered special pictures.

I am indebted to my wife Virginia, who read the manuscript with care and made valuable suggestions.

Perhaps most of my gratitude goes to hundreds of students both at the University of Illinois and Syracuse University. They showed me the steps needed to develop into competent editors.

Modern Newspaper Editing

4TH

EDITION

1

News editing
today and tomorrow

WHEN HE WAS PRESIDENT, John F. Kennedy described what an editor should be. In a speech at the University of North Carolina he said the press needed people "educated in the liberal traditions, willing to take the long look, undisturbed by prejudices and slogans of the moment, who attempt to make an honest judgment on difficult events." Such people, he added, "could distinguish the real from the illusory, the long range from the temporary, the significant from the petty."

These stiff requirements will always mean a shortage of ideal editors. If the democratic society is to function properly, however, it must have a sizable number of editors who come close to the ideal. Many of the highly qualified professionals at the close of the century will be men and women who today are journalism students or beginning journalists.

Because journalism professionals rise rapidly, the responsibilities of executive positions may come early. The city editor on a major newspaper can be a person younger than thirty. Sometimes the news editor on a quality, medium-sized paper is barely thirty. Higher administrative positions like managing editor or executive editor often come well before middle age. Increasingly, women are taking some of these key posts. If the journalists are to approach the qualities cited by President Kennedy, they must learn the skills of the reporter and copy editor rapidly and well. Rarely can a person leap into an executive position without solid preparation as a writer and editor. Nor should anyone wish to make that leap unprepared.

The ideal editor has been a reporter of various worlds: politics, government, social welfare, labor, and business. The reporter has followed such experience with a period of editing—working to improve the copy of others. Then the young journalist may be ready for the moves to city, state, or wire editor; then to news editor, managing editor, and, eventually, editor.

To grow professionally, young news people must learn each job well. They prepare for positions of greater responsibility by combining observation, reading, listening, discussion, writing, and introspection. They look about the newsroom and around their city to see how jobs are done and how they might be done better. They read about what they cannot observe firsthand. They open their minds by listening to others who report how the job has been done and how it should be done. They sharpen ideas and challenge each other's thoughts in discussions with professionals inside and outside of journalism. They examine themselves to recognize and reduce their shortcomings.

Men and women at every level of journalism usually find satisfaction in helping to inform thousands and possibly millions of people about vital public affairs. Magazines, books, radio, television, and word-of-mouth contribute, but much of what ordinary citizens know about current problems they have learned through the work of newspaper editors.

To meet this responsibility to the reader, editors at all levels must be thorough and painstaking. This is particularly difficult on daily newspapers or on radio/television news programs because there is little time to examine issues with scholarly thoroughness. In recent years, however, the better newspapers often have put less emphasis on speed. They have been willing to hold up a story for an edition or two, or even a day or more, until additional facts can be gathered. These papers make every effort to give reporters time to get the complete story so readers will not be misled by superficial information. Television also is willing to spend three or four minutes on a major story, blending graphics, voices, and pictures to provide a reasonably complete report. National Public Radio with its "Morning Edition" and "All Things Considered" offers detailed information. So does the "McNeil-Lehrer News Hour" on PBS.

Emphasis changing

Any news operation that strives to be thorough and honest risks antagonizing sizable blocs of people. Many readers want soothing news that ruffles no one, even when the community is plagued by severe problems or rampant injustices.

Note how disturbed many people get about a military plant closing, a modest tax increase, or some air pollution control. Journalists who report details on such subjects are bound to create enemies. Sometimes, of course, the honest journalist prints or broadcasts details of shady practices by prominent persons. Quite often those persons can arrange retribution. Some firms may quit their advertising; circulation may dip; and libel suits may be filed. The paper may successfully resist attacks, but the price in lost revenue and legal fees may be steep.

This kind of retribution or pressure rarely works against well-established and profitable papers. But the little weekly or the daily with competition may be hurt badly.

As an example, the *New London* (Connecticut) *Day* ran a series of stories on production problems at the local Electric Boat Company, which builds submarines. The company didn't like the series. It canceled its classified advertising with the paper. That meant a $10,000 yearly loss. The company also refused to talk to *Day* reporters, thus further harassing the newspaper. In another case, arsonists burned the plant of the *Mountain Eagle,* a feisty little paper in Kentucky. Other examples could be cited.

History shows that deep anger or even hysteria erupts periodically in the nation. In the McCarthy era of the late forties and fifties, a great fear of communism almost paralyzed the country. Newspapers that called for calm and a faith in democracy were denounced as communist publications. During the height of debate of Vietnam war policy in the late sixties and early seventies, many newspapers, editors, and reporters were vilified for questioning government decisions. Some of the attacks came from the White House itself. Those assaults did not seem to cause financial loss, but they often meant serious personal distress. No one knows when the next emotional binge will occur.

Pressures of these kinds, national and local, may seem remote to the young journalist, but they will soon appear. One must prepare to meet them confidently. Beginners practice reporting, writing, and editing, so they also might practice reacting to bribes—labeled gifts. And what would one do if a story should cost the paper an advertising contract? What if a group of furious business leaders descended on the office? What if someone called from the White House or city hall to complain about an editorial? Unfortunately, most journalists have not prepared for such occurrences, and the first one can be unnerving. To become a capable and trusted editor, the professional must learn to resist pressures with confidence and skill.

Cable television

The last decade has seen cable television become an important news source, with millions of people getting some of their news from a cable channel. Some publishers and other entrepreneurs are experimenting with a system in which viewers, by tapping a few buttons, may "call up" on their television screens certain information, such as baseball scores and election results, at any time of the day or night. Cable contributes to the glut of information poured out by newspapers, television, and radio. Some observers fear that the public, bombarded by news, pays little attention to any of it.

Others have wondered if computers will not virtually eliminate human editors. The computer has swept through American newspaper plants, scattering typewriters, Linotype machines, pencils, paste pots, and copy paper. Reporters write on keyboards linked to computers. Editors work at similar devices, and computers, indirectly, "set type" on a strip of paper. The computer can be programmed to write simple stories and provide information on a certain mix of stories. It reviews the number of stories in type and tells an editor how many inches of type are available.

So far, however, there is no indication that the computer can gather information, write it in fresh ways, and edit the material with all the subtle intelligence that the human brain can provide. But it is possible that in years to come the stolid and unimaginative reporter or editor, who does everything routinely, quite likely could be replaced by a computer.

Computers in perspective

The new technology can be so dazzling that the casual student may assume that the computer will make judgments, write most stories and headlines, and determine the layout of the paper. A closer inspection, however, may lead to these four observations:

1. Major technological changes are unlikely. The computer has revolutionized newspaper production, but experts generally agree that developments from now on will refine current technology. Newspapers already have computer capacity to handle most typesetting and even some information retrieval, such as getting material from their libraries.

2. Most newspapers could improve without more machines. Some people become entranced by technology and think that every word or calculation must be handled by a computer. They neglect simpler and cheaper methods? How many newspapers today make more than a minimal effort to collect facts that are not readily available? How many will spend the money, with present hands and equipment, to dig hard for information? In getting full information on a story, newspapers should first use money and people to check their own libraries, phone the public library, interview widely, and send queries to press services. When these elementary methods to obtain information prove inadequate, more sophisticated (and expensive) retrieval should be considered.

3. The computer can be a great aid for the working editor. If automated machinery is unlikely to emerge soon as the newsroom master, it can be a helpful servant. For example, even the experienced human brain is harassed in keeping track of the competing stories on a complex news day. But just as airline and hotel reservations become instantly available by pressing a computer key, the whole array of world, national, state, and local stories can be quickly recalled for human evaluators.

4. Human editorial judgment will remain essential to great newspapers. In this generation, it seems improbable that a robot will be created that can select and display news as well as a seasoned editor. Editing is less of a science than an art. Until computers can successfully make subtle distinctions in word choice, they will not be able to pull together into editorial choices all the variables that, consciously and subconsciously, mold the fine decisions required of editors.

An understanding of the complexity of news has advanced along with automation. Traditionally, the aim of journalism has been expressed in three parts: to inform, to guide, and to entertain. While those goals still serve well enough for a quick rule of thumb, modern editors have to weigh the news with at least nine purposes in mind, giving an edge one time to the serious, another time to the frivolous.

Goals for journalists

1. To inform. Transmitting the bare facts to people remains a major goal. Readers want, as fast as possible and in greater detail than broadcasting gives, the facts of life, such as stock quotations, ball scores, election results, and contest winners.

2. To alert. As watchmen, sentries, and runners have for ages brought vital news to leaders, the media of a democracy today alert readers to what they need to know. To assume that the headline-skimmer is uninformed is an oversimplification. For example, over a few weeks home owners may note several headlines on house sales or mortgage rates and barely glance at the stories; yet they are alerted to trends that are important if they ponder selling or renting. Even the lack of war headlines from an area may indicate to the reader that little fighting is going on.

3. To interpret. While the objective newspaper tradition of conveying only facts is still strong, for at least a generation editors have been emphasizing the need for interpretation. The facts alone may lie or distort. Someone must put them into perspective. To illustrate, a Washington reporter may learn that a federal program for the poor has been eliminated quietly. But perhaps its end was contemplated when work was undertaken by another department sometime earlier. What is needed is an interpretation of what all government departments are attempting to do about poverty.

4. To educate. Some editors would argue that education is the same as interpretation, but others would say journalism has nothing to do with education. It is true that many interpretative stories — for example, on urban problems or on measures to overcome poverty — aim to convey an accurate picture of a situation, which is teaching. But many features besides interpretative stories, such as medical columns, science cartoon strips, and income tax pointers, are printed primarily as education. The "Newspaper in the Classroom" seminars sponsored by universities in cooperation with the American Newspaper Publishers Association underline these educational potentialities. One newspaper critic, W. H. Ferry, goes so far as to suggest that the whole purpose of the press is educational: "My view is that mass-comm's social and cultural responsibilities are those of the largest and probably most influential educational system any society has known."[1]

5. To lead. Newspapers inevitably lead, intentionally or not. The presentation of news leads readers to think and act about some things rather than others. A paper that emphasizes crime, scandal, and sex directs readers' attention to such subjects. A more serious paper, with

1. W. H. Ferry and Harry S. Ashmore, *Mass Communications* (Santa Barbara, Calif.: Center for the Study of Democratic Institutions, 1966), 10.

a diet of more important civic issues, directs community concern by establishing the agenda of discussion. Too often journalists think of their leadership role as confined largely to the editorial page. In fact, headlines probably are more important in making both opinion leaders and ordinary voters sort out the vital issues. The Hutchins Commission on Freedom of the Press in 1947 noted that one requirement of the press is to present and clarify the goals and values of society.

6. To persuade. While persuading is, of course, like leading, there can be static leadership that merely points a direction for concern, as thorough coverage of a pickpocket epidemic would direct attention to solving the problem. But there is also persuasive leadership, which includes arguing and cajoling to get citizens to act. This is a normal function of a good editorial page. When a newspaper crusades, as it might by printing numerous stories on pollution, it is using facts to persuade.

7. To provide a forum. The letters-to-the-editor page is the most obvious platform for different points of view. But a well-edited paper aims to report all important shades of opinion on major issues. One evil of the press in an authoritarian country is that the news presents only the official line, a monolithic view. Most American papers could do a better job by giving a greater range of opinion instead of sticking to the popular or the view held by the community's power structure.

8. To inspire. When journalists speak of "inspirational messages," they usually are facetious, even though some of their work does inspire readers. A good editorial stimulates rededication. Even the news sections should contain some stories less important for their information and interpretation than for the bravery, courage, determination, or love they portray.

9. To entertain. Obviously cartoons and gossip columns provide entertainment, but human interest stories and feature pieces entertain as well as inform. Life is not all drab, as the serious and often gloomy news may imply, and editors should give their readers the amusing, the witty, and the whimsical.

Gatekeeping

The editor who puts out a paper that intelligently fulfills all these varied functions is a major figure in the community and in society. The term *gatekeeper* has been coined by some researchers to emphasize the editor's importance at a cutoff point where the decision is made to stop some items, to let a trickle of other news through, or to permit the flow of a story judged as important. Years ago Dr. David Manning White, then of Virginia Commonwealth University, analyzed the reasons a wire editor gave for rejecting copy and found them "highly subjective," colored by personal experiences and attitudes.

All the research in this area supports White's findings in deciding what news gets into the paper and what gets discarded. One researcher, the late Dr. Walter Gieber of San Francisco State University, observed, "News is what newspapermen make it."[2] How do the editors make their decisions? Why do they disagree so vigorously on what is news? We clearly need to know more about what influences gatekeepers, and gatekeepers need to analyze more carefully what influences their decisions. Society could use more editors who can attain maximum objectivity, who understand readers' needs, and who can produce newspapers to meet those needs.

Newspapers of quality

The emphasis on quality editors may seem to say that a news operation need hire only competent people and the customers will flock to buy or watch the product. That is rarely the case. The production and sale of anything good usually take time, so much time that editors trying to do a conscientious job become discouraged. The paper's sales may stay small, while a third-rate paper gains circulation. In other cases, a newspaper staff may spend a great deal of energy, resourcefulness, and money to get some outstanding stories, then find that few people bother to read them.

Rather than become needlessly discouraged, editors must ask themselves in such cases if they have done as good a job as they thought. Perhaps they had overestimated the readers' knowledge. Were the stories really easy to grasp? Were the editors expecting that a story or two would bring quick reaction in circulation figures? Was the news displayed so the reader could hardly avoid the stories? Or was the paper so deadly serious, so lacking in any humor or sprightliness, that people found it ponderous and tedious?

If editors with high standards are sometimes discouraged, they often can find cheer. Thoughtful people in the community, sometimes called "the creative minority," frequently will praise the coverage of local, national, and world events. Public officials may mutter harsh words, but they usually will work better when they are aware that what they do is scrutinized carefully but fairly. The business community is especially responsive because advertisers like to put their ads in carefully read newspapers.

What the public wants

Sometimes newspapers employ organizations that survey readership to "find out what the people want." Some successful editors suspect such surveys because people often consciously or subconsciously misrepresent their beliefs. They also are skeptical of surveys because people tend to like what they are accustomed to. If they have been taking a quality paper for years, they tend to like quality. If they have been handed a diet of comics, agony columns, and other fluff for years, they will find quality hard to digest.

---

2. Walter Gieber, "News Is What Newspapermen Make It," in *People, Society, and Mass Communications,* ed. Lewis Dexter and David White (Glencoe, Ill.: The Free Press, 1964), 173–82.

Editors who have drawn the greatest praise in the nation — people like Joseph Pulitzer, John S. Knight, Katherine Graham, Adolph Ochs, E. W. Scripps — have had concrete ideas on what a newspaper should be. They produced that kind of paper, and their journalism was successful, both commercially and professionally.

Editors who turn out "what the public wants" usually produce an insignificant paper. Believing that the public is bored by anything important, they fill their papers with the trite and the trivial. This formula was enormously profitable in the past. Circulations skyrocketed late in the nineteenth century on a news formula of love, lust, and lucre. The technique started to fade in the early thirties, and today it is usually the serious, thoughtful, and penetrating newspaper that shows the best gains in circulation, advertising, and influence.

The most spectacular circulation increase in the last thirty years has been made by the *Wall Street Journal,* a newspaper with three detailed, socially significant stories on the front page each day, plus several valuable minor stories and, of course, full financial reports. Its circulation, about two million, is the biggest in the nation.

Other serious newspapers have grown, and the more literate magazines at least have maintained circulation. Dozens of special interest magazines flourish. The Public Broadcasting Service draws 20 percent of viewers to its best television programs. Frivolous publications and TV programs still are with us but, in the main, quality is being demanded by an increasing number of Americans. An exception to the demand for quality can be cited in the circulation success of *USA Today,* a paper that only skims the news.

The new devices

Around 1965 it was fairly easy to describe the operations of the copydesk. Stories came on paper from reporters and the wire services. With a pencil, an editor corrected errors, sometimes shortened a story, and tried to improve the language. A headline was written, either typewritten or in longhand, and story and head were sent by a pneumatic tube to the composing room, where printers would set the stories and headlines into type.

No newspaper still functions that way. All of them have joined the technical revolution. Manual typewriters and pneumatic tubes are gone, pencils are used sparingly, and paper does not litter every desk. (See Fig. 1.1.) Today the newsroom is dotted with computer terminals, where reporters write their stories at computer keyboards. As they type, their words appear on the video display terminal (VDT) in front of them. If they don't like what they write, the press of a button takes it away. The reporter wishing to rephrase a sentence taps a few keys and the change is made. When the story is finished two or three more keys are pressed and the words leave the screen, resting inside a computer until the copy editor "calls up" the story for editing. (See Figs. 1.2 and 1.3.)

The copy editor touches a few keys and imprecise words or errant letters disappear and better words are inserted. A sentence can be eliminated or the lead changed. When the story is fixed properly, a

1.1. The old. The *Chicago Tribune* copydesk and newsroom looked like this in 1927. Note the formality of dress. (© Copyrighted, Chicago Tribune Company, all rights reserved, used with permission.)

headline can be typed onto the screen. All the words then are swept off the screen to appear on a strip of paper, almost instantaneously, in the composing room. That strip can be pasted, with a dozen other strips, onto a sheet of paper the size of a newspaper page. The sheet is photographed and a page plate is made. The plate, along with perhaps sixty others, is put on the press and the paper is printed.

Perhaps strangely, computers don't speed newsroom operations. They even take a little more time than the paper-and-pencil method,

1.2. Today's newsroom. The *Atlanta Constitution.*

for an editor can cut out or insert words more quickly with a pencil. The saving is in the composing room, and a mighty big saving it is. Not so long ago it took a Linotype operator about an hour to set a column of type. Some technical advances cut that time moderately. The latest equipment requires almost no time to set type — and almost no workers to do it.

The new devices can perform some of the tedious jobs once done on the desk, and on some tasks save a little newsroom time. No longer do copy editors have to figure out the length of the story or keep score on how much type has been sent to the composing room; the computer can do that. And if editors forget what one story is about, a couple of key punches on the VDT will refresh their memories, as the story once more leaps onto the screen.

But whether the copy editor uses a VDT key or a lead pencil, the job is basically the same. The task is to correct misspelled words, alter language, cut out redundancies, trim away surplus wording, or insert facts until the story is concise, accurate, factual, and appealing to the reader.

To attain this result the editor needs to combine an interest in the English language with an understanding of reporting, some knowledge of printing processes, a reasonably broad education, and a clear understanding of the newspaper's policy.

The path of copy

Regardless of the method of handling copy, all desks operate about the same way. They edit material from three, four, or five subeditors. (The term *subeditor* is descriptive but not much used in U.S. newsrooms. In Britain, however, a subeditor is a copy editor.) The city editor sends copy from city reporters. The state editor provides stories about events from the paper's circulation area outside the city. The wire editor delivers copy selected from wire services. Some papers have a suburban editor, who transmits news and features from the suburbs. The biggest papers have a foreign editor and, if so, the wire editor becomes the national editor.

In the paper-and-pencil days, copy editors encircled their chief, who sat in what was called the *slot*. The chief, naturally, became the *slot person*. Copy editors needed to be near to get paper copy from the slot and, after editing, to hand it back. Those editors sat on the *rim* of the horseshoe-shaped desk — or desks shoved near one another — and were called *rim persons*. The slot person had a key function at the hub of a wheel, and the rim persons were junior or subordinate to the slot. Modern usage keeps the terms rim and slot as if both positions were still physically tied together.

The electronic newsroom needs no such proximity, although copy editors still work close to one another. Nothing is handed to people on the rim. Copy floats about in the computer, and a copy editor could be a mile away from the slot, getting any instructions typed on top of stories. The slot may write instructions this way:

< hot story. read with care >

The message inside the special brackets would not appear in type. The slot also may type in a special blank space that the story should be 12.5 inches. The copy editor then reduces the story to that amount. Almost certainly the slot would order a certain size headline and the editor would write the assigned *head*.

If the copy editor runs across some mystifying facts in a story, a query can be typed atop the story and the whole thing can be sent back to the slot, who probably will send it to a subeditor, who may send it to the reporter who wrote it. All of this will be done by wire, with no paper or voices used.

Editorial teamwork takes place as a unit on medium and large newspapers. All local, state, and wire copy crosses the desk or group of desks of this editorial unit. Because stories from all three sources come from everywhere, the desk is called *universal*. Only sports, feature, lifestyle, and business news usually are edited at separate desks.

A few metropolitan newspapers receive too much news to use the universal desk system. They divide the flow of news into *city, national,* and *world* operations. Local, suburban, and state copy comes to the city desk; stories from Washington and the nation go to the national desk; and some wire news and stories from special correspondents go to the world or foreign desk. But in this system sports and lifestyle or features still remain apart.

Small newspapers, of course, do not use enough copy to keep a full desk busy, so each subeditor edits the appropriate stories from reporters or wire services. For example, city editors may edit the copy

1.3. Electronic reporter.
An *Arizona Republic* reporter writes on a VDT with her notepad propped against the machine.

written by three or four local reporters, while a wire editor may handle international, national, and state news from the wire, as well as copy from correspondents in nearby villages. An informal system of consultation is used so subeditors know how much copy is flowing and what the top stories are.

No matter how simple or complex the system, editors must concentrate on improving copy. They tighten, point up, trim, polish. But they should not make over stories by altering every one so it will read as if they wrote it. Reporters seethe when clever phrases are made prosaic or novel leads are made routine. All editors should change copy with care, for they should encourage originality. The best newswriting is sprightly and varied. An editor who makes all copy read alike mechanizes writing, and mechanical writing can be done by a machine.

The special qualifications of a copy editor bring advantages. In most cases the pay is better. Newspaper Guild contracts usually set the base pay of editors several dollars above the minimum salary for reporters. Salaries sometimes are pushed well above Guild scale.

The nature of desk work

The way to promotion most often is by way of the rim person's chair. Because copy editors usually have been reporters, the combination of reporting and desk experience makes a journalist valuable for higher positions. The first step for a copy editor usually is over the desk into the slot. But it may be that the copy editor will be boosted directly from the rim to such jobs as state editor, city editor, suburban editor, wire editor, or picture editor. The first promotion could be to assistant city editor or assistant state editor. These jobs then prepare the copy editor to move up to the more responsible and best-paid positions as editor, assistant to the publisher, executive editor, news editor, or eventually editor-in-chief.

Even at the beginning, in the informal atmosphere of the copydesk, the copy editor is in good company. Most desks are populated by bright men and women with superior wit and humor who appreciate a well-turned phrase. Copydesk wisecracks are told all over the newsroom, and from time to time show up in a local column. Most of the joking is done during lulls, for copy tends to come in spurts. After working at a good pace for an hour or so, an editor can take a few minutes to relax. During these breaks editors often spoof each other, rib the copy aides, or even comment on the boss's foibles.

If young journalists enjoy being up-to-date on public affairs and ideas, the copydesk puts them in the middle of news flow. The editors of small papers tend to be as well informed on the full range of human events as almost anyone in the community. They therefore have a special responsibility to stay up-to-date. On the large paper, desk people can become expert on a few specialties, although scholarship is an avocation to most editors.

Though it provides various rewards, copyediting also includes some frustrations. Editing is sedentary, and the lack of physical activity bothers some people. Egos also get little exercise, since the work is anonymous. The reporter can get a byline, but no one ever sees a story topped "Headline by Joe Guggenheimer." Since the fame of copy editors rarely extends beyond the newsroom, they have to be satisfied in large part by belief that they are doing an important job well. Editors find their egos strengthened most by the approving chuckles or praise from their associates or, best of all, from their bosses.

The person who enjoys being out where the news is made and hobnobbing with the big names as a reporter may miss the excitement when brought to the desk. Though writing headlines and reshaping stories has its creative possibilities, the copy editor who is at heart a writer may be unhappy without the creative challenge of writing news and feature stories. Not all journalists are cut out for copyediting.

Perhaps the greatest and most surprising drawback in desk work is inactivity. While breaks can be stimulating, long slack periods can be depressing. This is particularly true on the biggest newspapers, where there are several editions and the staffs are large enough to cope with almost any emergency. If a slack period comes at the end of the work day, most slot persons let a few copy editors go home early. If rim people can spend slack times reading magazines or books, they will turn a disadvantage into an advantage. Such people "get their reading done" on company time, and the paper gains from their widened knowledge.

Much of the negative side of copyediting can be eliminated by real appreciation from the desk person's editors and colleagues, a good principle for copy editors to recall when they move up the ladder. Praise when the copy reader has made a complex story readable or turned out an exceptional headline is worth almost as much as a raise in pay.

The *St. Petersburg* (Florida) *Times* underlined the value of accurate editing with a game of "killing enemy errors." "X-act Agent" buttons were distributed to 664 staffers, along with special blue pencils. The paper paid $25 to the one who circled the most errors. Perhaps the game was a corny gimmick, but it showed every reporter and copy editor that management cared about quality.

Reporters who appreciate the efforts of editors boost the morale of the desk, as an example at the *New York Times* illustrates. A member of the Washington bureau of the *Times* wrote a letter to the city room expressing appreciation for checking doubtful points with him. To the amazement of the desk crew, a breed accustomed to little praise, he wrote: "I read my story this morning with just the greatest pleasure, noting where, as always, you had smoothed some lumpy sentences, chopped apart some over-long ones, skillfully made a couple of internal cuts in exactly the right places and, in short, made the story better than the one I had written."

Whether working on small or large papers, editors have to keep tabs on themselves, for they can go stale on the job. A person who develops professional skill remains, it is hoped, a credit to the profession. But a lazy journalist can drift through several years, unaware of changes, oblivious to undercurrents in world affairs, and unwilling to prepare for more demanding tasks. The job is a dead end for such a person.

Editors with the brightest futures are readers. They read magazines and the best newspapers, and at least skim through the current books, while thoroughly reading some of the old ones. Their reading alerts them to change and to ideas. News almost by definition concerns itself with changes and ideas, and editors unfamiliar or uninterested in them become ineffective. They will gain neither responsibility nor respect.

Even competent editors can slip unconsciously into carelessness about the fine points of the job. They may allow grammatical slips because they let slide the occasional few minutes necessary for review. A well-thumbed book on grammar shows that an editor is concerned with details of quality and therefore probably concerned with quality in general.

A good desk person can obtain tips for quality writing and editing in three or four minutes of reading every day or so. One of the best sources is *Winners & Sinners,* "a bulletin of second guessing" issued forty times a year from "somewhere or other" in the *New York Times.* This one-sheet paper recounts the blunders and triumphs of *Times* staffers. The *Cleveland Plain Dealer* once published *Goods & Bads,* and a medium-sized paper, the *Wilmington* (Delaware) *News-Journal,* turns out *Hits & Misses.* These sheets help greatly in preventing editing mistakes. Books like Strunk and White's *Elements of Style* and Gowers' *Plain Words: Their ABC* (see Bibliography) prod the editor to make sure that words are used correctly and that language is simple and direct.

The conscientious editor makes the whole news picture clear as well as fair. But sometimes the news may not be clear to the editor either. Reporters may be unable to get complete information; some sources may have tried to mislead the press and the public; and the editor's own background may be inadequate to assess the news properly. Newspaper editors can't be sure of the accuracy of all the information received, nor can they usually be certain when attempts are being made to mislead. Neither are they so erudite that they can grasp the significance of every event or utterance. But all editors should strive to do the best job possible to make the news understandable. The reader expects and deserves reporting that makes sense.

The editor's job also requires sifting and organizing the news so the reader does not have to struggle to get information. All kinds of distractions affect the reader. Television, radio, other papers, general noise, and conversation lure the reader's attention. Newspaper editors must make the product easy-to-read and worth reading. They accomplish this by an intelligent selection of news, careful interpretation of it, serious but sprightly editorial comment, good writing, and attractive placement of these items on newspaper pages.

This is creative work, for it requires knowledge, imagination, writing skill, judgment, and an eye for design. An editor who combines these elements can create something significant—a paper that informs the public and guides citizens to intelligent decisions.

2

Editing the copy

IN THE ELECTRONIC NEWSROOM, inserts, deletions, and movement of paragraphs are made by a few VDT keystrokes. The slot still gives each edited story a swift check, but from then on no one spots errors until after the presses roll. Printers no longer see copy, for it is set in type automatically. Modern newspapers don't have proofreaders to check for flaws. What gets into the paper almost always is what the copy editor drained off the screen into the typesetter. This means that copy editors need to work carefully to eliminate both big and little errors.

Slot people generally agree on how they want their copy editors to operate. They want stories "fixed up," but, unless the writing is bad, they do not want them butchered and rewritten. Copy editors must learn the proper amount of editing required or allowed on a particular newspaper. They keep an eye on all the minutiae, at the same time watching to see that the whole story fits and flows together to give an accurate general impression. The copy editor combines good English and good sense with the paper's rules and traditions.

Story leads deserve particular attention, for a lead can make or break the reader's interest. If the lead seems clumsy, lacks facts, or misses the point, the editor certainly should revise it.

Good copy editors, unless squeezed by a deadline, read each story at least twice. Often errors show up in each reading. New sentences inserted should be read two or three times to make sure that the corrections themselves are not in error.

The editor ought to ask finally, "Does this story make sense? Is it clear? Are there any inadequacies? Will the reader have any important questions? Does the story read smoothly? Are all statements properly attributed? Is there any factual error?"

The desk person should check to see whether the story rambles on for ten or eleven paragraphs of details without getting essential information close to the top. This shortcoming often mars stories of strikes. The beginning usually reports who says what and how long the strike has been going on, but what the strike is all about may be buried or ignored.

The copy editor should make necessary changes and quit. This means hands off clear and accurate writing. *Winners & Sinners* has warned editors not to change language for the sake of change. One issue in preelectronic days noted:

> Itchy pencil . . . refers to occasional copy desk tinkering with copy for no apparent reason—a practice that sometimes makes the writing inferior, sometimes makes the copy outright wrong, and always baffles the writer. If a holdup man takes a picture of his colleagues with a Polaroid Land camera and the reporter writes that in that way "he was able to avoid taking the incriminating film to the corner drugstore for developing" what is gained by changing the final quoted phrase to "elsewhere"? There is actually a slight loss in sense.
>
> If a reporter writes about a chimpanzee at the Museum of Natural History that "whizzed across its acres on a red tricycle" why should "acres" be changed to "halls," which loses the idea of vastness? If a correspondent writes that a "betting man could get a dime to a nickel from almost anyone in the Western delegations" about the break-up of the Geneva conference, is there any improvement in making it "could get a wager"?
>
> Although the damage wrought in these instances may seem minor, the reader has been deprived of colorful detail; moreover, the cumulative effect on reporters of such tinkering is discouraging. Changes have to be made in copy, to be sure, but be certain that when you make a change it is definitely a change for the better and not just the work of itchy pencil.

The job of editors is to go over copy to correct grammar, to oust waste words and sentences, and to make the language more graceful. Every effort should be made to produce rhythm in language, so anyone reading a sentence aloud will not stumble.

Here's a simple example:

> "The women's basketball team plays well in the first half but bogs down badly in the second," said the coach, Wilma Andersen, today.

Smooth the last part by making it "Coach Wilma Andersen said today."

Editors should throttle clichés such as "run like a deer," "a dream come true," and "red as a beet," and hunt down ambiguous phrases and errors in syntax. Several editors must have been dozing when an AP story said, "The governor, often criticized for his freewheeling style, is the son of a Cajun sharecropper, a former Navy fighter pilot, a former Nazarene preacher, and a high-stakes Las Vegas gambler." Apparently that gave him four fathers.

Another story said, "Tall and slender, Jane Goodall's eyes, ringed by crow's feet, seem to dance when she talks about her chimps." Ah, those tall and slender eyes!

One editor was able to keep these boners out of his paper:

- Four juvenile boys admitted the theft.
- Manager Joe Jones relieved himself at third base.
- Passengers were treated to a mid-morning concert shortly after noon.
- The General Electric Advanced Electronics Laboratory shot its last employee Saturday as the company's flu vaccination program ended.
- A post-mortem autopsy was performed.
- The hospital reported she was pregnant but the injuries did not effect it.

Editors need a quizzical, skeptical approach if they are to catch errors. They must keep asking as they read, "Can this be right?" With this in mind, for example, they will question whether, as the story says, Edward Kennedy was born in California and the University of Michigan is in Kalamazoo.

The probing editor

Editors must check to see if needed information is omitted. A *New York Times* reporter once sent a note to the desk mentioning an editorial oversight: A story on a supersonic airliner gave only oblique reference — in the eleventh paragraph — to the name of the government agency that received the airliner designs from a manufacturer. Knowing this kind of error should be caught by the desk, he wrote in *Winners & Sinners,* "Every reporter is going to have an occasional lapse in fullest lucidity, and he would like to feel that he is securely backstopped. That, after all, is the copydesk's primary function."

If there is any doubt about the accuracy of changes in a story, the editor should check with the nearest authority — the writer of the story. The reporter might be asked, "Does this improve the meaning of the story? Have I made it clearer, or have I muddled the facts?" Reporters will be furious, and they have a right to be, if copy is revised into error. It makes them look like fools to news sources, and it embitters the staff when an accurate story is distorted by an editor who had no firsthand knowledge of the facts.

Where a reporter has used an inappropriate word, the editor should find the right one. This requires familiarity with semantics to be sure that the words convey the intended meaning. For example, where the reporter has written "dignitaries," the word "politicians" might be better.

There must be a steady watchfulness for libel. Every story that defames anyone — and many stories must defame — should be checked to see if the defamatory phrases can be used safely under law. Chapter 14 discusses in detail the legal pitfalls that always lurk near a copy editor.

Hoaxes are another thing to contend with. A naive reporter may write a story that sounds like a dandy. The more experienced copy editor, however, may recall that the same story ran a decade ago and was exposed as a fake. This story needs the oblivion treatment.

Unless editors are careful, a single story may get into the paper twice, causing merriment among readers, but not among top editors.

It is doubly amusing if the same stories get into the paper the same day. Occasionally, different reporters will write essentially the same story a few days apart. Although the writer of the second story should have read the paper more carefully, such an oversight is no excuse for the copydesk to repeat the error. An alert desk must likewise kill outdated stories that did not make the paper. A story announcing last night's event as "tonight" is bad news for the participants, the frustrated audience, and the newspaper.

Editors also have to watch for advertising that masquerades as news. Since newspapers sell advertising, news stories should mention advertisers only when they make news. For example, if a meeting is going to take place at a hotel, the reporter has to say which hotel. This "advertising" is unavoidable and therefore permissible. After the event, it is safe to say only that the event was held "in a hotel." Brand names like Coca-Cola, Buick, and General Electric should be eliminated unless they are essential to the story.

It is even harder but more important to eliminate propaganda. Many people try to sneak their points of view into the paper under the guise of news. This is most apparent during election campaigns, when dozens of events are staged to attract attention. The editor should sift through all the propaganda and stick to a factual report.

Sometimes an inexperienced reporter will quote a news source too much and let the source misuse the news columns to further an individual or a cause. The editor gives this material its proper weight, which sometimes is nothing.

Thirteen pointers

All editors should keep in mind this checklist:

1. Double-check names. If the copy editor has any doubt about the spelling of a name, someone should look it up. Be sure that a name is spelled correctly throughout a story; a person should not be Whelan in the first paragraph and Whalen in the second. The editor should watch for a common lapse associated with names: The reporter uses a person's full name in the lead but mistakenly substitutes the first or middle name for the last in the rest of the story. For example, the lead may refer to a university president as Dr. William Carson McDuff. From then on, however, he is Dr. Carson, instead of Dr. McDuff. The copy editor should catch this blunder.

2. Attribute facts properly. Almost anything that cannot be witnessed by the reporter should be attributed to some person. The "almost" is essential to remember because often stories contain facts neither observed by reporters nor found through records, and yet there is no attribution. Attribution is unnecessary when the source obviously is telling the truth. It is silly, for example, to attribute to a university president the employment of every single new faculty member. The university is not going to announce an appointment in a news release and then back out of it, so phrases like "the president announced" are unnecessary.

3. "Duck it." Sometimes an editor spots what appears to be a minor misstatement in a story, and the reporter is not around for verification. Any other check might take fifteen minutes. The item is not worth that much time, so the editor "ducks it" by omitting the statement. A story may say, "Jones, who moved here in 1973, has served on the county board for 17 years." The copy editor may trust "17 years" but doubt "1973." How could Jones have won an election so soon? So the editor ducks the problem by changing the sentence to "Jones has served on the county board for 17 years."

4. Simplify language. Newspapers are not written for morons, but for people who want easily read news and comment. Simpler words should replace involved ones like *inextricable, dichotomy,* and *tangential.* Language even for an intellectual audience should be precise and readable, not pretentious.

Reporters sometimes get caught up in the special language or jargon of the fields they cover. Court reporters, for instance, may write *filed a demurrer, stayed the execution,* or *granted a continuance.* Such terms may be hard for a nonlawyer to grasp, and the editor who thinks the story should interest the ordinary reader will either change the wording or send it back to the reporter for translation.

5. Recognize your own prejudices. Copy editors need to double-check themselves to be sure they do not make decisions to chop one story and inflate another because of personal prejudice. Some editors who control newspaper content favor stories that concern their personal hobbies. A person who loves to sail may run an unusual number of stories about boats and the sea. Such prejudices are basically harmless, although they could make the paper look amateurish. Sometimes, however, an editor may intensely dislike a senator or fear, let us say, that the nation is moving rapidly toward socialism. This person may edit the news to make the senator look foolish or to emphasize personal political views. This kind of editing is harmful and unprofessional. Editors must develop an attitude of detachment in handling news.

6. Don't trust your memory completely. A copy editor is often tempted to drop a fact into a story as a way to improve the article. These facts should be inserted, however, only when the editor is absolutely sure of them. If one isn't certain, it is essential to look up the information in the library or a reference book.

7. Be sure copy is fair and tasteful. Balancing objective reporting and interpretation is a continual problem, but even if a story is primarily interpretative it should be fair. Snide, belittling comments should be removed.

Rebuttal from criticized persons should be included or run as a separate story nearby. Copy also should remain in good taste. Taste is difficult to assess, but most editors have a rule of thumb: A paper read by all kinds of people, including children, should consider softening or eliminating the most brutal or intimate details.

8. Watch for doublespeak. The practice of using language to deceive has swollen so much in recent years that the term *doublespeak* has been adapted from George Orwell's *newspeak.* Much of this de-

ception may be unintentional — the speaker or writer was plain sloppy, as in the case of the senator who said, "We might ventilate the structure of campaigning." But much of the deception is deliberate. The military announces a *protective strike,* to avoid saying *bombing.* Presidents talk often of *national security.* Diplomats rattle off *balance of power.* These terms either lack meaning or are intended to fool the public. The copy editor should oust such phrases and encourage reporters to challenge sources who spout doublespeak.

9. Scratch euphemisms. A journalist learns on the first work day that people *die,* not *pass away.* But pass away is a simple euphemism, and the dictionary bulges with more complicated ones. The State Department doesn't *fire* people, it *terminates* them. *Poor* gets replaced by *low-income* or *culturally deprived; slums* become *inner city;* and *prisons* get named *correctional facilities.* The desk should serve as translators.

10. Check the facts. Sometimes through error or carelessness, a scrap of information gets passed as fact. For example, a reporter once wrote that one-third of dog food sold in slums was consumed by human beings. This was not true, yet it was widely quoted about the country.

In another case a reporter may quote someone as saying, "Crime costs the nation $100 billion a year." Who can have anything but a wild guess on what crime costs? Copy editors, always skeptical, should ask frequently, "Who said so? Where did the source get this information? How would anyone know that?"

11. Avoid fad words. Americans race from one fad to another in clothing styles, entertainment, food — and word usage. A word or phrase will pop into everyone's vocabulary and the meaning often is obscure. Words or phrases like *bottom line, in the wake of, unveil, arguably, linkage, parameters, back to square one, scenario,* and *paranoid* are misused or they quickly become tedious. Editors at the VDT should hit the delete key when they see such overworked or misused words.

12. Stay alert. It is easy to slide over copy, watching for misspelled words and getting the drift of the story. It also is easy at such times to let the mind nap slightly and let ridiculous errors slip by. One paper wrote that someone had been convicted of *negligible homicide* and another reported that a climber *peaked* into a volcano. A third used *collaborate* when *corroborate* was meant.

13. Dig for holes. Reporters occasionally omit essential detail, causing a hole in a story. One reporter referred to a *troy ounce,* without describing it. Another reported that a city had produced a special directory, but didn't tell where it could be obtained.

Copy editors must always think about how to make the news readable. They revive listless writing and chop out ponderous language to make sentences brisk and stories a pleasure to follow. They may add a phrase to make a story clearer or to tone down lurid writing. A good slogan is "Make copy brisk but not brusque — vivid but not lurid."

Color and completeness

The editor should make every reasonable effort to get a local angle high in stories, because readers tend to pay attention to stories that mention local issues or people. Localization can be overdone, of course. Here is an example from an Oshkosh paper:

> The brother-in-law of a man who lived in Oshkosh in 1929 was arrested today in Dallas on a charge of panhandling.

But if an Oshkosh native wins a Nobel Prize, the Oshkosh paper had better have his birthplace in the lead, not in the ninth paragraph as it probably came over the wire.

Localizing often requires some juggling of paragraphs. Sometimes it requires only a phrase inserted high in the story:

(including Tulsa)

```
    Fifteen cities have lost federal grants aimed at
reducing poverty.
```

Other stories will require considerable restructuring, perhaps rewriting the lead or inserting paragraph seven after paragraph one. Feature writers have a habit of writing long introductions before getting to the heart of the story. Often an editor can chop whole paragraphs at the beginning of such pieces and trim the tail end of many news stories.

Whenever possible the stories should be organized to pinpoint the significance for the reader. Most of us read stories, as the communications researcher Wilbur Schramm has pointed out, because we want to be rewarded. We want to know what will affect our pocketbooks, to know what has happened to our friends and acquaintances, to know what might please us or upset us. The reporter writes stories with these ideas in mind, and the copy editor fixes the reporter's oversights:

(property)

```
School taxes will go up $1.5 million next year, the board of
education decided last night.
```
The new rate means that a resident who paid $300 in school taxes this year will pay $324 next year.

Because editors know that every reader has certain areas of ignorance, they often explain what the reporter thought obvious. "Died of nephritis" needs an addition: "a kidney disease." If the story mentions District IV schools, tell the reader at least roughly what area District IV covers. If the story mentions Theodore Roosevelt, add an identifying phrase. The story must remind as well as inform readers, and even the brightest of them have knowledge gaps.

The reporter, as noted many times, is the eyes, ears, hands, nose, and tongue of the reader. If the reporter does not describe the look, sound, feel, smell, or taste of something that needs these descriptions, the editor should get this information in the story if possible.

But the copy editor occasionally thinks that a reporter, striving for vividness, has given an incorrect tone. Perhaps the reporter unconsciously chose the words the editor thinks will sound snide, superior, or patronizing to the reader. Words like *intellectual, radical, foreigner, dropout,* or *uneducated,* if used in certain contexts, may alter the story tone. For example, a story may start, "Militant environmentalists picketed city hall today, demanding an end to toxic waste dumping in the landfill." *Militant* is a loaded word, often evoking an emotional response. *Demanding* possibly exaggerates the pickets' position.

On the other hand, a reporter may turn in a biographical story filled with syrupy phrases that make a rather ordinary person appear to be a saint. The deletion of a half dozen adjectives in these cases usually makes the tone ring true. No one should assume, however, that the tone of stories need always be coldly factual. A funny incident should be reported in a funny way. A story on a political session may be irreverent. And a story on a funeral generally should be dignified and restrained.

The *New York Times* started a story on a St. Patrick's Day parade with: "Irishmen, regardless of race, creed or color, marched down Fifth Avenue today."

The late sportswriter Red Smith, covering a Democratic convention, wrote of the keynote address: "The Democratic party last night was smitten with the jawbone of an ass."

A somber funeral story might include: "The senator's wife sat dry-eyed through the services, occasionally biting her lip to keep back the tears."

Of course every story should have the essential facts as well as the right tone. Readers are interested in the overall view of an event, but they also expect the story to answer reasonable questions. If the reporter doesn't have the answer, the story should say so: "Petersen's age was not learned."

Sometimes the editor can't revive a story. The sentences are long winded, the quotes are ponderous, and the story seems to drone on. The copy editor has to read each paragraph twice even to begin to understand what the writer was driving at. The story demands rewriting, and it should go back to the reporter or another staffer with specific instructions on how to improve it.

Quotations that look brief in copy take up an alarming amount of space when squeezed into a column width. The copy editor can boil down long-winded quotations by combining material, omitting by ellipsis, or using partial quotes:

"The dam, which is designed to bring vast blessings to the

Balancing the reporter's judgment

Polishing pointers

25

people of Central Nebraska and which will avoid terrifying floods, will cost $8 million and be built within two years," the governor said.

The quote could be paraphrased:

The dam will cost $8 million and take two years to build, the governor said.

Another possibility would be:

"The dam . . . will cost $8 million and be built within two years," the governor said.

Quotation marks suggest authenticity, but too many of them make the report look patched together. Quotes are the seasoning of the story, not the meat.

Reporters who keep interrupting their own stories put the reader in a coma with the comma. An involved sentence that stitches facts together with commas needs editing:

```
    The Tobiason boy, 8 years old and a fourth grader at the
new Leal school, said that his mother, the former Ann Davis who
was Miss America 14 years ago, had planned to pick him up at
4 p.m. at the school.
```

The references to her former title, if essential, can be inserted elsewhere.

Other reporters string identifications of people throughout a story, particularly on the sports page. In the first paragraph the football player is simply "a halfback," in the second he is "the native of Florida," in the third "the 205-pounder," in the fourth "the Big Ten's leading ground gainer," and in the fifth "the junior economics major." Such detailed identification, if used at all, should form a separate short paragraph of background information.

Redundancies are harder to spot than quotes or identification tags, and they are more worrisome. They waste space and bring snickers from readers. Obvious ones like "killed to death" rarely creep into copy, but ones like "widow of the late John Smith" are unsettlingly common. "Autopsy of the body" suggests that autopsies are performed on things other than bodies. "Graves of dead soldiers will be decorated" indicates that some soldiers are buried alive.

The correct use of words can raise interesting problems. A dictionary, of course, is a good guide, but sometimes a correctly used word will convey the wrong sense. An editorial writer once referred to a major religious denomination as a "sect." If connotation is ignored, this is a correct use of the word. But many readers were incensed, for they viewed the word as a term for little flocks that convene in abandoned stores.

Copy editors may try to rewrite a few sentences in some stories and discover that one new sentence could include the gist of three or four. All copy editors spend much time reducing copy, because there simply is not room for all stories. Editing to save space means applying the scalpel, not the meat ax. Some copy butchers would merely whack off six inches from the story's end. Skillful editors, however, recreate, take off the last two paragraphs, remove the fourth, combine two rather long sentences into one of moderate length, take a phrase from two or three different sentences, and make a long quotation into a short one.

Ten more flaws

Several more difficulties face copy editors:

1. Subject-possessive pronoun agreement. It is not unusual to see a story that says, "The council went to *their* meeting." The singular subject, *council,* requires a singular pronoun, *its.* "The group will take cars to *their* hotels," however, is correct for *group,* in this case, refers to individuals.

2. Pronouns. Copy editors should check *he, she, it,* or *they* to see if the right person or thing is identified. If there is doubt, a suitable noun, not a pronoun, should be used.

3. Illogical modifiers and appositives. Watch sentences like, "A graduate of Harvard, he is the father of eight children." Being a father has nothing to do with attending Harvard. A similar problem is illustrated in this sentence: "While diving in the surf, the water knocked off his glasses," which says that the water dived into the surf.

4. Double meanings. There is always someone around who will spot the secondary—and possibly racy or bawdy—meaning of a phrase. These double meanings amuse readers, but they detract from professionalism. For example, one paper, on a food story, added this headline:

A Leek in the Soup
Is Worth Two in the Garden

5. Editorializing. Any trace of personal opinion or a value judgment should be eliminated, unless the story is an interpretative feature or news analysis.

6. Unlikely quotes. Sometimes reporters commit a sin by inventing quotes and the unfortunate result is a sentence or two with a hollow ring. A baseball team manager noted for his linguistic errors, for example, may be quoted as saying, "We were in a desperate position in the third inning, but Bocko Jennings, our superlative third baseman, made what must be the best play of the year, allowing us to escape without damage." This unbelievable quote should be scratched

and the facts put in as straight news: The manager said Bocko Jennings' spectacular play saved the game.

Occasionally, a reporter writes that more than one person said the same thing: "John Adams and Peter Farrel said, 'I think the foreign policy of the nation is clearly a menace.' " One of them might say it, but not both.

7. Series. Check a series of several items in one sentence for a surplus verb. "He is a determined golf player, a collector of antique clocks and often reads a detective story at night." To clear up the awkwardness, the copy editor could change it to: "He is a determined golf player and a collector of antique clocks. He often reads a detective story at night."

8. Punctuation and spelling. Commas, quotation marks, hyphens, semicolons, and apostrophes need special attention. *Its* and *it's* always require a third look, and every possessive ought to get an extra glance to make sure the apostrophe is in the right place. Hyphens are needed occasionally. There's a difference between a *short story writer* and a *short-story writer.* Names, as mentioned, must be spelled correctly. Other misspellings can easily slip by. Whenever you are in the slightest doubt, consult a dictionary.

9. Arithmetic. Many stories involve addition, subtraction, division, multiplication, and percentages. Copy editors need to run those figures through their heads—or calculators—to see if they make sense. For example, a *Washington Post* story once said the value of Argentine currency had dropped 100 percent. That obviously made the money worthless; 50 percent was the proper figure. If there is any question about the arithmetic, the copy editor should start computing.

10. Homonyms. It's easy to write *flare* when *flair* is meant, or *feet* for *feat, bear* for *bare, reigns* for *reins, peddle* for *pedal.* Editors must be on guard for these lapses.

More advice

In architecture we may speak of "gingerbread," meaning excessive decoration. Language, too, can be loaded with grand words and opulent sentences. Editors in most cases should eliminate the fancy in favor of the plain.

Sometimes reporters fall into the bad habit of making verbs out of nouns. *Impact* is a common noun misused as a verb, as in *the campaign impacted upon the voters.* A Secretary of State once even said, "I'll caveat that," perhaps making the most startling switch of noun to verb.

A noted columnist used *conglomerating,* and *concertize* slips onto culture pages, as though someone can *concert.* Someone even concocted *funeralize* and *strategize.*

Use of the passive voice should be discouraged, too. It is easy to spot writing that says something *is supported,* when *supports* is active and shorter.

Editors should watch also for *preposition pad,* in which a stream of prepositional phrases fills a sentence, as in *He ran into the store in the early morning after a quick breakfast during a rain shower, and in his haste in ordering* . . . Prepositional phrases often can be dropped by using the possessive: Instead of *the main points of the platform,* try *the platform's main points. One of the students* can become *one student.*

Copy is improved, too, by reducing the number of words ending in *ize.* The word *use* does nicely in place of *utilize* and *set priorities* is an improvement over *prioritize.* Only a few words should end with *wise,* so that rule should oust such creations as *moneywise, weatherwise,* and *transportwise.*

Here are two examples of the editor's finished work (circled words and numbers mean that they should be spelled the opposite way):

(— Homer, Chatsworth and Hansonville —)

Three area villages will get special federal grants to finance sewer reconstruction. ~~The grants will amount to 2,500,000 dollars. The villages are Homer, Chatsworth and Hansonville.~~

totalling $2.5 million

The grants will pay for construction ~~costs of a total~~ of (fourteen) miles of sewer line ~~replacement in the towns.~~ Some of the sewers are 60 years old.

new   (s)   current   a

Mayor Florence Stegeman of Homer said she had conferred with the mayors of the other villages and they agreed that the work could be finished in two years.

She ~~averred~~ said that the three towns will aim to let contracts within four months. She assumed contractors will start work about (6) weeks later.

~~Homer~~ The grant money is not divided evenly ~~between~~ among the towns. Homer and Hansonville will get ~~$900,000,000~~ $900,000 each and Chatsworth will get $700,000.

The school board ~~at its meeting~~ last night voted ~~by~~ 7 to 4 ~~margin~~ to raise ~~the~~ property tax by (two) percent.

The new levy is expected to produce $700,000 ~~in new revenue~~ and will help the board grant teachers a 9 percent pay increase~~,~~ ~~in the coming year.~~

~~The tax will be assessed on property beginning in July but~~ the extra tax ~~payments~~ will not be billed until October.

Charles C. Bigert, the president ~~of the~~ school board, said the increase should ~~give the board~~ produce a balanced budget in the next fiscal year.

~~The four dissenters were divided in their opposition to the tax increase.~~ Two dissenters ~~wanted~~ to raise taxes three percent and two wanted ~~the~~ a increase ~~limited to~~ one percent.

The ~~school~~ board only taxes property~~,~~ ~~to raise its revenue.~~ The rest of its income comes from state and federal aid~~,~~ ~~dispensed itself calculated basically on the number of pupils.~~ The property tax yields ~~only~~ 31 percent of the ~~school~~ budget.

The cutting may not seem like much, but in the second story it removed about six lines of copy. This means that the story in type will be about an inch and a half shorter. A dozen stories each shortened that much would make room for an eighteen-inch story.

Every newspaper should have a *stylebook* describing how capitalization, abbreviation, and punctuation are handled in news stories for that paper. Reporters are supposed to follow this set of rules, or *style,* but sometimes they don't. The editor, to correct their errors, needs to be thoroughly familiar with the stylebook but willing to look up an obscure point whenever there is any doubt or argument.

The consistency established by the stylebook prevents the careful reader from being annoyed when a story spells a proper name two or three different ways in as many paragraphs or abbreviates a word one time and spells it out the next.

If a newspaper does not have its own stylebook, the editors may use a book published by another paper, such as the thorough one published by the *St. Louis Post Dispatch.* The Associated Press and United Press International publish a widely-used stylebook that in-

Guidebooks for accuracy

cludes valuable advice on word usage. Most papers use the AP-UPI book, and since wire service staffers use that style, it would be wasteful to make many changes in it.

Accuracy of copy requires several other reference books. Two of them, a medium-sized dictionary and the *World Almanac,* should be at arm's length. The need for a dictionary is obvious; an almanac is the poor man's encyclopedia. It gives an editor quick access to thousands of facts on recent history, dates, biographies, and records. Today a one-volume paperback encyclopedia is available to save the editor from getting up to consult the multivolume set in the library.

A good, unabridged dictionary and the city directories should be close by. Most newspapers have such books in the middle of the newsroom where everyone can get to them quickly. In addition, some editors use a thesaurus to help find the right synonym for an awkward word in a headline or story.

The following essential but less frequently used books should be easily accessible in the newspaper's library or reference room, sometimes still called "the morgue."

> *Congressional Directory*
> Area telephone books
> Various kinds of *Who's Who,* such as *Who's Who in the East*
> *United States Postal Guide*
> *Blue Book* or *Red Book* for every state the newspaper serves — to provide information about state government
> *Dictionary of American Biography*
> *Current Biography*
> A grammar, such as E. L. Callihan's *Grammar for Journalists*
> *Facts on File*
> A complete, modern atlas, such as the *National Geographic Atlas of the World*
> *American Labor Yearbook*
> A geographical dictionary, such as the *Macmillan World Gazetteer and Geographical Dictionary*
> *New York Times Index,* and back issues of *Times* on microfilm
> *Statistical Abstract of the U.S.*
> *International Motion Picture Almanac*
> King James and modern editions of the Bible
> *Poor's Public Utilities*
> *Moody's Railroads*
> *Encyclopaedia of the Social Sciences*
> *Editor & Publisher Yearbook*
> *Bartlett's Familiar Quotations*
> *Yearbook of Agriculture*
> Various sports record books and military directories
> A book on good usage, such as *Current American Usage,* by Margaret M. Bryant; *A Dictionary of American-English Usage,* by Margaret Nicholson (based on a famous English work by H. W. Fowler); *A Dictionary of Contemporary American Usage,* by Bergen

31

and Cornelia Evans; *Modern American Usage,* by Wilson Follett; *American Usage and Style, a Consensus* (1980) by Roy Copperud; *The Careful Writer* by Theodore Bernstein.

The largest newspapers have even more reference books, and Dr. Eleanor Blum's *Reference Books in the Mass Media,* a paperback, lists all of them. Some are used so rarely that many newspapers don't need to own them. However, a telephone call or a quick trip by a copy aide to a public library can put an editor in touch with almost any reference book.

3

Word watching

MOST EDITORS-IN-CHIEF tell their copy editors to "use words correctly." Good advice, of course, but hard to follow. What is correct? Who said so? What about new words not yet in dictionaries? Which dictionary is correct? Not only are there new words, but also new meanings of old words, as with *bug, gay,* and *turkey.*

Newspapers use a standard for the meanings of words. If they did not, the reader would be confused frequently by jargon, slang, and malapropism. Usually the standard is the big dictionary in the middle of the newsroom, even if the edition is twenty years old. Some supplement is needed, however, to cover words newly accepted into the written language. Editors should take care to avoid words or meanings that they think will appear for a short time and then pass into obscurity even as they are being listed in a new dictionary. Perhaps a good guide to word usage in a newspaper would be to cling to the old, so the meaning of language does not change every generation, but adapt to the new if it brings freshness and vividness to the language.

Editors should not only be alert to changing usage; they also should spot redundancies, grammatical errors, and misleading language. The following tips on usage, grammar, and spelling should be valuable.

Actual fact or *true fact.* A *fact* is by definition *true.*

Advance planning. Planning implies advance work or thought. *Advance reservations* also is a redundancy.

Advise, for *inform.* "He was *informed* [not *advised*] of his wife's illness and *advised* to call her doctor immediately."

Allusion. A reference, as in "Her *allusion* to Hamlet . . ."

Alternative, for *alternate.* "He had an *alternate* [not *alternative*] plan. It gave the voter a choice of *alternatives.*"

Alumna. One female graduate; the plural is *alumnae. Alumnus* means

Words and phrases often mistakenly used

33

one male graduate; the plural is *alumni,* which also is the plural for a group including both men and women.

Amateur, for *novice.* A *novice* is a beginner; an *amateur* is one who works or plays for fun, not money; a *professional* works or plays for money. Because the professional usually is highly skilled, an amateur sometimes is complimented by being called "professional."

Amused. See *bemused.*

Ancestor. A person from whom one is descended.

And etc. Etc. stands for *et cetera,* which means "and the rest" in Latin, so the *and* is redundant.

Anxious, for *eager.* "He was *eager* [not *anxious*] to try, but his mother was *anxious* for his safety."

Ask. In its various forms it can often be dropped. "*Asked* what he thought about the game, he said he thought it was good" can be simply "He said he thought the game was good."

At the present time. Use *now* instead.

Author, as a verb. "He *authored* a text" should be "He wrote a text."

Baby girl (or boy) *is born.* Redundant, as no one is born fully grown.

Badly injured. No injury is good; say *severely injured.*

Balding. A person is either bald or getting bald.

Beautiful. The word involves a value judgment, and some crank is bound to disagree, especially over a "*beautiful* woman."

Bemused, for *amused. Bemused* means "dazed," "preoccupied," or "confused."

Boat, for *ship.* Technically, *boats* are carried on *ships;* generally, a *boat* is a small vessel.

Bridegroom. See *groom.*

Broadcasted. The past participle of *broadcast* is *broadcast.* "The program was *broadcast* daily."

Brutal beating. No *beating* is gentle.

Burglar. A person who breaks into a building with intent to steal something.

Calvary. The hill on which Jesus was crucified.

Cavalry. A military unit, originally riding on horses.

Celebrant. A person taking part in a religious rite. A *celebrator* whoops it up.

Cohort. A band; *cohorts* are not associates.

Collide. This verb refers to a bumping of two moving objects. "The car hit [not *collided with*] a telephone pole and then *collided* with another car."

Combine. Do not use as a noun, unless it refers to a piece of harvesting equipment.

Complected or *complexioned.* The noun *complexion* has no adjective form. "She is fair *complected* [or *complexioned*]" should be "She has a fair *complexion.*"

Completely destroyed. The *completely* is redundant.

Comprise. Means "contain," "embrace," or "include." The whole *comprises* the parts.

Consensus of opinion. Of opinion is redundant, as a *consensus* is a collective opinion.

Controversial usually is a waste word. "The crowd shouted down the *controversial* proposal" can be simply "The crowd shouted down the proposal."

Contusion. See *laceration.*

Convince. To overcome any doubt; different from *persuade.*

Crescendo. Means "rising" or "increasing," not "loud."

Critical, for *critical condition.* A sick person in *critical condition* is seldom *critical.*

Debark. Use only for those getting off ships or out of boats.

Decimate. To destroy one-tenth.

Descendant. An offspring, perhaps remote, of an ancestor.

Devout, for *religious. Devout* is an exceptionally high degree of devotion—too high for the layman to measure.

Diagnose. Conditions are *diagnosed;* patients are not.

Different than, for *different from.* "Each house is *different from* [not *different than*] the one next to it."

Disinterested. Impartial, unbiased. *Uninterested* means "without interest."

Dove, for *dived. Dove* is the colloquial, not the written, past tense of *dive.* "He *dived* [not *dove*] from the side of the boat."

Due to, for *because.* "He was late *because* [not *due to*] the battery went dead. He had been *due to* meet us at noon."

Eager. See *anxious.*

Elderly. Be cautious about this word, as even persons of seventy-five may be sensitive about being called *elderly.*

Enormity. Implies evil. *Enormous* means "large."

Esquire, the honorable, and other undefinable titles should be omitted.

Etc. See *and etc.*

Fewer. See *less.*

Finalize. Try *complete, end,* or *finish.*

Flaunt. Means "to disregard rules" or "make a boastful display."

Flout. Means to "treat with contempt."

Foreseeable future. Who can see into the future?

Forgotten. See *gotten.*

For the purpose of can be simply *for.*

Fortuitous. By chance, not by good fortune.

Freak accident is a cliché. Let the facts show that the accident is unusual.

Fulsome. Overfull or excessive because of insincerity.

Gauntlet, for *gantlet.* A *gauntlet* is a glove that can be thrown down;

a *gantlet* is a form of punishment that can be run.

Gendarmes. Only small French towns have them. Large French cities have *police.*

Gender. A grammatical distinction; *sex* refers to physiological differences.

Gotten, for *got. Gotten* is the colloquial past participle of *get,* but *forgotten* is the regular past participle of *forget.* "He had *got* the man's address but had *forgotten* to get his age."

Great Britain. A country that includes England, Wales, Scotland, and North Ireland. A *subject,* not a *citizen,* of the country is a *Briton.* Great Britain now is called *United Kingdom.*

Groom, for *bridegroom.* "The *bridegroom* had recently been employed as a *groom* with Smith Stables."

Ground rules. Except in reference to baseball games, skip the *ground.*

Half mast. Flags may fly at *half mast* on ships but at *half staff* ashore.

Hare-brained. Refers to a rabbit; *hair-brained* is incorrect.

Heart condition. Everyone has one; some have heart *disease* or heart *ailments.*

Hung. "Spectators *hung* over the wall to see the murderer *hanged.*"

If and when. Just *when* will do.

Inform. See *advise.*

Intrigue. As a verb, it means "to plot," not "to interest" or "to mystify."

Jewish rabbi. Rabbi is Jewish by definition.

Kin. Means "relatives," not "one relative."

Knot. A nautical mile an hour. *Knots an hour* is redundant.

Laceration, or *contusion.* A *laceration* is a cut; a *contusion* is a bruise.

Ladies, for *women.* All *ladies* are women, but not all *women* are ladies. So call all women *women.*

Lawmen. A vague term. Use *police, deputies, prosecutors.*

Less for *fewer. Less* refers to a general quantity; *fewer* refers to the specific items that make it up. *Fewer* dollars earned mean *less* money to spend."

Like. Don't confuse with *such as;* e.g., not "cities *like* Chicago," but "cities *such as* Chicago."

Litany. A prayer, not a list.

Litmus test. Use it only for stories about chemistry.

Livid. Black and blue or the color of lead; not flushed or red.

Located, for *situated. Located* means "found," and *situated* means "placed at." "He *located* the school, which was *situated* five miles from town." As in this example, even *situated* can often be dropped without loss of meaning.

Majority, for *plurality.* In an election, a *majority* is more than half the votes, and the *plurality* is the margin of victory. "Jones was elected by a clear *majority* (64 percent), rolling up a *plurality* of 115,000 votes."

Masterly. Skillful; *masterful* means "imperious or domineering."

Matinee performance. A *matinee* is a *performance.*

Media, for *medium. Media* is the plural of *medium.* "Television is an important *medium.*" And, "*Media* are a good source of information."

Menial. The word has degrading overtones; avoid using it to describe workers.

Militant, for *protestor* or for *rowdy.* A *militant* is a vigorous fighter for a cause and may be nonviolent; a *rowdy* fights for selfish reasons. A *protestor* may be against violence.

Monies, for *money. Money* is collective, so the plural is unnecessary.

More unique, or *most unique. Unique* is an absolute, so it cannot be modified.

Mourning dove. Not *morning dove,* for the sound is mournful.

Nee. Means "born"; only the family name should be described as *nee,* as "Alice Jones, *nee* Smith."

New record. When a *record* is set it is *new.*

Novice. See *amateur.*

Orientated, for *oriented. Oriented* is the preferred past tense of *orient.*

Panic, riot, disaster, etc., should not be used unless the facts clearly indicate the need for strong words.

Per (in *per year, per day,* etc.). Skip the Latin; use *a* year, *a* day. *Per annum* is doubly unfortunate.

Personal friend. No one is called an *impersonal friend.*

Persuade. To cause someone to do something.

Plurality. See *majority.*

Presently, for *now. Presently* is a long word meaning "soon."

Prior to should be simply *before.*

Professional. See *amateur.*

Protestor. See *militant.*

Query. A question, not an inquiry.

Raised, for *reared.* Children are *reared*; animals are *raised.*

Ravage. Destroy. *Ravish* means "to carry away with force" or "to rape."

Reason why. The *why* is redundant.

Red-headed, for *red-haired.* Be accurate. Do you mean the scalp or the hair? (*Red-headed,* like *tow-headed,* is figurative. It is best left to other forms of writing.)

Refute. To prove to be wrong. It does not mean "debate."

Religious. See *devout.*

Remand back. Skip the *back.*

37

Resides is a fancy way of saying *lives*.

Revert back. The *back* is redundant.

Robber. A person who threatens another in the act of stealing. An *armed robber*, of course, has a weapon.

Row. (Rhymes with *plow*.) An argument or to have an argument. Avoid, for readers easily confuse it with other meanings.

Ship. See *boat*.

Situated. See *located*.

Snow. It is not *white stuff*.

Sudden explosion is redundant.

Superlatives (like *eldest, fastest, biggest*) should be handled with care. Often someone will be challenged to find something that surpasses your example.

The before a plural noun is often, but not always, unnecessary. "*The* voters filled the polling booths" could be simply "Voters filled the polling booths." Let your ear be your guide.

Thief. A person who steals, but without threatening others and without breaking into buildings.

Thusly should be *thus*.

To death is often redundant, as in *strangled to death* or *drowned to death*.

Unaware of the fact that should be simply *unaware that*.

Unknown. Use sparingly, for usually someone knows what is labeled *unknown*: e.g., "her age was *unknown*."

Utterly, flatly, sheerly, categorically, definitely, and many other such adverbs pad most sentences.

Very should be used very seldom.

Watershed. Not to be used as a synonym for *high point* or *landmark*.

Whether or not, for *whether*. Because it implies an alternative, *whether* rarely needs to be followed by *or not*.

-wise. A bad suffix for general use. *Otherwise* is fine, but *healthwise, automobilewise, taxwise,* etc., smack too much of advertising shoptalk.

About may indicate approximation; *around* implies motion. "He weighs *about* 150 pounds and runs two miles *around* the track each day."

Adjective phrases should be hyphenated. "The *two-year-old* boy ran to the *sad-looking* man."

Adjective-noun agreement. *This* kind, not *these* kind.

Adjectives for adverbs. An adverb modifies verbs, so "She hits *good*" and "He plays *good*" are incorrect; for *good* here modifies verbs. Change the *good* to *well.*

Adjectives referring to health or emotion. See *feel.*

Affect is a verb that means "to have influence." *Effect,* as a noun, refers to a result. "His speech *affected* the audience deeply; the *effect* was a silence so profound one could hear the crickets outside the tent." As a verb, *effect* means "to bring about or accomplish." "His work *effected* a cure." Note that as a verb *effect* is usually unnecessary. "His work cured her."

Agreement. A subject and its predicate, and a noun and its pronoun, should agree in number. "The *group* of boys *was* trying to break down the door. The *girls* inside *were* screaming in panic. The *group* lost *its* steam when the dean appeared and told the *boys* he had called *their* parents."

Among. See *between.*

Apostrophe (to indicate possession). See *possessives.*

Around. See *about.*

As. See *like.*

Beside refers to nearness; *besides* means "in addition to." "*Besides* being sheriff he was dogcatcher, so he built the dog pound *beside* the jail."

Between refers to two persons or things; *among* refers to three or more. "The power of government is divided *among* the legislative, judicial, and executive branches. The legislative power is divided *between* the Senate and the House."

Capitalization (in quotations). See *quotations.*

Commas setting off appositives or interrupters come in pairs. "John Smith, senator from Vermont will speak today" should be "John Smith, senator from Vermont, will speak today." And "The meeting, surprisingly enough went off on schedule" needs a comma after *enough.*

Complement. Means "to accompany," or "enhance." *Compliment,* of course, "means to praise."

Contrary-to-fact statements. See *subjunctive mood.*

Double negatives. *Can't hardly* and *can't scarcely* are examples of redundant negatives.

Doubt, statements of. See *subjunctive mood.*

Effect. See *affect.*

Either pairs with *or; neither* pairs with *nor.* "*Either* he *or* I is at fault, but *neither* he *nor* I admits guilt." Note that both *either* and *neither* require singular verbs.

Farther refers to distance; *further* refers to thoroughness. "He wanted to check *further* on the flood damage, so he walked *farther* onto the bridge."

Feel, when it refers to health or emotion, requires an adjective, not an adverb. "I feel *bad* about not calling him back." "I feel *badly*" would imply an impaired sense of touch. The same rule applies to *look, sound, smell,* and *taste.*

Gerunds coupled with a pronoun require the possessive. "I could watch *his dancing* for hours."

Hyphenation, of adjective phrases. See *adjective phrases.*

It's and *its. It's* is a contraction of *it is; its* is a possessive pronoun. "*It's* too bad the store lost *its* lease."

Lay and *lie. To lay* is a transitive verb and therefore takes an object; *to lie* is intransitive and thus takes no object.

    Transitive: He *lays* bricks for a living.
                     He is *laying* the box on the counter.
                     Lay the box on the counter.
                     He *laid* the box down.

    Intransitive: He *lies* in bed till noon.
                     He is *lying* in the sun.
                     Lie down for an hour or so.
                     He *lay* down to rest.
                     His head *lay* on the pillow.
                     He has *lain* there long enough.

Like is a preposition and requires an object; *as* is a conjunction and requires a following clause. "She looks *like* her mother, just *as* [not *like*] we thought." *Like* may be used as a conjunction in a simile. "He performed *like* Peter Serkin."
Look, when referring to health. See *feel.*

Neither. See *either.*
Nor. See *either.*

Or. See *either.*

Parallel usage. Don't shift the form of construction in a sentence, as in "John was *tall and heavy and had a fair complexion.*" Instead, use "John was *tall, heavy, and fair.*"
Plurals. It is *courts martial, attorneys general, fathers-in-law.* But drop the final *s* from *somewheres, anywheres, backwards.*

40

Possessives. To form the singular possessive, in most cases, add an apostrophe and an *s*. "The dog*'s* coat is glossy." To form a plural possessive, in most cases, add the apostrophe. "The dogs*'* coats are wet." If a word ends with an *s* sound, add only the apostrophe if it has more than one syllable. "Rabinowitz*'* book is well-written; Ross*'s* book is dull."

Prepositional object. When a pronoun is the object of a preposition, it should be in the objective case. "The decision was between *him* and *me*."

Pronouns. They should match the case of the nouns to which they refer, as "we students" and "she told *us students*." Pronouns must be used with care to assure clearness. This sentence is confusing: "Deborah told *her* mother *her* purse was stolen." Whose purse?

Quotations.

A quoted sentence needs only one capital:

"It is a difficult problem," Smith said, "but we can solve it."

Two quoted sentences require two capitals:

"The well is dry," she said. "We must get water elsewhere."

A quote within a quote takes single quotation marks:

"New devices let people 'hear' atomic explosions thousands of miles away," he said.

When quoted material continues for more than one paragraph, save the *ending* quotation marks for the end of the quoted material:

"The well is dry," she said, "so we must get it elsewhere.

"Maybe we can get it at the next farm."

Set and *sit*. *To set* is a transitive verb and thereby takes an object; *to sit* is intransitive and thus takes no object.

Transitive: He *sets* tile for a living.
He is *setting* plants in the garden.
Set the box on the table.
He *set* the box down.

Intransitive: He *sits* here regularly.
She was *sitting* in the chair.
Sit down, please.
He *sat* in front.
Have you *sat* there before?

Smell. See *feel.*

Sound. See *feel.*

Subjunctive mood. The subjunctive mood expresses wishes, doubts, or things contrary to fact. It requires a plural verb. "If he *were* seven feet tall, he would be on the basketball team for sure" (contrary to fact). "I wish I *were* old enough to be President" (wish). "He acts as if he *were* unable to speak" (doubt).

41

Taste. See *feel.*

That. A restrictive clause (essential to the meaning of a sentence) is introduced by *that* and does *not* take a comma. I entered the building that was air-conditioned. (There are other buildings.) A nonrestrictive clause is introduced by *which* and takes a comma: I entered the building, which was air-conditioned. (There is only one building.)

Touch. See *feel.*

Try. Make it *try to,* not *try and.*

Voice. Don't shift voices in the same sentence, as in "He *will travel* to Maine (active), and *will be traded* to New Orleans."

Were. See *subjunctive mood.*

Who. This word should be used as the subject of a sentence or a clause, as in "*Who* will come? *Whom* is used when the objective case is required, as in "They wondered *whom* she would choose."

abbot	cemetery	inaugurate
abscess	changeable	independent
absence	cite, site, sight	innocuous
accidentally	compliment,	inveigle
accommodate	complement	irrelevant
accumulate	conscious	judgment
across	consensus	knowledgeable
advice, advise	coroner	lessen, lesson
adviser	corps, corpse	libel, liable
advisory	council, counsel	loose, lose
allege	defendant	lovable
all right	desert, dessert	lying
allotted	develop	mantel, mantle
amateur	dyeing, dying	marshal
arctic	emigrate, immigrate	mileage
appellate	embarrass	missile
apologize	endurance	misspell
ascend	envelop, envelope	necessary
athlete	equivalent	Niagara
baptize	existence	nickel
believe	exorbitant	obscene
benefited	extravagance	occasion
bridal, bridle	eyeing	occurred
Britain	familiar	omitted
Briton	flew, flu, flue	ordinance, ordnance
calendar	gauge	paid
canceled	guerrilla	peaceable
canvas, canvass	guillotine	penitentiary
capital, capitol	height	personal, personnel
category	hemorrhage	Philippines
cellar	hypocrisy	picnicked

42

plaque	scion	there, their
potatoes	scissors	tomatoes
prairie	seize	traveled
precede, proceed	separate	truly
preventive	sergeant	unnecessary
principal, principle	sheriff	vaccinate
privilege	sizable	vane, vain, vein
questionnaire	soccer	varicose
rhyme	sophomore	vermilion
rhythm	stationary, stationery	weird
ricochet	strait jacket	wholly
salable	superintendent	wield
sauerkraut	supersede	your, you're

4

The basics of printing

COMPUTERS DOMINATE the modern newspaper plant. Classified and display advertising, news, columns, and editorials all funnel into computers, which send signals to phototypesetting machines. Those machines send forth the ads and news on photopaper that can be pasted onto *camera copy.* (See Fig. 4.1.) That copy is photographed, a printing plate is made, and the plate is put on a press. Newspapers spin off the press by the thousands.

A visitor to this kind of plant usually is told almost immediately, "All this is obsolete." The statement is true, for every company making

4.1. A *Baltimore Evening Sun* editor directs a printer as a front page is pasted up. (*Baltimore Evening Sun*)

printing equipment is preparing to turn out even faster machines or new machines that will abolish one or two steps in the printing process. As examples, engineers are trying to perfect *plateless printing* in which microscopic jets of ink will be sprayed onto paper to form letters. Printing plates—and presses—would no longer be used.

Engineers have developed *pagination,* which lets an editor, at a special VDT, guide a computer in making up newspaper pages. Editors, in effect, make up the pages. Only a few papers use pagination because of the expense and because so many technical problems remain, but the number is sure to increase every year.

Engineers also are striving to create a printing system called *computer to plate.* As the name implies, this system would let a computer create press plates, thereby eliminating all printers.

Printers used to say, with some bitterness, that they were an endangered species. They are close to being extinct now, and even the International Typographical Union, which once represented nearly all the nation's printers, has been folded into the Communications Workers of America.

Even though most current printing equipment is termed obsolete, the devices in use tend to dazzle almost anyone. The idea of tapping a few keys and having columns of news glide out of a machine startles even people who have seen the process operating for years.

The changes put new responsibilities on editors. In effect, they run the typesetting machines and no one—neither printer nor proofreader—is there to prevent errors. Editors must be as sure as they can be that errors do not slip past them.

Step-by-step

Newspapers did not shift overnight from the old style printing to the new. Most of them rather timidly bought one piece of electronic equipment, then a few more until much of the paper was tied into computers. Wherever possible newspapers tried to keep using existing machinery, so long as it could perform adequately. As a result, many papers have hybrid operations, making use of some modern, some old, and some middle-aged equipment. The one piece of machinery that has tended to stand firm is the press, for presses are big, expensive, and durable. New presses are not much faster than old ones. A new press requires a place to put it. The paper can't be shut down for six months while the old press is removed and the new one installed.

Let's say, however, that a newspaper is using all the latest equipment. Chances are good that it will function this way: Reporters write their stories on VDTs. Copy editors, on other VDTs, edit reporters' copy. Much advertising also is prepared on these screens. Wire copy comes directly into the computer, to be called up onto the VDT. Copy editors write their headlines on the screen, too, and if the headline is too long or too short, the computer will say so.

The slot person pushes a VDT key and in another room the edited stories appear on paper in the desired column width. A dummy, showing printers where to put those stories, headlines, and ads, is sent to the composing room. The printer pastes ads and stories onto paper the size of the newspaper page. This page then is called *camera-ready copy,* a *mechanical,* or a *keyline.* The page is put before a machine, and laser beams scan the page. This process takes two minutes. In another four minutes the laser machine has completed a plate with a raised surface. These plates are put on a *letterpress* press and the paper is printed. The press is called letterpress because paper is squeezed against inked letters. Those letters are raised surfaces, which look something like a rubber stamp.

After the camera-ready copy is prepared, a majority of American papers make *offset* plates and put them on an *offset* press. The plate is made by photographing the camera-ready copy. The negative from the photograph is put above a page-size piece of thin, specially treated aluminum that resembles a cookie sheet. Light is shined through the negative for a few minutes. A quick chemical treatment makes an image of the page appear on the sheet. This *smooth* plate is put onto the offset press. A letterpress press uses only ink. An offset press uses both water and ink. Images of letters and pictures on the smooth plate will attract ink and the surface that is free of images will attract water. Paper does not touch offset plates. The turning press plate sets off — *offsets*—the image onto another cylinder and the paper rolls against that offset roller. Progress is coming to offset, too. Some new offset presses are called *dry offset,* for they use no water, saving a lot of adjustments by press operators.

If a laser plate is not made for letterpress work, camera-ready copy can be photographed and the negative placed in a special machine to make a thin plate with raised surfaces.

Like most new equipment, the computer-era machinery required painful adjustments. The first devices were sensitive and broke down often. Some of them were produced by people who knew nothing about newspaper operations, and keyboards and codes were awkward. Now the devices are durable and efficient. Anyone who can type can learn the basics of VDT operations in a few hours, although grasping the full potential of VDTs may take several days.

Some early claims for computers have not worked out. The time lag between newsroom deadline and press time has not been cut by much. Some editors report a fifteen-minute reduction, but it still takes about an hour to get the last bits of type set, pages pasted, and plates made and locked onto the press. The reader is not getting any fresher news, in the main, than before.

Other developments help the reporter and editor, even though they have little bearing on printing. A portable VDT is available for reporters covering events far from home. A box holding the device, no bigger than a portable typewriter, can be unfolded, plugged into electricity, and attached to an ordinary telephone. Reporters can write on the VDT and have the signals sent over a telephone line to the computer in their newspaper's plant.

VDTs provide a paper copy of a story. An editor or reporter pushes a button labeled "Print" and out comes a copy from a sister device. Such copies help editors who want to show the story to someone far from the screen.

Some computer systems include software that corrects misspelled words, although they have trouble with homonyms. Others even correct style errors.

In the early 1980s, some business firms started to use inexpensive computers and a laser printer to turn out newsletters, reports, and brochures. The devices produced camera-ready copy. The equipment took up so little space that the process was called *desktop publishing*.

Several years later a sizable number of weeklies and even some tiny dailies adopted the system. A human printer only made a printing plate and ran the press.

Computer experts foresee bigger dailies making some use of desktop publishing, particularly for tabloid-size inserts like health or business magazines.

Computers produce all kinds of graphics, which help explain complicated material. They are so easy to make that some papers slip a graphic onto nearly every page, badly overdoing the usage. It seems likely that use of graphics will moderate in the future.

Anyone laying hands on a VDT should know printing measurements. The machine needs to be told how many *picas* wide it should make the column and how many *points* high it should make headlines and body type.

Printing measures

Points and picas are the two main printing measures. In general, a point refers to vertical measure. One point equals 1/72 inch. Seventy-two-point type, then, is 1 inch high. Thirty-six-point is ½ inch. Twenty-four-point is ⅓ inch. Most *body type*—the type for news stories—is 8- to 10-point. (See Fig. 4.2.)

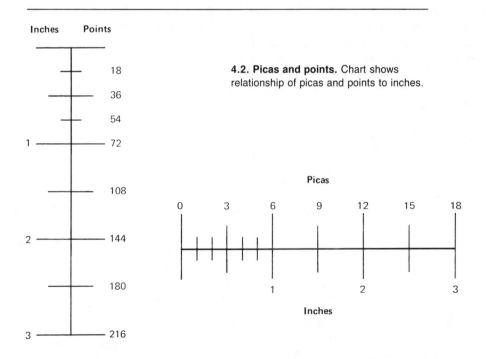

4.2. Picas and points. Chart shows relationship of picas and points to inches.

The measure for horizontal distance is *pica*. A pica is ⅙ inch (or 12 points), so a column 2 inches wide will have type set 12 picas wide. A half-column picture in such a column width would be 6 picas, or 1 inch.

A few simple problems and answers will help make these measurements clear.

1. If body type is 9-point, how many lines will there be in 3 column inches?

2. If a picture is 3 inches wide, how many picas is it?

3. If the body type of a story is 9 inches long and the story has a three-line 36-point type headline, what is the total length of story and headline in inches?

4. How many inches of type will eighteen lines of 8-point make?

The answers: 1. 24; 2. 18; 3. 10½; 4. 2[1]

A pica sometimes is erroneously called an *em*. An em technically is the square of the type. Thus, an em of 18-point type is 18 points square—18 points by 18 points. An em of 12-point is 12 points square. A 12-point em, of course, is also a pica wide, because it is ⅙ inch. (The em got its name from the letter M, which usually looks as wide as it is high.)

In B.C.—before computer—copy measurement was done approximately, so a story often was ½ inch or so longer or shorter than expected. Makeup editors then would throw away a sentence or two so a long story would fit. A too-short story would be lengthened by slipping thin pieces of *lead*—type metal is mostly lead—between paragraphs or between lines of the first paragraph. This process is called *leading* (pronounced "ledding"). In cold type the same technique is used, except that a printer takes a knife and cuts away a bit of the story to shorten it, as directed by an editor. If the story is too short, paragraphs can be cut apart and each graf separated a tiny bit from the piece ahead of it. So instead of pieces of lead, white space is used. Even with cold type, however, this process still is called leading.

The well-edited paper does not use so much lead that white spaces noticeably fragment the stories. Neither does it stick meaningless little fillers into the bottoms of the pages to report, say, that Sumatra has twenty-eight species of monkeys. A good staff, with VDTs, can edit copy to fit most holes exactly.

Quality newspapers usually spend much effort on the appearance of their pages. Part of this job is the selection of type. (See Fig. 4.3.) At the turn of the century body type was small and crowded. Headline faces were squeezed thin, and there was so much of this type that the reader could hardly make out what was printed. Gradually

Types of type

1. Nine-point type yields eight lines to the inch (9 divided into 72). Three inches, then, would require twenty-four lines. 2. Since an inch is 6 picas, 3 times 6 is the number of picas in 3 inches. 3. Three lines of 36-point take 108 points. Seventy-two goes into that 1½ times. So add 1½ inches to 9 inches to get the total. 4. Eight times 18 points gives 144 points. Divide by 72 to convert to inches.

the 7-point body type was replaced by 7½- or 8-point type, and that frequently gave way to 9. Today many papers use 9½- or 10-point; or they may use 9-point on a 10-point line—meaning that the type is 9-point with a point of leading. Similarly, the old all-capital headlines, with layers of decks, have given way to simple, neatly designed type faces and headline forms in caps and lowercase that can be read at a glance. The result has been pages with white space for "air," body type that can be read without squinting, and heads with clean beauty. (See Fig. 4.4.)

1. 𝕿𝖊𝖝𝖙
2. Roman
2a. Oldstyle
2b. Modern
2c. Mixed
2d. *Italic*

3. **Gothic**
3a. Sans Serif
3b. Sq. Serif
4. *Script.* Cursives
5. NOVELTY

4.3. Races of type. Five major subdivisions, or *races,* of type are illustrated. Square serif type, here a subcategory (3b), is sometimes called a race. The fifth race, novelty, sometimes goes by "ornamented" or other names. Most newspaper usage is obviously in categories 2 and 3— roman and gothic. In newspaper parlance "italic" is not a subdivision of roman, as shown, but a slanted, or nonperpendicular, form of roman or gothic faces.

Tax cuts to favor wealthy

Bodoni

Money isn't sole trouble for pensions

Times Roman

Financing still No. 1 car factor

Century Bold

Stock prices weaken

Helvetica Bold

Dog proves a hot shot, wounds man

Helvetica Medium

4.4. Headline faces. Races of type (see Fig. 4.3) are divided into families. Loosely called simply *faces,* they often bear the name of the designer. This illustration shows some common headline faces in use. Note that some have serifs—finishing strokes on letters—while others, like Helvetica, are sans serif.

Pictures, collectively called *art,* once were prepared for printing by having acid etch hundreds of little grooves into a zinc plate to produce an *engraving* or *cut* with a pattern of tiny raised dots. The dots on paper produced shades from dark to light to make what is called a *halftone*—halfway between white and black. The darkest grays of the picture provide bigger black dots and smaller white areas among them; the lightest grays of course make very small dots against relatively large untouched areas. These massed points of black and white are so tiny, however, that the eye mixes them optically to form the illusion of continuous tones of gray. (See Fig. 4.5.) A machine now makes plastic engravings for letterpress operations.

4.5. Halftone screen. This picture employs a gross halftone screen. The dots are magnified for this illustration. To see how the eye blends the dot patterns used in the screens of ordinary engravings, look at the page from eight or ten feet away.

The dots are made by photographing the picture through a *screen.* When no screen is used to produce a halftone, all background material is removed, leaving only certain lines, as in cartoons, fashion drawings, or some courtroom sketches. There are, of course, no dots. These *line cuts* produce black on white, or gray if the artist has put black lines close together. (See Fig. 4.6.)

4.6. Artwork. The artist can be useful to the newspaper for humor and variety. This is a line engraving, to be distinguished from a halftone (cf. Fig. 4.5). (Reprinted with permission of the *Los Angeles Times*.)

Pictures that appear in offset papers are handled differently. When the camera-ready page is being prepared, a piece of red or black paper the size of the picture is pasted onto the camera copy. The paper is called a *window*. The camera-ready page is photographed and the window is removed from the page negative. The picture is photographed through a screen and the resulting negative is pasted into the place vacated by the window. The whole page negative then has light shined through it to make a page plate. The little dots for the picture appear on the page, just as they do in letterpress engraving. The quality, however, is better in offset pictures because the paper is smoother and shinier than paper used in letterpress operations.

Laserplates handle pictures with no difficulty. The screened picture is simply pasted onto the full-page camera copy, along with the cold type, and the laser beams pick up the lights and darks just as they appear on the copy. The great advantage of laser platemaking is that two steps are eliminated: photographing the pages and developing the film.

Engraving for offset

The comic pages of newspapers pioneered color reproduction, but magazines long ago passed the dailies in use of color, and color television has contributed to making the newspaper's gray image look old-fashioned.

Color printing is increasingly popular as editors compete with television images. The process was a separate press plate for every basic color: red, yellow, and blue—with black the fourth color. Other colors are made by overlapping the basic colors. When two color plates are to print overlapping impressions, great care must be taken to get the plates in *register*. This means, for example, that the blue and yellow impressions must coincide exactly to produce a green. Otherwise the printed picture will appear fuzzy. To illustrate, a register only slightly off on the picture of a woman's green dress can give the garment two distinct hemlines, one yellow and one blue.

Register is so difficult that once a color picture or ad is adjusted properly no editor should tinker with it. If, for example, a color picture is running in columns one through four on page one in the first edition, it had better stay there in later editions—unless an editor is willing to argue with an outraged pressman, who probably has a large metal tool in his hand.

It is perhaps surprising that some of the biggest papers don't use color. Neither the *Wall Street Journal* nor the *New York Times* is equipped to use color in regular news pages. The *New York Daily News* and the *New York Post* were late in providing even spot color. But many papers now use up to two thousand color pictures a year. Smaller papers use three or four a week, plus various color and cutoff rules.

The death of the newspaper has been predicted off and on for half a century. First, radio was going to kill newspapers. That didn't happen, but doomsayers after World War II were convinced that television would make the printed word obsolete. When that didn't happen, cable television was expected to sound the death knell.

Radio, television, and cable have had their effects. They have contributed to a stagnant newspaper circulation for the last twenty years. Still, sixty million newspapers are sold every day, one for every four Americans. Network television is getting its jolts, too. Instead of only three networks available fifteen years ago, a majority of homes now receive cable, offering thirty or more channels. To add to the network problems, a growing number of viewers spend their evenings watching movies transmitted through video cassette recorders.

There is no doubt, however, that television gobbles up time that viewers otherwise might spend reading, and newspapers must struggle to lure viewers away from the TV screen for thirty minutes a day to read. A person usually can read a whole newspaper in the time a half-hour news broadcast provides only sketchy information.

Newspaper publishers have been quick to capitalize on satellite technology. The *Wall Street Journal* uses satellite transmission to send pictures of its pages to about twenty satellite printing plants all over the nation, in Europe and Hong Kong. The *New York Times* sends pictures of most of its pages to eight cities where editions are printed and distributed. Both the *Journal* and the *Times* are available in news racks in nearly any city of size. The *Detroit News* has its main plant downtown, a satellite plant twenty-five miles away, and another eighty miles away near Lansing, the state capital. The *Los Angeles Times* has satellite plants in Orange County, about sixty miles south of Los Angeles, and in the San Fernando Valley, about twenty miles northeast of the main plant. The *New York Times,* in addition to other plants, has a printing factory twelve miles from Times Square in New Jersey and plans another in the area. Page pictures are sent there by microwave, the same system used for some long-distance telephone calls.

Whether readers will get their news from newspapers or television, or both, there should be plenty of jobs for copy editors. The task of selecting, condensing, revising, and fitting news to space *or* time will require a growing number of people who can write, edit, make news judgments—and operate modern equipment.

Changes produced by new technology came to pass because publishers seized upon inventions, such as the computer, and adapted them to newspaper use. Most newspapers seek even more printing changes.

Journalism students today are bound to be plunged into these technical changes. This does not mean that they will have to learn how the new technology operates any more than automobile drivers have to know how to fix the newest car. Journalists, like car drivers, need a basic knowledge of what the machines can do. They must consider not only how the machines can work for them, but also how they can work in the best interests of the public.

The basics of graphic arts will be important to any conceivable graphic presentation of the future. A few students see no practical use in learning about type and design, but on the job the background has proved useful in unexpected ways—such as making graphics for television programs!

5

Writing headlines

HEADLINES HAVE BEEN COMPARED to road signs, advertising slogans, and store windows. All these have the common task of seizing attention and putting a message across swiftly. That is what a good newspaper head does. The first and most important purpose of a headline is to inform readers quickly. The well-written head immediately tells them the gist of the accompanying story.

When we say we are a nation of headline skimmers, the tone is usually derogatory. The other side of that criticism, however, is that skimming heads makes possible rapid news comprehension, since literally no one can read all the stories processed each day. If the heads do their most important job—rapid summary—the careful skimmer will get the general drift of events and slow up for a story that may be worth careful reading.

A second important goal of headlines is related to their billboard function. Headlines must sell. On newsstands in competitive cities, front page headlines tend to sell one paper instead of another. In monopoly cities they may push a reader to buy a paper instead of skipping it. But on the inside pages of every newspaper, headlines sell the reader to start reading a story. Philosophically, the primary function of the free press in a democracy is not to make money but to inform citizens. But in our society the paper must be profitable to remain alive and lively, so headlines must help sell individual stories as well as the whole paper.

Relating to both informing and selling is a third function: grading, or evaluating, the news. One head shouts that this story is important. Another suggests quietly that this one might be of some interest as well. Even the size and style of type help communicate to the reader the importance and quality of the news—whether it is a cataclysm or a pleasant afternoon tea. A more extensive explanation of how the editor evaluates the news appears in Chapter 8.

A final purpose of headlines is to stimulate the reader's artistic sense. Dull heads make a dull page. But graphic artistry is much more complex than merely replacing dullness with brightness. Headlines may add to the clutter of ugly or confusing pages. But when heads are well written and well placed in styles that have been thoughtfully designed, the pages are clean and good looking. Indeed, the personality of a paper, in part, is set by the consistent use of heads day after day, and a sudden, drastic change in heads may make a subscriber feel that a familiar friend has moved away.

Hazards in heads

One of the newspaper's most vulnerable points is the headline. Readers may grumble about the way a paper covers the news, but often their complaint boils down to dislike of the heads.

Simple inattention can make heads read two ways, sometimes ludicrously. Here are two examples:

Downtown hogs grant cash

**Life sentence
stretched by
cursed judge**

Often reporters complain that their stories were all right — but the heads were distorted. Reporters often have had to explain to sources that they had nothing to do with the headline. When the head doesn't quite match the story, the reporter is embarrassed and sources are irritated or even angry.

Let's say, for example, that a governor named Becker is caught up in an emotional campaign to weaken the state's water pollution law. The governor may want the law strengthened, if it is changed at all, but powerful people in and out of the legislature want the law virtually repealed. The issue rages in the news media for weeks, with much of the public choosing sides in the argument.

The governor, eager to cool the debate, suggests in a speech that a minor compromise might satisfy reasonable people in both camps. In such a case the headline should be something like one of these:

**Becker proposes
step to soothe
pollution debate**

**Becker suggests
three changes
in water law**

Instead, some papers may come up with these:

**Becker concedes
to opposition
on water law**

**Becker relents
in his battle
on water law**

The inaccurate headlines could cause a storm. Those favoring strong antipollution laws would think at first glance that the governor had betrayed them. Those wanting a weaker law would rejoice—and later perhaps feel that the governor had tricked *them*.

The governor would be furious, because the inaccurate headline further snarled a difficult political task. He might be so angry that in a press conference a few days later he would charge newspapers with distorting his position.

Such attacks by prominent figures erode the public's confidence in newspapers. Admittedly, some headwriters do distort the news, or they editorialize. Even careful copy editors face built-in dangers. They have to struggle with the limitations of both space and brief words to convey a fair and accurate impression.

Perhaps oversimplification is the greatest threat in headlines. When the news is complex, the reporter often oversimplifies in writing a tight lead. The copy editor's job is to polish and tighten that more, if possible. Then the task requires further condensation into a half dozen words or fewer for the headline. The subtleties inevitably get squeezed out. The honest desk person should change the headline angle if necessary to keep from oversimplifying.

A second danger in headlines is emphasis on a minor angle of a story. A common complaint of speakers is that a reporter takes some minor point, even an aside, and builds a big story around it. The fault is compounded if the head plays up this angle, perhaps in oversimplified form. What the speaker and audience both understood as almost a joke may, for example, be blazoned:

Denounces Bleeding Hearts

Readers who were there—and perhaps the speaker's future audiences—will be re-convinced that newspapers distort and sensationalize.

Distrust of headlines has caused many serious newsmakers to try to avoid distortion. They greatly fear that an unusual but insignificant point will be emphasized. Some of these people have pleaded with editors for a headline that reflects the heart of the story. Others have insisted that magazines put a serialized book into only two or three installments, so newspapers taking excerpts from the installments would have fewer chances to exploit the bizarre. Some editors are aware of the problem, and for complicated stories they will ask the reporter either to write the head or to approve it.

Another danger in headlines is overplay. Too much emphasis on a story usually results from a bad choice of type, but vivid headline words also may overdramatize. Another factor is news flow. A story that would deserve a small one-column head inside on an ordinary day may be overplayed under several columns on the front page when news is dull. According to a tradition, which is passing, a few newspapers run a full-width banner head across the front page every day. (The *banner* is also called a *streamer* or *line*.) This tradition inevitably overplays some stories. A reader might suspect that some of the banners in Figure 5.1 distort the news.

Underplay, of course, is also a threat. Admitting that there is no

5.1. Banners or streamers. Few are used today. (These illustrations, of course, have been reduced to fit this page.)

universal standard of correct play, fair-minded editors nevertheless acknowledge that some papers do not give certain stories the space or heads they deserve. This may be policy or ignorance—maybe the desk person does not realize that the coup in such-and-such a country really affects local readers. Some editors knowingly order small heads on racial strife in other communities, on the theory that large heads would stir things up at home.

Heads of quality

Notwithstanding criticisms, most newspaper head writers do a good job, day in, day out. They may often compose routine or dull heads, but they are accurate. Nothing better illustrates such good, ordinary headlines—unimaginative, perhaps, but fair—than the latest edition of any large daily.

Kudos for head writing usually go to the writers who have a flair for saying the difficult with style. The head that draws the envy of other professionals usually displays unique imagery or wit. Neophytes who want to distinguish themselves as head writers should try to develop a colorful way of putting things in a few words; they will sometimes write corn, but they may develop a valuable talent. The head writer should probe nearly every story for something amusing or clever that can be brought up to a headline. In some instances, as in an obituary, it would be in bad taste. So would heads that make puns out of a person's name. But some real effort to be droll or even funny will produce an occasional gem.

The *Los Angeles Times* put this head on a story noting the decline of musical comedies:

The Dying Strains of the Musical

And this on a story showing slowness in hiring minorities:

The Action Doesn't Look Affirmative

On an editorial condemning a baseball executive's statement on blacks:

Hall of Shamer

and this pun:

'Star Wars' Politicizing Science in U.S.

and this witty one:

Libyan High School's 3 R's: Reading, Riting, Rocketry

The *Wall Street Journal* put this atop a story on animals in films:

**These Agents Supply
Actors That Cluck,
Moo, Roar and Bark**

The *Washington Post* headed a story on the disappearance of the old TV dinner tray:

It Came, It Thawed, It Conquered

And in a teaser, without a verb:

The Poet, the Biographer and the Pulitzer Prize

The *Post* also had a story about Chief Justice Rehnquist's son, a basketball star:

Rehnquist's Son Supreme on Court

One paper used this on a crime story:

Diamonds Are a Thief's Best Friend

The grand champion headline appeared in the *New York Daily News*. President Ford in 1975 curtly rejected New York's appeal for financial aid. The *Daily News,* in 144-point type, proclaimed:

FORD TO CITY: DROP DEAD

Width

The head writer is helped because most papers use horizontal headlines. The traditional "Civil War head" of numerous parts was one column wide and, it seemed, almost a column long. Today only a few papers still hold to a tradition of frequent one-column heads. Most papers use heads of two, three, four, or even six columns.

Style

Aside from the number and length of lines, several other elements set the style of an individual headline.

One factor is arrangement of lines. Should they be even on the left or should they step in on one side? Or should they be stepped in on both sides? The answer will determine how modern a head looks. The *flush left* head — all lines even at the left — has been most popular for decades now, because it can be written more speedily and it looks good. The *lowercase* head has become popular because the letters take up less space. It uses only capital letters for the first letter and for proper nouns. Other words are lowercase for quick reading.

Even before the words of a head are chosen, several other decisions face the copydesk. Normally the slot person or news editor makes these choices almost automatically. Here are some brief guidelines on modern practice.

Type face and size

Modern newspapers use head types that are clean and easily readable, as noted in the chapter on printing. *Sans serif* types (without finishing strokes on each letter) are popular; so-called *modern* or *transitional* types — especially Bodoni — also are often employed because their sharp, bold lines are quickly grasped. Condensed type (squeezed so that many letters will fit into a column) was popular a few decades ago, but the trend is to larger sizes. This movement toward display types that are big, legible, and attractive complicates the problem for the writer who has much to say in little space.

Number of lines

The spread of horizontal makeup, which uses multicolumn heads almost exclusively, brings wide use of the single line three or more columns wide. But two-line heads are by far the most frequent. Though three lines in major headlines are still common, probably less so than a generation ago, four lines are rare.

The other most obvious variable in determining the shape or appearance of the head is the number of parts. Accompanying the main head may be one or more smaller headings to lead the eye down to the story. These parts of a headline are called *decks* (or sometimes *banks* or *drops*). The strong trend has been toward the single deck, especially in one-column heads. The *Wall Street Journal* and the *New York Times* are the only major papers that cling to heads with three decks. Typically the story is told in the first part, or *top,* and further detail follows in the second part, which is sometimes called simply *the deck*. (See Fig. 5.2.)

As decks declined in popularity, the *kicker* for a time became popular. It is a head of from one to several words, frequently with an

Modern head styles

Telephone Switch

ITT-CGE Deal Shows
The Change Buffeting
Telecommunications

High R&D Costs, Difficulty
Of Winning Orders Leads
To Cross-Border Linkups

The Talks That Led to Alcatel

'Faint Noise' Recorded on Doomed Jet

**Crew Conversation
Yields Nothing; No
Sign of Sabotage**

PROBLEMS PLAGUE AMNESTY PROGRAM FOR AIDING ALIENS

LAW TAKES EFFECT MAY 5

Counseling Units Cite Delays
and Confusion — I.N.S.
Concedes Difficulties

underlining rule above the main head. Writing of decks and kickers will be considered later.

In summary, a head in small type, narrow measure, with several decks of stepped lines, looks old-fashioned. The modern head tends to be in a large and clear face, flush left and several columns wide, in lowercase, and accompanied by not more than one subordinate deck. The few newspapers that still have subordinate decks use two or three lines in a variety of ways.

Head schedules

Every newspaper has a variety of headline type faces. Editors choose from the styles and sizes available to produce headlines that please readers' eyes. Most papers list the head styles on a *headline schedule,* so staffers can see what they look like. The schedule shows a sample of each face and lists the size of the type and the number of characters, called the "count," that can be squeezed into one column.

Perhaps most headlines are called merely by the size, such as "36-point," and a two-column headline would be labeled "2/36." Some newspapers use a code, letting an "A" headline equal two columns and two lines of 36-point, a "B" head signifying a one column of 30-point with three lines, and so on.

60

The electronic newsroom has largely eliminated close attention to count, for the computer does the job. Copy editors, having a rough idea that a four-column, 42-point head takes around thirty characters, will write a head with five or six words. They hit a couple keys and find out immediately if the headline fits. The VDT screen will say "long" or "fits" or "minus 2" (characters) after each line, telling the writer whether the headline must be revised to fit the space.

Sometimes typographers may propose a complete redesigning of the type dress. They usually choose types that harmonize, and that usually means sticking to one family of type. The regular face is used in different sizes, and more variety is introduced by using italic, bold-face, ultrabold, and condensed versions of the basic face. Sometimes a second style of type will complement the basic one, as, for example, sans serif with a modern face. Use of three or more faces leads to a muddle.

A knowledge of type enables the copy editor to write off-beat headlines. While one must take care not to introduce confusion and ugliness, the imaginative deskperson occasionally can create variety and freshness with unorthodox heads, such as some of those in Figure 5.3.

The importance of being Harry

In Line With
The Literati
Writers to Confer at the Library

So you want to
write a screenplay?
Stretch Fabric E x p a n d i n g

5.3. Unusual headlines. The second head uses no verb. The last one, by spacing, cleverly displays the head's message.

Many of the world's papers have accustomed readers to heads that are mere labels. A London paper, for example, may proclaim in 18- or 24-point type, **Parliamentary Debate** or **Death at Chamonix.** Most American readers find such label heads dull, but an editor overseas can argue with some point that they do not give away the whole story. There may even be some tendency in the United States, as newsstand competition diminishes, for the American editor

Basic rules for heads

to use more label heads. Some editors see no point in insisting on heads with verbs on certain feature stories. So they use verbless heads, much like magazine article titles:

Love's Labors Loft

Berlin: East Side, West Side

Punchy heads

The mainstream of American head writing, however, emphasizes the vivid, dramatic, summary headline. American readers would immediately sense something wrong if they met this headline:

**The Congressmen Were in a Disagreement
On the Housing Legislation**

It is wrong because it is past tense; it has no active verb with object; and it has several articles. Furthermore, most of the words are too long for a conventional head.

Americans feel more at home if they see the subject summarized this way:

**Solons Split
On Home Bill**

This head is in the present tense; a concrete noun is followed by a strong, active verb; and articles have been sliced out. This same example, however, has some head-writing weaknesses. "Solons" is *headlinese,* or jargon, which many copydesks dislike. "Split" may be read here as a verb in the past tense or an adjective, and it doubtless overstates the debate the reporter discussed. And while "home bill" has punch, it introduces an oversimplification and perhaps even connotations that the more complex language avoids.

The severe space restrictions for headlines bring forth dozens of short words that the headline writer weaves among longer words so the heads will fit. Stewart Benedict, a copy editor for the *Jersey Journal* in Jersey City, wrote for *Editor & Publisher* this spoof of the copydesk's short-word vocabulary.

Q. – So you work as a copy reader?
A. – Yes.
Q. – What does your work involve?
A. – Fix copy, write heads.
Q. – Are you considered a sort of executive?
A. – No. Aide.
Q. – If things go well, how do you describe your day?
A. – OK.
Q. – And, if they go badly, what emotion do you experience?
A. – Ire.
Q. – But, if you aren't quite so angry, what is your state of mind?
A. – Irked.
Q. – And if you're only slightly irritated?
A. – Miffed.
Q. – After work, when you drop into a bar to unwind, what do you do?
A. – Parley.

62

Q. — But, if you don't run into any of your friends to converse with at the bar, what do you do while you're having a drink?
A. — Mull.
Q. — What is your marital status, sir?
A. — Wed.
Q. — And how would you describe your wife?
A. — Top gal.
Q. — Do you and your wife ever have any disagreements?
A. — Tiffs? Sure.
Q. — What do you do about your concerns?
A. — Air them.
Q. — And what is the next step?
A. — Close them.
Q. — Do you have any children?
A. — One tot.
Q. — How would you describe your abode?
A. — Fine site.
Q. — But, back to your work. What's the first thing you do on getting a piece of copy?
A. — Eye it.
Q. — Suppose you get a story so badly done that it seems hopeless?
A. — Kill it.
Q. — But, if it can be salvaged, what do you do to the reporter?
A. — Flay him.
Q. — And what does he do to his story then?
A. — Alters it.
Q. — Do you find that your work has any drawbacks?
A. — Unquestionably. The limitations incumbent upon me to eschew polysyllabic vocabulary and linguistic esoterica are inhibiting. Frequent animadversion about my inability to transcend these aforementioned restrictions has, I fear, produced in me a somewhat pessimistic Weltanschauung. A consolation, however, is my perhaps utopian expectation that some hitherto anonymous philanthropist will establish a periodical in which only sesquipedalianisms will be tolerated.
Q. — Uh — check. Thanks.
A. — 30.

Abbreviating

How do copy editors decide what to put in the headline's abbreviated key sentence?

As reporters try to get the gist of the story into a lead that summarizes the event, head writers boil that sentence to fit the count. In theory, at its simplest, they switch the sentence into the present or future tense and eliminate articles and time-place references. The remaining skeleton is typically subject, verb, and, perhaps, direct or indirect object.

Assume the wire carries this lead:

WASHINGTON — The House today launched into a bitter debate on a bill to set up a new version of the Job Corps.

A copy editor might write a two-line head:

**Job Corps Bill
Debated in House**

The second line is a little long, so it can be altered easily to make it fit:

**House Debates
Job Corps Bill**

Some slot person may argue that this does not reflect the ire the bill has produced—and it starts with a flat word: "House." Another might do the job:

**Job Corps Fight
Erupts in House**

But maybe this one is too strong. A calmer head might be tried:

**Job Corps Bill
Debate Fiery**

This one only implies the verb *is,* so another one is tried:

**House Wrangles
over Job Corps**

This starts with "House" but it may indicate the intensity of the debate, without exaggeration. It would fit and tell the story.

Rules and reality

These illustrations reveal two points about head writing:

1. "Inviolable" rules sometimes collide head-on, and a choice has to be made as to which is more important.
2. Since tastes of copydesk chiefs vary, the head writer has to be alert to the dictums and prejudices of each particular boss.

In the American fashion, headlines "give the story away," so skimmers can decide what they want to read in detail. But *feature heads,* another whole category of headlines, give only a hint of the story. In magazines, of course, these are simply *titles.* Such heads do not summarize but rather try to capture interest. They may lack verbs or subjects, as sometimes mere fragments arouse the reader's curiosity.

Traditional headlines usually go on spot news stories. Feature-head treatment best fits material like the human-interest story or the personality sketch. It may pun. It may twist a common phrase or aphorism. Such heads require imaginative or witty deskpeople. These editors also can apply their talent to the occasional straight news story when a traditional summary head doesn't provide insight into the story. A clever, catchy head may do the job. Some editors, to describe this situation, have a slogan: "If you can't tell it, sell it."

An example of the "sold-not-told" head could be:

**Ah, There, Doomsayers!
You Forgot $42 Million**

"Almost anything goes" is the motto for the writer of feature heads. But copydesk traditions are quite firm about news headlines. Beginning copy editors must have the rules firmly in mind before they can decide which may be broken safely.

Cardinal rules

The previous discussion suggests the two cardinal rules of the news headline:

1. State (or imply) a complete sentence in the present or future tense.
2. Eliminate all articles and most adverbs and adjectives.

The first rule notes that to imply a complete sentence, as with an infinitive or an understood verb, is permissible:

**Senator to Speak
At Senior Dinner**

**Guerrillas Aiming
For April Victory**

Usually the subject of the sentence is vital to a headline, but sometimes the alert slot person will accept a head that clearly implies the subject. Here are borderline examples:

**Weighs GOP
Industrial Plan**

**Enjoins Strike
In Second Day**

Beware of heads that seem to command action from the reader. This one sounds like a plea or command rather than a report:

**Hit Democrats'
Housing Proposal**

Some editors, to whom such headlines are anathema, suggest that too much permissiveness may lead to the ridiculous:

**Attack 3 Women
With 6 Children**

The second rule, banning articles, also has exceptions. Sometimes a head reads and fits better with an article:

**Judge Charges Teenagers
'On the Loose' at Night**

65

Major rules

Beyond these two cardinal rules lie five other head writing guidelines. Most of them stem from the discussion of good and bad heads and are given here more or less in descending order of importance.

1. Be accurate. If necessary, sacrifice color and drama in a headline to avoid leaving an erroneous impression.

Accuracy may force the copy editor to sift the story for the kernel of the news. Of course if the lead is buried, the good copy editor revises the story, putting the major news at the top and then drawing the head from the revised lead. But an interpretative news story may properly start with a less pointed lead than a spot news story. Then the head writer has to grasp the full meaning of the story and try to summarize it accurately.

Here, for example, is the lead of a story in the *New York Times:*

> ALBANY, April 24—Evidence that the Legislature is embroiled in its adjournment rush is visible and audible this week.
>
> Absent members are being voted "aye" by the leadership to pass favored bills. Legislators cannot get copies of bills even as the bills are being passed, lobbying is rampant and many legislators have dropped all pretense of parliamentary politeness and are literally snarling at each other. . . .

The *Times* copy editor summarized the whole piece with this head:

Tension Rises as Windup Nears at Albany

2. Be specific and concrete. *One-eyed thief* is better than *robber* or *man; 3,000 bales* is better than *cotton; killed* is better than *died.* Increasingly, it is difficult to write heads that tell the story on complicated economic issues, international tensions, or environmental legislation. A single word such as *economy, accord,* or *nature* rarely gets across what the subject is about. Vague, abstract words make headlines without punch. But blunt words that fit may mislead.

3. Use strong verbs. Avoid jelly words such as *discuss* and *indicate* and forms of *to be.* As in good news story style, use strong verbs in the active voice—*slash, pinpoint, reveal, assail, hit, kill.* Some otherwise good words have been used so much that good editors avoid or ban their use; these include *rap, sift, probe,* and *flay.* Remember that verbs must be accurate as well as active. So perhaps *assail* should be replaced by *criticize,* or *denounce* by *chide.*

4. Start with the news. The first line of the head should tell readers what they want to know immediately. A short noun followed by a short, active verb will usually do:

Pope Decries . . .

Teachers Revolt . . .

U.S. Shifts Lead . . .

Of the five Ws used in the lead, the top line of the head summarizes the *who* and *what*.

But sometimes the group acting is less important and newsworthy, at least in a label word, than is the body acted upon. So, as indicated already, *congress* and *legislature* as the first word of a head probably will have less pulling power than the tag for the legislation passed, as with *pollution bill* or *teen draft act*. Though such a subject forces the verb into the weaker passive form, strength can still be given, as with *debated, argued,* or *killed.*

5. Punctuate correctly. Some beginning head writers mistakenly cut out punctuation marks as well as articles. As Figure 5.4 shows, punctuation is the same in heads as other copy, except that the period almost never ends a headline. Commas are often necessary, as in other writing. Semicolons join independent clauses, but a semicolon in the middle of a line splits the reader's attention. To save space and improve appearance, single quotation marks replace the traditional double ones. The dash has many good head uses, but since words are not split at the end of the line in the heads of the well-edited paper, hyphens appear only between words.

Whether periods mark a head abbreviation is a question of the paper's style; it may be Y.W.C.A. or YWCA. Sometimes a paper will use periods in one group of initials but not in another, according to a

---

Canton Man, 32, Found Guilty Of Armed Violence, Battery

Fire away!

space shuttle

test succeeds

Havana Rolls Past VIT, 84-51

5.4. Punctuating headlines. Punctuation, as in these heads, generally follows the conventions of English sentences, but without the ending period.

Wayzata man found guilty of murder, attempted murder

When 'dog bites man' is startling news

tradition that the writer must learn. Similarly, abbreviation is according to style. *Prof.* without the name, *yr.,* and *Dept.* are typical abbreviations that many newspapers would ban. But, *Dr.* and *Rev.* and *Co.* (with appropriate names) or *Pct.* or *U.N.,* would be used without hesitation. Nicknames, like *Maggie* or *Jerry,* as well as first names alone or initials only—like *FDR, Abe,* and *Teddy*—are taboo on some papers, though frequently used by others.

All sorts of other traditions and preconceptions hedge the major rules. One paper may avoid the verb *eye* in heads; another will use names of only the most prominent personages in headlines. But all agree that numerals may be used in heads, even to begin a line.

Minor rules

Most editors would further agree on these seven minor rules:

1. Don't split. *Splitting* a head means dividing a natural grouping of words by the end of a line. The most heinous split puts the "to" of an infinitive at the end of one line and the verb on the next:

**Mayor Promises to
Study Rent Frauds**

Splitting prepositional phrases is almost as bad. But it is also poor practice to sever "have" or "will" from the rest of the verb or to separate an adjective from the noun it modifies. (To keep headline writers sane, editors usually allow splits in decks or between the second and third lines of a three-line head.)

2. Don't repeat. A good headline, like a good sentence, avoids simple-minded repetition. **Fair Manager Tells Plans for Fair** obviously is awkward. Copy editors also should skip awkward repetition of sounds, as in **Legislators Eye New Racing Legislation.**

One of the greatest temptations is to repeat a word from the head in the deck. Even use of a synonym sounds strained, so the deck should usually reveal a second angle.

3. Don't overpack. It is good advice to try to get many ideas into a head; good practice avoids padding and thinning. Yet one can cross a line where the head becomes so packed with ideas that the reader has trouble translating it. Piling up nouns as modifiers makes awkward heads. **State Police Investigators** is clear to most. **State Police Traffic Toll Investigators** is more difficult, but **State Police Major Highway Traffic Toll Investigators** is impossible.

4. Don't use headlinese. Good English is best. As indicated already, headlinese is the language of overworked words. They may be the short, punchy verbs, so some editors object to even *hit* and *gut* as headlinese. Certain nouns, such as *cops* and *tryst,* are overworked and slangy. Stay alert to usage; when a word becomes a cliché, avoid it.

Homely words become headlinese when used for their size and not their sense. One of the most infelicitous such uses is *said* for *termed, called,* or *described as.* Those who employ this poor English can argue that it is short for "is said to be," but the mind swirls at fitting in the missing words, as in this head from an Eastern paper:

**Red Bloc
Trade Said
Beneficial**

Called counts only 1½ characters more than *said* and in this instance would have fit. (Words like *called* or *labeled* are considered attributive words. They indicate to the reader that someone is making a statement. Without such words the headline would become a flat statement, like **Red Bloc Trade Beneficial**, which would be an *editorial* head appropriate on the editorial page but not over news stories.)

5. Don't be ambiguous. Mushy words leave mushy meanings. The many legitimate meanings of a single English word make the writer's job difficult. The verb *will,* in faulty context, may appear to be a noun, which one reader may mistake for *determination,* another for *legal document.* Humor sometimes results from unexpected double meanings:

**Roberts Will Suit
Stalls over Horses**

Precision is essential in heads, as illustrated by earlier discussion of Governor Becker's trouble over a water pollution bill.

6. Avoid lazy techniques. Some headline writers will snap off anything that will fit, even if the reader is puzzled, as in these outrages:

Pimples good for you: Study

Panel: Chemical waste harmless

7. *Don't repeat wording in lead.* A story may begin: "Despite $25 tickets, business is booming among Broadway theaters." But readers hear an echo if the head reads:

Despite $25 prices, Broadway theaters booming

Beginning headline writers, like beginning newswriters, tend to produce vague copy. They appear to be reluctant to get to the meat of the story. For a story of a crash that killed fifteen people in Los Angeles, for example, they may produce heads that say:

Plane crashes at airport

Jet crashes on runway

These obviously won't get much news across to the reader. The head writer might turn to the story lead and write a digest of that paragraph:

15 killed in L.A. air crash

This way the reader knows immediately the seriousness of the accident, what kind of accident it was, and where it was.

Headline writers should say to themselves as they tackle a head: What's the real news? How can I tell it in a few words? How can I squeeze in more information? Will it be essential to tell where something took place? If headlines only skirt basic facts, readers sense that the paper is bland and dull.

In paper-and-pencil editing days editors had to know which letters were fat and which were thin. With computers, as noted, editors let the machine worry about the width of letters. Once in a while, however, someone editing a newsletter, a little magazine, or a circular actually will have to count the letters. In that case the rudiments of type size must be understood.

Each small letter counts one character, except that *l, i, f, t,* and usually *j* and spaces are thin and count only ½ character. Also, *m* and *w* are fat and count 1½. So do all capital letters, except *M* and *W,* which count 2. A headline starting *Simple Simon* counts 12, and it will fit nicely if the column can accommodate 13 characters.

Making heads fit

Some headlines come easily and naturally and fit the first time, but often copy editors have to ponder several possibilities. They should try to put the whole head together at once and make space adjustments afterward. If they tinker to make the first line perfect before going on to the rest, they will likely find it impossible to fit other lines to the first line.

Flexibility is most important. The copy editor should try not to get the mind locked in on a particular wording. If a pet phrase doesn't work after a bit of trying, the head writer should stop wasting time with it and use a new approach. The key statement of the lead may have to be abandoned and the writer may need to rethink what the story is trying to say.

Developing the knack

Three pointers

Here are three tips on the knack of writing heads, probably in the order the copy editor will use them.

1. Try for good short synonyms when the head doesn't fit. Since English has many short verbs, these can probably be juggled more easily than others: e.g., *criticizes, assails, slaps, raps, quits.* Sometimes a slight loss in clarity is unavoidable when substituting, as when

"School Superintendent" becomes "School Chief." Initials and nick-names can be used, though good desk procedure requires that they be immediately clear to readers and that they not become too numerous. (Such means may be the only feasible way to distinguish among news figures with the same name; in a city with a mayor named Rudolph Hammerhill, head writers may use "Rudy," "Ham," "Mayor," and other such codes to communicate the right name quickly.)

2. Reverse the head if the first subject-verb pattern doesn't fit.

**Diplomats Foresee
Middle East War**

will fit if changed to

**Middle East War
Feared by Envoys**

3. Look for a new angle. If the one on the left won't do, perhaps the other one will:

**Nation found
suddenly upset
over economy**

**Jobless rise
seen causing
wide anxiety**

Kickers

Another subordinate head is the kicker. (See Fig. 5.5.) Almost all newspapers use this device of a little head above the main head, though research shows that kickers are seldom read. They do, how-ever, provide a ribbon of white space above the head and thus help attract attention. So they should be kept short, to emphasize the white space, and their wording should stir interest with a new angle or touch. Words that would make a good, crisp flush-left second deck probably also will make a good kicker, but it should be a little more striking or dazzling than the typical deck. Sometimes dropping the verb will do the trick, for labels are more readily accepted in kickers. A conservative kicker looks like a regular head:

Detectives Spot New Evidence

But a kicker can display more vigor:

Mysterious Time Bomb

A quote draws attention to the main head:

'I Was Framed!'

Symbol or Substance?

Misgiving, Lawsuits Greet Freeze on Federal Hiring

Unorthodox Scientist

Going Out on a Limb on the Origins of Man

Interpreting the news

Marginally poor would lose most

FAMILY ASSISTANCE STRESSED

Juvenile Court Changes Urged

5.5. Kickers. Note that if head is roman type, the kicker is italic, and vice versa. The kicker usually takes up only half the space of the full headline and is half the type size.

The kicker should not read like the beginning or end of the headline or as a substitute for attribution:

And choked with junk
Inky Creek found laden with acid

Zefoss Says
Board filled with tightwads

One form of head, still used a little, is the *subhead*. Ordinarily it is simply two or three words of boldface, the same size as the body type, in the body of a story. Subheads help break up the monotony of large blocks of type, although many papers simply use a little extra white space between paragraphs to accomplish the same thing.

Rules for subheads are the same as for major heads: present tense, no articles, active voice. If used at all, the subhead is typed into the story on the VDT every fourth or fifth graf. It should refer to the material in the next couple of grafs. (See Fig. 5.6.)

Subheads and jump heads

The Beavers scored 9 straight points — 5 by Radford and 4 by Johnson — to go ahead, 48-47, and seemed to have taken control.

Miller Shakes His Head

But then they ran into problems. Sitton was called for an offensive foul, his fourth, and was replaced by McShane.

Stories continued inside the paper need some heading for the continuation, or *jump*. The *jump head* usually repeats basically the front page head. Some papers now use a smaller head for the jump. It typically has a "better count" than the one on the front page, and the copy editor may be able to get ideas and precision here that were abandoned in writing the main head. (A reverse "logo" — white letters on a dark gray background — sometimes helps the eye spot the jump.)

The jump word is often a single key word. It may be employed with a jump head, but more often it stands alone. Like the slug, this word should distinguish the story from all others that day. The jump word is set in larger type or caps; and a box, rules, or white space should make it easy to spot. (See Fig. 5.7.)

Oregon State is No. 1

Continued from Page B 11

CHICKEN: Out of Frying Pan, Into Profits

Continued from 6th Page

Diabetic

Fires set at 2 cabins irk officials

From Page 1

Chop shops

Continued from page 1

★ Sizzler

(Continued from Page 1A)

Prince

(Continued from Page 1A)

Monkey in 2nd Day of Mission

FROM PAGE 1

5.7. Jumps. Editors have developed ingenious heading devices for inside pages to help readers find continued stories. Regular heads are often used to emphasize the news content of these pages. Many editors also use a gimmick, such as a reverse plate so that the reader's searching eye can spot the jump quickly. A slug word, perhaps with rules, attracts a reader's attention easily.

A few papers use a headline called a *readout*. This head accompanies a *line* (or *banner* or *streamer*) and provides supplementary information. It gets the name from the fact that it "reads out" of the main head and tops a story that will run vertically down the page. It looks and reads like this:

JOBLESS RATE IN NATION REACHES 7.2 PCT.

Area around
Great Lakes
hardest hit

This discussion of headlines has moved from theory to the nuts and bolts of head counts and then to the lowly subhead and jump head. A copy editor may similarly leave broad principle behind and become involved in the minutiae of quick writing—"anything that fits." Professional editing, however, keeps to the high purpose of the newspaper. Even though a head must fit a space and flag attention, its main purpose is to inform quickly and truthfully. The best head writer produces accurate heads so regularly that applying rules becomes as habitual and automatic as hitting the "head fit" key on the VDT.

6

Designing the pages

GOOD NEWS COVERAGE, news selection, editing, and headline writing are four of the five essentials of an excellent newspaper. The remaining element of excellence is good typographical design—the choices of type and the placement of type and pictures. *Makeup* is the designing process; *layout* and *dummying* are part of makeup, but the terms are loosely used to refer to the whole process.

Good design attracts readers and makes reading easier. A well-designed newspaper encourages readers to look at every page. They will find that they need not squint to read the material and that the various blocks of type are arranged to convey news values.

There is no set way of accomplishing these aims, just as there is no set way of painting a picture. Yet as painters learn form, color and shading, newspaper designers learn principles of readability and attractiveness. They use findings in art and psychology to test intuitions on how best to get information from the page to the reader. Researchers have found that today's readers won't take time to read small type, so body type sizes have been increased to 9-, 9½-, or 10-point. (See Fig. 6.1.) Researchers also have discovered that moderately large headlines

It is of course right that the British and Irish governments should have close contact on all matters concerning Northern Ireland. It it a profound mistake, however, to conceal from our own people and from the people of Northern Ireland the broad lines of the contents of these discussions about which many are clearly apprehensive and about which they have a perfect right to be informed.

Editors at Knight-Ridder Newspapers have also developed a comprehensive, 3½ hour test for prospective copy editors, and editors at Knight-Ridder's Philadelphia Inquirer say the testing program — combined with efforts to encourage better writing — has produced a steady improvement in the quality of the paper's prose.

6.1. The 7-point, unleaded type from the *Times* of London, left, is less readable than the 10-point, leaded type in the *Jackson* (Mississippi) *Daily News.*

of both capital and lowercase letters are easier to read than those in all caps. The better papers use headline types that are easy to see, but not so large that they shout at the reader. Many papers, as noted, have put all headlines in lowercase, capitalizing only the first word and any proper nouns. These moves reflect our experience with print and handwriting: Words are made up mostly of small letters. Designers believe we are more content following familiar patterns.

Until recently, newspaper designers contended that much typographical ornamentation hampered readership. To separate stories, they advised eliminating stars, dashes, asterisks, and cutoff rules in favor of ribbons or small blocks of white space. The result was called a "clean" design. In recent years, however, many papers have restored a few lines and cutoff rules. Their editors said that white space had been overdone.

Some researchers have found that the eye tends to scan a page in a line that resembles a reversed numeral 6. (See Fig. 6.2.) The reader looks toward the upper left of a page first, shifts across to the right, to the lower right, to the lower left, and then loops to the center of the page.

The reverse-6

Why, then, do newspapers put their best stories in the upper right, the number two position? Custom, or habit. For years newspapers ran banners on page one. When reading English, people move their eyes from left to right. When they finish reading the banner, their eyes are at the right of the page. Editors argued that it was foolish to send the reader back to the left to read the story, so the story "read out" of the banner down the right column. Most papers have nearly given up the banner but still cling to putting the lead story in the upper right. A few have discarded the idea. They make up page

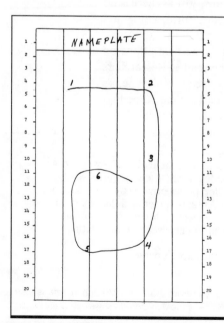

6.2. The reverse-6 pattern. Some researchers find that readers' eyes usually land first about Point 1 and travel to the right, down the page, across the bottom, and back to midpage. Editors often put key stories or pictures at the numbered points. Photographs and color, of course, upset the pattern to some extent.

one with the main story at top left and other strong material at lower left.

Horizontal makeup, which is now easy to use with modern presses, means a fairly long story can appear complete on one page, without a jump. While the stories often are long, they do not seem lengthy. The few inches of copy in each column encourage the reader to absorb the whole story rather than to stop with the first few paragraphs. Avoiding jumps is desirable because only the most determined readers will turn from page one to page twenty-one and back to page one again.

Some years ago newspaper designers took a careful look at the American newspaper and realized that the narrow columns looked jammed with type. The reader had to focus carefully to read the stories. A rather simple test showed that most readers did not read one line at a time. The narrow, 11- or 12-pica column in eight-column newspapers was a trifle long for one glance and not quite long enough for two. (Since a pica is ⅙ inch, a 12-pica column is 2 inches wide.) So the six-column newspaper was born. The columns widened to 16 picas (2⅔ inches), which allowed rapid, comfortable reading and permitted better head counts, resulting in more accurate headlines.

Unfortunately, economics interceded. Newsprint costs soared and, to save paper, column widths were reduced a little every year or two. Now most papers use six columns, with each column only a little more than 12 picas, putting the column width almost back to what it was when papers used the eight-column format. The narrowed page, however, makes the paper easier for the reader to hold.

Changing styles

Makeup styles come and go. For a time, one style will be the rage, and hundreds of papers will shift to it. Then another style comes along and most editors switch to it. The current favorite is *modular,* a system that uses modules, or rectangles, to form blocks that, pieced together properly, form a pleasing combination of type and pictures. Modular design borrows heavily from contemporary architecture and other modern art forms.

One main advantage of modular style is the way the whole story fits into one compact unit, instead of having part of the story in one column and a longer part in another. With modular, the eye is less likely to be diverted from the module than it is from any other design form.

Modular designers have some problems, however. They often lapse into stacking one module atop another until the page looks like a bunch of packing boxes in a warehouse. They also like to develop a neat design for the front page and then shop around for stories to fill the modules they created. Once those are found—probably with distorted judgment on news values—they are reluctant to change anything for new stories. (See Fig. 6.3.) A few papers, notably *USA Today,* have used vertical design. Some researchers contend that readers find modular angles a bit too neat.

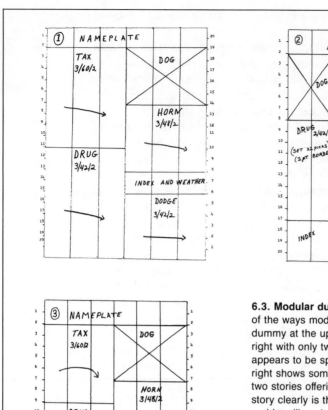
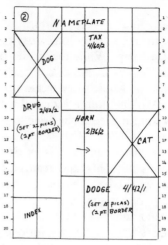

6.3. Modular dummies. These designs show some of the ways modular makeup is used. In No. 1 dummy at the upper left, the design is heavy to the right with only two stories at the left. The page also appears to be split into two segments. No. 2 on the right shows some variety, with borders around the two stories offering nonstandard widths. The lead story clearly is the best, because of its placement and headline size, and the page is neatly anchored at the bottom, avoiding a top-heavy appearance. At the lower left No. 3 dummy also provides a solid anchor, with the type set 24 picas, requiring three "legs" of type under the six-column head. The column widths of type normally would not appear on dummies. The required border size would.

Page one of the six-column modular paper can use two or three pictures and five or six stories. This method leaves plenty of good stories for the inside. Readers sense that they are getting a lot of information for their money—and they are. Most users of this format try to put out a newspaper that looks like a big magazine and gives readers both the news of the *day* and the news of the *times*. That is, readers get, clearly spread out before them, the news of the previous twenty-four hours. In addition, they receive information about trends in local and world events that may have been going on for the last three months or the last three years.

Other terms describe design styles or techniques. Applying names to those styles is difficult because one category shades into another. Those who actually do the day-to-day job of designing pages may rarely use the names of the categories, if they have ever heard of them, for editors make up pages by judgment or "feel," not by labels.

Everyone concerned with design, however, refers frequently to *balance.* The term is so common that it has come to describe a particular kind of makeup. In this system the typographic display on one side of a page balances, or nearly balances, a similar display on the other side. Fifty years ago a picture often occupied the exact center, with headlines of equal size on either side. At the bottom a double-column headline would go on one side and another double-column head on the other. The idea was to achieve perfect symmetry.

Perfect balance, however, has serious drawbacks. In judging the day's news, editors usually decide that one story is clearly better than all others. They want to say so by giving it the biggest headline. But in balance they must give the same headline display to a lesser story.

Strict balance has another shortcoming. The eye finds it hard to focus on anything so exactly proportioned. A balanced page calls attention to a pattern but not a point. Every cluster of type is tempered by another exactly the same. Some critics have contended that looking at a balanced page is a bit like looking at a checkerboard.

For these reasons formal balance was replaced largely by *asymmetrical* or *dynamic balance.* This method includes balance but not exact counterbalancing. A two-column picture may balance a three-column headline in the adjoining quarter page, or quadrant. Or a two-column headline may adequately balance a three-column head. In this system, the lead story is clearly the lead, for it has the biggest headline.

Another makeup style is called *focus* or *brace.* The names suggest the heavy focus of attention at the top and the way the big headline there is braced—or supported—by sizable heads beneath it. The big headline and its satellites dominate the page. Few newspapers use this style because the banner head is used so rarely. The *Chicago Tribune,* however, often displays a banner and the larger heads below make an attractive page.

Circus, the opposite of brace, scatters big headlines all over the page. Its detractors sometimes call circus the "gee whiz" method. Half of the front page stories are headlined as though each were an advance on the Second Coming. Traditional circus is now the province of foreign newspapers, and even there it is declining. (See the variety of designs in Figs. 6.4 to 6.16.)

Los Angeles Times

Circulation: 1,336,813 Daily/1,421,711 Sunday   Tuesday, November 29, 1988   CC1/ 96 Pages   Copyright 1988/The Times Mirror Company   Daily 25¢ / Designated Area Higher

Gillette Plant Issue

U.S.-French Ties Take on a Hard Edge

By RONE TEMPEST, *Times Staff Writer*

ANNECY, France—When the 400 workers of the Gillette razor blade factory in this picturesque lakeside city heard rumors early this fall that their American parent corporation planned to close the plant, they launched an energetic counterattack.

They dipped into union funds to take out full-page advertisements in Paris newspapers charging that Gillette planned to "shave" France of an important employer. They staged a highly publicized "reverse strike" in which they posed before television cameras toiling "harder, longer and better" than ever before.

Finally, on the eve of a crucial meeting between Gillette management and the French minister for industry in Paris, four plant workers climbed to the summit of nearby 15,771-foot Mt. Blanc, Western Europe's highest peak, to unfurl a banner protesting any closing of the plant. Television crews filmed the event from hovering helicopters.

A Fantastic Success

As media campaigns go, it was a fantastic success. No wonder Minister of Industry Roger Fauroux entered the meeting with Gillette officials last September charged with patriotic, protectionist zeal. Talking to reporters afterwards, Fauroux said he told Gillette Vice Chairman Derwyn Phillips, president of the company's European operations, that "if he closes the factory at Annecy, he will not enter into a conflict with the unions from the plant, but with France herself."

Then, in language that sounded to everyone around very much like the threat of a state-endorsed boycott, Fauroux, a former manager or of one of France's largest industries who until that point had been considered a friend of American business, went on to say:

"The French market is very important to Gillette in Europe; it would be very irresponsible for the company directors to run the risk of losing it. . ." He told Gillette officials not to ensure back until they had come up with a proposal to save the Annecy facility, which produces double-edged razor blades and a few other toiletry items.

Strong Talk

According to the American officials and business leaders in Paris, it was some of the strongest talk in years from a French government that has been increasingly open to foreign investment.

"Fauroux brandished the threat of a boycott weapon as though it would be condoned by the government itself," one American business leader said. "It was like using the atomic bomb to kill a mouse."

As a result, the relatively small matter of the closing of a medium-sized manufacturing plant in a remote city has escalated into a serious free-trade conflict between France and the United States. Fauroux elevated the issue into an affaire d'état between the two countries.

At the heart of the conflict is the right of foreign businesses in Please see GILLETTE, Page 6

Bush, Dole Vow Harmony; Fitzwater Keeps Press Job

By JAMES GERSTENZANG, *Times Staff Writer*

WASHINGTON—All smiles and good humor—could it be that these two men were the bitterest of campaign rivals only months ago?

President-elect George Bush and Sen. Bob Dole, the Republican Senate leader whose cooperation is crucial to the new Administration's legislative fortunes, claimed Monday to have buried their substantial

Picture on Page 2.

differences and pledged to work together in the upcoming session of Congress.

Bush and the GOP contender he defeated and then passed over as his running mate echoed the oft-common harmony after a long-anticipated fence-mending meeting in the vice president's office. It came as Bush labored to heal political wounds and fill out his

$38.5-million painting—Picasso's "Acrobat and Young Harlequin" set a record for 20th-Century art prices when it was auctioned off to a Japanese department store. (Story on Page 5)

Stop Selling at Inflated Rates, 2 Insurers Told

State Farm, Safeco Targeted by Gillespie Order; Commissioner Also Considers Refunds, Fines

By KENNETH REICH and PHILIP HAGER, *Times Staff Writers*

State Insurance Commissioner Roxani Gillespie on Monday told State Farm, the biggest seller of auto insurance in California, and Safeco, the 12th-biggest, to stop selling to new customers at inflated rates or respond within 10 days why they should be permitted to do so.

The commissioner said she is prepared to call hearings on the matter and may order the companies to refund any excess money they have collected from new customers as compared with old ones.

If the companies violate such an order, they could be fined up to $100,000 for each operating subsidiary, an aide said. State Farm has two such subsidiaries and Safeco has three.

Tells of Her Resolve

"The law says—same rules, same rates," Gillespie declared. "Unlawful or unethical business practices will simply not be tolerated."

The commissioner's action came two weeks after State Farm announced it would sell new policies only through its 20% higher-priced State Farm Fire and Casualty subsidiary. It said its old customers would continue to pay the more common, lower State Farm Mutual rates. Gillespie officials, meanwhile, quietly told some of their agents to stop selling policies at lower "preferred" prices.

In a terse statement, Gillespie announced that she had "notified

both insurers that they are violating California-insurance-laws which require insurers to offer similar rates to policyholders with similar risks."

She added that the new sales policy of State Farm and Safeco that followed passage of Proposition 103 "unfairly discriminates against new policyholders."

Both companies quickly indicated that they would stick with their sales policies pending the response that Gillespie invited them to make.

"We obviously don't believe that we have done anything illegal or we wouldn't have done it in the Please see INSURANCE, Page 20

Pushiness Seen as Kiss of Death for New U.S. Jobs

By PAUL HOUSTON and JOHN M. BRODER, *Times Staff Writers*

WASHINGTON—He ran as a halfback at three Rose Bowls. He ran a couple of businesses. He ran successfully for local and state office.

And now, armed with a thick folder trumpeting these accomplishments and name, Los Angeles County Supervisor Pete Schabarum is running to be George Bush's transportation secretary. Well-placed friends are distributing the promotional folder to even better-placed contacts—including, Schabarum hopes, the President-elect himself.

Schabarum's campaign, brassy though it may be, is only one of a host being conducted by people Please see JOBS, Page 14

OPEC Agrees on Quotas, Cut in Production

News of Oil Accord Helps Boost Prices on World Markets

By WILLIAM TUOHY and DONALD WOUTAT, *Times Staff Writers*

VIENNA—Freeing itself from the grip of the Iran-Iraq War, the Organization of Petroleum Exporting Countries took a big step Monday toward re-establishing its credibility and market clout with a unanimous agreement to slow its production of crude oil.

Despite prospects of a worsening of the old glut in the near future, news of the accord immediately drove prices up 7%, to just over $15 per barrel on U.S. markets, as OPEC appeared to close ranks after two years in disarray. The agreement eventually could cause gasoline prices to spurt by 5 cents to 10 cents a gallon.

But analysts viewed the pact as more noteworthy for the OPEC unity it showed than for any dramatic effect it might have on world oil prices. Even strict adherence to the new set of production quotas might not result in OPEC reaching its $18-per-barrel target soon.

Saudis Drove Down Prices

And that would remain far below the $30-per-barrel price that prevailed as recently as November, 1985, when Saudi Arabia, the cartel's biggest producer, flooded the market with oil and drove prices as low as $9 per barrel.

Also, numerous problems went unaddressed in the agreement, especially the continuing demand by the United Arab Emirates for a dramatically higher quota and the issue of the large pending increases in Iraqi production capacity.

Nonetheless, the oil ministers' agreement after 12 days of wrangling at their winter meeting here marked the first time in two years that an OPEC agreement has been Please see OPEC, Page 10

Saudi Oil Minister Hisham Nazer discussing OPEC accord.

Shultz Ignored Senior Aides in Barring Arafat

By NORMAN KEMPSTER and ROBIN WRIGHT, *Times Staff Writers*

WASHINGTON—In deciding to prevent Yasser Arafat from addressing the United Nations in New York, Secretary of State George P. Shultz overrode the argument of his top Middle East experts that a snub to the PLO leader would damage Washington's standing as Middle East peacemaker, Administration officials said Monday.

Shultz's decision, culminating a week of bitter bureaucratic combat, showed that the fight against terrorism has assumed precedence over almost all other foreign policy objectives in the closing weeks of the Reagan Administration.

By denying Arafat's request for a U.S. visa, Shultz angered much of the Arab world—including many traditional American friends as Saudi Arabia, Jordan and Egypt—and may have shattered the U.S. role as mediator between Israel and its Arab adversaries. Paradoxically, the decision may make it easier for President-elect George Bush to make a conciliatory gesture toward the Arabs because Shultz so completely deflated their expectations.

'Could Have Overruled It'

White House spokesman Marlin Fitzwater said Shultz did not consult with President Reagan before making his decision. Fitzwater said the President "could have overruled it . . . but he did not want to." He added that Reagan "supports this decision."

According to State Department officials, Shultz was persuaded by his counterterrorism chief, L. Paul Bremer III, that the United States should make a dramatic gesture against terrorism—especially in the wake of the Iran-Contra controversy, in which the Administration, albeit indirectly, violated its own rules against dealing with kidnapers and terrorists. In announcing his decision Saturday, Shultz accused the Palestine Liberation Organization of terrorism against Americans and others. Arafat, he said, was "an accessory Please see ARAFAT, Page 13

U.S., Soviets Extend Grain Deal 2 Years

By MICHAEL PARKS, *Times Staff Writer*

MOSCOW—After eight months of hard bargaining, the United States and the Soviet Union agreed Monday to extend for two years a pact under which Moscow will buy at least 9 million tons of wheat, corn and soybeans annually.

The agreement will assure American farmers a major share of Soviet grain purchases in what is likely to be at least one year—and probably two years—of extensive food imports by Moscow as the government here seeks to make up for poor harvests and to raise living standards.

Alan F. Holmer, the deputy U.S. trade representative who negotiated the agreement, said it will "stabilize grain trade between our two countries, ensuring a secure source of supply for Soviet grain imports and a secure market for U.S. grain exports."

For the Soviet Union, the purchases will play an important role in President Mikhail S. Gorbachev's drive to solve what is known here as "the food problem"—the inability of this still heavily agrarian country to feed its 285 million people.

Soviet officials said the grain imports are intended as an interim Please see FOOD, Page 8

Banks Push Prime Rate Up to 10.5%

4th Hike in Year; Key Interest Figure Is Highest Since '85

By PAUL RICHTER, *Times Staff Writer*

NEW YORK—Major U.S. banks raised their prime lending rates Monday to 10.5% from 10%, the fourth such increase this year, bringing the prime to its highest level since January, 1985.

Chase Manhattan Bank led in increasing the rate, which is closely watched because it is the benchmark for a wide variety of loans to medium-size and small businesses and consumers.

Quickly following suit were much large lenders as Citicorp, Bank of America, Manufacturers Hanover, Chemical Bank, Security Pacific, Wells Fargo and First Interstate.

Inflation Rekindled

The Federal Reserve Board has been tightening credit for the last eight months in an effort to contain inflation, which has been rekindled as the economy has strengthened. Many economists believe that key interest rates will continue to rise at least through the early part of next year and that the prime may cross the 11% mark within months.

"We think you're going to see another round of tightening before these moves start the slowdown in borrowing that the Fed wants," said Kenneth Ackbaradi, senior economist at First Interstate.

The prime rate hike had been expected by the financial markets and had little effect on them. In stock market trading, the Dow Jones industrial average rose a modest 5.76 points for the day, closing at 2,081.44.

With the latest increase, the prime rate has risen 4 full 2% since early May, when it stood at 8.5%. The lending rate was increased to 9% on May 11, to 9.5% on July 14 and to 10% on Aug. 11.

Consumer Credit Affected

Many average consumers will feel the prime's rise in the monthly payments they must make on the adjustable home equity loans that have become so popular in the last year and a half. The prime is also the benchmark rate for some adjustable auto loans, credit card interest rates and a few home mortgage loans.

This latest prime rate hike should be felt by consumers with adjustable-rate debt within 30 to 60 days, bankers said.

A look at a typical home equity loan shows what this year's 2% increase in the prime would mean for some borrowers.

A consumer making interest-only payments on a $10,000 home equity loan would be paying $70.83 a month at an 8.5% rate, but $81.50 a month at a 10.5% rate, according to the Federal Reserve Board.

Such increases may seem modest, and economists say this year's rising rates have had very limited effects for most consumers. But the general upswing of rates may strain those consumers who have borrowed heavily and face hikes in Please see INTEREST, Page 16

City, State Efforts Lag

L.A. Rental Crisis Swells Ranks of the Homeless

By JILL STEWART, *Times Staff Writer*

Jackie Leo and her five children sat on a bus bench on Jefferson Boulevard 19 months ago, homeless and heading wherever the next bus would take them. A man pulled up and told the distraught mother about a place that would help. Peering into his eyes, the grateful woman decided he was sincere and accepted a ride.

Lee, 29, today is a "house mother" who looks after other homeless families at the Bible Tabernacle in Venice, the shelter that helped her through the frightening first months of homelessness.

A former customer service representative, Lee once had a decent home in Southwest Los Angeles. But when she and the children's father broke up, she found she could not afford rent.

"My dream is to let my babies have a home again," Leo said. "My prayer every night is, 'Lord, just give me back what I had. And if me and their father don't get back together, then at least make me strong.' "

Her story is told every day in a city where an estimated 35,000 are

THROUGH THE ROOF
L.A.'s Crisis in Rental Housing
Last of three parts

homeless and the streets are no longer the lonely outpost of alcoholics and schizophrenics. One in five homeless people is believed to Please see HOMELESS, Page 2

primary transition near its second month.

In an appointment to one highly visible job, Bush announced that Marlin Fitzwater, now the chief White House spokesman, would retain that role. Fitzwater, formerly Bush's vice presidential press secretary, took over as President Reagan's top spokesman nearly two years ago during the President's most troubled months in the midst of the Iran-Contra scandal.

Fitzwater has been credited with relieving to a degree the angry tenor of relations between the White House and the Washington press corps at a volatile time. Under Bush, he will get the title of press secretary, which has been held by James S. Brady for the eight years of the Reagan Administration. Brady has been recovering Please see BUSH, Page 17

INSIDE TODAY'S TIMES

Abby	VIEW	3
Ann Landers	VIEW	8
Astrology	VIEW	8
Bridge	VIEW	8
Comics	VIEW	7
Crossword	CLASSIFIED	14
Deaths	PART I	22
Editorials	METRO	6,7
Entertainment	CALENDAR	
Letters	METRO	6
Tangle Towns	CALENDAR	
TV-Radio	CALENDAR	8,9

WEATHER: Sunny and windy through Wednesday. Civic Center low/high today: 49/76. Details: Part B, Page 8.

Actor John Carradine Dies
John Carradine, a veteran actor who appeared in movie, stage and television productions, died in Milan, Italy, at age 82. **Page 3.**

Soviet Changes Approved
The Soviet party leadership announced changes that President Gorbachev called essential to the nation's democratic goals. **Page 7.**

More S&L Capital Urged
Regulators proposed requiring savings and loan firms to increase their capital by as much as 50% over four years. **Business.**

6.4. Balance. The *Times* displays nine stories and two pictures in basic balanced page. Note the multicolumn heads at the bottom and the paper's serious tone. (Copyright, 1988 *Los Angeles Times;* reprinted by permission.)

6.5. Modular. These modules tend to divide the page into three layers. Each module, however, seems nicely separated from others. Note the refer line.

OFFICE OVERLOAD

The right people to find the right people.

The Globe and Mail

IMPERIAL REALTY GROWTH FUND
A MUTUAL FUND INVESTMENT PROVIDING:
• Income • Stability • Growth
• RSP Qualified
Toronto (416) 865-0655 Winnipeg (204) 949-1220

145th YEAR, NO. 43,301 ■ FRIDAY, SEPTEMBER 16, 1988

50¢ Mon.—Sat.

World spotlight focuses on Seoul

The 16-day Seoul Olympics, which start tonight with the opening ceremonies, give South Korea a chance to impress the world with its technology, pageantry and hospitality.

The Land of the Morning Calm, despite tight security barriers, hopes to bring down international fences with an athletic showcase promoting peace and harmony.

Starting on Page A15, The Globe and Mail's Olympic crew — James Christie, Mary Hynes and Murray Campbell — previews the medal prospects and sets the scene for the biggest Games in history.

Cabinet shuffle upgrades 2 junior ministers

BY RICHARD CLEROUX, ROSS HOWARD and CHRISTOPHER WADDELL
The Globe and Mail

OTTAWA

With a federal election in the offing, Prime Minister Brian Mulroney produced a minor shuffle of his Cabinet yesterday, raising the profile of two junior departments and loading yet another portfolio on to the back of his Deputy Prime Minister.

Two Ontario members of Parliament, John McDermid (Brampton-Georgetown) and Shirley Martin (Lincoln), were brought into the Cabinet as Minister of State for Housing and Minister of State for Transport, and the responsibilities of eight other ministers were changed.

The reorganization keeps the Cabinet size at 40 members and appears designed to respond to outstanding commitments made by the Government to establish a separate forestry department and reward a couple of backbenchers for past work.

It may also shore up Tory electoral prospects in urban areas, with a new ministry solely responsible for multiculturalism and a minister for housing.

It also gives a higher profile to some MPs likely to face tough re-election battles.

Mr. Mulroney rejected suggestions that the shuffle had an electoral flavor.

"These days if you change shirts it's considered an electoral move," he said.

The new ministers were sworn in at a late afternoon ceremony at the Rideau Hall residence of Governor-General Jeanne Sauve.

Afterward, Mr. Mulroney pointed out to reporters the number of Cabinet members from British Columbia, citing ministers responsible for Science and Technology, Fisheries and Oceans, Forestry and the Treasury Board.

"I hope British Columbians will be pleased," he said.

But when asked if the appoint-

CABINET — Page A9

ANALYSIS

PM tries to shore up weak areas

BY HUGH WINSOR
The Globe and Mail

OTTAWA

Yesterday's realignment of the Cabinet combines the traditional practice of injecting new faces on the eve of an election with an attempt to broaden the Conservatives' election platform beyond the potentially volatile free-trade issue.

While some of the changes have been dictated by resignations, the political strategy behind Prime Minister Brian Mulroney's rejigging of departmental responsibilities appears to be an attempt to shore up areas in

SHUFFLE — Page A2

REPORT ON BUSINESS

■ Walwyn 'in order'
The Toronto Stock Exchange has found the "house is in order" at Walwyn Stodgell Cochran Murray, a broker rumored to be in trouble. B1

■ Principal Group
Principal Group investors got something unusual yesterday: good news. They'll be getting another $50-million. B1

■ Steinberg Inc.
Steinberg has found something else it might want to sell, Smitty's Super Valu, the top food retailer in Phoenix. . . B13

A NATION OF RISK-TAKERS
Why are so many taking the entrepreneurial plunge? And how are they doing? Report on Business Magazine has the answers. Also: arts and the hard sell; how Don Mazankowski runs the government; rough times in the rag trade; the high cost of divorce among the rich.

QUOTE OF THE DAY

"Well, we don't talk about it . . . well we do. . . . He's got his own views, I've got mine."
— **Justin Trudeau**, 16, says he supports John Turner although he and his father, the former prime minister, do not necessarily agree on that topic. A11

NEWS

Citizens want to save Old Port area of Quebec
Citizen groups in Quebec City want to block a federal Government plan to sell a piece of riverfront in the city's Old Port District to a developer who is also a Conservative organizer. . . A8

Ramsay in hot water over parks promise
Northern Ontario groups say Cabinet minister David Ramsay has endagered his credibility by promising a review of provincial parks policy that the Government is not going to permit. . . . A11

INDEX

Births, Deaths	A23
Challenge Crossword	A8
Comics	A10
Contract Bridge	A22
Legal Notices	B18
The Far Side	A10
Didn't you used to be?	A2
Sport	A12-A18
Michael Valpy	A8
The Arts	A18, A19

YOUR MORNING SMILE

You know kids have entered adolescence as soon as they start thinking their par-

Hurricane hurls floods at Yucatan

Associated Press and Reuter

CAMPECHE, Mexico

More than 50,000 people fled rising flood waters yesterday as Hurricane Gilbert battered the Yucatan Peninsula and its posh resorts. Two babies drowned.

Gilbert, the strongest storm on record, left much of Yucatan without communications, electricity or drinking water. Airports were closed, most roads were blocked and supplies were running short.

Red Cross and government officials said rescue work was hampered by blocked roads and serious damage to airports.

Looting was reported in the resort city of Cancun on the east coast of the peninsula, and officials said many people were afraid to leave their homes for fear of burglars.

In Campeche, on the peninsula's west coast, "there is no light, there is no radio, there is nothing," said Ramon Castillo, a night watchman at the newspaper Novedades de Campeche. "The whole city is flooded. Everything is dark. I've lived here all my life and I have never seen bad weather like this. People are scared."

Later yesterday, the storm continued toward northern Mexico and the coast of Texas.

"It's still moving west-northwest, which is good news for Texas but not so good news for the northern part of Mexico," said Robert Sheets, director of the U.S. National Hurricane Centre. He said it appeared that the storm was strengthening.

Over land, the hurricane had weakened and been reclassified from a Category 5 storm — the most dangerous — to Category 3. But it remained a formidable threat, and its 1,600-kilometre-wide storm system blanketed almost the entire Gulf of Mexico from the Mexican coast to Florida.

U.S. and Soviet military aircraft, co-operating by radio, flew into

MEXICAN — Page A5

BERNARD BENNELL/The Globe and Mail

Following the devastation caused by Hurricane Gilbert, residents of Kingston make their way across a flooded street. As the map illustrates, hurricane is making its way toward United States.

Texans flee towns along Gulf coast for higher ground

BY COLIN MacKENZIE
Globe and Mail Correspondent

PALACIO, Tex.

Amid mosquitoes only slightly discouraged by 60-kilometre winds, the residents of the flat Gulf coast of Texas made their preparations for Hurricane Gilbert yesterday.

Plywood and tape covered windows in the towns along a coast accustomed to the threat of hurricane season.

More than half the population of towns like this shrimp-boat community of 4,000 on Matagorda Bay have left for higher ground. The rest were preparing to do so.

"This is the first time we haven't had to issue an evacuation advisory," Palacios Mayor Leonard Lamar said. "When they saw those pressure readings over Jamaica, everybody must have started paying attention."

Situated midway between Galveston and Corpus Christi, Palacios had a shrouded, Sunday-afternoon look yesterday. Stores and schools were closed. The only activity in the 35-degree heat was some last-minute window-taping at the fire hall and at a few homes.

"It's not meant to hit us, but you never can tell with these suckers," Mr. Lamar said, between attempts to reach the owners of a Ford dealership that went out of business last spring.

"If they don't get those showroom windows covered, there's going to be an almighty mess out there," he said.

Mr. Lamar and his emergency team were prepared to move to the highest point in town if the weather got rough.

At five metres above sea level, however, that is little comfort.

The hospital was emptied yesterday morning, as was the local nursing home. Most businesses closed early Wednesday to let employees join the exodus.

"Nobody was doing any work anyway," said Herbert Hodovsky, manager of the local fishnet factory. "They were all talking about the storm, so I let them go."

Roads away from the coast were all jammed yesterday afternoon as thousands of weather-wise Texans left their homes under the scudding clouds and showers that are Gilbert's harbingers. Hotels as far away as Austin, 450 kilometres to the north, reported they were filled with refugees.

Palacios was flattened in 1961 by Hurricane Carla and has been battered by near misses regularly since then.

The major fear locally is that Gilbert may knock down the month-old $95,000 pavilion on the town dock that is the long-awaited replacement for the structure Carla destroyed 27 years ago.

Although the hurricane is now expected to hit the Texas coast around noon today near Brownsville on the Mexican border, the vigilance further up the coast is undiminished.

"You just can't tell," said Rosa Hernandez, surveying the empty shelves of Fenton's Mini-Mart on the edge of town. "It could just skip up the coast the way one of them did five years ago."

The fear is well founded. Not only are hurricanes notoriously unpre-

TEXANS — Page A2

Prime rate jumps to 11.75 per cent

Consumers and businesses are facing yet another increase in the cost of loans, after the prime lending rate jumped by half a percentage point to 11.75 per cent, its highest level since April, 1986.

The cost of mortgages and other personal loans is expected to rise in response to signals from the central bank, which remains concerned about inflationary pressure in the Ontario economy.

Several chartered banks increased the cost of loans to their best corporate customers early yesterday, even before the Bank of Canada rate's rise to 10.57 per cent.

Details on Page B1.

Finding birth parents could take 8 years

Adopted people swamp ministry

BY DOROTHY LIPOVENKO
The Globe and Mail

Thousands of adopted people in Ontario face an eight-year wait to find their birth parents under new disclosure legislation because of a backlog in the provincial ministry doing the searches for them.

Since the law came into effect last year, the Ministry of Community and Social Services has been besieged with 3,500 requests from adopted children to search for a biological parent or for a relative related by birth.

The ministry has only three search officers to do the legwork (one of whom left last month and has not yet been replaced) and has completed only 300 investigations.

Most searches have ended successfully, with the birth parent agreeing to a reunion or more restricted contact, such as a letter, from the child given up for adoption.

Michael Kurts, an assistant to the minister, John Sweeney, said the ministry, which estimated it would receive 7,000 requests for searches by 1991, has been surprised that half the expected number have come in during the first year since the new laws took effect.

"We're faced with a greater demand than anticipated and than we put aside resources for," Mr. Kurts said in an interview yesterday.

"From the time a person puts in a request for a search until the time it is completed, we're looking at eight years," he said.

It is not only Queen's Park that is feeling the impact of the recent changes to the disclosure laws. Adopted people eager to satisfy their curiosity about their biological background have created other waiting lists for information at children's aid societies.

The Metro Toronto CAS cannot begin to make a dent in the 800 to 900 requests it has received, mostly

Heavy demand for adoption Page A11

from adopted people, for "non-identifying" information about their backgrounds.

The waiting time has increased to 2½ years to get the information, which is not specific enough to reveal the identity of natural parents but can help in locating them by revealing the professional background of the birth mother's family, how many siblings she had and the family's medical history.

"We're not making any headway into getting that waiting list reduced," says Peter Hagedoorn,

REQUESTS — Page A2

Radios for army to cost average $72,222 each

BY PAUL KORING
The Globe and Mail

OTTAWA

The Canadian army will get 18,000 radios worth $1.3-billion, Defence Minister Perrin Beatty announced yesterday after Cabinet approved spending $81.7-million for a five-year program to define what types of communications equipment the army needs.

Although 5,400 of the new hand-held and tion's defence, the other 12,600 will be used by the regular forces, who currently number 20,185.

Defence department spokesman Captain Donald Roy said a ratio of nearly two radios for every three soldiers wasn't unreasonable "when you realize that they will be of several types. A single truck might have six or seven radios in it," he said.

"Canada needs a well-equipped army, in-ty said in a statement announcing the program.

It was the third major defence equipment program announced by the minister in the last six weeks. Earlier he said the Government would spend $850-million on 820 tracked troop carriers and a dozen minesweepers. However, the choice of British or French nuclear powered submarines — the most controversial of Mr. Beatty's plans to rebuild Canada's military and at an estimated $8-bil-

The radios are just the first element in a three-phase plan that will include, at extra cost, mobile microwave stations mounted on trucks for area communications and an automation system that will allow data exchange. The entire project is expected to be completed over 15 years.

The $1.3-billion radio contract will be awarded to a "Canadian-based" company in 1991, the Defence Department announced. "Cabinet has requested that bidders include

6.6. Canada style. This Toronto paper uses the left column for reference to inside pages, then as one of several modules. Top of page looks a bit cluttered.

THURSDAY

Woman worries as rapist nears parole Colorado Living/ 1G

Dorsett wins starting job over Winder Sports/ 1F

Viola wins 20th as Twins rout Rangers 10-1 Sports/ 1F

Showers, Cooler Highs 75-80

THE DENVER POST

SEP 7 1988 LB

September 1, 1988

Voice of the Rocky Mountain Empire

Final Edition / 25 cents

Fiery Texas jet crash kills 13

Concerns over safety nearly shut down Flats

By Gary Schmitz
Denver Post Washington Bureau

WASHINGTON — Safety violations at the Rocky Flats nuclear weapons plant earlier this year nearly led to an unprecedented shutdown of the facility, federal officials said Wednesday.

The safety problems were blamed on "lax attitudes" among employees and managers of Rockwell International, the corporation the Department of Energy pays to operate the plant west of Denver.

Agency officials said they know of no similar federal facility that has come under such a threat.

'Close to a shutdown'

"Rocky Flats came very close to a shutdown; it was very real," said Tony Lane, deputy energy secretary for military applications. The revelations came during the first examination of Rocky Flats by the department's newly formed Advisory Committee on Nuclear Facility Safety.

The enforcement action was considered in February immediately after an inspection team from agency headquarters in Washington discovered that nine safety violations first uncovered in 1986 still had not been corrected.

Problems cited were: an incomplete emergency response plan; lack of "enforceable safety rules" plantwide; inconsistent management review of safety shortcomings; four instances of failing to certify the precision of radiation monitoring equipment; lapses in security on the grounds, and insufficient barriers to guard against fires.

While potentially serious, officials said those violations alone were not severe enough to warrant as stringent a response as closing the plant.

However, because the same problems were found repeatedly across the plant for several years, officials said they were confronted with a clear pattern of inaction. Taken together, they said, the violations suggested Rockwell was paying too little attention to the overall issue of safety.

'Teach Rockwell a lesson'

Safety experts in the Energy Department pushed to have the facility closed until the problems were fixed, "to teach Rockwell a lesson," sources said. However, officials in charge of production objected, warning that halting work could compromise national security.

Rocky Flats is the only plant in the nation to manufacture and assemble plutonium components for nuclear bombs and warheads, and is the primary center for reprocessing the plutonium recovered from outmoded weaponry.

The dispute over Rockwell's safety performance went to the "the highest levels" of the federal agency, sources said, and a decision was made to keep the plant

Please see FLATS on 19-A

INSIDE

DENVER WEATHER: Scattered showers developing, cooler. **Highs 75-80; Lows 50-55.** Details/**8B**

INDEX

BUSINESS	1-5D
CLASSIFIED	7-18D, 1-8E
COLORADO LIVING	1-8G
COMICS	6-7G
CROSSWORD	8B
DENVER & THE WEST	1-5B
MOVIES	4-5G
OBITUARIES	6D
OPINIONS	6-7B
PEOPLE	20A
SPORTSTODAY	1-8F
TELEVISION	8G

TO CALL THE POST

MAIN NUMBER	820-1010
NEWS	820-1201
CLASSIFIED	825-2525
HOME DELIVERY	825-7678

Associated Press

CHARRED: Wreckage attests to heat of fire when Delta jet crashed during takeoff Wednesday.

Perfect day hid horror to come

By The Dallas Morning News

DALLAS — The Delta 727-200 jetliner eased onto the runway at Dallas-Fort Worth Airport just before 9 a.m. on Wednesday morning. It was a beautiful/morning for a flight.

But in just a few minutes, the placid beginnings of Flight 1141 would give way to a harrowing experience of fear and courage.

□□□

Frank Nix let his wife, Jean, have the window seat on row 29 in the smoking section. He sat between her and Edmund Fadel, a good friend from Waco, Texas, who, along with his wife, Marion, was joining the Nix family on a pleasure trip to Lake Tahoe, Nev.

Nix, a troop carrier pilot during World War II, sensed something was wrong the instant the plane took to the air.

The jetliner shuddered, and as he stared out the window, Nix could see the plane's flaps vibrating violently. Nix feared the worst.

Then, from the rear of the pl.ne, there was an unnerving boo:-

□□□

Gene Metzig, sitting on a commuter flight that had just landed at D-FW from Wichita Falls, Texas, was riveted to his window.

He was watching a plane in

Please see SURVIVE on 18-A

Associated Press

PILOT AIDED: Flight Captain Larry Davis, 48, is rushed to hospital.

94 survive crackup on takeoff

Denver Post Wire Services

GRAPEVINE, Texas — A Delta Air Lines jet with 107 people aboard crashed and burst into flames shortly after takeoff Wednesday morning, killing 13. But 94 people got out alive.

Many walked away unscratched, with some flying on to their destinations later in the day.

It was just three years ago that 137 people died in the crash of another Delta plane at the same field, Dallas-Fort Worth Airport.

Airline officials said the Boeing 727, bound for Salt Lake City, began to shake wildly on takeoff and then crashed, breaking in two and bursting into flames about 1,000 feet past the end of the runway at 9:03 a.m.

Many survivors, who clambered from emergency exits and a hole in the roof, expressed amazement that so many people came out alive.

"From the time it took off there was something wrong," said Jerry Galloway, 27, a professional rodeo clown bound for Twin Falls, Idaho. "The sound was like a flat tire running down the road."

According to witnesses, the jet, a 15-year-old Boeing 727-300 series, never got more than 50 feet off the ground, dropping suddenly as it approached the end of the runway.

As it touched down, the aircraft dipped left and right, then skidded sideways, plowing through the deep weeds at the south end of the airport before breaking up and bursting into flames.

By the time the jet came to rest, its right wing was sheared, its nose was broken and one of its three rear-mounted engines lay alone 150 yards to the north. The Boeing's twisted and broken tail was engulfed in flames.

Some questions were raised about the three engines on the tail of the plane. One surviving passenger, Norman Newcity of Atlanta, said the plane shook on takeoff, and he heard three loud backfires

Please see CRASH on 17-A

INTENDED DESTINATION Salt Lake City, Utah
FLIGHT ORIGINATION Jackson, Miss.
CRASH ON TAKE-OFF Dallas, Texas
Terminal Bldg.
1985 Delta crash site
Runway
Runway
Delta Terminal
Dallas-Ft. Worth Intl. Airport
Airfield Drive
WEDNESDAY'S CRASH SITE
½ mile

The Denver Post/ Jerry Lundwall

AIR CRASHES:
Prosecutors begin investigation of air show tragedy./ **12A**
Incidents tarnish Delta's image./ **16A**
Probers won't speculate on cause of Dallas accident./ **17A**
Denver denies runway had role in Continental Flight 1713 crash./ **1B**

Assault suspect quizzed in deaths of prostitutes

By Thomas Graf
Denver Post Staff Writer

Denver police are investigating the possibility that one man is responsible for the murder of six or seven suspected prostitutes, whose bodies have been found throughout the metro area in the last several months.

Officially, Denver police will neither confirm nor deny an investigation even exists. However, police sources on Wednesday confirmed that detectives are heading up a large-scale investigation of the murders.

Lindstrom

The investigation was unintentionally revealed after the weekend arrest of a 36-year-old California man in the sexual assault of several prostitutes and other women in Denver.

Gerald Lindstrom was arrested Saturday night and is being held in the Denver City Jail on a $250,000 bond for investigation of five counts of first-degree sexual assault.

Lindstrom has admitted to police he sexually assaulted several women since moving here from California in December, but he denies any involvement in the slayings, said Denver Police Sgt. Byron J. Haze.

Haze said Lindstrom told police, "I'm sick and I need help."

Lt. Tom Haney said Lindstrom is not yet a suspect in any murder investigation.

Whether he will be "included or excluded" from any homicide investigation should be determined

Please see SUSPECT on 19-A

Crested Butte to be lab for woodburning air test

By Mark Obmascik
Denver Post Environment Writer

Crested Butte will turn into a giant air pollution lab this winter under a first-in-the-nation program to replace homeowners' old woodburning stoves with cleaner appliances.

The state Health Department plans to conduct extensive air pollution tests this winter in the southwestern Colorado mountain town that sits under a brown cloud. After scientists study those results, more than 350 homeowners will get high-tech stoves next year for as little as half price from an industry trade group.

State officials and industry executives hope the new stoves, which spew out only 15 percent as many pollutants as the traditional heating fixtures, will greatly improve Crested Butte's air.

"We want to prove that the advanced technology really works," said Carter Keithley of the Wood Heating Alliance in Washington. "We believe in it and want to demonstrate it."

If the $300,000 experiment proves successful, it would provide a big incentive for many cities with woodburning pollution problems to ask homeowners to switch to the cleaner stoves. Less than 2 percent of the 14 million wood stoves in the United States employ the new technology.

In Denver, woodburning is be-

Please see TEST on 19-A

DRUG CRACKDOWN IN PARK

The Denver Post/ Duane Howell

Patrolman William Yeros arrests John Earl Tatum, 30, of Denver in City Park Wednesday as a suspect in possession of a controlled substance. Yeros is a member of the Gang Task Force that is conducting drug crackdowns in the city.

Bakker's offer of $165 million tops PTL bids

By Knight-Ridder News Service

CHARLOTTE, N.C. — Jim Bakker is now the leading candidate to buy PTL's assets and soon may be back in charge of the television ministry and Christian retreat.

PTL trustee M.C. "Red" Benton said Wednesday that Bakker's offer — a package worth up to $165 million — is the best to date.

He said that if he gets no better offer, he will recommend that U.S. Bankruptcy Judge Rufus Reynolds approve the sale to Bakker.

"It's a good proposal. And it's the best proposal we have today," Benton told reporters after meeting with Bakker and his attorney, Jim Toms, for 2½ hours at Heritage USA, south of Charlotte.

Canadian businessman Peter Thomas, who has offered $113 million, said he won't raise his offer. His Samoth Capital Corp. has offered $46 million in cash and $67 million financed over five years.

Bakker, who is expected to submit his formal bid today, intends to offer at least $70 million in cash and as much as $15 million more to pay off debts owed to Kansas contractor Roe Messner, who once was PTL's chief builder.

He also plans to obtain an $80 million mortgage on 1,000 undeveloped acres at Heritage USA. The money is a guarantee that he will restore benefits to PTL's lifetime partners.

Typical lifetime partners paid $1,000 in exchange for free lodging at Heritage USA. "I would put Mr Bakker's proposal ahead of Mr. Thomas'," Benton said.

Bakker has refused to say where he is getting the money. He has identified his financial backers only as overseas lenders. Toms said they are "Greek investors with lots of money."

Bakker was PTL's leader until he resigned in March 1987 because of his 1980 sexual encounter with Jessica Hahn.

6.7. Splashy. All pictures, the reference box, and the index are in color, perhaps overpowering stories. The three headline faces detract from appearance. Map ties nicely to lead story.

6.8. Unusual. Almost no newspaper except the *Chronicle* puts index atop page or uses the kind of head in upper right. Two big heads under nameplate tend to tombstone.

AN INTERNATIONAL DAILY NEWSPAPER   Wednesday, January 25, 1989   50¢ (60¢ Canadian)

THE CHRISTIAN SCIENCE MONITOR

COPYRIGHT © 1989 THE CHRISTIAN SCIENCE PUBLISHING SOCIETY
All rights reserved

VOL. 81, NO. 41

⚶ PICTURES/ARTURO ROBLES

A TALE OF TWO COUNTRIES

Gorbachev Scrambles to Bridge Reform Divide

By Paul Quinn-Judge
Staff writer of The Christian Science Monitor

MOSCOW

AT a recent public meeting Grigory Baklanov, a writer and editor who has been one of the most consistent advocates of political change, remarked that the letters he receives at his journal Znamya these days seem to be written by people "from two different countries."

In what threatens to be the most difficult period yet of his four years in power, Soviet leader Mikhail Gorbachev is trying to reconcile the "two countries" – the people who are disturbed at the lack of real progress in reform, and those who are incensed at the transformations it has already wrought.

In a speech published Tuesday, Mr. Gorbachev once again reiterated his commitment to far-reaching change. The Soviet Union, he told the Moscow city Communist Party, "will never be the same again." At the same time, he warned, there would be no quick fixes – like buying consumer goods from abroad.

Gorbachev's speech appeared just as an article in the Leningrad journal Neva began to attract attention here. The author of the article, Sergei Andreyev, takes the highly unusual step of criticizing Gorbachev by name, suggesting that some of his comments on economics have been woollyminded.

Mr. Andreyev complains that the economy has slipped even further into crisis, and says that the top political leadership is still

"groping" for a policy. The Andreyev article is unusually harshly phrased, but reflects a feeling that is widespread among intellectuals who support radical reform: the need for the leadership to act fast and resolutely if perestroika (restructuring) is to succeed.

The strongest supporter of radical reform in the top leadership, Alexander Yakovlev, made a similar point in a speech last month. Reformers had perhaps two to three years left to prove

GORBACHEV: The Soviet Union 'will never be the same again.'

that socialism as conceived by the leader of the Bolshevik revolution, Vladimir Lenin, could actually work, Mr. Yakovlev said.

Andreyev views things in an even bleaker light: The first signs of "incipient decay" in the reform program are already visible, he writes.

Over the weekend, yet another prominent economist voiced deep concerns about the situation. In a newspaper interview Oleg Bogomolov, director of the Institute for the Study of the Economics of the Socialist System, estimated inflation to be running at an annual rate of 5 to 7 percent.

He hinted that the government may be fueling the problem by printing more money, and wondered out loud about the desirability of one of the most expensive parts of the Soviet space program: "We don't have to be the first people on Mars when the shelves in our shops are completely bare?" He predicted that the country's budget deficit would reach 100 billion rubles ($166 billion at the government-set exchange rate) next year.

The situation could be rectified in the near term, Mr. Bogomolov said. But to do so, "firm political will," was needed.

The existence of the deficit was only revealed last October, when it was set at just over 36 billion rubles ($60 billion). Unofficial estimates of the annual inflation rate suggest that the real figure is around 10 percent.

Gorbachev's speech was in part an effort to answer growing concern among specialists about the state of the economy. He gave his address last Saturday, but it was only printed in the central media Tuesday. (Such delays have in the past indicated either that the speech was extempore, or that it was being edited for wider distribution).

At the same time Gorbachev warned ordinary Soviet citizens, who are increasingly unhappy about the shortages of such everyday needs as washing powder, not to expect any overnight improve-

See **SOVIET** next page

NICARAGUAN SOLDIERS AND PEASANTS: Class divisions grow starker.

COMRADES AT ODDS

Nicaragua: a Revolution Betrayed?

By Brook Larmer
Staff writer of The Christian Science Monitor

MANAGUA, NICARAGUA

TWO worlds converge at Managua's exclusive "dollar" store.

Strolling through the air-conditioned aisles inside, well-dressed Nicaraguans stack their grocery carts with expensive American goods that can only be bought with United States dollars or government coupons. In the parking lots outside, bedraggled children badger shoppers for coins, food – anything to help them survive.

Such stark class divisions are merely considered an unfortunate fact of life in many other developing countries. But in Nicaragua, where the 1979 communist revolution promised to

erase class barriers and lift the living standards of poor workers, the resurgence of social inequality is provoking an intense internal debate on the nature – and future – of the revolution.

"The revolution now finds itself at a crossroads," says Francisco Lopez, director of the National Institute for Social and Economic Investigations, a hardline socialist think tank. "The government has thrown so many bones to the producers and the professionals that they've become elites. . . . It's a total contradiction of our revolutionary ideals."

For the most part, Mr. Lopez and other economic experts say, the widening social gap stems from a government austerity program to lift Nicaragua out of it's worst economic crisis ever.

So far, the market-oriented policy has flopped.

See **NICARAGUA** next page

From Drought of '88 to Drought of '89?
Lack of winter rain or snow in parts of the US could threaten spring and summer crops. Much of the Midwest is drier than normal
7

Marian McPartland's Career in Jazz
Pianist and long-time radio host talks about hurdles she's faced – and cleared – on the way up
10

A Poet Dresses Georgia O'Keeffe
. . . in the flora that Arcimboldo, a 16th-century Milanese painter, might have used
16

INSIDE

3	THE WORLD
7	THE US
9	THE ECONOMY
10	ARTS
12	IDEAS
14	PEOPLE
16	THE HOME FORUM
18	OPINION
20	EDITORIAL

6.9. Tabloid modular. Even the small size of the *Monitor* allows for three distinct modules. All pictures are in color, making a lively page. Note the excessive white space in the upper right.

TULUAT

PARTLY CLOUDY
Partly cloudy tonight and tomor-
row with patchy morning fog.
Highs, lower 50s; lows, upper 30s
to 40 degrees.
DETAILS, F4

'YOU MAKE
YOUR OWN
PARTY'
Rap music is more
than a trend/D1

WHY
MIKE
MOORE
LEFT M's/F1

GNP
SLOWS
RATE OF
GROWTH/B1

The Seattle Times

25¢
50¢ outside Seattle metro area
52 pages

WASHINGTON'S LARGEST NEWSPAPER ■ COPYRIGHT© 1988, SEATTLE TIMES COMPANY

TUESDAY
November 29, 1988

High school principals seek stiffer gun rules

Seattle administrators want expulsions to be automatic

by Constantine Angelos
Times staff reporter

Seattle's public high school principals, disturbed by incidents in which students have brought guns to school, are asking their district to toughen its weapons policy.

Under current policy, students are usually suspended, not expelled, for bringing a gun to school. In a memorandum to Superintendent William Kendrick, the principals ask that possession of a gun by any student in the district bring on-the-spot expulsion and filing of a criminal complaint.

The principals' memo says, in part:

"Given the increase of weapons, particularly guns, loaded or unloaded, being
confiscated by
schools; given
the awareness of
the increase of
weapons being
carried by teen-
agers in and out-
side of school,
and given the in-
creased availabil-
ity of guns, the
high school ad-
ministrators rec-
ommend that the
school district re-

> On April 21, a student
> at Hamilton Middle
> School brought a gun,
> and the weapon acci-
> dentally discharged in
> a crowded classroom.

view its policy on the normal sanctions for criminal behavior as it relates to weapons and explosives."

Sharon Green, West Seattle High School principal, and Joan Butterworth, Chief Sealth High School principal, drafted the proposed policy. They said the principals do not want to be arbitral, but want to make it very clear to any student who brings a firearm to school that "this is what we're going to do."

Green said the principals stress guns specifically because of any weapon a student might carry, a handgun is the most frightening, whether a real firearm or a toy. "You don't know whether a gun is loaded or unloaded," she said.

Jim Simmons, principal of the Seattle Alternative High School and chairman of the principals' group, said the administrators are not reacting to any particular situation, though school and police records indicate several incidents involving guns have already occurred in city schools this year.

■ On April 21, a student at Hamilton Middle School brought a gun to the school and the weapon accidentally discharged in a crowded classroom. No one was hurt.

■ On May 10, a student at Hamilton Middle School who had previously been expelled brought a gun to school and threatened another student.

■ On Sept. 9, a student at Mercer Middle School, involved in a shoving match with another student, jumped out the window of the vice principal's office and escaped after he made gestures and threats with what appeared to be a handgun.

■ On Oct. 13, a loaded .22-caliber handgun was confiscated from a student's briefcase at Rainier Beach High School.

■ On Nov. 3, a 15-year-old West Seattle High School student was expelled for bringing a handgun to school. The boy told police he brought the gun because of threats from several youths who were not students.

Superintendent Kendrick, attending a National Community Education Association meeting in Orlando, Fla., was not available for comment on the principals' proposal.

Deputy Superintendent Arthur Binnie said that what the principals are asking for sounds like "the Milwaukee Plan."

Binnie said Milwaukee school officials have told him that "they didn't have a (gun) problem because it was clear that any possession of a weapon meant immediate expulsion. The student could return to an alternative school but not to a regular high school."

Boost to victory

16-month-old Taylor Matthew gets a lift from his dad, Steve, at the Kingdome.

Replays: Seahawks lost their appeals, won game

by Bob Sherwin
Times staff reporter

Imagine if we all could use replays in our lives. What if we could take back what we've said in anger? What if you had asked someone else to the Homecoming Dance? What would your kids look like now?

Unfortunately, we don't get a second chance in life. But you do in the National Football League. The Seattle Seahawks and the Los Angeles Raiders discovered that four times last night before 62,641 deeply involved fans at the Kingdome and a national television audience on ABC's Monday Night Football.

The NFL's replay rule, which allows certain plays to be reviewed on videotape (and, if need be, reversed) came under one of its most serious tests last night in Seattle's 35-27 victory over the Raiders. There were at least three time-consuming and generally unpopular replay decisions that had an impact on the game.

"I think it's tough to beat the referees and the Oakland Raiders at the same time," said Seahawk partisan Brian Dit-

■ More Seahawks coverage, Sports, F1.

Please see SEAHAWKS on A 6

$1 billion cut in Medicaid proposed

Plan would pay states less for medical care of needy

by Spencer Rich
Washington Post

WASHINGTON — The Office of Management and Budget (OMB) has proposed cutting $1.1 billion from projected 1990 federal payments to the states for Medicaid, the medical assistance program for 22 million low-income people, according to documents obtained yesterday.

Unless the plan is reversed before President Reagan sends his final budget to Congress in January, it is certain to set off a bitter fight with Congress. The states would have to make up the lost revenue or cut their programs from levels they would reach under current rules.

"If these reports are true, it's an outrage," said Rep. Henry Waxman, D-Calif., chairman of the House subcommittee with Medicaid jurisdiction.

"Over the past six years, the Congress has moved away from these shortsighted and mean-spirited cuts in the Medicaid program. The program administrators oppose them, the governors oppose them, the Congress opposes them," Waxman said.

Recalling that Reagan in 1981 won approval of a similar plan that was later killed by Congress, Wax-

man said, "To bring these irresponsible proposals back now after Mr. Bush has talked about expanding Medicaid to reach the poor and uninsured, would only make a mockery of this campaign promise to make a kinder, gentler nation. I hope he dismisses them without any consideration at all."

Bush transition aides had no comment on the OMB proposals yesterday.

In addition to the Medicaid cut, the OMB also has proposed reductions in projected Medicare outlays of $5.2 billion in fiscal 1990, almost entirely by cutting payments to doctors and hospitals for services to 33 million aged and disabled Social Security recipients.

The American Hospital Association and Federation of American Health Systems said they would fight such cuts.

The OMB also has backed $1.4 billion for AIDS research and related programs in 1990, compared with $1.9 billion sought by the Department of Health and Human Services (HHS). The fiscal 1989 appropriation was $1.3 billion.

Under the existing Medicaid program, the federal government

Please see MEDICAID on A 12

U.S. feels isolation after banning Arafat

Only Israelis giving full support to visa denial

Times news services

UNITED NATIONS — Secretary of State George Shultz's decision to bar Palestinian Liberation Organization leader Yasser Arafat from coming here this week has thrown U.S. and Israeli diplomats into a degree of isolation at the United Nations that they have not experienced in years.

Even some close U.S. allies reportedly are likely to support a resolution, which Arab representatives agreed today to introduce, which would condemn the U.S. action, postpone a debate on Palestine scheduled for Thursday and urge the State Department to grant the visa.

The U.S. isolation was palpable in corridors, hallways and formal meetings yesterday, as only Israel was wholeheartedly supporting Shultz's position.

"This is the only friendly conversation I've had all day," said one low-ranking U.S. diplomat, breaking off from a chat with an Israeli aide in a U.N. corridor.

In informal discussions and

speeches yesterday, the U.S. was urged by allies and foes alike to reverse the decision and allow Arafat to address the General Assembly, despite Shultz's ruling Saturday that Arafat is not entitled to a visa because he supported terrorism.

Arafat had sought the visa so that he could speak at the U.N.

Please see PLO on A 12

CLOSE-UP / A3

■ George Shultz overruled top Middle East advisers when he denied Yasser Arafat's visa.

■ U.S. counterterrorism specialists say they have no hard evidence that Arafat has recently condoned terrorist acts.

Could boy's death have been averted?

Chance events foiled CPS plan to shield 4-year-old

by Stephen Clutter
Times East bureau

The man arrested in connection with the apparent beating death of a 4-year-old Kirkland boy did not take classes on being a better parent — as told to by state officials — because the class was canceled at the last minute.

died Thanksgiving day from head injuries received in an apparent beating.

Bailey, the boyfriend of the child's mother, was to attend a "parenting class" as part of a program designed for him by the state Child Protective Services to protect the child and teach Bailey better child-rearing skills.

day-care worker found bruises on the youngster's body then.

But the plan began to fall apart when the nine-week class, which was scheduled to begin in October, was canceled at the last minute by Children's Home Society of Washington officials.

Charlie Langdon, president of the nonprofit group which provides counseling and other services to parents, said the class was canceled after all but two of the 17 people who signed up

have been sitting in class tonight instead of in the King County Jail.

Langdon said both Bailey and Landon's mother, Kimber Davidson, met with the director of the group's Eastside office on Sept. 29. The director, a clinical psychologist with 22 years' experience, interviewed Bailey and determined he was a good candidate for the class.

Langdon said the course is offered to the general public, and

INDEX

Arts, entertainment	D section
Bridge	D 11
Business	B section
City Gritty	D 3
Classified ads	D 10-12, E section
Classified index	D 10
Comics	D 8, 9
Crossword puzzle	F 4
Dear Abby	F 3
Deaths, funerals	E 8
Doonesbury	E 8
Editorials	A 10
Going Places	D 6
Horoscope	F 3
Northwest	C 1-5, 8
Puzzles and Predictions	F 4
Scene	D 1-6
Sports	F 1-5, 6-8

6.10. Vigorous. The picture-story, boxed, provides this page's focus. All other modules are well-defined. Note that long story at left does not jump.

THE MILWAUKEE JOURNAL

Monday, November 28, 1988 — Latest Edition III

Human error in cockpit eludes FAA expertise

Washington Post service

Washington, D.C. — Each of the past three fatal air crashes involving major airlines occurred on takeoff, and each involved lapses in pilot attentiveness shortly before he pushed the throttles to the wall.

The similarities raise troubling questions about the state of airline pilot discipline and training.

Consider this:

■ In Detroit in August 1987, two Northwest Air Lines pilots forgot to set the jet's wing flaps. Their plane crashed onto a freeway off the end of the runway.

■ In Denver, two months later, two Continental Air Lines pilots, waiting to take off

in a snowstorm, chatted with a flight attendant instead of monitoring the jet's wings for signs of icing. They crashed near the end of the runway.

■ In Dallas on Aug. 31, three Delta Air Lines pilots carried on a wide-ranging and lengthy conversation with two flight attendants while taxiing to the runway. The plane slammed to the ground shortly after becoming airborne.

As the National Transportation Safety Board convenes a public hearing Tuesday into the cause of the Dallas crash, the inquiry into the retracted position, and investigators are exploring the disturbing possibility that the aviation system in one year suffered two

accidents in which the pilots did not set the flaps.

The industry has known for years that roughly two-thirds of aviation accidents are caused by pilot error. Yet the study of human performance is in its infancy compared with the advance of technology.

Billions of dollars have been spent since the dawn of the jet age perfecting the machine, while little has been invested in exploring the dimensions of the human mind.

"In almost every phase of aviation, we have pushed the frontiers of human knowledge. But we have not pushed the frontiers on human behavior," said Clark Onstad, an

Please see Pilots, Page 6A

The perfect tree

Nationwide sales
Percentage of total trees sold, by species

36%	Scotch pine
20%	Douglas fir
8%	Balsam fir
8%	White pine
28%	Other

How to determine tree's age

Natural vs. artificial

38%	34%	28%
of households have a natural tree	have an artificial tree	have no tree at all

Journal graphic

3 teens sought in arson at elementary school

Milwaukee police were searching Monday for three teenagers seen near Hampton Elementary School Saturday night shortly before an arson fire extensively damaged the school.

Deputy Inspector Rudolph Will said that a witness had provided descriptions of the teenagers. They were described as white males between 14 and 16 years old.

The teenagers are suspected of breaking a window and entering the school after a janitor went home at 5:30 p.m., stealing several videocassette recorders and tapes, and setting a fire to cover up the crime. Damage was estimated at $750,000.

Please see School, Page 10A

Perfectly natural
Yule trees still need grower's hand

By ELIZABETH CULOTTA
Journal science reporter

How do you grow the perfect Christmas tree? In Wisconsin, the recipe begins with traditional methods of tree farming. Add a hefty dose of hand labor and a dollop of biotechnology and you have the tree of someone's dreams.

Please see Trees, Page 10A

Major US banks increase prime lending rate to 10.5%

Washington, D.C. — AP — Several of the nation's biggest banks raised their prime lending rates Monday to 10.5% despite good news about the trade deficit.

Please see Economy, Page 6A

SUITE DREAMS — Dreams of ballerinas and a floral paradise have been transformed into colorful reality for the Christmas show at the Mitchell Park Domes. 524 S. Layton Blvd. The show, which runs through Jan. 8, includes

Journal photo by Bruce Halmo

poinsettias, decorated spruce trees and scenes from "The Nutcracker." The Domes are open 9 a.m. to 5 p.m. weekdays, 9 a.m. to 6 p.m. weekends, and 9 a.m. to 6 p.m. Christmas Eve, Christmas Day and New Year's Day.

Italian center scales back lakefront project

By FRAN BAUER
Of The Journal staff

A $5 million Italian Community Center is about all that remains of plans for a $250 million development at the lakefront.

Please see Center, Page 6A

Saving for kids' college may break piggy bank

Madison, Wis. — AP — Parents who aspire to send their children to college should start saving money well before they buy their children's first microscopes or chemistry sets.

INSIDE

Sack time for Majkowski

Green Bay quarterback Don Majkowski lost control of the football after being dropped for a loss at the 1-yard line by Chicago's Al Harris (90) and Steve McMichael in the fourth quarter as the Bears beat the Packers, 16-0. The victory was costly for the Bears, who lost quarterback Mike Tomczak and defensive end Richard Dent to injuries. **Sports, 1C**

Claims questioned

A new infant formula may be called Good Start, but some pediatricians are questioning whether the product delivers what it promises. **Health, 1D**

OPEC agreement

OPEC oil ministers agreed Monday on a plan to reduce production and raise crude oil prices. The agreement could raise crude prices by $1 or $2 a barrel, analysts say. **Page 3A**

WEATHER

Milwaukee-area forecasts from National Weather Service

Tonight — Fair early. Becoming cloudy, a 20% chance of light snow toward morning. Light southwest winds.

Tuesday — Cloudy, a 50% chance of light snow. Details on Page 5B.

Projected college costs

6.11. Serious tone. The modules here are a bit less precise. All pictures are in color, which tends to draw attention. The page tone is both serious and modern.

FRIDAY, SEPTEMBER 23, 1988 PORTLAND, OREGON 35¢

AM
NORTHWEST EDITION

The Oregonian

WEATHER: Cloudy; cooler; high 67, low 47; Page A2

OLYMPIC UPDATE

A hug for gold

U.S. swimmer Janet Evans (right) hugs teammate Tami Bruce after Evans' world-record effort in the 400-meter freestyle Thursday night in Seoul. Evans' time of 4:03.85 broke the world record she set in 1987. Bruce finished fourth in the event. Page F1

READY TO RUN

Twenty-five world record-holders stand poised for an East-meets-West duel as track-and-field competition gets under way. Page F6

VIOLENCE AFTER THE FIGHT

South Korean boxing coaches storm the ring and attack a referee in protest of a loss. Page F1

THE GAMES ON TV

KGW (8) continues its coverage Friday (events subject to change):

6-9 a.m., 2:30-3:30 p.m., 4:30-9 p.m., 9:30-11:30 p.m.: swimming, boxing, basketball, gymnastics, track and field, table tennis.

TERRY FREI IN SEOUL .... Page F1
COMPLETE RESULTS .... Page F9
FRIDAY'S SCHEDULE .... Page F9
SPORTS HOT LINE 221-8100

STOCKS

Market down 10.49 points; closes at 2,080.01; trading light. — Page E3

NEWS IN BRIEF

Time's running out for river bill

Disagreeing over treatment of the Klamath River, Senate and House committees drafted different versions of the Oregon Wild and Scenic Rivers bill Thursday. Failure to agree on the Klamath, where the city of Klamath Falls wants to build a hydroelectric project, sets up a deadline faceoff between Sen. Mark O. Hatfield and Rep. Peter DeFazio, the most senior and most junior members of the Oregon delegation. Page D1

Unrest mounts in Soviet region

Radio Moscow said protesters attacked a prosecutor's office in the disputed Soviet region of Nagorno-Karabakh, which officials have sealed off and put under curfew. One person was reported killed and 48 injured in clashes between Armenians and Azerbaijanis. Soldiers cordoned off city streets and were checking identifications. Page A8

S&Ls still lose, but slower

The nation's 3,000 savings and loans lost $3.6 billion from April to June, which was a slight improvement over the first quarter when they lost $3.9 billion and the last quarter of 1987 when the loss was $4 billion. In a speech for delivery in the Senate, William Proxmire, D-Wis., said it was his "reluctant but profound conviction" the problem "has grown beyond industry resources." Page E1

INDEX

SECTION A		Forum	11,13
News in brief	3	Obituary	8
Foreign	4-8	SECTION E	
Nation	10-22	Business	1-6
SECTION B		Classified	7-22
Living	1-8	Funerals	7
Crossword	6	Metro/NW	7
Radio, TV	7	SECTION F	
SECTION C		Sports	1-12
Advertising	1-12	Comics	10,11
SECTION D		SECTION G	
Metro/NW	1-10	A&E	1-28
Editorial	12	Movies	11-17

Seven sections — 126 pages

Classified advertising 221-8000
Circulation hot line 221-8240
News department 221-8188

Copyright © 1988, Oregonian Publishing Co. Vol. 137 — No. 45,902

House OKs tough drug bill

The anti-narcotics measure offers rehabilitation for addicts and now faces resolution with conferees on the Senate's version

By LARRY MARGASAK
The Associated Press

WASHINGTON — The House on Thursday approved an anti-drug bill that would punish offenders from the smallest users to the major dealers and provide for the rehabilitation and treatment of those hooked on illegal narcotics.

The vote was 375-30.

The Senate has yet to begin consideration of its own anti-drug bill, and a conference will likely be needed to iron out differences during the remaining days of the 100th Congress.

Several sponsors of the bill said some of the provisions might prove to be unconstitutional and expressed hope that such language would be eliminated in conference.

The Democratic floor manager, Rep. Charles Rangel, D-N.Y., said "at least all of us can go home" and say "we responded to our constituents and the nation."

"We have made some effort to address the problem as Republicans and Democrats, and we have set our labels behind us," Rangel said.

The bill would give new money to federal law enforcement agencies and to local law enforcement and would give states money for anti-drug education, rehabilitation and treatment.

We "can go home and say we responded to our constituents." — Rep. Charles Rangel

Before the final vote, the House amended the bill to give states additional highway money if they take away driving privileges of convicted drug offenders. The amendment was an alternative to a tougher proposal that would have withheld a portion of highway money unless states agreed to suspend or revoke drug offenders' drivers' licenses.

The vote broke a string of decisions by the House to enact the toughest possible measures against both drug dealers and those who simply possess illegal narcotics.

The House took two amendment votes. In the key vote, the House adopted 281-119 the incentive approach proposed by Rep. Glenn M. Anderson, D-Calif. A second, technical vote of 392-8 formally inserted the language into the drug bill.

The wide margin for the highway fund incentives reflected opposition by conservatives who voted for previous amendments to toughen the drug bill.

Rep. Tom DeLay, R-Texas, expressed their fears, arguing: "We're forgetting the passionate states rights argument and trampling all over the division of powers.

"You can blackmail the states for a bad purpose, or you could blackmail them for a good one, but it's blackmail just the same."

Please turn to DRUGS, Page A22

Spill slows I-84 traffic

The Oregonian/DOUG BEGHTEL

A worker pours absorbent material on Interstate 84 near Northeast 148th Avenue, where an eastbound McCall Asphalt Co. tanker carrying liquid asphalt overturned about 4:30 a.m. Thursday. No injuries were reported, but the accident blocked one lane, slowing traffic on the freeway until after noon.

Did copter buzz ranch in Oregon, fire 'shots'?

The FAA and an Air Force Reserves unit launch an investigation into the low-flying incident near Bend

By ROBERT E. SHOTWELL
Correspondent, The Oregonian

BEND — The Federal Aviation Agency and the Air Force Reserves are investigating reports that an Air Force Reserves helicopter recently buzzed a Central Oregon ranch and possibly fired a burst of gunfire while doing so.

Peter Hiatt, who lives on a ranch between Bend and Sisters, said Thursday he had filed a complaint with the Federal Aviation Administration flight standards office in Portland after the helicopter startled his mother at about 5 p.m. Saturday while she was watering his horses at the ranch.

"She wasn't frightened; she was angry," Hiatt said. "As the (helicopter) flew over the house, she thought she heard a short burst of gunfire — 10 or 15 rounds. We figured it was because she shook her fist at the pilot."

Hiatt said that in scrambling to get a number off the tail section of the helicopter, his mother stumbled and fell, bruising her hip.

Lt. Col. William E. Scarboro Jr., safety officer for the Portland-based 939th Aerospace Rescue and Recovery Group of the Air Force Reserves, said Thursday it's possible the aircraft was from his unit.

"Our aircraft were flying in the area, and we did have a helicopter armed with an M-60 machine gun, armed only with blanks," Scarboro said. "It's likely the incident did involve one of our aircraft, but I don't have any specifics from the crew. I haven't had a chance to talk to them. We are conducting an internal investigation of the unit itself."

Scarboro said there is an area near where the incident occurred that is used by his unit as a search and rescue training site.

"Last weekend, we were doing low-level ingress and egress training into a particular landing zone, which is up in the Black Butte area," Scarboro said. "The pilot flying the helicopter with the M-60 machine gun did do some low-level firing, but I can't believe that any of our crews would fly low over a farmhouse and fire off blank ammunition.

"If anything, it was probably an inadvertent overflight, because these pilots don't fly over any structures or even in close proximity to structures," he said. "For one thing, it's against Air Force regulations."

Hiatt had originally filed his complaint with the Deschutes County sheriff's department. A sheriff's dispatcher said Hiatt's was the only complaint filed Saturday, but that "many calls were coming in most of the day Sunday, from Sisters, Bend and Alfalfa (east of Bend)" about helicopter noise.

Scarboro said he tried to talk to Hiatt on the telephone, but said Hiatt told him (Hiatt) would write it all in the complaint.

The incident comes on the heels of another incident involving military aircraft in Central Oregon. In that instance, two Oregon Air National Guard jets made a low pass over the Mount Jefferson Wilderness Area July 28 and frightened some horses. Two people riding the horses, Cole and Charlotte Still of Prineville, were thrown and seriously injured.

"We were the people who went in and rescued those injured riders," Scarboro said.

Sandra Burger, spokeswoman for the Air Guard in Portland, said Thursday that incident still is being investigated.

David Duff, a spokesman for the FAA in Seattle, said Thursday the incident involving Hiatt is "being investigated as rapidly as possible. We have received his complaint in our Portland office, and we have identified two possible helicopters that may have been involved. That's about all we have right now."

Please turn to COPTER, Page A19

Wright denies he revealed classified information

Republicans quick to call for an investigation after the speaker outlines CIA operations in Nicaragua

By JIM DRINKARD
The Associated Press

WASHINGTON — House Speaker Jim Wright denied Thursday that he had revealed anything classified when he criticized a covert CIA operation in Nicaragua, while Republicans pressed for formal ethics and intelligence investigations of the speaker's remarks.

Wright, who has become a lightning rod for Democrats on Central America policy, found himself again embroiled in controversy for his revelation two days earlier that the Central Intelligence Agency had instigated demonstrations aimed at provoking the leftist Managua government and sabotaging peace talks with the Contra rebels.

Jim Wright

"I didn't say anything that was revealed to me as classified."

The speaker repeated that assertion to reporters, but contended such CIA activity already was well known through news reports.

"I didn't say anything that was revealed to me as classified information," said Wright, D-Texas.

While he denied breaking rules against disclosing secrets, Wright did not specify how he had learned of the covert operation in Nicaragua. He and other Democrats sought to focus attention on the administration's action rather than the propriety of Wright's disclosure.

Please turn to WRIGHT, Page A19

Political parties effectively ignoring voter sign-up

The unusual campaign strategy is expected to continue the 24-year decline in Election Day turnout

By JEFF MAPES
of The Oregonian staff

After being heckled by angry shipyard workers in Portland earlier this month, Vice President George Bush shrugged it off as no great loss to his campaign.

"It's part of the action. . . . All I need is 51 percent of the vote," Bush said after his confrontation with the union workers at Northwest Marine Iron Works.

The Republican nominee could have added that this figure also may come close to representing the percentage of American adults who will even bother to go to the polls Election Day, Nov. 8.

Bush's "us vs. them" comments also underline a basic strategy that several voting experts say is being followed diligently by both Bush and Democratic nominee Michael S. Dukakis.

Instead of making major efforts to increase the number of people registered to vote, both candidates and their parties are focusing their money and attention on identifying their supporters and getting them to the polls.

This lack of interest in voter registration is just one of several factors that appears to be leading to a continuation of the 24-year decline in voter turnout. Since 1960, when nearly 63 percent of eligible adults voted, turnout has steadily declined to about 53 percent in the last two presidential elections.

Oregon, with its tradition of civic involvement and relative ease of voter registration, has had a better record. An estimated two-thirds of eligible Oregon adults voted in the 1984 presidential election.

But it may be difficult to get as many voters to the polls in Oregon this year, because of a new law that ends voter registration 20 days before an election. Four years ago, Oregonians could register as late as election day, but concern about Rajneeshee importation of new voters led first to a day-before deadline and then, under a 1986 ballot measure, to a 20-day cutoff.

"I don't think there's any question that the 20-day cutoff is a barrier," said Secretary of State Barbara Roberts. "By the time many people become aware and excited about the election, it's too late."

Nationally, "my sense is we're going to have a low turnout," said Curtis B. Gans, director of the non-partisan Committee for the Study of the American Electorate. "The main factors are the long-term trend of weakening voter identification with either party. . . . compounded by one of the more vacuous presidential campaigns of my lifetime."

Bush's slashing verbal attacks, combined with Dukakis' hope of running a low-issues campaign, is "not destined to draw out" a large turnout, added Gans.

In addition, neither the Republican nor Democratic campaign apparatuses have launched major voter registration efforts this year. In 1984, the Republicans spent about $8 million on a sophisticated voter registration drive after Democrats had announced their own effort to sign up new voters. The Democratic drive fizzled because of the party's money troubles, but a number of conservative and liberal groups conducted their own campaigns, ranging from efforts to sign up new voters from evangelical Christians to poor clients of government social-service agencies.

Those drives added anywhere from 4 million to 7 million registered voters, depending on who does the counting, and appeared to produce a slight upward blip in voting — from 52.6 percent of eligible adults in 1980 to 53.1 percent in 1984.

"Neither party is doing as much this year," said Gans, explaining that Dukakis and Bush instead are focusing on identifying favorable voters and getting them to the polls Nov. 8.

Please turn to VOTE, Page D7

6.12. Overpowered. The strip at left is blue on yellow, making the rest of page look tame. Note the double border around picture and cutline. Deck heads probably are not read well.

6.13. Restrained. This page, without color, looks a bit old-fashioned. The stories tend to form layers and the nameplate dominates the page. (Reprinted courtesy of the *Plain Dealer*)

The Boston Globe

Telephone 929-2000
Classified 929-1500
Circulation 929-2220
Customer Service 929-1818
© 1988 Globe Newspaper Co.

Vol. 234; No. 139

WEDNESDAY, NOVEMBER   1988

*15 cents at newsstands beyond 30 miles from Boston

100 Pages • 25 cents

Fall downhill from here
Wednesday – Partly sunny, 50s
Thursday – Clouds, showers, 60
High tide – 3:53 a.m., 4:04 p.m.
Full report – Page 64

Sudan snarls aid in red tape

By Thomas Palmer
Globe Staff

ABYEI, Sudan – Three desperately needed nurses and a doctor arrived in this refugee-packed village 10 days ago, but they were unable to work.

Instead, they were confined grim-faced to the area around their tiny quarters, swatting mosquitoes and trying to disguise their frustration with patient, restrained comments.

"The security officer told us we needed a 'stay permit,'" said one medical worker. "In Khartoum we asked for that, and they don't know what it is."

All around them, in the bush, in grass huts and in a hospital that is just a warehouse for the dying, Sudanese who have been routed from their homes by civil war were suffering from malaria, malnutrition and other diseases.

A bureaucracy as virulent as the indigenous diseases has frequently paralyzed foreign assistance efforts by agencies such as Oxfam, the European consortium, Doctors Without Borders and Catholic Relief Services.

"We just want to work," said one nurse, sipping tea with local Abyei officials. All of those interviewed insisted that using their names would only infuriate the bureaucrats and security officials who must grant permission for expatriate relief efforts.

Although the graveyard in

SUDAN, Page 22

A malnourished Sudanese baby yearns for his mother's milk after rejecting food.

State revenue forecast may be cut $300m

By Bruce Mohl
Globe Staff

The governor's Revenue Advisory Board, whose revenue forecast for this year is already $117 million less than that of the Dukakis administration, is sending strong signals that it may soon cut its projection by as much as $300 million.

Two of the five board members said yesterday that they think the board's revenue projection should be cut $300 million. Two other members said they were reserving judgment on the precise figure but indicated a cut is in the works.

The sobering news came as Gov. Dukakis delivered a warm speech of thanks to a joint session of the Legislature for its help during the presidential campaign and assured lawmakers that he is not underestimating the seriousness of the state's budget problems.

"I've tried as best I could to play my part over the last 20 months," Dukakis said. "But it's you to whom this state and I owe a great deal of gratitude."

Dukakis said on Monday that he is not making any revision in his forecast of 10.9 percent growth in tax revenues for this year until he hears the next report from his Revenue Advisory Board, scheduled to meet later this month or early next month.

But Robert T. Capeless, a board member and former Revenue Department commissioner, said nearly every budget observer inside and outside of state government has failed to recognize that the advisory board's current estimate is below $117 million below the governor's.

"They're sticking with what is their number," Capeless said, referring to the Dukakis administration. "They're not sticking with our number. They've never accepted our number, and we have real questions about whether we'll reach our number."

Capeless' assessment of the revenue picture was supported by board members Jerry Hausman, an economist with the Massachusetts Institute of Technology, and Robert Zevin, an economist with US Trust Co. Both men said the board's revenue estimate is lower than the administration's and both said they were prepared to cut it by $300 million when they meet again.

"I think that we now have more per-

BUDGET, Page 7

Nursing homes say they'd sue

By Charles Stein
Globe Staff

The head of the state's nursing home industry yesterday said his group would sue the Dukakis administration, if necessary, to force the state to live up to a promise to pay nursing homes an estimated $200 million in Medicaid money.

"We are asking our largest customer – the state – to pay its bills," said Alan Solomont, president of the Massachusetts Federation of Nursing Homes. "Right now, that customer is a deadbeat and is looking for excuses not to pay us."

Administration officials denied the charge, but they could not say when and if the homes would be paid.

The nursing home dispute strikes at the heart of the state's fiscal crisis. Massachusetts already has borrowed $1 billion this fiscal year to make up the gap between tax revenues that are lower than projected and spending that is exceeding targets.

Medicaid, the state's largest budget item, accounts for a good part of the overspending. In the first four months of the fiscal year, Medicaid spending was 25 percent, or $118 million, above last year's pace. Nursing homes receive roughly 40 percent of the $1.5 billion annual Medicaid allotment.

MEDICAID, Page 16

Brady will keep Treasury post

By Walter V. Robinson
and Diane Alters
Globe Staff

WASHINGTON – President-elect George Bush yesterday selected Treasury Secretary Nicholas F. Brady to retain that post, and sources said an announcement that Gov. John H. Sununu of New Hampshire will be the White House chief of staff is imminent.

In a busy first day after a long weekend in Florida, Bush sidestepped questions about Sununu while using the announcement of Brady's retention to send a message to jittery financial markets that reducing the federal budget deficit will be his immediate priority as president.

In going to the ranks of his close friends for the second time in a row to fill an important Cabinet post, Bush underscored his interest in resolving a looming impasse on the deficit. But when a reporter asked how a solution could be achieved without raising taxes, a step he has said he will not consider, Bush shut back: "Just watch what we do."

BUSH, Page 10

AFP photo
President-elect George Bush shakes hands with Treasury Secretary Nicholas F. Brady. The Globe's John Robinson writes that Brady shares with Bush an early life of Eastern privilege and educational opportunity. Page 10.

Prime faces takeover bid

By John Wilke
Globe Staff

A California computer company armed with junk-bond financing yesterday launched a $970 million hostile bid for Prime Computer Inc. of Natick, one of the Bay State's largest corporations.

The surprise $20-a-share offer turns the tables on the minicomputer maker, which late last year launched a successful $435 million hostile bid for Computervision Corp. of Bedford.

Bennett S. LeBow, who controls MAI Basic Four Inc., a Tustin, Calif., computer maker, said in a letter to Prime president Joe M. Henson that a merger "makes excellent strategic sense."

But Prime is more than four times the size of Basic Four, which would shoulder an enormous debt load to close the deal.

A Prime spokesman said the offer and art in the best interests of the shareholders, customers

PRIME, Page 69

Arafat claims mandate to search for peace

By Mary Curtius
Globe Staff

ALGIERS – The chairman of the Palestine Liberation Organization, Yasser Arafat, said yesterday that the resolutions adopted by the Palestine National Council gave him a mandate to seek a peaceful settlement to the Palestinian problem.

He said he would "pursue a political settlement and secure the rights of the Palestinian people to self-determination and statehood. We are not begging for peace. . . . We are seeking peace on an equal footing with the other parties concerned."

On Monday, the Palestine National Council adopted versions of UN Security Council Resolutions 242 and 338 as the basis for an international peace conference while declaring an independent Palestinian state. "The ball is now in the American court," Arafat said. The Palestine National Council is regarded as a parliament-in-exile by the Palestine Liberation Organization.

"It is true that this is the intifadah session that gave the PNC, but it could also be the session of peace if the US administration and the Israelis wish," Arafat told a press conference. Intifadah is the Arabic word for the uprising in Israel's occupied territories.

Arafat spoke after laying the cornerstone here for the first Palestinian embassy. Algeria was the first nation to recognize the Palestinian state declared early yesterday.

Arafat appeared in good humor as he spoke in English and Arabic to several hundred reporters in the room.

PLO, Page 18

INSIDE
Today: Food

Celtics beat the Heat
Boston snapped a 4-game losing streak with an 84-66 victory in Miami. Page 51.

Grand old send-off
Retiring Republican national committeewoman Polly Logan got a glowing salute yesterday. Living, Page 83.

Abuse victims
Women who were sexually abused as children are twice as likely to give birth to babies who are premature or have medical problems, researchers report. Page 12.

Guide to features
Arts/Films 85	Deaths 60-61
Ask Globe 62	Editorials 14
Bridge 82	Horoscope 62
Business 67	Living 83
Comics 62-63	Sports 51
Crosword 74-82	TV/Radio 85
Classified 74-82	88-100

Heart attack treatment may be overused, study implies

By Richard A. Knox
Globe Staff

WASHINGTON – Confounding the assumptions of many heart specialists, a large new study has found that it does not pay to use a popular technique called balloon angioplasty to clear the diseased coronary arteries of a heart attack victim as soon as possible.

About 1 million Americans suffer heart attacks each year, and US specialists are increasingly subjecting such patients to the kind of all-out intervention that the new study has found is often unnecessary.

HEART, Page 6

Boston schools short of books despite a $350 million budget

By Patricia Wen
Globe Staff

Despite a $350 million budget, the Boston public school system has a shortage of basic textbooks that principals, teachers and parents say is compromising the quality of education.

Martin Luther King Jr. Middle School in Dorchester has spent $15,000 to copy parts of textbooks the school cannot afford to buy. At some schools students are not allowed to take books home. A second-grade class in Dorchester had to share math books at the start of the year.

Some school authorities say there are not enough funds to buy books; others say the money is there but politicians have not made it a priority.

"Some people don't get their priorities right," said Michael Fung, community superintendent for District E, the citywide magnet school district.

"How can a kid do homework without a book?" asked Lena Freeman, a King School parent who plans to bring the matter before the School Committee. "To expect our children to do anything academically, we have to give them materials," she said.

At Mather Elementary School in Dorchester, Mary Stroup found another teacher with some

BOOKS, Page 13

Mary Stroup, a second-grade teacher at the Mather School in Dorchester, says that when a student takes a book home, "it's considered a prize." Here she instructs Nyeia Milton at the blackboard.

6.14. Five column. The *Globe* often widens its columns to aid reading, and the result is a five-column paper. All pictures are black and white but the page looks lively. It does seem cluttered in midpage. (Reprinted courtesy of the *Boston Globe*)

On Today's Editorial Page
Voters Sent No Message
Editorial
A Turn For The Worse
In Afghanistan
Editorial

ST. LOUIS POST-DISPATCH

★★★★★

Vol. 110, No. 318   SUNDAY, NOVEMBER 13, 1988   710 Pages   (6)   Copyright 1988 $1.00

U.S. Considers Suing E. St. Louis For $9 Million

By Safir Ahmed
Of the Post-Dispatch Staff

The U.S. Department of Justice is considering going to court to collect debts totaling $9.5 million from East St. Louis, the debts resulting from what federal authorities say was mismanagement of jobs program grants in the mid-1970s.

But the department has yet to act on the debts, partly because the city is in dire financial straits, a source at the department told the Post-Dispatch last week.

"We really don't want to rain on their parade, we think they've had

plenty already," the source said. "And a debt like this could break the city. It's a serious debt."

The debt stems from $22 million in federal grants the city received between August 1974 and September 1979 under the Comprehensive Employment and Training Act, the federal jobs program known as CETA. After audits in the early 1980s, the U.S. Department of Labor "disallowed" $5.15 million that was spent but not accounted for. With interest, the figure now stands at about $9.5 million.

The Labor Department turned the

matter over to the Justice Department for litigation. Amy Brown, a Justice Department spokeswoman, said the case was "still under review, and it is being studied."

Mayor Carl E. Officer says that he knows about the debts but that he is not about to agree to any payment plan. The debts precede Officer's administration.

"I think it would be irresponsible of me in chief executive to go into an agreement just because the Department of Labor says I owe (the money), and they can't back it up with records," Officer said. "I would have

in challenge the initial finding."

The initial finding was for a disallowance of $4.5 million and was made after the Labor Department completed an audit in 1982. When the city failed to exercise its right of appeal, the department made a formal determination in April 1983 that the city owed $4.5 million.

Since April 30, 1983, interest started accruing on the debt at an annual rate of 13 percent. Today, the principal plus interest stands at about $8.8 million. Interest on the second disallowance, of $651,354, started accruing on Feb. 5, 1987, at an annual rate

of 7 percent, bringing that total to about $733,000.

The disallowances arose in the administration of former Mayor William E. Mason, who preceded Officer. The Labor Department curtailed the city's participation in the CETA program on Sept. 30, 1978, because of "fraud, thefts, kickbacks, nepotism, patronage and poor record-keeping," the Justice Department source said.

Mason, who operates a consulting business, said he was unaware of any disallowance of CETA money. Mason said it was unfair for the federal government to try to collect it from the city now.

"This is the first I've ever heard about it," Mason said Friday. "For them to come now and pick on a city that's already crippled is unfair — it's unfair to my administration, to the present administration and to the city."

Officer said: "They seem to be finding new-found interest in going back into history. I imagine they'll go back through the city's 112-year history and find more debts incurred that we owe for some horses and hay."

See DEBT, Page 10

Richard F. Daykin
"Why in the world would I?"

Daykin Let Jobs To His Son's Bosses

By Deborah Peterson
and Louis J. Rose
Of the Post-Dispatch Staff

©1988, St. Louis Post-Dispatch

Richard F. Daykin, St. Louis County highway director, gave the County Council to award more than $1 million in no-bid contracts to two engineering firms that employed his son, Richard J. Daykin.

The elder Daykin says he did not tell the County Council that his son worked for the firms when he proposed that the council give the companies contracts over the last five years. Daykin has been the county's highway director since 1967.

"I have no obligation under the laws of the state or the county to advise the council," Daykin said. "I didn't feel I ought to advise them. Why in the world would I?"

Daykin said he saw no conflict in proposing that the companies — James B. Becker Consulting Engineers and Stock & Associates Consulting Engineers Inc. — get the no-bid work while his son worked for them. He also said no favoritism had been shown to either firm.

The six contracts involved represent roughly about one-fifth of the Highway Department's spending for engineering services in the last five years, one Highway Department official estimates.

The Becker firm was awarded four contracts totaling $613,759 from 1984 through 1987, while Daykin's son worked there, records examined by

See DAYKIN, Page 10

5 Perish In Mobile Home Fire

By Carolyn Bower
Of the Post-Dispatch Staff

Five people — a man, a woman and three children — perished early Saturday in a fire at a mobile home at the La-Cal Trailer Court in Herculaneum.

Officials would not make public the victims' identities. All five were pronounced dead at the scene, off U.S. Highway 61-67.

Neighbors said the man and his wife, Paul and Marie Adams, both in their 20s, had lived in the home with their three children for about a year.

The neighbors identified the children as Brian, 4; April, 2; and Anthony, 9 months. They said Paul Adams worked at an auto-repair shop in Arnold.

The blaze was reported at 5:09 a.m. Bill Haggard, the Herculaneum fire chief, said. When firefighters arrived at 985 La-Cal Court at 5:13 a.m., he said, "There was lots of smoke. The front room was on fire. How long it had been burning, we don't know."

Haggard said firefighters had needed several minutes to bring the fire under control.

Ralph Williams, the Herculaneum fire marshal, said the family had no electricity or gas in the trailer home.

Officials initially suspected that the fire had been caused by candles used to light the trailer. But later in the day, they ruled out the candles as the cause of the blaze. Haggard said.

Inspector J. Trent Ford of the Missouri Division of Fire Safety said that while only a small part of the home burned, the smoke damage was heavy. He said the cause of the fire was still under investigation.

Haggard said the victims had been found inside the front (or) rooms of the trailer. He said they probably had died of smoke inhalation.

Annalie Watkins, who lives in a trailer directly across from the charred green trailer, said she had been awakened by someone who "banged on my door and yelled, 'Fire! People, I have a phone,'" she said.

Watkins said she had called the Herculaneum Police Department. "I practically just hung up the phone when an officer arrived, and the firefighters were right behind him," she said.

Watkins said she had seen new flames except for some running along the bottom of the trailer.

"It was raining," she said. "There was lots of smoke. We didn't think it was that bad."

She added, "It's awful. There were three little kids."

Neighbors said the fire had melted

See FIRE, Page 11

Neil Rasnic and his daughter, Tabitha, standing outside a trailer in which five people died in a fire early Saturday. The

Karen Elshout Whiteley/Post-Dispatch

Rasnics also have no electricity or hot water in their trailer because they have been unable to pay their electric bills.

2nd Trailer Family Using Candles

By Carolyn Bower
Of the Post-Dispatch Staff

At least one other family in a mobile home park in Jefferson County where five people were killed in a trailer fire Saturday is without electricity and uses candles for light.

"It's a damned shame," said Neil Rasnic, who lacks electricity and hot water in his home at the La-Cal Trailer Park off U.S. Highway 61-67 in Herculaneum.

"For my to make it, and you can't." Five other people live in a trailer with Rasnic, including his daughters Tabitha, 4, and Crystal Gayle, 6, his wife, Barbara; and her father and stepmother. They live on $396 a

month in welfare, $260 of which goes for rent, Rasnic said.

Rasnic said he had tried to find a job but has been turned down because of medical problems. He said, "Everybody says it's easy to pay bills. It's not."

Rasnic lives next door to the trailer at 985 La-Cal Court where two adults and three children perished Saturday in an early morning fire.

Authorities were investigating the cause of the fire. The trailer was lighted by candles, which may have fallen from a wall. Earlier, authorities said the candles had not been the cause of the blaze.

Neighbors said the couple who

lived with their children at 985 La-Cal Court, Paul and Marie Adams, had been unable to pay their electric bills and had had their electricity shut off.

"I'm in the same fix," said Rasnic. "We can't pay the bills, and we have to run extension cords to other trailers sometimes to get lights. Sometimes we have to use candles, which is dangerous."

Rasnic said he had sought help from charitable groups and the state Division of Family Services. He was given $200 to help pay his electric bill, but he said he still owes $462.

"It's like some people don't give a damn," he said. "They're making it fine. Why should they worry?"

Rasnic said his biggest concern was for his daughters, who watched the bodies of the children next door being taken out of the charred trailer Saturday morning.

"My little girl cried," he said. "They all played together.

"I looked at those kids, and I thought, 'They could have been my kids.'"

Ralph Williams, the Herculaneum fire marshal and building commissioner, said people should report families who are living without electricity or gas by calling 479-4447, station 10, because such conditions are

See CANDLES, Page 11

PLO's Arafat Urges Bush To Rethink Israeli Policy

Compiled From News Services

ALGIERS, Algeria — PLO Chairman Yasser Arafat has urged President-elect George Bush to re-examine U.S. policy toward Israel.

Arafat made the appeal in a speech Saturday, the first day of a meeting of Palestinian officials.

He told the Palestine Liberation Organization would challenge Israel with "the rifle in one hand and the olive branch in the other" in the PLO's quest for an independent state.

He addressed the Palestine National Council, the parliament-in-exile of the PLO. He said Palestinians wouldn't stop fighting until their final blow over Jerusalem.

Before her four-day gathering, Arafat was asked for his opinion of the outcome of the American elections. He responded, "It makes no differ-

Arafat

ence. The United States is pampering the Israeli military junta with a baby by giving them all the weapons they ask for."

But in his opening remarks to the conference, Arafat seemed to write upon the occasion to appeal directly to Bush for a change in U.S. policy.

"I am asking President Bush that he should have a new policy, not a policy aligned toward Israel," Arafat said. "We are standing on the side of justice."

The Palestine National Council is expected to issue a unilateral declaration of independence for the occupied West Bank and Gaza Strip, where a Palestinian uprising has been under way for 11 months.

But the four-day meeting has wider significance, because it will determine the extent to which the PLO can make well Western demands for its new over Jerusalem.

See ARAFAT, Page 17

● ISRAEL CLOSES off Arab areas to prevent protests.............Page 17A

Wellsville, Mo., Finds Itself Dogged By Issue Of Strays

By Terry Ganey
Post-Dispatch
Jefferson City Bureau Chief

WELLSVILLE, Mo. — All is not well in Wellsville. There is Trouble here. With a capital T, and that rhymes with D, and that stands for dogs.

The trouble seems to have begun Oct. 24, where a special state prosecutor filed four criminal charges of animal abuse against the city.

But there are those who say the trouble was stirred up the month before, when a Humane Society investigator from St. Louis came to investigate allegations that police were abusing the stray animals on an obscene gesture.

Others believe the trouble began so long ago as in 1978, when the dogcatcher quit and the decision was made to pay police an $3.50 bounty for each animal they brought in dead or alive.

Whatever the roots, there is no question now there is trouble in Wellsville. It was easily measured at the well-attended City Council meeting last Wednesday night.

Montgomery County was hit with a severe thunderstorm that night. But it was nothing like the storm clouds that gathered in the sunroom fire department garage, where the meeting was moved to accommodate the 65 who attended.

Just before the meeting began, at the request of Alderman James T. Mottaz, police frisked a man in the audience. No weapon was found, and later during the meeting, the man repaid Mottaz with an obscene gesture.

"I've been chief of police six years and I've never witnessed more unrest since I've been here," said Daryl Keithley, the head of Wellsville's six-member

See ANIMALS, Page 14

Voters Showed Caution Despite Shifting Blocs

By Bob Adams
Post-Dispatch Washington Bureau Chief

WASHINGTON — It was, in the end, as uneasy affirmation of the status quo.

There was no crashing wave of conservatism, as in 1980. There was an overpowering mandate for change, as in 1932. There was, instead, a solidifying of the core of President Ronald Reagan's conservative coalition — along with some fraying of that coalition around the edges.

It was a cautious, pragmatic, why-rock-the-boat vote. And it was, perhaps unintentionally, another vote for divided government, with Americans sending Republicans back to the White House but Democrats back to Congress and the statehouses.

Perhaps surprisingly, it was the first election since 1972 in which the presidential candidates did not run against Washington. On the contrary, both Vice President George Bush and Gov. Michael S. Dukakis of Massa-

★ ★ ★ ★ ★ ★ ★
CAMPAIGN '88
News Analysis

● PROFILES of Barbara Bush and Marilyn Quayle.............Page 4A
● DEMOCRAT WON'T push Bush on tax increases.............Page 6A
● GOP'S WIN in Illinois tied to low black turnout.............Page 10B
● WOMEN SHOW gains in congressional races.............Page 8

chusetts stressed their experience in handling the problems of government.

Thus it may have, without fanfare, marked the passing of the anti-Washington atmosphere that has been a feature of every campaign since the Watergate scandal in the mid-1970s.

That is the broad assessment of Tuesday's election results by political scientists, politicians and others who

See ELECTION, Page 6

SCORES
College Football
Oklahoma 10   Missouri 7   Arkansas 25 ... Texas A&M 20
Michigan 35   Illinois 9   LSU 20 .... Miss. St. 3
Wash. 6, Lee 17   Wash. U. 13   Syracuse 45 ... Boston Col. 24
Nebraska 7   Kansas St. 7   Clemson 40 ..... Maryland 25
Kansas 14   Kansas 24   Alabama 17 ... SW Louisiana 0
Nebraska 7   Colorado 0   Wash. St. 36 ..... Oregon St. 27
Michigan St. 36   Indiana 12   Youngstown 31 ... S. Illinois 14
Minnesota 7   Minnesota 7   SW Missouri 21 ... Illinois St. 10
Ohio St. 34   Iowa 24   Boise St. 17 .... E. Illinois 7
Northwestern 28   Purdue 14   W. Illinois 22 ... Wayne St. 8
USC 50   Arizona St. 5   SE Missouri 42 ... SW Baptist 6
West Va. 35   Rutgers 25   W. Missouri 24 ... Mo. Western 21
UCLA 27   Stanford 17   Detroit in Sports, Section D

SUNDAY

WEATHER
Sunny, Pleasant
Forecast for St. Louis:

Sunday: Patchy fog in the morning, otherwise sunny with light winds. High 58. Low Sunday night 38.

Monday: Sunny and warmer. Breezy in the afternoon. High 63.

Other Weather on Page 2A

 DOGGONE!

INSIDE
Automotive 45G
Books 5F
Business 1-10E
Classified 1-72G
Commentary 3B
Editorials 2B
Everyday 1-14F
Movie Listings 11F
Music/The Arts 4F
News Analysis 1,4B
Obituaries 10C,13C
Real Estate 1G
Reviews 2C
Sports 1-16D

THE REAGAN LEGACY

President Ronald Reagan's foreign policy kept its triumphs and failures, described in the first of a five-part series assessing the Reagan record.
PAGE 1B

FEATURES

 Happy 75th

St. Louis musician Russ David was this time out from her busy schedule this week to celebrate his 75th birthday.
PAGE 1F

6.15. Layered. This page also forms layers, although the mug shot breaks up the pattern a little. All pictures are in color and a blue strip tops the refer box at the bottom.

Today: Partly sunny with a chilly wind. High 56. Low 36. Tuesday: Mostly sunny and cool. High 52. Wind 8-16 mph. Yesterday: AQI: 10. Temp. range: 43-54. Details on Page D2.

The Washington Post

A News/Editorials
B Sports/Comics/Classified
C Style/Television
D Metro/Obituaries
Inside: Washington Business
Detailed index on Page A2

111TH YEAR · No. 352 · © 1988, The Washington Post Company · MONDAY, NOVEMBER 21, 1988 · Prices May Vary in Areas Outside Metropolitan Washington (See Box on A6) · 25¢

Senate Leadership Race Promises Change in Ways

3 Democrats Stress 'Quality of Life' Issues

By Helen Dewar
Washington Post Staff Writer

The candidates are promising more jobs, better working conditions, longer weekends, negotiating clout and conciliatory prowess.

Campaigns for Senate majority leader, one of the two or three most important elective jobs in Washington, have often been likened to the selection of a pope—almost mystic in their secrecy, ritual and sense of celestial importance.

But in their bid to succeed Majority Leader Robert C. Byrd (D-W.Va.) in a secret-ballot vote of their Democratic colleagues Nov. 29, Sens. Daniel K. Inouye (Hawaii), J. Bennett Johnston (La.) and George J. Mitchell (Maine) might as well be running for shop steward of Senate Local No. 1.

Pressed for institutional reforms by the large group of new Democrats elected when the party regained control of the Senate in 1986, they have tried to outbid each other with proposals to improve working conditions and make the Senate more efficient—from shorter hours to better computers.

The frenzy of bidding over "quality of life" issues, coupled with promises of power-sharing, more collegial policymaking and skill in dealing with a Republican White House, has virtually assured major changes in the way the Senate will do business next year.

But it has not produced a clear favorite in the seven-month leadership race, the winner of which will instantly become a key figure in Democrats' party-rebuilding efforts in the wake of their latest presidential defeat.

While Johnston and Mitchell are assumed to share a lead over Inouye, neither has scored a knockout, and Inouye is said to have a long-shot chance.

Aside from the one-upmanship on institutional reforms, all have strengths and weaknesses that will sway their colleagues—five newly elected Democrats as well as 50 incumbents—to varying degrees.

Inouye, 64, the eldest of the three, is first in seniority and secretary of the Democratic Conference, third-ranking on the party leadership ladder. Well-liked and respected among colleagues for his insider skills, he was once assumed to be the heir apparent to Byrd, and some senators are said to view him as a short-term transition leader, a plus in the eyes of those with leadership ambitions.

But some criticized his chairmanship of the Senate Iran-contra investigating committee, and he was embarrassed by the disclosure that he tucked away funds in a spending

See SENATE, A4, Col. 1

SEN. DANIEL K. INOUYE
. . . says he feels "very confident"

SEN. J. BENNETT JOHNSTON
. . . "very close" to locking up win

SEN. GEORGE J. MITCHELL
. . . "it's going very, very well"

GORBACHEV, GANDHI AGREE

UNITED PRESS INTERNATIONAL/REUTER

Soviet President Mikhail Gorbachev and Indian Prime Minister Rajiv Gandhi issue joint plea in New Delhi for the U.N. secretary general to speed the quest for an Afghan government acceptable to all parties. Story on Page A15.

Lab Work Evaporating From Schools

Safety Fears, Computers Help Deprive Youths of Hands-On Experience

By Boyce Rensberger and Barbara Vobejda
Washington Post Staff Writers

The most effective method ever devised for teaching science—having students do experiments in a classroom laboratory to enable them to see the results—is slowly vanishing from American schools.

The proportion of science classes that use "hands-on" activities has dropped between 15 percent and 27 percent, depending on the grade, during a recent 10-year period, according to a nationwide study done for the National Science Foundation.

The result is obvious to David Walker, a teaching assistant at the University of Maryland who supervises labs for students in introductory chemistry.

"They don't know how to use Bunsen burners, pipettes . . . we would expect them to know how to use a balance, burettes to titrate, read volumes, how to light Bunsen burners," Walker said. "You could talk to any teaching assistant and they would agree that students don't have very good lab skills."

Graduate student Dan Hatten has seen the same problems in the physics lab courses he teaches at the university. "A lot of them are not good with equipment . . . . They lack a sense of wiring simple circuits from a diagram, which is quite straightforward." He said the students are missing the scientific common sense they should be gaining from high-school physics courses.

Walker and Hatten are witnessing first-hand the results of what a number of studies report as a dramatic decline in the amount of time high school students spend in labs. In 1977, for example, 53 percent of the high school science classes surveyed included some form of laboratory exercise. When the survey was re-

See LABS, A10, Col. 1

Discontent Thrives in Polish Worker Hostels

Barracks, in Lieu of Housing, Serve as Breeding Ground for Strikers

By Jackson Diehl
Washington Post Foreign Service

WARSAW—Jaroslaw and Andrzej, two young Polish steelworkers, often spend their evenings sitting on the beds in a tiny room they share here with another worker, passing the time the best way they can without television or the luxury of privacy.

If their monthly payday has been recent, they might have a bottle of vodka to pass around. If not, they simply sit, talking about their jobs in the huge Huta Warszawa steel mill and their lives as bachelors in a factory dormitory without women, money or much hope of change.

One recent evening Jaroslaw, Andrzej and a friend from upstairs, Janusz, were talking when a visitor asked about a speech publicized that day by Polish communist leader Gen. Wojciech Jaruzelski that mentioned the privations of "workers' hostels" such as theirs.

"It is hardly surprising that there is widespread disenchantment in workers' hostels, occasionally erupting into open rebellion," Jaruzelski said. "Yet it is we who should call out to those young people, especially young workers, 'Come on, join us on our march to socialism, which is a good system, and don't go along those roads that will take you nowhere or even astray.' "

The general's words appeared to reflect real concern about the pressures that have made young workers the driving force of two waves of strikes in Poland this year. But the sentiment was lost on these young men. Not only had they not heard of the party leader's speech, but the three also appeared to be uninterested in any statements or promises Poland's communist leaders might have to make.

See POLAND, A21, Col. 3

Mulroney Ahead on Eve of Vote

Polls Show Turner Trailing in Canada; Free-Trade Debated

By Herbert H. Denton
Washington Post Foreign Service

TORONTO, Nov. 20—Canadians ended a bitterly contested election campaign today and prepared to vote Monday in an election that will determine the fate of Prime Minister Brian Mulroney and the controversial U.S.-Canadian free-trade agreement he negotiated with President Reagan.

The most recent public opinion surveys show Mulroney ahead in the three-way race, but most analysts said they could not calculate whether he and his Progressive Conservative Party could win the majority of seats in the House of Commons needed to ensure ratification of the trade deal.

The trade agreement, which would remove virtually all hindrances to the flow of trade between Canada and the United States over the next decade, was easily approved by both houses of Congress earlier this year and signed by Reagan. But it has been an explosive issue here and almost the only topic of debate in the 50-day election campaign.

Opposition Liberal Party leader John Turner's accusation in nationally televised debates last month that Mulroney had "sold out" Canada by negotiating a trade agreement he claimed would jeopardize Canada's generous social programs and its political independence, had propelled his party from third place in preelection polls into a dead heat with Mulroney's Conservatives.

Both Turner and Ed Broadbent, leader of the socialist New Democratic Party have said they would scrap the agreement if either of them forms the next government and that they would combine their numbers in the House of Commons to vote it down if Mulroney tries to form a minority government.

In a last-ditch appeal, Turner said today that the only way to defeat the trade agreement and "keep Canada Canadian" was to vote for his Liberal Party.

Meanwhile, Mulroney told a news conference in Montreal that if he is returned to power, he will recall Parliament as soon as possible to win approval of the trade agreement. Appearing confident, Mulroney grinned broadly as he campaigned in Montreal's east end, giving the thumbs-up sign to crowds

See CANADA, A18, Col. 1

A Case of Divided Loyalty

Ghanaian Is Torn Between Wives, Cultures

By Blaine Harden
Washington Post Foreign Service

Dawu, Ghana—Kwasi Oduro's face went slack with shock.

He had come home to his village in the Ghanaian forest for just three days to pay his respects to his family and to help out with medical bills. He had brought along Stella Adgei, his longtime girlfriend, to introduce her to his kin. He had expected nothing more trying out of the long weekend than his usual guilty discomfort over being unable to afford more than a fraction of his family's demands for money.

Certainly the last thing he expected was for his wife, Margaret, the mother of his five children, to follow him here from the capital, confront him publicly and accuse him of adultery.

Yet there Margaret was, standing defiantly in the middle of Dawu's one dirt street, with her baby boy, Yaw, strapped to her back. Shouting at the top of her lungs, she threatened Stella with physical violence and her husband of 15 years with divorce.

Oduro, 38, a lecturer in sociology at the University of Ghana in Accra, had approached Stella's parents in the traditional way last year, asking for her hand. He had been accepted and had told a few friends that Stella was his second wife. He always had been reluctant, however, to have a public wedding or to inform Margaret about the marriage.

He said he knew she wouldn't like it.

Oduro is like many village-born Africans whose education and ca-

See GHANA, A18, Col. 1

AN AFRICAN HOMECOMING
Last of two articles

BY BLAINE HARDEN—THE WASHINGTON POST

Teacher Kwasi Oduro holds his 1-year-old son, Yaw, at his Accra, Ghana, home.

Heritage Is Slipping Away From Cambodian Refugees

Decade in Camps Uproots Culture, Morals

By Keith B. Richburg
Washington Post Foreign Service

SITE 2 REFUGEE CAMP, Thailand—When Luy Chanphal talks about Cambodia to his two young daughters, he spreads out a large map on a table. "Here is Tonle Sap, where there are so many fish," he explains, pointing to western Cambodia's large lake. "And here are the rice fields of Battambang. And here is Kompong Speu," he says, searching for his native village.

Luy Chanphal's children, 7 and 5 years old, were born here on the Thai-Cambodian border, refugees from a country they have never seen and know nothing about. They have never seen Cambodia's expansive rice paddies or its quaint Buddhist pagodas. For them, home is a crowded, dusty camp enclosed by fences, where rice is delivered from the backs of trucks and the distant thud of artillery shells rings out from across the surrounding mountain range.

"I am always worried about my two daughters because they have nothing to do for their future," said Luy Chanphal, who left Cambodia in 1981. "If we remain here much longer, they won't know anything about the Cambodian people, the country, the culture."

The people in the camp, he said, ... up, sleep and get up, and they get their rice from the United Nations."

He added, "The culture of the Cambodian people is breaking down."

Nearly 10 years after Vietnam invaded Cambodia and sent a human wave of refugees fleeing into neighboring Thailand, the border camps have developed into veritable cities unto themselves, seemingly permanent entities with markets and blacksmith shops, with fire stations and clinics and heavy bicycle traffic—and with their own unique social pathologies.

Crime is rising, with roving teams of armed bandits terrorizing camp residents.

International relief workers say that domestic violence has increased, with the frustrations of the cramped conditions leading husbands to beat their wives and small quarrels with neighbors to develop into violent attacks.

Hospitals have treated refugees who were cut with axes and knives in fights. Some relief workers said alcoholism is increasing, as are suicide attempts. Some relief workers and Cambodians are also worried that the traditional culture and devout Buddhism may be slowly eroding.

With the problems mounting, almost everyone here agrees that the border refugees have reached

AIDS Tests Often Performed Without Consent

By Sandra G. Boodman
Washington Post Staff Writer

When Robert S. Church was admitted to the National Hospital for Orthopaedics and Rehabilitation in Arlington early this year with severe back pain, he thought that the tests performed on his blood were standard procedure before possible surgery.

But Church soon learned that one of the tests—and the impact it ... had tested positive for the human immunodeficiency virus, which causes AIDS. He was immediately moved to a private room away from other patients in a vacant wing of the hospital. Bright orange "isolation" stickers were affixed to all his property including his comb, toothpaste and cigarette lighter. And, he said, he was shunned by several members of the hospital staff, including his doctor.

Church, who did not know he had ... asked me I probably would have agreed to it," he said. "But I'm completely outraged at the way they did it and at the way I was treated."

Church's experience is not unique, according to doctors and lawyers who work with AIDS patients. They say that hospitals and physicians regularly flout guidelines issued by the American Medical Association, the American Hospital Association and the federal Centers

INSIDE

Pakistani Discussions

■ Pakistani President Ghulam Ishaq Khan has summoned rival political leaders for talks on a new government. Page A15

The Washington Post
Washington Business

■ Textile industry officials are

6.16. Busy page. Seven stories and five pictures make for too much activity. It is doubtful if the deck heads get much readership. All pictures are black and white and, with all the stories, make for a serious paper.

While design aims primarily at making news easy to read, it has several other functions. One is to reflect a newspaper's personality. The *New York Times,* a serious paper, would be unwise to adopt a frivolous design. Its makeup has been modernized on some special pages, but the paper still radiates a no-nonsense approach. Much of this serious impression stems from typography, for the type and the layout indicate tradition and formality. On the other hand, the design of the *Minneapolis Tribune* suggests not a "paper of record" but a paper filled with alert, lively, clever writing. Newspapers that cling to the policies of love, lust, and lucre have page designs to match: Headlines and pictures scream for attention.

Another function of design is to tell the reader what editors consider the day's most significant stories. As noted in Chapter 5, headline size does most of this job. Usually, the bigger the head, the more important the story. But not always. A short story on page one with a small but special headline tells the reader that the story is short but important. The size of pictures, use of color, and length of stories also indicate news value.

Placement cues the reader. A story on page one rates high. On the split page — the first page of another section — it also rates. But if it is three paragraphs on page fifty-three, the reader realizes the editor considers the item little more than a filler.

Good design provides other aids for the reader. The various sections — editorial page, comics, sports, etc. — should be in about the same place every day so the reader doesn't have to hunt for them. Related stories, such as reports on state legislative activities, should be grouped. If this is not possible, a *reference* or *refer* (pronounced "reefer") can be inserted in the story:

State unemployment rate drops from 7.7 to 7.6 percent. Story on A9

Another design goal is to offer variety. Unless the makeup varies at least slightly every day, it lulls readers into thinking that they saw the same thing yesterday. The main picture may be in the first two columns one day and in columns three to five the next. One day there will be a banner and the next a five-column, two-line headline will cover the lead story.

Typography should enhance the appearance of the paper, but never at the expense of misrepresenting the importance of the story. Readers accustomed to banners that signify little will learn to underestimate headlines that are really important. Readers are just as ill-served if a story of considerable significance is underplayed.

News before beauty

It is easy for editors to get so enthusiastic about newspaper design that they let makeup overshadow content. They concentrate on how the paper looks, not on what the words or pictures tell. Their newspaper makes a good first impression. Readers eagerly pick it up because it looks so appealing. But their eagerness changes to disgust if they find the news play clumsy, the stories disjointed, and important items buried or even omitted. Editors infatuated with appearance may refuse to change one day's makeup when a breaking news story demands it. They are so smitten with page design that alteration cannot be tolerated.

Makeup always should be an adjunct to news coverage. Editors must first consider the news. They must select it, weigh its merits, and decide what stories are most important. Then they will decide the typographical display of the most important stories and pictures. No matter how clever the makeup, the editor must be willing to scrap or revise it whenever news events demand. Revising makeup is itself a skill, and it is covered separately in Chapter 13.

Dummying

The process of designing each page is called *dummying*. The editor uses a diagram called a dummy to send the printers instructions on where the type and pictures are to go. Some papers refer to the dummy as a *map,* and the description is apt. The printer looking over the dummy is really reading a map.

The dummy, usually an 8½-by-11-inch sheet, has columns with measurements, signifying inches, at the sides. (See Fig. 6.3.) The newsroom gets dummies for all inside pages from the advertising department, which has marked ad space. The news department fills the remaining space with news and pictures.

Computers, as mentioned, list the exact length of stories, making dummying easier. Headline space is easy to tabulate. If a headline is 24-point, three lines equal 1 inch. If a story with a three-line 24-point head takes up 8 inches, the total length, obviously, is 9 inches. The editor simply provides the equivalent of 9 inches of space on the dummy.

Several editors usually prepare various dummies on a big paper. The sports editor and the lifestyle editor will dummy their pages. The city editor probably will do it for the city news section. The state and suburban editors will handle a few, and the news editor or slot person probably will lay out page one plus several other pages. On some newspapers the wire editor makes up page one and other major pages.

The wire service *news digest* lists the important stories to be filed that day. It gives editors an early view of what state, national, and world stories will be available. If a newspaper puts any local or regional news on page one—and every paper should—the person dummying the front page will have to confer with the city editor and state editor to see which of their stories may warrant front page play. From the wire editor comes information on what unexpected stories arriving on the wires are worthy of special attention. Available pictures are inspected and a mental note is made on pictures that might arrive by deadline.

The editor then makes a series of decisions almost automatically. The day's best story is picked and a headline assigned. The editor decides the headline size by comparing the merit of the story to top stories on other days. If the story is unusually good, it gets bigger display than an average lead story will receive. If it is less worthy it will draw a smaller headline, and the editor will mumble, "Nothing much going on today."

The editor quickly sketches where pictures will go and, holding all the major stories in mind for comparison, decides which story ranks second. A head to that story is assigned and dummied, probably near the top left but perhaps under a picture. The "play" of the number two depends on how far it ranks in news value behind number one and how attractive the headline on it will be. The number three story may get a three-column head at the lower right, and number four may get a two-column head and be placed in the lower left. These decisions are made while the rest of the main stories are kept in mind.

From there, the priority system is a bit blurred. The other stories may be unconsciously rated "good," "fair," and "expendable." Five stories may about tie for fifth place. The editor may put three or four of these onto page one, until all the available niches are filled. The rest and other good stories can be saved for inside pages where fair and even expendable stories may appear. The editor, of course, works from a list of stories and pictures to make sure nothing is forgotten.

Beginners in dummying tend to put all display at the top. They methodically march down the page, filling the space with lesser stories until they hit the bottom. The result is that the top of the page looks good but the bottom is covered with minor, one-column stories and looks ragged.

This tendency of beginners reveals their limited vision. They work with one story at a time and do not consider or even see the whole picture as they select the news. They need to think of *all* major stories as they sketch their design.

The skilled editor looks at the available stories and mentally roughs out the makeup for the front page, putting the key stories at various spots on the page. This means that stories with good-sized headlines land at the top right, the top left, in each of the lower quarters of the page, and beneath pictures placed at the top. As a result, five or six important spots are filled and the open space, if any, will be filled later.

Typographical devices

While the number of ways dummying can be done is not limitless, a good designer guards against having only four or five basic patterns. Like some musical composers, the designer strives to weave seemingly infinite variations on basic patterns. The variations can be supplied by several typographical devices, although editors should use them sparingly, to avoid wearing out their welcome:

1. Boxes. Borders can be placed around stories to form a box. Boxes can be single-column, double-column, or even six-column.
2. Wide measure. This is type set wider than usual, probably one

and a half columns to divide into two wider columns under a three-column head.

3. "One-up." Five columns of type, for example, go under a six-column head. The extra white space between columns attracts attention. This technique often is used above the nameplate on page one.

4. Headlines with kickers. The extra ribbon of white space above the headline makes it stand out to attract the reader.

5. Color borders. These strips may go around a whole story or only at top and bottom to call attention to it.

6. Centered headline. A centered headline in a page of heads set flush left makes an effective contrast.

7. Art work. A little sketch inserted into stories relieves the monotony of solid type.

8. Unusual pictures. Some could be only partial outlines of figures or silhouettes.

To supplement these devices, an editor may put a six-column head over a story at the bottom of the page; the next day each lower corner may get a two-column head. To draw attention to the lower left, a picture may be used on some days and a three-column head on others. (A wide variety of typographical display appears in the illustrations of front pages.)

The editor does well to dummy the front page with variations in mind. Thus, the tentative sketch of the first five stories in the dummy might look something like Fig. 6.17. If the dummy of these five is satisfactory, the editor sifts through second-level stories—the ones that are good but not outstanding—and fills the rest of the space with them, as in Figure 6.18. All the type must be arranged so no gaps are plugged with dinky fillers, and there should be few jumps, especially jumps of only an inch or two, which especially irritate readers.

For layouts that neatly fill the page with stories the editor must

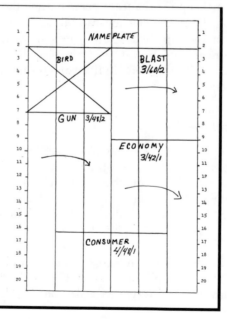

6.17. Makeup process. The news editor may start by putting the best story upper right and a big picture upper left. Another good story may go under the picture, a third under the top story, and still another to anchor the bottom.

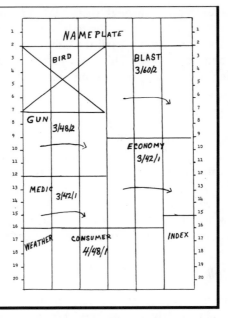

6.18. Makeup process. The editor finishes by blocking in other stories to fill the page and to achieve a modular page.

juggle type, shorten some stories, and move others. Sometimes it means that a story intended for page three must be switched with a story planned for page one. If both stories have about equal news value, the transfer is easy. But sometimes the shift forces alteration of the editor's original judgment of importance.

Fitting stories to space

Makeup would be easier if there were an endless number of good stories of various lengths. Then the editor could readily choose the right one to fit a certain hole. The story desired for a specific place, however, is almost invariably too long or too short. Three choices remain: Select another story; shorten or lengthen the one in hand; or shorten an adjoining story to make room for the one that didn't fit. Editors usually don't have the time to lengthen stories, so they keep shortening, choosing, and juggling until the page is filled.

The dummy should provide only basic information on picture placement (shown by crossed lines plus an identification word), headline size, slugline or guideline, and how multicolumn stories move from one column to another. Any other mark on the dummy makes instructions confusing. For example, it is usually unnecessary to note whether heads are roman or italic type or bold and medium faces, although most papers use all of them.

It also clutters the dummy to draw all kinds of lines indicating that type goes to a certain point. Under a single-column head, the printer will know that type is to be placed there so it is unnecessary to make any mark in that area. Leave it blank. The little arrows on multicolumn stories tell the printer exactly where type is to go.

The job of fitting copy to available space in a limited time requires a system. Most papers work the system something like this: Various editors are assigned to fill a certain number of pages. They

97

then review stories that roll through their VDTs and note the stories expected by deadline. Often an editor tells reporters what length to write their stories, and they must tell the editor if a story is running long—longer than anticipated. This information enables editors to begin dummying their pages, making minor, and sometimes major, adjustments as news develops.

When editors want a story cut to a certain length, they put the desired figure at the top of the story. The copy editor calls the story onto the screen, noting the headline orders and the story length. The copy editor then trims a few phrases or sentences to shave the story by an inch or so. If that isn't enough, a paragraph or two may be deleted and, possibly the last six paragraphs removed. At various times in this cutting, the copy editor will push the "copy fit" key to find how many inches the story, as trimmed, will produce. The copy is slashed and pared until it is exactly the length the editor demanded.

Avoiding pitfalls

Anyone making up pages should keep in mind the knowledge of typography accumulated by researchers. For a newspaper to gain maximum impact with the reader, most experts in typography advise certain guidelines in makeup. Here is a list of things to avoid:

1. Don't "tombstone." Heads of similar size and weight side by side resemble grave markers in old cemeteries. (See Fig. 6.19.)

Shasta County D.A. Removed From Office

Redding,
Shasta County

Shasta County District Attorney Will Hawes has been removed from office after a judge denied his request for a new trial on misconduct charges.

Newspapers Team Up on Production

Seattle

The Seattle Times and the Seattle Post-Intelligencer have agreed to a joint operation, which would combine production, circulation and advertising functions of the two newspapers.

6.19. Tombstones. Putting the same style heads side-by-side distracts the reader. Eyes tend to stray from one to another.

2. Avoid "squint-size" headlines. The reader should never have to squint to read headlines. Twelve-point heads are all right on one- and two-paragraph stories, but a longer story ought to have a bigger head. Multicolumn heads should be at least 30-point, unless there is a corner above an ad to fill on an inside page.

3. Never crowd the page. Headlines should not take up every millimeter of space, and cutlines should not be jammed against their pictures. On the other hand, too much air gives readers the feeling that they bought a lot of blank paper.

4. Avoid letting headlines "bump." Heads should be separated vertically by body type or art so each one stands clearly by itself. This sometimes is impossible at the top of a page, but even there the heads can show contrast. (See Fig. 6.20.)

6.20. Bumping heads. Even differing type sizes, side-by-side, do not provide the proper contrast. Nearly all bumping heads should be avoided.

Woman Fights Eviction by Religious Sect

Woman Who Died In S.F. Car Crash Is Identified

5. Stop body type from forming ponderous blocks. Several strips of white space or graphics should break up the gray, or type should spread over several columns. As mentioned, this gives the impression that reading the story will not be arduous. Even an editor, upon seeing a long, ponderous story in print, tends to say, "That looks interesting. I'll have to read it when I have more time." It never gets read.

6. Avoid top heavy or bottom heavy pages. Top or bottom headlines so big that one area overpowers the rest of the page are only appropriate if the paper's policy is to have brace makeup—and few do.

7. No headline should "cry wolf." If a story is of little consequence, let the headline admit it. A reader justly feels cheated if the head grossly exaggerates the story's value.

8. Repress dingbats. Most stars, asterisks, dashes, and rules can be scrapped. Most newspapers have eliminated column rules and do not end stories with dashes. It is clear to the reader when the stories end, and a little ribbon of white space usually does a better job of separating stories than a rule ever did.

9. Don't let a story escape its headline. Tucking the last few lines of a story someplace in an adjoining column is sloppy design. It confuses the reader and makes the type look sidetracked. Keep the story under the shelter of the head.

Taking positive steps

Other rules accentuate the positive:

1. Try to put associated stories together. Otherwise insert a refer somewhere near the beginning of the major story.

2. Liven the corners of the pages. They can look like dead space unless strong typography is planned to give them life.

3. Choose headline type faces that contrast but don't conflict. Perhaps this harmony of type can be explained by comparing it to harmony of dress. A man who wears a plaid jacket with a vertically

99

striped shirt and a diagonally striped tie may find the combination overwhelms the eye.

4. Use few type faces. A paper displaying half a dozen different type faces can be as upsetting as a woman wearing an orange hat, a blue blouse, a brown skirt, a purple scarf, yellow shoes, and a green coat. Editors of the *Los Angeles Times* fill that huge paper with only two type faces. For contrast, type is varied in size and font (roman and italic).

Some editors take pains with front page makeup but throw together the inside pages. Readers may get the impression that the inside is a snarl of words not worth reading. So good editors work nearly as hard on the inside pages as on page one.

Newspapers with vigorous inside pages continue the reverse-6 system, which means that each page has a strong left side with a good-sized headline or a large picture in the upper left. The rest of the page offers such variety that no story, except perhaps a tiny one used as a filler, will be lost. (See Fig. 6.21.)

Inside pages

6.21. Reverse-6 inside. The moderately strong head at the left lures the readers' eyes, which then can swing to the right, down the page, and back toward the top. (The *Washington Post*)

Editors making up pages on a big newspaper usually have a large selection of photos from wire services and staff photographers. Even if there are only a few really good pictures on a given day, the editor tries to avoid printing any poor art and aims for a large proportion of excellent photographs. The average quality is kept high this way, even though the number of pictures may have to be reduced some days.

Some papers have a rigid policy on art: There must be a picture on every news page. This restriction frequently forces the editor to use poor pictures. A better policy would be to have a picture on every page if a good photograph is available. Well-designed papers that try to mix art and news are not bothered if several pages lack art. Their editors believe that a solid page of type is better than one diluted with a photographic cliché, like city officials sitting around a table or a governor signing a bill.

Increasingly, editors print a few pictures of beauty or to illustrate some offbeat scene, such as railroad freight yards or water gushing through a hydroelectric plant. The beautiful and the odd may not offer much information, but they can provide a change from the conventional news photo. Many papers now print striking color pictures that help make the newspaper compete better with television.

The major change, however, is the use of graphics (mostly charts and graphs) that help illustrate a complicated business, economic, or consumer story. These, too, are "art," and they often provide information that a picture cannot. Some papers use short items under a special head to attain a little variety, as in Figure 6.22.

Pictures in makeup

Business digest

The markets

■ **The Dow Jones** industrial average closed at 1,993.95, up 19.12 from Tuesday. Advancing issues outnumbered declines by nearly 3 to 1 on the New York Stock Exchange, with 1,212 up, 442 down and 366 unchanged. Big Board volume totaled 190.87 million shares, against 189.30 million in the previous session. The NYSE's composite index rose 1.62 to 146.43. At the American Stock Exchange, the market value index was up 5.38 at 278.86. The Murphey Favre Northwest 50 stock index rose 10.75, to 944.52. **Page D9**

■ **The dollar** rose against most major currencies in sometimes hectic overseas trading Wednesday. Gold prices fell. In London, gold closed at $399.75 bid a troy ounce, down from $401.40. The Zurich closing price was $399.50 bid, down from $401.50. Silver traded late in London at $5.37 bid a troy ounce, down from $5.42.

The world

■ The Indian government Wednesday charged that Union Carbide Corp. was aware of a potential disaster before the Bhopal gas leak disaster, but failed to design its Bhopal plant to safeguard against it. The government filed a 93-page reply in Bhopal district court in response to Union Carbide's statement in December that the gas leak was caused by sabotage.

■ **West German** Finance Minister Gerhard Stoltenberg, rejecting French pressure, said Wednesday calls for a realignment of the European Monetary System are "not opportune" at present. His pronouncement followed an earlier statement by Economics Minister Martin Bangemann that there would not be any revaluation of the mark.

6.22. **Squeezing in a lot.** The *Portland Oregonian* condenses business items this way, quickly giving readers needed information in a few sentences.

The term *makeup editor* may suggest a person who dummies the pages and controls the placing of news. This editor rarely has this much authority. Although this person may make frequent appearances in the newsroom, headquarters are in the composing room. The news editor dummies much of the paper. The makeup editor makes the little last-minute adjustments that fit all the stories, ads, and photos on each page. Suppose a story dummied for 16 inches really measured 16½. The makeup editor then checks the story as it is being pasted up to see if four lines can be cut without damaging the story's meaning. These expendable lines are called *bites*. The printer is told, "Bite it here." The printer then slices off the expendable type. Sometimes a *window,* shown in Figure 6.23, emphasizes a longer story.

Soviet Psychiatrist Gets OK to Emigrate

By WILLIAM J. EATON, *Times Staff Writer*

MOSCOW—Anatoly Koryagin, who disclosed how the Soviet regime abused dissidents by confining them in psychiatric hospitals and who is now a candidate for the 1987 Nobel Peace Prize, will be allowed to emigrate, his government announced Thursday.

Tass, the official Soviet news agency, broke precedent by announcing that Koryagin, one of the best-known dissidents, will fly today to Switzerland, where he will make his home.

In most cases, Soviet citizens who leave the country are either ignored or denounced. According to prevailing orthodoxy, anyone who wants to move away from the motherland is a traitor.

Koryagin, a 48-year-old psychiatrist, was pardoned by the Supreme Soviet last February after being imprisoned since 1981 on charges of "anti-Soviet agitation and propaganda." His offense was to have written an article for a British medical journal documenting cases in which individuals who dissented politically with the Soviet regime were punished by confinement in psychiatric hospitals and by the administration of mind-altering drugs.

Western governments have been pressing for Koryagin's release, and he is also on a list of political prisoners whom dissident physicist Andrei D. Sakharov has asked to be released. His Nobel nomination for this year's peace prize follows a similar nomination last year.

Koryagin apparently was granted an exit visa along with his wife, Galina, their three sons and his mother.

He was sentenced in 1981 to seven years in a labor camp and five years in internal exile for accusing Soviet authorities of using psychiatric hospitals to punish dissenters.

Koryagin's case was complicated

The announcement set a precedent, an indication of Koryagin's special status.

because his 18-year-old son, Ivan, also was serving a prison term after being convicted of "hooliganism," a charge his family denies.

On March 25, however, in the midst of the younger Koryagin's three-year sentence, Soviet authorities released him from a labor camp near Kharkov.

Anatoly Koryagin, unlike most of the political prisoners who were released in the opening months of the year, was freed without asking for a pardon or acknowledging any guilt.

The announcement of his departure and his direct flight to Switzerland—bypassing Vienna, the usual gateway to the West—also indicated his special status.

Koryagin has said he would like to work eventually as a psychiatrist in the West.

His time in confinement was harsh, according to statements he made in letters smuggled out of confinement.

For example, in a document made public late last year, he said he was placed in solitary confinement for three years and put in a punishment cell for six months.

He quoted a prison camp commandant as saying, "You are going to drop dead here."

His permission to emigrate was apparently part of a trend initiated by Soviet leader Mikhail S. Gorbachev to show some leniency toward dissidents who have big followings in the West. Sakharov and his wife, Yelena Bonner, have been released from their sentence of internal exile in the remote city of Gorky, and dissident scientist Natan (Anatoly) Sharansky was freed from prison and allowed to emigrate to Israel.

Koryagin's wife reportedly told friends that her husband was released from prison on condition that he leave the Soviet Union immediately.

6.23. Another insider. One story fills an inside hole at the *Los Angeles Times.* The *window,* the material in bigger type, helps fill the space and "breaks up" the body type

The makeup editor's biggest job is keeping everything straight in a developing story or during a major change in deadline. In these cases stories may be cut drastically or *time copy*—really timeless—may be inserted. New dummies may be sent from editors in the newsroom. The stories should be inspected carefully in paste-up to make sure they make sense.

The job of makeup editor varies with the size of the paper. A paper that usually runs fewer than fifty pages would not have enough work for such a person. And on a big paper the makeup editor usually does not supervise the makeup of special sections. The sports department will send a copy editor to the composing room for perhaps half an hour to check the makeup on sports pages. Individuals from the financial, features, lifestyle, and editorial page departments will do the same for their sections. Still the makeup editor on a big paper has plenty to do.

On medium-sized and small papers each subeditor goes to the composing room to make sure the pages get put together the desired way. Each of them may spend no more than half an hour at the task. Printers, following dummies, may have the pages nearly ready by the time the editor arrives. Only a few adjustments may be required of both editor and printer. On small papers, the managing editor, who may write editorials as well as manage the news operation, may also be the one who dummies the key pages and supervises their makeup.

Inside page design follows principles used on page one: No crowding, a mix of stories and art, a variety of headline sizes, and, in most cases, multicolumn heads. Fitting copy to the news hole on a page can be done quite simply. The editor totals the available space. It may come to 32 inches. The editor may put a four-column head on a 17-inch story. That leaves 15 inches. A 9-inch, two-column story might be placed beneath the four-column head and a 6-inch, single-column story inserted in the remaining space. Samples of inside page dummies can be seen in Figures 6.24 and 6.25. A list of stories available, noted in Figure 6.26, aids editors as they choose which stories to put where.

Whoever goes to the composing room to make up should remem-

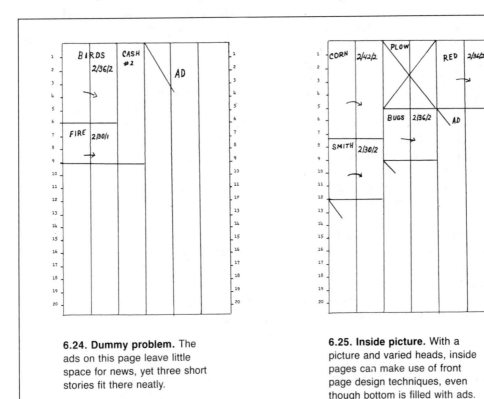

6.24. Dummy problem. The ads on this page leave little space for news, yet three short stories fit there neatly.

6.25. Inside picture. With a picture and varied heads, inside pages can make use of front page design techniques, even though bottom is filled with ads.

103

6.26. Copy control. Most computers will provide information something like this, listing story slug, head size, and story length. Designers may refer to the list as they lay out the pages.	President	3/60/2	14 inches
	Court	3/42/1	12.5 inches
	Medic	2/36/2	11.5 inches
	Waste	4/42/1	16 inches

ber not to touch type without permission of the printer. That prohibition is a printers' union rule and a reasonable one. Editors would not like a printer messing with their papers or VDT, so editors should not interfere with the printers' work.

Persons supervising makeup should listen to advice from printers. Since most printers are intelligent people who take pride in their craft, they often can suggest ways out of a problem. The makeup editor should accept with thanks the good suggestions and reject others gracefully.

Future makeup

When a newspaper staff decides to try improving typography, changes probably should be made gradually. Readers are creatures of habit who, if confronted by a revolutionary makeup, may rebel. So most papers revamp their makeup piecemeal. The headline type faces are altered, and a few months later the body type is modernized. The nameplate may be next, but each shift comes only after the readers have adjusted to the preceding change.

Staffs of a few papers, however, have decided to make all the changes at once, hoping that the sudden alterations will dramatize the paper's eagerness to adjust to change. "Why cut off the dog's tail an inch at a time?" they ask. Each method has its merits, but most editors take the gradual approach. Substantial changes, regardless of how sweeping, should be accompanied by a news story announcing them. The paper may even use pictures to contrast examples of the new and old. The readers then see the improvement and perhaps will recognize their newspaper as more than a fusty relic frozen in tradition.

Most typographers look at today's best-designed pages with satisfaction. The type is easy to read; white space separates headlines from stories; and nothing looks crowded. The design pleases the eye. Best of all, it gets across to the reader the news of the day.

No one should believe, however, that perfection has been attained. Editors must stay alert to the typographical changes other editors make. They need to find new ways to get people to read and to understand what they read.

Editors also must study the findings of psychologists, communications specialists, and newspaper researchers. While some findings will be of little value, they will find some pearls that will help them help the reader. More thought and study on how human beings respond to the printed page will stimulate hundreds of fresh ideas to help the modern reader both survey and absorb the news.

7

The editor and journalistic writing

NEWSPAPER EDITORS traditionally have dealt with writers and writing after the fact, by trying to patch poor or mediocre writing at the copydesk. The success rate has varied, with some copy editors performing brilliantly in sharpening sentences, spotting holes, rewriting leads, and juggling paragraphs, while others have only corrected spelling errors and caught an occasional gross blunder.

In recent years, some editors have realized that work on writing should be done before the reporter turns to the VDT to write a story. This emphasis on improved writing has resulted in a few papers' hiring writing coaches or directing a copy editor to spend at least a couple days a week helping reporters with their writing. Sometimes the training consists of a coach sitting down with a reporter and carefully going over copy. Each sentence is evaluated and story deficiencies are explored. The coach emphasizes getting more information and figuring out ways to make maximum use of all the facts. At other times, the coach might bring a half dozen reporters together to consider how sentences can be more concise and leads less stereotyped. Before these training sessions start, top editors must determine what kind of writing they want—sprightly or serious, detailed or almost superficial—and encourage the whole staff to aim toward the desired writing style. Editors will not need uniformity, of course, but will strive to avoid excessive variety in styles.

In some cases the copy editor may operate as head of a committee in developing significant stories. In consultation with the managing editor, the committee may decide to have two or three reporters investigate some problem. Together they can decide what facts to get, how the stories should be written, and what pictures will be needed. The copy editor can lead in shaping and editing the stories to attract the most readers.

It can be argued that interpretative reporting is just good reporting. It is true that *in-depth* or *enterprise reporting* or *backgrounder* may simply be a fancy title for the old-fashioned digging that was a part of good newswriting anytime. Yet the complexity of modern issues and the social need to understand them require more resources, more reporters, more thought, and more leadership. This means that staffers confer on how story angles can be nailed down, what sources can be found, what records to inspect, what history to examine, and who can best run down facts for one or two parts of the story. Sometimes one reporter, given careful instructions as facts dribble in, can do the main job, given two to four weeks. In other cases, a team of a half dozen is needed.

This kind of planning and diligence netted the Sun Newspapers, a group of weeklies in the Omaha area, a Pulitzer Prize for their investigation of the famous Father Flanagan's Boys Town in Nebraska. The story became known as the "exposé without bad guys," for no real scandal was uncovered, but the inquiry opened the Boys Town books and brought a dozen reforms.

The Sun group had been curious for some time about where Boys Town spent the money it raised in mail appeals. It was obvious at the start of the investigation that officials at the home would give no information. So, in the best investigative technique, reporters began nibbling around the story's edges. The best edges turned out to be reports filed by Boys Town with governments or governmental agencies. Boys Town is an incorporated village, so it had to file a budget and an operations report. It had its own post office, and it had to file a few reports with the postmaster general. Since Boys Town is a school, certain state reports were required. Because it is a nonprofit corporation, various other information had to be filed with the state. It is a child care operation, so reports were given to the state welfare department. Since the home had bought land, records of deeds, purchase prices, and tax records were available.

Reporters barely out of college started gathering material for a "general historical piece" on Boys Town. They quickly found that the home received some $200,000 each year in federal and state subsidies, although the home claimed that it "got no funds from church, state, or federal government." The school also said it trained 1,000 boys, when the real figure was 665. Boys Town property was valued at $8,400,000, nearly all tax-exempt.

A few staff members at the home talked guardedly to reporters about low pay, rejection of innovative suggestions, and discouragement to boys who wanted to go to college.

It was learned that Boys Town sent out 34 million fund appeal letters in one year. Professional fund raisers estimated that perhaps $15 million would be attained by such voluminous mailings. It became obvious to the staffers, checking various figures, that Boys

Town spent no more than $5 million annually. Without counting bequests, the staffers decided it appeared that the school had accumulated $100 million over the years.

Unexpectedly the investigators found that Boys Town had filed a ninety-four page form with the Internal Revenue Service. The form was public information. When the form's figures were digested it was clear that Boys Town's net worth was not $100 million as first assumed, but $191,401,421 — and that it was rising at the rate of $17 million a year.

By this time the papers had a big story, but it was only fair to seek comment from Boys Town officials. So reporters questioned the archbishop of the diocese, the director of the home, and, finally, members of the board of directors. No one contradicted the facts gathered by reporters. But the reporters did not get any extra information either.

In a few days the papers carried a front page special report. The headline read:

BOYS TOWN
America's Wealthiest
City?

On page two was a copy of a fund-raising letter, "There will be no joyous Christmas season this year. . . . " Page three had a reproduction of the IRS form's first page, showing both the net worth and $25,900,000 annual income. The story, plus sidebars and art, covered eight full-size pages.

Within days, wheels started to turn at Boys Town and in a few months the board canceled fund raising for the year, announced a $30 million endowment of an institute to treat speech and hearing defects in children, promised $40 million more for a national center to study child development, and hired a management firm to reexamine the home's whole program. Other reforms followed.

The investigation showed that a small staff, working together, could marshal facts for a story the public needed to know.

Investigative leadership

Editors supervising investigations function as any good team leader does: goading, persuading, inspiring, and pushing. They guide the collection of information because they usually have more experience and can be more dispassionate than the reporter on the hunt. Furthermore, two or more editorial heads generally are better than a single reporter's. Editors work over story drafts to make sure there are no holes — and no libel. They question the investigators, and they suggest lines of inquiry that reporters may have missed. They tap their own experience as reporters and editors to make sure the best job is done. Most important, perhaps, they keep telling themselves and the special reporters that there must be no mistakes. They realize that one error in a story may cause the whole investigation to collapse. The

107

people being investigated will shout, "See, the paper's making up the whole thing!"

As mentioned in the Boys Town story, editors advise investigators to start by asking seemingly innocuous questions at low levels. Underlings, unaccustomed to dealing with the press, often spill facts that higher level people would keep to themselves. As the story forms a pattern, reporters move to quiz more informed people and to seek more crucial documents. The best human sources are the disgruntled, the idealists, or those who relish a kind of conspiracy role. The disgruntled often seek revenge; the idealists seek justice; the "conspirators" hope to be anonymous sources of information. Each type may be overly zealous, and may give false or distorted details. This is why investigators often insist on corroboration of a fact before it is printed. If reporters cannot sift their information for truth, the editor should.

In the search, it is not enough to get oral accusations. Documents are essential — letters, memos, canceled checks, and official reports. All may be crucial. Editors and reporters should realize that their greatest ally here is the copying machine, for it will duplicate evidence in seconds. That evidence often makes previously silent people decide to tell reporters their whole story.

In the enthusiasm of cracking a big story, journalists may forget a sense of ethical conduct. Theft, lies, fakery, or threats may be precisely what is being investigated. A journalist either should not use these shabby practices or should use them only after full soul searching. Some reporters and editors have wrapped themselves in the flag of "public interest" and dashed off to commit shady or even criminal acts.

Editors should realize, too, that many investigations do not look for scandalous or illegal conduct. What may be sought is evidence of ineptitude or incompetence. Or, as in the Boys Town story, evidence of money seeking, improper power, and hoarding. This is why editors and reporters should take care to avoid accusations and strident language in their stories.

Sometimes editors must use a firm hand to get the news the community deserves. In one middle-sized city the social welfare reporter got the go-ahead to do a series on black employment in local business and industry. He was so thorough that he conducted scores of interviews over several weeks. As time passed, the information in the early interviews began to get stale. The paper's interest flagged, perhaps in part because the lengthy investigation brought worried inquiries from industrial leaders. When the brief series finally appeared, it was weak — much weaker than if it had been done with more dispatch. Perhaps the city editor should have assigned a second reporter to help collect information. Perhaps the editor should have told the reporter at a certain point, "You've got enough material. Write it!" In any event, firm editorial leadership was missing.

Aides of the team

Editors also have leadership roles with various nonstaffers. The staff editor may have to teach the basics of straight writing. Steady, clear communication is essential to lead a team of part-time reporters, called stringers. Similarly, a good foreign desk provides leadership for its correspondents — staff and stringer. A major complaint of reporters who write abroad is that the home office leaves them too much on their own.

Free-lance writers and photographers also can be valuable. They should be treated courteously even if the paper can use only a little free-lance work, and they should be encouraged and guided if the quality of work is poor but promising.

Amateurs should be given pointers about producing the articles or pictures the paper can use. The magazine of the *Houston Chronicle* has a form that explains its needs in subjects, pictures, manuscript preparation, and deadlines, and its method of payment. Queries on ideas should be answered, not ignored. Rejected material should be sent back promptly, even if the editor is busy and overburdened, and checks for accepted material ought to be mailed quickly. Smart editors supplement their regular staff operations when they provide effective leadership for part-timers and free-lancers.

Editors serving as teachers must make clear that instructions for handling simple stories don't quite work for the complex story. The inverted pyramid diagram for a news story quickly breaks down in longer stories.

The editor as teacher

Traditionally, the feature story has always been an exception. Writers can start features with a question or an anecdote or a quote, among other devices, and may write chronologically or according to some other nontriangular logic. Sometimes features are diagrammed as pyramids sitting on their bases, but this pattern is no more applicable universally than the triangle is to news stories. An editor who started to revise a feature to fit any such preconceived pattern would soon stop, frustrated and foolish.

What, then, can editors discover about the structure of complicated stories, and what can they hope to teach advanced reporters?

In his popular English textbook, *The Practical Stylist,* Professor Sheridan Baker of the University of Michigan argues that the writer should find a *thesis* to begin a piece. A thesis can be stated as a debate resolution, "Resolved that . . . " When writers thus clarify their aim, they find that the supporting information falls into logical order, into an outline.

This approach has some validity for most news stories, since the beginning states the point of each piece. The concept is most applicable to the work of the editorial writers when they attempt persuasive editorials, but in the newsroom Baker's thesis on theses is generally valuable. It reminds editors to look for a clear statement of the main point close to the top of a story.

Another rhetorical tradition classifies writing forms, such as the essay, into a natural (and obvious) pattern of three parts — beginning, middle, and end, standing like three rectangular blocks piled one on another. The middle might be subdivided into several paragraphs of development. The bottom block is conclusion. This plan fits nicely with Baker's if the top contains the statement of thesis.

This tripartite form again may seem more suited to essays for the editorial page than for front page news accounts. The shift toward more and more interpretation, however, makes this observation less certain. What is a series of articles but a number of blocks? And as background, depth, and perspective become writers' watchwords, they are less concerned with the first-paragraph vigor of the inverted pyramid and more concerned with the clarity emphasized in the beginning-middle-end structure.

Complex patterns

Analysis of news stories over many decades shows that actually they are not simple triangles. Usually they are a number of triangles on a string, like fish. The story unfolds in two or three paragraphs, then recaps with more detail, explains at length in a third triangle, and perhaps adds minor detail and color in still another. Consider the story of a major fire in three or four buildings. The first section quickly recounts the deaths and damage. The next section reveals how it started and spread and how fire-fighting forces were marshaled. The next triangles tell who discovered it, what efforts were made to confine it to the first building, and who made a call for outside help. There may be a snippet about two suburbs that sent equipment and firefighters. A block of type may inquire into insurance. Then in more leisurely fashion the writer may quote the passerby who thought he saw smoke, the watchman who opened the inner doors and discovered the blaze, or the woman who threw her baby into the fire net.

The story may form a more complicated pattern than even a series of triangles, as Figure 7.1 suggests. A triangle that tapers off to the inconsequential point would bore a reader. Rather, each triangle becomes blunt bottomed. Some are hardly triangles at all. Can a chronological account be called a triangle, since start, middle, and finish are equally essential to the tale? Is a list of injured a triangle? Blocks and wedges are more appropriate to clear portrayal of the way a long story is put together.

The copy editor who sees news articles in some such schematic fashion will understand better how they can be rearranged and tightened. Perhaps the inner logic requires that a paragraph or two near the end be moved to a higher position, even though these sentences are in themselves almost trivial. Or perhaps killing a minor detail in the heart of the story will strengthen the whole.

An editor able to analyze advanced writing can quickly show reporters where their work is solid and where it is loose or rambling. This analytic skill is especially useful in working with an investigative team. Structuring the long series becomes similar to outlining a

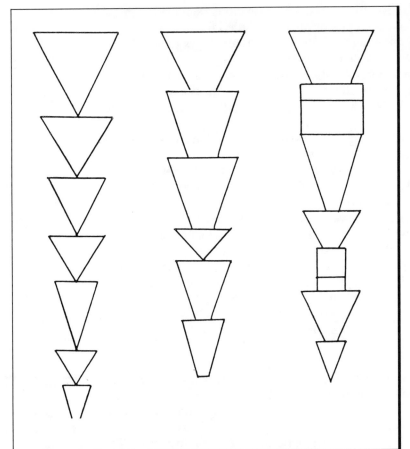

7.1. Story patterns.
These patterns are a more realistic picture of complex news stories than the traditional inverted pyramid. The more complex the story, the more likely it is a combination of triangles, wedges, and rectangles. Copy editors who recognize these variations will be able to reshape a story effectively.

lengthy magazine article or a book. Formal logic has to be related to the likelihood that a reader's interest will wane, and to the technical demand that the individual pieces be of a certain length. "Can we shift this block into the first article in the series, and can we give the third piece some punch by building up this anecdote?" an editor might ask. Sometimes these deceptively simple questions lead a writing team into a kind of outline they had hoped to leave in Freshman English.

It may be useful to think of the complex story not as a triangle but as a freight train: The diesel supplies the power and the pace, and a series of boxcars follow with the information. More than other types of writing, news stories have minimal transitions and internal references. With little concern, a copy editor can rearrange paragraphs; the boxcars of many stories seem almost interchangeable.

Whatever the pattern, the story needs logic, but not the I, II, III type. It can be chronological or sequential, moving the reader from one point of interest to another. The chief sin is rambling, with the story drifting into subtopics or quotes of little value.

Reporters rarely think of the most effective ways to structure a major story. They tend to turn swiftly to the VDT to start writing, as though they were pounding out a routine, three-graf story. As a result, too many potentially excellent stories miss connections with readers. The editor-teacher must jog both writers and copy editors to strive for patterns that will communicate best.

More should be done on newspapers to discover fresh ways to present material related to a central story. Instead of one long story, why not five short stories, sidebars to each other? Why not play three or four related stories, perhaps with a box or editor's note to explain their common theme?

Magazine editors appear to be more ambitious in developing new patterns of presentation. They have tried boldface summaries, called *precedes,* at the top of articles in trade magazines. They have boldfaced the first paragraph of new sections. Some have tried narrative, near-fiction techniques. Others have paired two pieces, one light and illustrated, the other serious and editorial. Newspaper writers may find stimulating ideas for writing patterns and related graphic displays in the best-edited magazines.

Style is used by newspaper editors in at least two senses. The uniform system of spelling and capitalization is called style, as mentioned in a previous chapter, but the form and presentation of newspaper prose are also style.

The meanings of style

Good journalistic style is not florid, ornate, or rhetorical. The late journalism dean Frank Luther Mott used to say the best journalism is also good literature, as clearly demonstrated in the reporting of Ben Franklin, Stephen Crane, and Ernest Hemingway. English professors have long contended that good prose is usually plain and straightforward and therefore clear. "The approach to style is by way of plainness, simplicity, orderliness, sincerity," says William Strunk, Jr., and E. B. White's *The Elements of Style.* It is to good newspaper style too.

Effective prose communicates ideas and information. It might be argued that some writing is used to convey an ambiance or feeling without presenting much fact. But such usage in news reports is rare. Journalistic style has to be functional. The need to convey ideas quickly from one mind to other minds underlies the need for simple, clear writing.

What language scholars call *standard English* is appropriate to newspapers. Neither the formal English of the academic book nor the nonstandard or colloquial dialect of folksy talk has much place in newspaper pages. For most purposes, reporters and editors should choose their words from the broad range of language understood by most moderately educated people.

Standard English is threatened on the one side by jargon and gobbledygook. Reporters close to many professions may fall into legalese, academic pudder, or bureaucratic gibberish. On the other side is a threat from what has traditionally been known as slang—faddish talk. The young and academics, for example, sometimes aim to have their own secret language. The young use their special slang while academics develop obscure words and terms that have meaning only to a specialized few. Newspapers must avoid both kinds of fringe English if they are to communicate with a diverse readership.

Advocates of plain, simple style sometimes face the objection that this kind of writing is dull and lifeless. It need not be. Concrete nouns and strong verbs close to human experience can make a simple sentence vivid and lively. Yet sometimes even a good writer will fill a story with the stereotyped and obvious until it shrivels and dies.

Some editors, aware that too many stories jam one fact upon another, try to get some personal touches into copy. They seek a few quotes that show sources as human beings who laugh and cry. They introduce a bit of levity—or passionate concern—over some issues. As so often happens, some editors overdo it, saturating stories with personal details. But the best editors get stories with dashes of warmth and humor among the cold facts.

An examination of style by editors comes down to their analysis of the grammatical ingredients of the story—paragraphs, sentences, and words. There is a mystic quality in the overall effect of writing, for the whole somehow turns out to be greater than the sum of the parts. Still, some of the mystery can be penetrated by seeing how individual blocks fit together.

The sources of style

Paragraphs

In most writing the paragraph is an obvious block. The formal outline of an essay or a book divides into topics, subtopics, and sub-subtopics; each sub-subtopic may be treated as a paragraph, which might run various lengths. In type, long blocks look forbidding, so journalists use shorter paragraphs, often only one or two sentences long.

Copy is not effectively formed into short paragraphs by haphazard chopping, as some reporters and copy readers apparently suppose. The best procedure is to search the "normal" paragraph of the topic-sentence variety for the clusters of ideas within it. Thus a twelve-sentence unit may prove to be made up of four to six smaller pieces. Each piece then may become a newspaper-type paragraph, and each may run one or two, perhaps three, sentences, but rarely more. If writers see the relation of these shorter paragraphs to the overall pattern, they are able to write in a more logical style.

Sentences

A paragraph rarely should run more than fifty words. If such a paragraph has even two or three sentences, they must obviously be

113

short—perhaps an average of fifteen words, though no such figure should be taken arbitrarily. Length is thus one criterion of the good sentence, and newspaper sentences are usually short compared with those in books or scholarly magazines.

Sentences also should be straight: clear and to the point. Good examples of such sentences can be found in nearly every newspaper. The editor's job, of course, is to make sure that all sentences are straight. Though grammatically most straight sentences are simple, few compound, and even fewer complex, journalists might pay more attention to what is known in English classes as the periodic sentence, building from beginning to end, so the last element is the climax. For example, "Mayor Jones paused over the document, frowned, and then, as his face reddened, shouted, 'Never.' " Of course, putting an idea at the start of a sentence also can have impact: "Cut taxes."

Clogged, overburdened, and *too-complex* sentences muddle too much journalistic writing. *The clogged sentence* simply packs too much information between the capital letter and the period. No desk should pass this lead:

> In preparation for a predicted ordeal of total war, on the home front as well as on the battlefield, the leadership of the United Arab Republic is moving to organize citizens' war committees to cope with bomb damage and casualties, survivors and refugees and, after the war, the reconstruction of towns, factories and housing.

Editors of the *New York Times* cited this example from their own paper, noting that the sentence should have ended with the word "committees."

The overburdened sentence, although like the clogged, is not so much packed with facts as overstuffed with ideas. The writer loads too much freight onto the sentence before hitting the period key:

> Like the legislature's redistricting plan of 1981, the proposed new constitutional amendment now before the Senate Judiciary Committee, and soon to go before the House Rules Committee, not only deals with the congressional district problem but also the issue of one-voter-one-vote, according to regulations set by a previous ruling of the Supreme Court.

Break it up; simplify.

The too-complex sentence resembles both the clogged and the overburdened. Its writer is following the dictum to get away from the simple Dick-saw-Jane sentence. It is good advice, especially for essays and editorials, but the newswriter can overdo by throwing in too many clauses and phrases. Note these examples that need to be broken up:

> Mr. Salant, who took the unorthodox step of joining the competition when CBS's mandatory-retirement policy ended his long career as president of CBS News, said his other major goals—some of which he conceded might be difficult to achieve, given the nature of the television business—included the following. . . .

114

Since tension has developed in the Persian Gulf with its obvious dangers to the American oil supply, and with the need for careful diplomacy with the Arab world, divided as it is, and the great distance the gulf is from the United States, a viable military posture has been difficult to attain.

Writers of these three faulty types of sentences all tried to pack much information into a short space but they made the stories opaque. The antidote in each case is to lighten the load of each sentence. Even the most intelligent readers need frequent periods to catch their breath.

A fruitful suggestion for better writing is summarized in the slogan, "One idea, one sentence." News elements in the preceding examples should be cut away from their accompanying verbosities. The main idea of each sentence then will stand out so the reader can grasp it quickly.

New York Times editors have pushed the one-idea-to-a-sentence theme for years. Their second-guessing bulletin, *Winners & Sinners,* has occasionally pointed up the value of the concept with illustrations from the paper. Here is one example:

The special House committee set up in September to investigate possible election fraud may be abolished this month, according to many senior House members, and its plight, only six months after it was established by a vote of 280 to 65, provides an insight into the workings of Congress and the relationship between its members and their staffs.

Here is another sinner from the *Times:*

In Montreal, leaders of the American Bar Association killed Wednesday a resolution denouncing a key provision of the civil rights bill aimed at preventing discrimination in the selection of Federal jurors.

Of the second example the *W & S* editor commented: "The facts are all there, but the reader has to go to work on them. He has to take it from the bottom: The bill is against discrimination. Fine. But the resolution denounces this provision. Uh-huh. But wait a minute—the bar leaders have killed the resolution. So it's fine again, eh? In other words, the bar leaders took a stand in favor of preventing discrimination in the selection of Federal juries. Why not say it in some form similar to that?"

Words

The strength of sentences depends ultimately on the choice and arrangement of words. Good editors become expert on these basic blocks. Instead of the vague, the abstract, and the unusual, they seek words that are *direct, concrete,* and *familiar*—words that build vivid and accurate pictures for most readers.

Accuracy and strength, as well as commonness, should guide

115

word choice, and vitality in verbs is especially important. Forms of "to be" are generally static so editors prefer strong verbs that act and suggest movement. One-syllable words often generate the most power. Reducing the sentence usually adds strength. Pare weak or unnecessary adjectives and adverbs.

Choice of the right word is complicated by rapid changes in language. Again, a number of guides are available. Dictionaries are one, although editors may wish to choose an edition that evaluates word meanings strictly or loosely. A good guide to modern American usage is the *Dictionary of Contemporary Usage* by Bergen and Cornelia Evans. Also valuable is the revision by Sir Ernest Gowers of the famous *Dictionary of Modern English Usage* of H. W. Fowler, a classic in England. Theodore Bernstein of the *Times,* quoted earlier, has left five helpful books, the first based on *Winners & Sinners: Watch Your Language, More Language That Needs Watching, The Careful Writer, A Modern Guide to English Usage,* and *Miss Thistlebottom's Hobgoblins.*

One of his points is that the writer should note what makes for clarity, precision, and logical presentation. New word uses, or even new words, may clarify but they also may confuse. Sometimes a fussiness over exact word usage may seem picky, but carelessness or a casual attitude on the subject can strip language of meaning or effectiveness.

A final word on jargon

As noted, jargon confuses more than clarifies. In medicine or law, to be sure, a specialized word may add precision. But even there problems exist, for lawyers may rattle off *en banc* or *nol prosse* and only confuse other people.

"When you get your degree you can't wear it around your neck to prove you're educated," the late urban reformer Saul Alinsky wrote in *Harper's* magazine, "so instead you use a lot of three- and four-syllable words. Of course, they aren't any use at all if you really want to communicate with people. You have to talk straight English, using a small word every time you can instead of a big one."[1] Such advice is good not only for educators, economists, and sociologists, for example, but also for reporters and editors.

In a computer age when so much of life is quantified, it is tempting to analyze and measure language in the search for better communication. Can English be approached scientifically? Can the clarity or interest of a piece of writing be weighed or measured? Yes and no. No calipers or scales exist to indicate accurately whether sentences convey their message well. But quantification of newspaper copy may help a writer analyze style.

Theories of readability

1. Saul Alinsky, "The Professional Radical," *Harper's,* June 1965, 39.

What can be measured? The stylists and critics mentioned here indicate the qualities journalists might hope to quantify: difficulty of words, complexity and density of sentences, use of clichés or jargon, strength of verbs, and so on. The problem with measurement is that many of these stylistic qualities defy objective judgment.

Readability theorists who search for objective measurements have centered on judging the difficulty of words and sentences, which is certainly a key consideration. This factor is measured in the *fog index* developed by Robert Gunning (explained in *The Technique of Clear Writing*) and in the *Flesch formula* described by Rudolf Flesch (in *The Art of Readable Writing* and other books). After study of these and other practical applications of readability theory, Dr. Jeanne S. Chall of Ohio State University identified four significant reliable measurements: vocabulary load, sentence structure, idea density, and human interest.[2] The first two relate to the Gunning-Flesch work, and the third is associated with clogging and overburdening. The fourth, human interest, will be considered later.

The Flesch formula

In the late forties, AP hired Flesch to advise on improving writing. Practical journalistic use was made of a readability formula he had devised. His scheme rests on two assumptions. First, the number of syllables in samples of 100 words each increases as the writing becomes more difficult. Second, the more short sentences in the samples, the easier the reading. Actually, short words in short sentences can be hard going, but since the opposite is more often the case, the assumptions seem justified.

Starting with these two assumptions, one can randomly choose a few samples from news stories, interpretative stories, or editorials. The writer counts the syllables and the number of sentences (to find average sentence length) and works out the Flesch score according to the mathematics or charts in Flesch's books. If the sentences average 15 to 18 words each and if there are 145 to 155 syllables in each sample, the writing scores as *standard* and is suitable for much newspaper writing. Such sentences are not very long, obviously, and such a vocabulary includes a great many one-syllable words. However, using more long words or making the sentences more complex (and therefore longer) will almost certainly make the writing more difficult.

Paring sentences to an average of 12 words each and vocabulary to 130 or 140 syllables per hundred words results in what Flesch rates as *easy*. If news stories were written at this level—and few are—less-educated readers would doubtless grasp them more readily.

---

2. Jeanne Chall, *Readability: Research and Application* (Columbus: Ohio State University Press, 1958), 41–47.

Applying the test

Using the Flesch method, two researchers compared news stories to editorials in several West Coast dailies. They found both forms difficult, but the news was, surprisingly, less readable than the editorials. Any editor would want to correct such a shortcoming immediately, possibly by calling a staff meeting to discuss the problem. The task of writing at a level to please all readers confounds most journalists these days, for most editors realize that many high school graduates are poor readers. Journalists are in a quandary, however, on how they can write more simply without irritating good readers.

Recognizing that some writing passes muster as readable but is still dull, Flesch later developed a human interest formula. The most important factor in these measurements is the use of what he calls *personal words*—he, she, Mrs. Brown, Susan, etc. He also counts, but gives less weight to, *personal sentences,* which include quotations and direct address to the reader. Fortunately, news stories deal with people, so a degree of human interest comes naturally. However, some writers tend to abstractions, especially in writing of such subjects as government finance or sociology. To counteract this, editors can remind reporters that they must bring human beings into their copy.

Assessing the audience

Attempting to make newswriting easier and more interesting does not mean editors must seek the lowest level of readership. True, they should provide some material, aside from most sports and comics, which is clear even to poorly educated readers. And they should try to reach a broad readership. But some papers that have directed all content toward the "average" person have declined in circulation and general economic health. The successful papers of today continue to improve the quality of content a notch or two every few years. If a newspaper chose stories for only a ninth grade audience, it would omit much information on science, the arts, serious economics, the inner workings of politics, and dozens of other subjects.

To argue that because the average formal educational level of a community is only 10.3 years the paper must be written for high school sophomores assumes that people learn nothing after they leave school. It also assumes that those with little schooling and little experience are newspaper readers. Editors know that those above average in education and intelligence are the most avid readers. While still including news of interest for those who are not so lucky or concerned, the mix of content should emphasize news for the best readers. Nonetheless, editors should insist that stories always are lively and clear, as well as fact-filled. Even the most intelligent readers who are able to cope with scholarly journals may be pestered with distractions while reading the newspaper. Like everyone else, they must sometimes get the facts from the paper without much concentration. This means that the writing must be appealing and easy.

But Tom Wicker of the *New York Times* is right when he says:

Nobody yet ever made a writer out of a hack by setting up rules. . . . And to the man who tells me that every story can be written in 600 words, or 750, or whatever, I say that that is merely a rule; and I take my stand with Joseph Pulitzer, who said with a writer's exactness and a lawyer's flexibility that the prescription was 'terseness — intelligent, not stupid, condensation.'

Neither readability nor human interest concepts should be viewed as magic cure-alls. They can help journalists check on their talent for good copy, and no more. The good editor, as team captain, must above all continue to study overall story organization and the effective use of style.

8

Evaluating the news

THE DEFINITION OF NEWS has changed, causing editors to reject some stories that once made the front page and to use others that in the past would not have been written.

Business news thirty years ago often consisted of puff pieces on companies and executives. Today business activity is reported almost as thoroughly as government. Science stories some decades past were so carelessly done that most scientists dreaded talking to reporters. Stories on the arts once were limited to reports on the theft of a painting or on the selling price of an artwork. Today science and art are generally covered extensively and well.

Today reporters often are specialists, able to ask searching questions because they know so much about their fields. No longer are police stations, firehouses, city hall, and the courthouse the major news sources.

News definitions have shifted largely because editors give a little less attention today to *oddity* and *conflict*. Almost from the time of the first newspapers journalists have sought the peculiar, the dramatic, the quarrel, the battle, the outrageous, the victory, and the defeat. Journalists weren't alone. Historians, in the main, used similar evaluations, citing wars, elections, assassinations, discoveries, and plunder.

Both journalists and historians have shifted gradually to reports on economic and social movements, such as race relations in the United States and elsewhere, the struggles of immigrants, the plight of refugees, the rising American underclass, and dozens of other sweeping changes. Few of these movements started with one or two big front page stories. Almost all of them resulted from a long series of minor events, often so small they didn't even make a little inside story in a newspaper. Together, of course, they produced important political, social, and economic shifts. Journalists call them *trend stories,* for they show readers what has been happening, not just today, but over time.

Obviously, stories about odd occurrences and conflict cannot be ignored. News of tornadoes, accidents, wars, threats of war, presidential races, and congressional tangles attract almost everyone. Editors run these stories in detail. What needs to shrink are stories of little consequence, the petty quarrels, the sniping, the minor flood, or the record-breaking cucumber.

In particular, editors should avoid spending much space on *rigged oddities*. Two examples will suffice. In one state a gubernatorial candidate named Walker took advantage of his name and walked all over the state, wearing blue jeans, heavy boots, a chambray shirt, and a red bandana. Hundreds of pictures, showing him walking along the highway, chatting with a farmer, sipping lemonade in a little town, appeared in newspapers and on television. His opponents, wearing conventional clothes, never had a chance.

A few years later another candidate campaigned in an open jeep with a big, friendly dog sitting on the back seat. His pictures got big play. He won easily. Editors in both cases should have smelled the free advertising trick and used only one or two pictures.

Rigged oddities

Of course, conflict does attract us all. Pedestrians pause if two drivers, after an accident, stand in the street and bellow at each other. The issue is whether conflict stories are overdone. Since the days of Lincoln editors have given top priority to wars, foreign leaders' threats, or to a city council member's squabbles with the mayor. Editors are well aware that public interest wanes when there are no bitter contests, no wars, or no hot issues that turn a city's residents into jangling factions. Peaceful events and eras, like placid marriages, are considered normal—and dull. If classes go routinely, college students tell parents that there's no news. But if a professor is fired or students demonstrate against a dean, there will be plenty of news.

Journalism students, many of whom will edit the news well into the twenty-first century, may ask if the public is overdosed on conflict. Intelligent readers know that a dog fight is less important than medical advances gained by research on dogs. They have had their fill of conflict in Central America and the Middle East. Research indicates that long reports on war and bickering are not read as well as most editors assumed.

Through habit, some editors make up pages as if bombings and threats of bombings were the most important news. Certainly conflict is significant; yet readers hunger for news of the relief or end of conflict, perhaps just because peace is uncommon.

Journalism critics often complain that the press does not print enough good news. Of course a lot of good news is printed and often what is bad news to one is good news to another. Still, editors might assay their papers' content to see if they have overdone accidents, crime, and corruption. Critics might do the same to see if they can find as much bad news as they assumed.

Though sometimes editors act as if the choice of news were decreed by the stars, it is men and women who make the decisions that

Conflict

make news. They base their decisions on theories and intuitions that are subject to analysis and criticism. What are these foundations for decisions? Is news the bizarre or the hopeful? Editors might keep a little checklist in their heads as they judge the news: Is it accurate, fair, and thorough? Will it appeal to a sizable number of readers? Does it throw light on an old subject or present something new? Is it misleading? Does it focus on the concerns of many people? Does it handle human relationships with sensitivity? Balancing these criteria and making judgments on story play and length become the almost constant task of an editor.

The nature of news

News is current information of interest to readers (or listeners or viewers). That definition is not meant to be a legalistic pronouncement but a stimulus to thinking about events. The concept *news,* like the concepts *mental health* or *spirituality,* is more easily recognized than precisely described. That first brief statement is meant to center attention where the editor's attention must be centered: on the reader's concern to be informed more than on the source of information or the incident itself.

The deciphering of an ancient hieroglyphic or the release of secret documents from World War II is clearly news, though the event was long ago. The information is fresh and current to the reader today. There has been a tradition of trying to get *today* into the leads of stories about news a day or even a week old: "It was learned today," or "Washington sources said today." But editors are sensibly coming to accept perfect tense forms as equally newsy: "Ancient secrets have been deciphered." If the information is of fresh interest today, it's news to the reader, regardless of the date of the event.

It may be objected that the definition, by emphasizing reader interest, minimizes the significance factor in news. However, if an item is truly important to a reader, it will interest the reader too. How could it be otherwise? There is no dull significant *news:* there is only dull significant *newswriting.* If an epidemic threatens a reader's town or if a change in the federal budget affects taxes or services that concern the reader, the medical or fiscal details should be presented in an appealing way. If an epidemic is far away or if the budget change really will not affect the reader, it deserves little attention. Why should an editor sweat over it? This does not refer, of course, to readers concerned only with themselves or perhaps their immediate families. Typical readers, with some concern about the whole nation and the world, must still focus on what is most significant for them, and the editor should try to help them see and understand that significance.

Editors may fail in taking the easy way out. They know most readers are interested in the rape-murder—or at least tradition says they are interested—so they print it. More significant stories tend to be more difficult to develop. The news staff concludes too quickly that the reader has no interest in or concern about a development in foreign aid or a cabinet change in some remote country. In this age of interpretation, however, the editor's job often is to probe for the relationship of distant or obscure events to the reader, indirect as it may be, and then to explain that significance.

This approach to news also helps the editor determine the importance of a story. Newswriting textbooks sometimes list qualities that will help the beginning reporter recognize the difference between a big item and a little one. *Proximity* is one, for example; others are *size* and *recency*. A flood killing five hundred persons is a bigger story than one killing five. A wreck killing five persons in our town means more to us than a wreck killing five outside Cologne. The death of a businessman an hour ago is more newsworthy than the death of a businessman two days ago. All such evaluations of course are made as if all other factors are equal, but usually everything else is not equal in the news that editors handle. Editors minimize the rules and categories and judge news as it touches current needs and interests of readers.

The desires of readers for the superficial as well as the heavy therefore are taken into account. Readers will identify with some stories, and such material—appropriately called *human interest*—will always be used. Reader needs, whether or not the reader recognizes them, are even more important. As pointed out in Chapter 1, people have less time to keep up with more news in a world whose horizons now extend far into space. An intermediary must alert them to the news they need. The editor is the person who decides which messages from Asia and the United Nations and Washington and Main Street are important to the paper's busy readers. The aim is to alert the reader, and this goal, like the other goals of journalism—to lead, to educate—would not be valid if the editor ignored readers' needs.

The evaluation network

Rarely does one person alone decide which stories will reach print. Except with routine local news in small papers, a whole network of writers and editors normally selects stories for the daily press. How vast the problem is can be seen in the fact that a big city daily may receive nearly two million words a day but can print "only" 100,000!

Suppose, for example, that a snowslide in the Swiss mountains kills and injures several tourists. Depending on such factors as the number of deaths and the prominence of the people, the local correspondent or stringer will get out the news. For a wire service the copy would most likely go to Berne or Geneva, probably by telephone. The editors there doubtless would send a full story to a central desk in London. If the dead were Latin Americans, the most complete story might go to South America.

Let's assume a prominent business executive from San Francisco is among the dead. London then sends quite a complete story to New York, and this story goes out on a West Coast regional wire. A much abbreviated item will go to most of the other dailies in the country. Wire service editors become involved in deciding how much of the story should move to papers and, finally, news editors decide how much, if any, of it fits their papers. In San Francisco, it is obviously a major story, but editors in most other cities will throw it out.

The fate of this story, moreover, depends on the flow of other news. At each point—Berne, London, New York, and on the wire desk—editors have to compare the news value of the story with other stories that reach their desks about the same time. This variation in the flood of news means that one day a relatively small story gets a big play, while another day a significant item is buried.

While the wire editor selects from AP or UPI, a city editor dispatches reporters to newsworthy events. Writers on beats decide which events they find deserve coverage, and how much. The city editor evaluates the overall flow of city news from these local sources while a state editor weighs copy from the state or region, and a sports editor evaluates sports news. Other editors and writers—the business editor, church editor, and lifestyle editor—survey their fields for news significant to their readers.

But who decides whether the accident in Switzerland deserves more or less space than a local court trial? In part this question is solved or evaded by departmentalization. The city editor, for example, typically will have a page or two for display of local news, and the sports editor and lifestyle editor have special sections for their copy.

On the front page, however, the biggest stories from all the channels meet in competition. Here the mountain accident faces the local murder, the bill in the state legislature, the statement from the president, and perhaps a World Series game. The newspaper has to have clear staff organization to decide how the stories should be played.

The *managing editor,* as the title suggests, is the person responsible, but on larger papers "the ME" rarely makes hour-by-hour decisions on all the major stories from varied sources. These routine decisions are left to a news editor. (The wire editor may in fact fill this role, or may, as an assistant to the news editor, make most decisions on wire copy.)

On a typical paper, the news editor considers the space and position requests of the city editor and wire editor. Perhaps the state editor, sports editor, or other subeditors will bid for front page space too. There may be discussion, and even vigorous argument, in which the city editor claims that the new break in a murder case deserves top play, while the science editor contends the new research on cancer is the most important story of the year. The news editor has to decide.

On most papers four or five key editors will meet in the managing editor's office several hours before deadline to look at the probable flow of the day's news and decide how the main stories will be played. This system provides greater objectivity in evaluating news, for the enthusiasms and foibles of a single editor can be contained. As the news flow continues, changing stories moderately or dramatically in the next few hours, two or three editors again may confer for a minute or two on how to handle the latest developments.

In some ways, this is judgment by committee, and no committee can edit a paper continuously. Individual editors must have the responsibility to make rapid decisions required by the varied flow of news. They operate something like people going through a cafeteria line, deciding swiftly which foods to select and which to reject.

Wire editors, for example, have to run their eyes quickly over a stream of story summaries on the VDT screen. They must pass over a half dozen and take a slightly longer look at the seventh story. The eighth may require the revival of a story already cast aside. Experience is essential, for there is little time to ponder for more than a few seconds what is going to be done with most of the hundred or more stories popping onto the tube.

Weighing news values

Story significance is the most important consideration on a well-edited paper. Closely related to news importance, as was argued previously, is usefulness to the reader. Any change in the Social Security law, as an illustration, will attract thousands of readers because the news is useful to them. A story that is not of world significance nevertheless may be highly significant to an individual reader. Parents with a daughter in Tanzania, for example, will pore over a story about a storm in that country. Other news is printed for its sheer entertainment value. Each story represents a mix of importance, usefulness, and interests, and the biggest stories have the most of each quality. No formula or rule can guide the news editor to infallible choices. Only experience sharpens judgment and produces pages that withstand critical examination a month or a year later.

Typically the news editor not only chooses the news but also decides on treatment. If the paper has only one wire service supplying news, the editor sees only the story filed by that service. But on larger newspapers a decision must be made on whether to print the Associated Press story or the United Press International version. Or should someone on the desk be told to combine them? Is copy from a special service, such as the *Christian Science Monitor* or the *Los Angeles Times–Washington Post News Service,* better than an agency story? Can spot copy from the wire and a backgrounder be used as a sidebar? Editors first decide what is significant and interesting and then decide how their selected stories will appear in the paper. They first choose the stories, then decide how they will be displayed. The chapters on headlines and makeup have shown the several ways the editor quickly directs readers to the major stories and keeps them aware of the minor items.

Gatekeeping

As mentioned earlier, the people who open and close the gates on the flow of news are known to researchers as gatekeepers. The many decisions constantly made by writers and editors clearly mean that countless gatekeepers influence the amount and quality of news in every newspaper. But for the readers of a daily, that paper's most important gatekeeper is the news editor, a person unknown to most of them. How does this editor go about the task of decision making? How do stories rank in importance? How do they get modified?

In theory, the news editor coolly and objectively decides on the value and display of news, without fear or favor. In fact, varied pressures squeeze the editor most of the time. News sense may be shaped or even seriously distorted by three general kinds of pressure: economic, traditional, and personal.

Economic pressure

"The advertiser made them use that story," one reader observes. "They'll do anything," says another, "to sell papers." Such frequent comments from newspaper consumers point to the supposed influence of profit on news decisions, because the two sources of newspaper income are advertising and circulation.

The threat of the advertiser in influencing news coverage is exaggerated in the public mind, however. On the well-run newspaper, the advertising and editorial departments are separate and distinct. Good journalists would repulse an advertising representative who approached asking favors. In fact, some editors would make a point of doing the opposite of what an ad person asked. There are doubtless cases where a big advertiser asks and gets favors in the news columns, or where a weak editor gives the advertiser free space or kills a story, though the advertiser may not even have asked. But such toadying is much more rare than it used to be.

One journalistic practice that muddies public thinking in this area is the issuing of special supplements. Since advertising of real estate, resorts, or insurance supports these sections, they often are filled with newslike puffs about such businesses. The decision by many papers to stuff regular columns with handouts, not only from charities but also from businesses, likewise demonstrates the strength of commercial pressure.

A greater economic threat to objective news coverage is the publisher's role as capitalist or business leader. Decades ago, the famous editor and political leader from Kansas, William Allen White, spoke of the "country club complex" that publishers and editors develop by mixing socially with the wealthy. Every year rising capital costs of newspapers increase this identification of the press leader with the money or power structure. The newspaper's management and top editorial staffers do not think as blue-collar workers or as union members, or even as teachers and doctors, but as well-to-do business leaders. So department store owners, for example, may rightly feel they do not even have to mention the ads they buy to get the news treatment they want. News editors may have to work consciously to play the news straight when they know that those above them assess events in much the same way as the more widely feared advertiser.

Until fairly recently, most newspapers tended to ride along with the status quo, which is largely set by the people of substance. Criticism of business and probing investigations of government were rare. Much of that has changed. A generation ago few papers ran much on the three giant electrical corporations convicted of price-fixing, with some of their corporate officials imprisoned. Today few businesses are immune from detailed reporting on the quality of their products.

12

Skepticism about government claims is almost the first rule of reporting, although too few reporters follow through on their skepticism to dig deeply for the truth.

Editors should keep asking, "Who are the sources and what is their motive in giving information? Is the story planted as a diversion, to take the public's eye off an embarrassment? Is it the result of some public relations 'spin'? Are some facts deliberately omitted or exaggerated? Is the story based on a 'media event,' a contrived happening to attract press attention?"

If purity toward advertisers is easy to preach about, the issues involved in keeping circulation up are more complex and more subtle. Everyone on a paper agrees that it has to sell, whether the aim is to make money, to convey news, or to wield great social influence. A paper that does not sell will die. And if it barely sells, neither the business nor the editorial staff is happy. This pressures every editor to print "what the public wants."

Editors often argue that the public wants serious, solid news coverage. On the other hand, many journalists say that the public interest is shallow, as shown by the great interest in comics and agony columns. That view may be too cynical. The *Los Angeles Times,* the *Wall Street Journal,* the *Philadelphia Inquirer,* and the *New York Times* are all serious yet successful. The *Journal,* with the nation's largest circulation, runs no sports, comics, or pictures.

Papers in small cities might break even imitating the *New York Times,* but the pressure on almost all newspapers is to build circulation and profit. Circulation can be built legitimately with stories of human interest. A few news editors will go further, giving in to circulation pressure to print a heavy diet of murder, sex scandals, and other sensations. Successful pandering may win a narrow kind of success, although the few papers that have turned to this formula have found no gold mine.

The emphasis on sensationalism, going back to the "penny press" of the 1830s and the yellow journalism of sixty years later, rests on a low opinion of humankind. Perhaps today the masses are more enlightened than when Barnum profited on the theory of a sucker born every minute. If human nature has not improved, at least education has spread. Idealistic editors also suggest that more serious and less sensational editing attracts the serious readers that management and advertisers both crave.

One pertinent aspect of this argument is the growing press monopoly. In the competitive twenties, sensation was an important weapon for survival. But publishers of monopoly papers with high home delivery now often argue that they can provide higher quality coverage when they have no competition. A monopoly lifts some of the pressure to strive for sensational headlines that sometimes raise street sales.

The other side of the monopoly coin, however, reveals the pressure to become lazy, self-satisfied, and careless because regardless of the paper's quality the money keeps rolling in. It is not hard to find examples of this kind of newspaper.

A relatively new economic development does not involve pressure. Instead, it is a conscious decision by many publishers and editors to take their papers "upscale." They deliberately want stories selected that will appeal to the better educated with high incomes. These top executives talk about "areas of dominant influence," usually meaning prosperous suburbs. They realize that circulation in those regions is more valuable to advertisers and that means more advertising and more profit. It also means that people in the lower middle class and below are almost ignored.

Traditional pressure

The pressure of "this is the way it's always been done" pushes the editor to evaluate news traditionally. For example, newspapers for generations have leaned strongly to government news. As history books have long been bound up with the dates of military and political events, newspapers have traditionally blanketed government offices, from the White House to the town council chambers. Even now, only a few journalists think that a newspaper should have reporters cover science laboratories as closely as they cover police stations. Coverage of the arts is often scorned by old-style journalists even though millions attend concerts, plays, and dance performances and visit museums.

There are, of course, good reasons—in terms of reader interest and concern—for keeping an eye on our political machinery. But suppose a news editor reached the objective conclusion that developments in, say, medicine and education deserved more regular front page space than did a feud between politicians. The mind-set of the whole profession would be upset. City editors habitually have reporters cover government offices, and press services send out daily news budgets heavily weighted with government coverage.

Since a democratic society requires a great deal of government news, a still more troublesome tradition is the habit of giving excessive coverage to certain kinds of unimportant and even trivial material. Most papers give sports more space than interest justifies, but since sports interest often is intense, many papers have increased sports coverage. Heavy coverage, of course, does develop a little more interest in sports news, but there are still frequent complaints that some towns simply will not support this or that sport. All the free publicity fails to spark much interest.

Tradition says also that certain events always deserve picture coverage and February 2 always has its Ground Hog Day story. Fall and spring bring out a rash of stories about small boys who hate school, apparently because some editor at the time of the Civil War hated school. It is, of course, unthinkable that the authors of such pieces might have enjoyed school writing!

Editors who look at news in these routine ways would have as much difficulty defending their practices as in justifying that newspapers have for years printed astrological predictions—during this scientific age. Such editors are dated, even though astrology still has avid followers.

Personal pressure

"The boss" is a near and vital concern of the news editor. The superior may be an absentee owner, local top management, the editor-in-chief upstairs, the managing editor in the next office — or a composite of them all. Usually when one or another of these delivers an opinion, the staff transforms this dictum into dogma. Thereafter *this* kind of story *must* be printed, and that type must *not* — and so the newspaper's sacred cows grow up from calves. *That* boss likes cats, and *this* boss has a feud with a particular politician, so journalists open the gates to cat stories and close them to mention of the politician.

Worship of a sacred cow is often foolish, as the presumed need for it and even the boss who created it are long dead. Moreover, sometimes the boss's bias is not dictated — the staff merely senses it. If, for example, a Republican paper endorses a Democratic candidate for president, the staff quickly feels the changing wind and is tempted to react in stories, columns, and news play. The same kind of bias is possible wherever a publisher takes a strong position on a candidate or issue. Conscientious editors can at least check to see whether ethics will permit them to go along. If they are professionals, they will resist the biases that would distort the news flow — or look for jobs elsewhere.

Research has shown that publishers do become involved in news direction — "interfere with" may be too strong, though it may seem so to the editor. Significantly, in contrast to popular supposition, publishers interfere less on the big papers than the small. At least one researcher found that publishers became more involved when local issues were being reported.

Chain owners seldom pass on specific orders on how to treat certain political or business leaders. Many of them boast of granting autonomy to their various newspapers. Chain operators, of course, have few local sacred cows, possibly because they almost never meet local people. Clearly, publishers have constitutional and economic rights to exert control, but they can cause the newsroom executives both ethical and practical problems if, trying to usurp their professional functions, they pressure journalists to act for the publishers' business interests rather than the public interest.

The narrowness of reader interest can apply severe pressures upon editors to emphasize trivial information rather than news of genuine significance. The staffs of the better newspapers today are made up of sophisticated and educated men and women. Specialists report on education, politics, science, and foreign affairs. Yet many readers dislike or even resent accurate reports about a world they can't quite understand. They yearn for a diet of little stories about opossums living under someone's porch and a firefighter's rescue of a faithful dog.

But sophisticated journalists sometimes add to the difficulty by affecting in their writing and editing a condescending attitude toward people of less education and breadth of experience. They rattle off phrases like *supply-side economics, tax losses,* and *détente* as though everyone should know what they mean. A respect for all readers and an understanding of their fears and desires can help a newspaper reduce the pressure to turn out a soothing, innocuous product.

Public pressure—the pressure from readers—also may tend to distort an editor's judgments. If subscribers cancel when reporters delve into pet subjects, the editor may soft-pedal these topics. But the pressure may not be so overt. Merely knowing reader attitudes may tempt editors to compromise. If they know, for example, that most readers are social and political conservatives, they may ignore some news of reform or revolt, or play such stories unsympathetically. Such bias is unprofessional. Wise editors, however, will note these public attitudes and avoid unnecessarily riling most readers. They still will select the news so readers may get a realistic picture of the world they live in. The goals of journalism include leading and educating, not giving in to narrow prejudices and preconceptions. Sound, objective news evaluation should not bend far, even before the tyranny of the majority.

Guidelines of judgment

The editor makes news evaluations most of the time with little concern over pressures. Several guidelines help in deciding what gets printed. One guide advises against printing the *obvious story;* events as predictable as the sunrise aren't news. Other obvious stories might be in the "What did you expect him to say?" category. If the Chamber of Commerce Secretary predicts a booming Christmas business, no one should be surprised. Should one expect any other prediction from this person? If the president, back from a trip, announces that he had a "valuable discussion" with the prime minister of Outer Nostrum, the editor probably has to print something, because the president spoke officially. But his statement is barely newsworthy because no one would expect him to say anything else. The only newsworthy prediction by a political candidate about a coming election would be, "I'm gonna lose."

The editor also should beware of fads. A particular social problem tends to become a national pastime, and the press reflects the current rage by carrying all kinds of stories about it. It may be popular during one period to write at length on juvenile delinquency. This fad may hold sway for six months or so before being replaced, perhaps, by a great concern for missing children. After giving that subject a good run, attention might focus on cholesterol, problems of the elderly, or women's rights. All of these subjects are important, but the good editor will print only the most valuable stories once the issue has been beaten almost to death.

When editors decide a subject is good enough for detailed coverage, they apply another guideline: story stamina. Will the issue have long-range interest or will it be forgotten in a few days? Subjects with staying power have been the perils of cigarette smoking and drug addiction. Some subjects of continuing interest have their vitality limited to short bursts of coverage. The ups and downs of the stock market may be everyone's concern for a few days but major daily coverage for weeks on end is too much for the ordinary citizen. A subject with long-term potential may even be killed by too much coverage. Readers can stay interested in events, such as local airport development, if major decisions are not lost in a stream of unimportant daily stories.

Good editors also strive to stay alert to change. Our society changes rapidly, yet anyone concentrating on the daily events might miss the economic and social alterations occurring over several years. Most editors were a bit slow to realize that a substantial portion of the population was keenly interested in retirement income, pensions, and estate planning. Only after the stories were dumped into their laps did they provide better coverage. Editors also dawdled in reporting how the electronic industry has altered manufacturing and marketing. Others have neglected to report on the growing black and Hispanic middle class or the rising economic power of Asian countries other than Japan.

Some editors ignore competition and others jump nervously in anticipation of what another paper or television will do with certain stories. The best editors will note the competition and adjust the news play accordingly. Obviously an afternoon paper will not print almost exactly, in the same position, what a nearby morning paper had. Neither will a paper print, as a breaking story, news that radio and television have had for ten hours. Good editors, of course, will not leave out stories just because the competition had them.

Journalists always should be checking to find whether their stories are what various blocks of readers want. Guesses, conversations with a few friends, and "logic" won't do the job. Some solid research, as described in Chapter 18, is necessary if editors are to know with some accuracy how well their stories are being read and what readers desire in their newspapers. Good journalists, naturally, will resist turning out a bunch of fluff just because researchers say the public finds the news too serious. Their sense of professionalism will require them to give the basic information that any citizen must have.

Bias and business

For years press critics charged that the news media were soft on business. They contended that stories about the perils of cigarette smoking got casual treatment and that lawsuits against business, like the price-fixing story, saw little print. Any careful reader realizes that these charges are far less true today than they were a generation ago. Dangers to health from smoking, air pollution, food additives, and pesticides are in literally hundreds of stories. Lawsuits against big automobile and tire companies make front page news and seriously damage company sales. The consumer information submitted by Ralph Nader, once studiously ignored, now gets into newspapers. Many papers have consumer reporters and, while some deal only in innocuous material, a good many dig for facts, even when the facts disturb powerful forces.

131

Tradition still plays a role, however, for often there is reluctance to battle the established and the powerful. Opponents of nuclear power contend that their charges of possible dangers and excessive costs were largely ignored by the press until Three Mile Island nuclear power plant came close to a meltdown. Even then, they say, the story soon faded and was revived after the 1986 disaster at the Russian nuclear plant at Chernobyl.

Others insist that proposals by government and big corporations often are described and lauded by the press with little effort to search for possible opposition. Critics point to how "crime in the suites" gets so little news coverage. They charge that a kid who steals a car for a night's joy ride may get six months in prison, with the details printed on a somewhat prominent page, while corporate thievery gets little attention. Part of the reason for this disparity, of course, is that white-collar crime rarely is prosecuted. An auditor for one large firm succeeded in spotting thieves within his organization and realized that over the years perhaps a hundred had been caught. "Only one case hit the newspapers," he said. The rest of the crooks were simply fired quietly and, when possible, persuaded to return the money.

Similar attitudes persist on welfare cheats, the critics say. A person found to have bilked the welfare department out of $200 gets a story about the fraud in most newspapers. A big food company that puts rotten tomatoes in its catsup, however, escapes without a line, largely because reporters and editors ignore all but the severest cases handled by the Food and Drug Administration.

Judging at a distance

News judgment is usually easier when the event is close to home. The facts are clearer and can be obtained more quickly. The news from far away, however, is more difficult to evaluate. Who can judge the accuracy or completeness of the information filed by wire services from, say, Ethiopia? How informed is the reporter? Does the reporter know the nuances of politics in the country? Are the cited news sources adequate?

Editors who judge the merits of such stories have to rely on their experience, of course, but they can take some conventional precautions. The byline is an obvious clue. They may know that the writer is new in the country and therefore inexperienced. The dateline is another clue. Where the story was filed tells whether the story is a firsthand report or a synthesis of information from second- and third-rate sources. Names of people quoted in a story can help as editors sniff for authenticity. If it quotes "reliable sources," editors should be at least wary. If refugees are quoted, editors should immediately be on guard, for refugees or exiles are hardly objective observers.

When editors are dubious about the reliability of the facts or the sources in a story, they should edit it with great care. Their editing should include a warning to the reader of their doubt. A thoroughly suspicious story goes into the editor's wastebasket. Even conscientious editors, however, have bitten hard on stories that should have raised suspicions at a half dozen places.

A leading example occurred in 1983 when Yuri Andropov became the Soviet Union's leader. Not much was known about him, so journalists traced the few threads available. It was difficult to get facts in the Soviet Union then, but many writers and editors didn't let that stop them. Stories said Andropov, who had been head of the secret police, was a liberal. It was hard to think that by American standards such an official would be liberal. Stories also said he liked American jazz and detective stories. Sources were lacking on all this material. As it happened, the stories caused little damage but they still misled millions of readers. Editors would have done better to print: "Andropov ran the KBG, but little else about his life or career can be discovered."

Hostility between the United States and the Soviet Union has declined markedly, but for forty years the friction contributed to other blunders. American editors, fearful that they would be beaten on some major story, printed rumors or the sketchiest reports from communist countries. Granted, it is hard to pin down rumors in such nations, but editors would save themselves embarrassment if they did not print these flimsily documented stories or warned readers that sources were impeachable. Russian, Chinese, and Yugoslav leaders have been reported dead several days or several years before their actual deaths. Reports of uprisings, famine, and natural disasters too often have been printed and then found to be false or grossly exaggerated.

Wishful editing

The mishandling of some foreign news brings into focus another difficulty that faces editors: wishful editing. Like nearly all citizens, editors possess an element of nationalism. They want to report events that they and their government wish would happen. Such wishes can impair judgment. Since nearly all Americans oppose communism, it is tempting to print stories that make the communists look bad, even when the stories are inaccurate.

Wishful editing, of course, eventually damages American society, for citizens develop perceptions based on faulty information. After all these years of occasional wishful reports from the Eastern bloc, probably a sizable majority in the United States believes that people there are close to starving, live in wretched conditions, and go about in the shabbiest of clothing. It is a jolt, then, to see television reports of people who are apparently fed and clothed moderately well and riding public transport that equals or surpasses some of the systems available in the United States. Fortunately, most editors and foreign correspondents are more cautious about wishful stories than they were a decade or two ago, and some countries are much more open to American reporters than they were in the depths of the cold war.

To make proper decisions on news play of major stories, editors must take a little time to reflect. Unfortunately, some veteran editors tend to think that decisive editing means fast editing. The best editors, however, know when decisions require delay. They read sensitive stories two or three times and even discuss them with a colleague. The interests of both the newspaper and the reader are best served by editors who have confidence in their judgment and who take time to let it operate effectively.

Some editors recognize that their own biases form one of the greatest pressures toward slanted coverage. How else can they view the news except through glasses colored by their own opinions and prejudices? Maybe they can see how the staff plays to their views on cats or airpower or pollution controls. Complete objectivity is impossible, but they can strive for it by regularly analyzing their feelings and checking influences on their judgments. They can watch the news play in other papers, including great foreign ones like the *Globe and Mail* in Toronto or the *Times* in London. Finally, they can check their perceptions by conferring with other staffers.

But even the way colleagues view the news is not sufficient for really self-critical editors. Colleagues also have their local or national biases. Editors can try sometimes to imagine how a person in Asia or at the United Nations would view the news. Other cultures do not operate as the American culture does, and American journalists should not assume that a foreign nation's ways are clumsy, wasteful, or evil. Regular exercise in trying to rise above their own biases, and even those of their profession and nation, would be salutary for news editors.

Such detachment is possible, and research has shown that editors with strong positions on an issue still can fairly handle a story on that subject. In fact, they might even do a better job simply because they are concerned enough to know whether the story adequately gives the facts.

These varied pressures on every journalist can distort evaluations of the news. Professional integrity, therefore, is the ultimate safeguard of the news stream.

For many Americans, the Golden Rule is the ethical touchstone. Wouldn't a newspaper be ethical if editors handled the news as they would want news of themselves handled? Not necessarily. The principle is not easily applied to the evaluation of news for a large public. Whether a story sees print would depend on how much pull a person can develop with the editor, who takes pity on friends. To be an impartial gatekeeper, the ethical editor in a sense has to be without friends — or enemies.

What news of arrests, lawsuits, bankruptcies, or other unhappy incidents would be printed if the rule were the desire of editors to have such news left out about themselves and their friends? The printing of most spot news items probably makes someone unhappy, and papers would go out of business if they did not seek a higher principle than saving someone's feelings. Sometimes they must print news that hurts

Professional integrity

individuals. So they apply a standard of fair-dealing to all, regardless of the editor's friendships or compassion.

Sound evaluation of news is bound up in professionalism. Professional editors come to look at their tasks not as plumbers contemplating a neat fit, important as that is, but as physicians or educators contemplating their role in the improvement of society. Such editors use as a frame of reference for decisions, not the personal tastes of advertiser, publisher, or themselves, but the professional ideals held by the best practitioners of the news profession.

9

Editing wire news

WIRE EDITORS, sometimes called news editors, decide what state, national, and world news gets in the paper. They select and edit perhaps twenty-five to sixty stories each day so those stories will give readers at least an adequate report on what is happening in their world. To accomplish this goal a good wire editor must have wide knowledge, careful news judgment, an eye for typographical display, and a skeptical attitude.

Knowledge lets the editor understand what is going on in the newspaper's state, as well as the nation and world. Knowledge of history, politics, and social change helps put the news in perspective. Skepticism helps keep the editor from being misled or even fooled by inaccurate or false information. Judgment lets the editor apply the knowledge to the stories at hand, so the information is clear, fair, and reasonably complete. The typographical eye helps the editor envision how certain stories will look on newspaper pages.

People who like to deal with national and international news often seek the wire editor's job. They relish the task of reading hundreds of stories each day, selecting the ones they consider most significant, and trimming them to fit the available space. On small papers wire editors may edit the news, write headlines for the stories, and even report some local news or edit city copy. On papers with circulations of 15,000 to 50,000 they probably concentrate on the wire editing and headline writing. On somewhat bigger papers they only skim most of the wire stories, select the ones they want, and direct copy readers to edit the stories and write the heads.

On the largest metropolitan papers the wire news may be divided, the city editor or state editor getting the stories that originate close to home, and other copy going to foreign, financial, and national desks. Sports wires feed directly into the sports department. Copy streams into the newsrooms of the biggest papers from a half-dozen wire services.

Wire editors once were called telegraph editors, a term stemming from the days when newspapers got their nonlocal news over telegraph wires. Each paper had someone listening to Morse code dots and dashes and typing or copying by hand what was received. It was a major advance when the Teletype was invented, for the new machine spun out a ribbon of paper, filled with stories from around the world. The Teletype is close to extinction, for most wire copy now comes directly to a newspaper's computer and from there to the VDT screens.

When copy poured from Teletypes, the wire editor was surrounded by paper. Stories were everywhere and new *leads,* (called *first lead, second lead,* etc.) *inserts, adds, corrections,* and *subs* (substitute material) seemed to spurt endlessly from the machine. To avoid chaos, editors tossed unwanted stories into a special basket or rammed them onto a spindle. That way they could concentrate on stories they intended to put into the paper. Editors pasted those new leads, inserts, and adds above, into, and below the stories to make them timely, correct, and complete.

The computer changed all this. Adds, inserts, and corrections appear on the VDT screen, but they rarely stay there long. A wire service editor will make the required alterations and within a few minutes a revamped story will appear with the additions, substitutions, and insertions all in place. On *hispeed wires* a corrected version of a story with one error may be transmitted, rather than force an editor to make the required change.

Wire services

The Associated Press and United Press International dominate wire services. Other services lack the breadth of coverage provided by AP and UPI. These two organizations cover events in the smallest towns and the biggest cities. They have full-time correspondents in most major cities and in lesser places, at home and abroad, they have part-timers, called stringers, to file stories whenever events warrant. In the United States nearly every daily newspaper or sizable radio station has a staffer stringing for AP or UPI. (See Fig. 9.1.) Also, newspapers can use what are called *electronic carbons* to send their own stories to a wire service, assuming the service might be interested.

9.1. Home base. Associated Press headquarters in New York City.

More than a century ago, when telephone and telegraph facilities were primitive, some wire reporters were forced on occasion to employ carrier pigeons to convey the news and others used boats or horses in attempts to beat any competition. While these struggles often were romantic, dozens of little news-gathering services failed. But new ones continued to be formed because editors realized that they had to have some kind of cooperative reporting service. They recognized that each could not afford to have correspondents all over the world and that some news association would have to provide nonlocal news.

After several starts, the first being in 1848 in New York City, the Associated Press formed in 1892. The United Press was organized in 1907, and Hearst's International News Service in 1909. INS was sold to UP in 1958, and the merged organizations took the name of United Press International, or UPI.

The AP is a cooperative, with each paper paying for service at a rate determined by circulation and the service received. UPI is a private business and calls its customers "clients," not members. It also charges only by circulation.

Because the papers share the cost of gathering wire news, they are a minor expense to newspapers. Their cost will vary from little more than $500 a week for papers with less than 10,000 circulation to several thousand dollars for the metropolitan papers. Even though the total cost for the giants may seem high, no newspaper could afford to duplicate the news coverage of the wire services.

Some wire editors have the impression that the two services have personalities. AP is known for its reliability, UPI for its bright writing and Latin American coverage. Researchers examined these impressions in a series of studies, and found that the impressions don't match the facts. Each service appears to be of equal accuracy and brightness, so far as that can be measured. There is no clear evidence, either, that UPI has a superior Latin American report.

In the early days of teletype transmission, words came via telephone lines onto teleprinters at forty words a minute. Later the rate became sixty-six words a minute, and today that service is called the *slowspeed wire*. Now, however, hispeed wires deliver 1,200 words a minute, enough to fill a column and a half in a newspaper. Nearly a hundred papers can receive copy at 2,400 words a minute on another special wire. Transmission into VDTs is so fast that time is insignificant. A tremendous number of stories are swimming inside those computers awaiting inspection by wire editors.

Supplemental services

While AP and UPI are the only services in the United States that try to cover almost all the news of the nation and world, a dozen or more special organizations provide news by wire.

The *New York Times* sells its own service to more than two hundred American and Canadian papers. Each subscriber gets almost all the news the *Times* has, except some from New York City. The stories are transmitted over both AP and the UPI fast wires.

The *Washington Post* and *Los Angeles Times* have teamed up to send special articles from their own Washington and foreign correspondents. The *Chicago Sun-Times* and the *Chicago Tribune* offer services, and the *Tribune* wire includes copy from Knight-Ridder newspapers.

The *New York Daily News,* the Scripps-Howard chain, and the Newhouse newspapers have services. The British news agency, Reuters, supplies a modest number of American papers. The North American Newspaper Alliance (NANA) also sends feature stories by wire.

Though none of these services provides complete reports, as AP and UPI do, more and more papers are subscribing to them to supplement AP and UPI. Their cost usually is lower and their coverage frequently more penetrating than what the two all-purpose wire services provide. Stories from supplemental services often are slightly editorial, in contrast to the studied objectivity of AP and UPI stories, and some editors think readers find such stories stimulating.

Both AP and UPI provide far more than straight news reports. Both have feature staffs, picture services, and a special wire for radio and television stations. The radio wire provides national and state news, and every hour a number of news items, taking about four minutes to read, are pieced together. With one minute of commercials they make the five-minute newscast. This has led to the scornful term "rip and read," in which an untrained person rips the five-minute newscast off the Teletype and reads it over the air. The skilled electronic journalist, of course, rewrites some of this material, replaces other parts with local news, and uses good judgment on news selection before heading to the microphone.

The satellite

Until about 1980 news came over telephone wires to Teletypes and computers. Now nearly every newspaper buying wire services has a satellite dish perched atop the building to receive stories from space. A transmitter in New Jersey shoots signals to a satellite cruising thousands of miles above the earth. Those signals, bounced off the satellite, reach those newspaper dishes and are stored in computers, awaiting an editor's command. The satellite travels at the same speed as the earth turns, so in effect it is stationary. This system greatly reduces transmission costs to newspapers. The wire services also have a back-up satellite if something happens to the main satellite. If transmission is shifted to the substitute, a thousand newspaper people will hustle to their buildings' roofs, wrenches in hand, to turn their dishes slightly to catch the signals from another satellite. If the back-up satellite also fails, a lot of newspapers will not make their deadlines that day, for they will have to revert to getting stories over telephone lines.

The daily routine

Wire editors who work on afternoon papers arrive at work early in the morning. They tap a few VDT keys and up pops the *news digest,* which once was called the *budget.* (See Fig. 9.2.) Newspaper

```
         PM-News Digest

Here are the top stories in sight for PMs.



     ROME--Desert locusts, breeding at alarming rates in
Sudan, have spread across the Red Sea to the Arabian
Peninsula and threaten South Asia, experts warn. Slug AM-
Locusts Plague. New, will stand. About 750 words.


     WASHINGTON--State and federal officials declare war on
hustlers trying to gyp Americans by telephone by using phony
prizes, cheap products and high-pressure sales tactics. Slug
AM-Telephone Fraud. Should stand. 600 words.


     WASHINGTON--The Internal Revenue Service is sicking its
computers on tax cheats who don't even bother to file
returns. Slug PM-Tax Cheats. Sent as a0417.


     WASHINGTON--A civil rights lawyer says the Supreme
Court's latest ruling restraining prosecutors from
disqualifying potential jurors based on race could mean new
trials or freedom for hundreds convicted of crimes. Slug PM-
Scotus-Juries.


     WASHINGTON--The tax systems in most states are so
unfair that the super-rich pay a significantly smaller share
of their incomes than do the poorest families, according to
a private study released today. Slug PM-State Taxes.
```

9.2. Partial news digest. The terms *will stand* and *should stand* mean that no changes are anticipated.

editors still often call the digest the budget. The digest summarizes the major stories likely to be filed that day. Editors skim these summaries to get a feel for the day's activities. Their thought processes go something like, "Hm-m-m, the Supreme Court story may be the best. I'll watch that to see if a landmark decision will be handed down. That story about the Secretary of State doesn't sound like much and neither does the Queen of England's visit to Ottawa. Congressional action on National Park Service legislation looks good, though."

The digest may include a dozen items, and most editors will print nearly all of the listed stories. In addition, the wire service will provide *advisories* every few hours, notifying editors that other important stories are in the works. With this information editors can get a quick summation of the day's news and plan which stories will get good display on their pages. They can get more specific details about the day's events by hitting a few more keys to glance at the first paragraph of all stories filed to date. It is even possible to have the computer list separately the Washington, world, and national stories. A printout of these summaries can be made for easy reference or to show to other editors.

Next, wire editors choose lesser stories and send them to the copydesk with instructions on headline size. Someone on the rim will edit the story and write the head. The slot person will check the story and head and direct the computer to set both in type.

Stories of moderate news value will be placed in a special *queue,* or collection, for the news editor to inspect. That editor will decide how long to make the story and what size headline to order. The stories wind up in the copy editor's queue for processing. Eventually those stories get in type and, following the news editor's dummies, placed by printers on inside pages.

The most important stories are discussed at about 8 A.M. in an editorial conference, probably also attended by the news editor, picture editor, city editor, state editor, and managing editor. The best stories in each department and the best pictures would be described briefly. After some debate, the managing editor might say, "Do we agree that we should lead with the proposal for a new city tax? And put on page one the Park Service story, the fire at the tire factory, and the governor's plan to increase the state budget only two percent. Two pictures on the fire. If the Supreme Court story amounts to much we will bump the Park Service piece."

The wire editor then works on the top ten or twelve stories, cutting them a little if necessary, and putting them into the news editor's queue. Those stories, with headlines assigned, go to the copy-desk, and more dummies are sent to printers. Within a couple of hours the stories are pasted onto layout sheets, printing plates are made, and the presses roll.

On smaller papers there may be no news editor, and the editorial conference may consist of a little conversation among editors at their desks. The wire editor or city editor may dummy the key pages, and each editor writes headlines.

On morning papers the process is about the same, except that the wire editor might come to work between 10 A.M. and 2 P.M., and the editorial conference may be around 6 P.M.

In paper-and-pencil days, editors struggled to cut wire stories, scratching out a sentence here and there, marking out a paragraph, and scribbling between lines to make one sentence take the place of three. The result often was a mess that a typesetter had to try to decipher. No wonder there were mistakes. Besides, after all that scratching, some editor had to estimate story length. The estimates easily could be off by several inches, resulting in too much or too little type to fill a hole. In contrast, the computer always gives a neat, clean picture of what is left after editing. If a sentence is ousted, the screen neatly reveals what is left of the story. There are no smudges and no scribbles. And, best of all, the computer tells editors exactly how long the story will be in type. There's no guessing, so type should slide almost exactly into the allotted hole.

How services operate

The computer also can do amazing things for the wire services. The little daily, for example, may want the cheapest service, but one that will give basic national, world, state, financial, and sports stories. The computer can be coded at AP or UPI so this customer gets that basic information. The little paper probably will use 75 percent of the information received.

A medium-sized daily needs two or three times as many stories because it has a larger news hole. The biggest papers, of course, order almost every service AP and UPI have, receiving perhaps five to ten times as much copy as they will use. Editors inspect all these stories (at least quickly), making sure they don't miss any item they consider important.

The services divide their work into various *wires*. The *A* wire contains the most important national and world stories. Regional wires have different labels, and they provide news of a state or region. One regional wire covers all of New England. Pennsylvania and Delaware make up another region. The *F* wire contains financial news and the *S,* sports. The wire services also code into their stories a letter that indicates the importance of each. At AP, a *D* label means that the story is in the computer but is *deferred*. It will not be transmitted as long as higher priority stories are available. An *R* means *regular,* so it will be transmitted whenever there is nothing more important to send. A *U* means *urgent,* and, obviously, will be sent ahead of *R*. A *B* stands for *bulletin,* and will be sent as soon as the story being transmitted has been filed.

Normally two or three bulletins may be sent each day. An *F* equals *flash,* and years may go by without its use. Only the most spectacular story, usually with historic significance, rates the flash. When President Kennedy's motorcade was fired upon in 1963, UPI, then using all capital letters on the teletype, filed a few *urgent* paragraphs about the event. This story was swiftly interrupted with a flash, explaining that the President had been shot. (See Fig. 9.3.) UPI uses a similar coding system but *L* stands for *lowest, O* for *ordinary, M* for *messages* sent between UPI offices, *B* for *bulletin,* and *F* for *flash*. The services run two *cycles,* one for morning papers (AMs) and the other for evening papers (PMs). The morning paper cycle starts about 12:15 P.M. and ends about 5 A.M. (EST). The cycle for PMs starts at 11:30 P.M. (EST) and ends about 5 P.M. A numbering system

```
LINKS."  THE DEFENSE HAD IMPLIED IT WILL TAKE THE LINE THAT CAROL'S

DEATH AFTER A SAVAGE BLUDGEONING AND STABBING IN HER HOME WAS THE

RESULT OF AN ATTEMPTED            MOREDA1234PCS

UPI   A7N   DA

          PRECEDE KENNEDY

    DALLAS, NOV. 22 (UPI)--THREE SHOTS WERE FIRED AT PRESIDENT KENNEDY'S

MOTORCADE TODAY IN DOWNTOWN DALLAS.

                    JT1234PCS
```

```
UPI    A8N    DA

            URGENT

     1ST ADD SHOTS, DALLAS (A7N) XXXDOWNTOWN DALLAS.

     NO CASUALITIES WERE REPORTEDZ.

     THE INCIDENT OCCURRED NEAR THE COUNTY SHERIFF'S OFFICE ON MAIN

STREET, JUST EAST OF AN UNDERPASS LEADING TOWARD THE TRADE MART WHERE

THE PRESIDENT WAS TO MA

FLASH

     KENNEDY SERIOUSLY WOUNDED

                    PERHAPS SERIOUSLY

PERHAPS FATALLY BY ASSASSINS BULLET

               JT1239PCS
```

9.3. Flash. The word *MORE* in the third line of this UPI transmission marks the start of material leading up to the flash on President Kennedy's assassination. (Symbols used to head these fragments no longer are used.)

is used for each day. AP starts with 001 while UPI begins with 200. AP's *A* wire, for example, starts A001, A002, etc.

A piece of AP copy is illustrated in Figure 9.4.

In a developing story the services keep filing *new leads* as new facts are found or as more events occur. For example, on the night of a presidential election the first lead on the election result story might say that the Democratic candidate has taken a lead in Massachusetts. The second lead may indicate that the Republican has gained strength

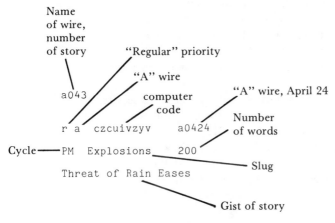

```
          LOUISVILLE, Ky.  AP  - While fears eased that rain might overload
          Louisville's devastated sewer system, city officials said they hoped
```

to complete emergency sewage trenches within 10 days and end a health
threat to 25,000 residents.

John Tierney of the Metropolitan Sewer District said it could take
longer than 10 days to complete 30-foot-deep open channels that would
carry rainwater and sewage to sewer lines undamaged by an explosion
Friday.

However, he said, authorities hoped the estimate was a good one.

Meanwhile, other officials were exploring the possibility of getting
government aid for repairing the extensive damage to sewer lines,
streets, homes and businesses.

The Friday blasts blew off manhole covers and tore up about two
miles of streets, hurling pavement chunks through roofs and walls in
the area.

9.4. Wire story with its code explained. Note the all-cap dateline that heads
nearly all stories filed by Associated Press and United Press International.

in New England and may take three states there. The third lead may
indicate that while the Republican is doing well in New England he is
getting beaten in Pennsylvania. The leads would keep pouring forth
every forty-five minutes or so, even after it is clear who the winner is.

Special services

The services, in addition to news stories, offer a variety of material. Both AP and UPI offer columnists who deal in humor, foreign
affairs, business, Hollywood, TV, finance, agriculture, and religion.

The services also have departments that provide detailed timely
and time features. Both services file *advance stories,* many for use in
Sunday papers. These often are filed two, three, or four weeks in
advance of the publication date. Sunday feature stories are in particular demand because most Sunday papers are bulky, yet little news is
made on weekends. By getting such stories early, the newspapers can
set them in type during slack periods and "close" some pages a few
days early.

AP and UPI gather news at their domestic bureaus and AP stories with national interest are sent to New York headquarters for
further editing. Regional stories are handled within their areas and
New York doesn't see them. Stories from abroad come directly to New
York, usually by another satellite, and then are sent by microwave
signals to the transmitter.

Sometimes editors combine reports from different wire services
to make a balanced story. They might lead with the first two paragraphs of UPI, for example, then insert a couple from AP, and close
with a half dozen from the New York Times News Service. The job
requires a little transitional writing to make sure that the language
moves smoothly and that essential information has not been left out.
When compiling or interweaving wire stories, the editor should be
sure to cross out the various wire-service logotypes and write across
the top of the patched-together story something like "From our Wire
Services" or "Compiled from Wire Dispatches."

144

Many newspapers have split screen VDTs, allowing an AP story to appear on one side and a similar UPI story on the other. It is easy to blend a few paragraphs from each to make a thorough story.

In some instances the editor can insert parenthetically a fact gleaned from another service. If the main story is from AP it may be strengthened with a paragraph from UPI: (United Press International reported, meanwhile, that the president had decided to stay two more days in Hawaii.) In this case there is no need to drop the AP logotype.

When editors rewrite wire stories, they omit the logotype but insert early in each story a phrase of acknowledgment, such as "United Press International reported." This phrase informs the reader that the facts came from UPI but they now have a different emphasis.

Some stories are *undated,* without a dateline. Usually they pull together information from several different areas, so that the story has no particular place as its focus:

By United Press International
Fighting broke out in four places in the Middle
East today, apparently for four different reasons . . .

Occasionally, the dateline of a story will change. If a major unexpected event occurs in Lynn, Massachusetts, the first news may be filed from Boston. An hour or so later reporters may have firsthand reports in Lynn and can dateline stories from there. The wire service will write "Precede Boston" on top of the Lynn stories. This simple instruction tells the editor that this story supplants the one from Boston.

Sometimes a wire service discovers that it has made a serious error, one that would cause embarrassment or possibly produce a libel suit against the service and all papers using the offending story. In that case a *bulletin kill* actually blinks on VDT screens all over the country, advising editors to kill a story or part of one. If the errant story should have happened to get into a few papers, the fact that the service filed a bulletin kill might reduce damages in any libel suit. Introduction of the bulletin kill as evidence in court would indicate that the service made a serious and speedy effort to correct the error.

As mentioned in an earlier chapter, all editors want to watch for ways to localize stories. The wire editor, in particular, should remain alert for ways that the reader can say unconsciously, "Ah, here's a story close to home." Such stories get read much better than ones that seem to have no direct interest to readers. An Oregon newspaper, for example, might handle a wire story this way:

The original:	The revision:
WASHINGTON – (UPI) – Three states have been granted $11 million by the federal government to run experimental drug treatment centers.	WASHINGTON (UPI) – Oregon and two other states have been granted $11 million by the federal government to run experimental drug treatment centers.
The grants went to New Mexico, New Hampshire and Oregon.	The other states are New Mexico and New Hampshire. Each state

Each state will set up several centers in key cities to test "aversion therapy" to addicts who volunteer for the treatment.

will set up several centers in key cities to test "aversion therapy" to addicts who volunteer.

Criticism of wire services

Wire services have improved considerably in the last twenty-five years, as many newspapers have. Stories are more carefully written, with more valuable detail. A wider range of stories is filed. Investigations have revealed scandals in the General Services Administration, the government's watchdog, and a lack of fire safety in nursing homes. The space program is reported in depth, and during election campaigns the positions of even minor candidates are carefully reported. No longer do wire service reporters faithfully copy what a public official says and put it on the wire. They may include a phrase something like, "Three months ago he took the opposite position."

The services also transmit much more about the arts and recreation. Many big city bureaus file a story every Friday on weekend activities available in Big Town, for they know that thousands of people may come to the city to visit museums and art shows and to attend plays, concerts, opera, dance recitals, and sports events. The services' play and concert reviews are often used by an increasing number of papers.

The flaws of the services might well be the flaws of newspapers generally. Newspaper editors often cling to the stereotypes of news, demanding a stream of stories that report conflict, oddities, and speculation. Many of these stories are read today and forgotten tonight. Since many papers want this kind of story, the wire services are bound to give it to them, but gradually newspapers, in the main, want stories with more meat, and the services provide that kind of reporting, too.

Nationalism has been reduced in wire service copy; during the cold war, AP's general manager had to warn the staff to report international conflict fairly, without cheering for one side or the other. Still nationalism does creep in. It is not unusual to read that "Communist tanks were moving into Afghanistan today." Yet any American reporter would feel foolish writing, "Capitalist ships moved into the Persian Gulf." Third World citizens sometimes contend that American reports give the impression that non-Westerners are backward, inept, and corrupt. Those residents often sense that American journalism is tinged with arrogance in reporting about the rest of the world.

Similar reflex reporting can creep into copy when handling stories about countries with different forms of government. Ideologies rarely are simple, and reporters should avoid giving them simple labels, such as pro-American or pro-Chinese. It probably is fair, however, to describe a country's position *on a certain issue* as pro-American. Perhaps it would be more helpful for the reader if reporters abroad did not scurry about with some kind of invisible measuring device to see whether another country's policies are favorable to the United States. A report on *what* happened and *why* it happened

146

would be better. Wire editors would be advised to sniff copy carefully for nationalistic bias and eliminate it.

The wire services some years back used to get frequent complaints of bias from members or clients. Some of those complaints were petty or ridiculous. Wire service staffers say that they get few such complaints now. If a charge of bias is filed, however, AP or UPI will try to investigate the charge. If the complainant appears to be correct, the word goes out to be more careful next time. Usually, it is too late to print a correction.

The wire services, like the better newspapers, also have moved to eliminate any hint of payoffs to reporters. Free lunches, a packet of free football tickets, and free trips once were common. Now the wire services accept free entry to a game or a theater to cover a legitimate event but all other "freebies" are banned.

AP and UPI are not totally to blame when significant information does not reach readers. Wire service writers and editors know that sometimes their best stories remain in the computer, never seeing print. One enterprising AP bureau did a thorough job of finding that almost a quarter of the property in the state was not assessed or was grossly underassessed for tax purposes. Many papers in that state ran the stories but several others did not. And few followed the state information with careful evaluation of tax assessments in their own communities. Fortunately, wire service staffers contend that an increasing number of papers print the best wire service copy. This stimulates the staffers, for they know that millions of people have access to their stories.

Individual wire editors must struggle to give readers full, accurate, and important news within newspaper space limitations. They may accomplish this by careful use of AP and UPI. They may persuade the publisher to buy a supplemental service. They should broaden their own knowledge by spending an hour a day reading other newspapers. This reading will help them test their own news judgment. Editors in the East should read the *New York Times, The Wall Street Journal, Washington Post,* and the *Christian Science Monitor.* In the Midwest they should read at least a couple of Eastern papers, plus Chicago publications and the *St. Louis Post-Dispatch.* In the South they should check the *St. Petersburg Times,* the Miami papers, and the *Atlanta Constitution.* In the West they should examine the *Los Angeles Times,* the *Denver Post,* and the Dallas papers.

In addition, as mentioned before, good telegraph editors need to cultivate these qualities:

1. Knowledge. They keep up in the social sciences, particularly the history of the world during the last fifty years.
2. Wariness. They are cautious in handling fad stories, such as child abuse, juvenile crime, or high school dropouts. They remain skeptical of unsubstantiated reports, stories based on unnamed

Some guidelines

sources and tales of medical "cures." Planted stories, trial balloons, "media events," and calculated leaks should trigger sham-detectors.

3. Awareness of goals. Their picture of needed coverage should encompass tomorrow's world as well as today's.

4. Alertness. They spot the news that will attain maximum readership in their areas.

5. Organization. Stories need careful placement in the news pages, rather than being dropped helter-skelter into any hole that fits. Related stories should be kept together.

6. Balance. They should mix major and minor stories effectively and be able to leaven the basic seriousness of the paper with humorous items.

An editor who successfully does all these things will present the information that the public needs to function as citizens in a democratic society.

10

The subeditors

IN ADDITION TO THE WIRE EDITOR and picture editor, newspapers have four and sometimes five other subeditors. Each supervises a staff that may range from one to fifty or more persons, and each is responsible for a certain part of the paper.

The best known of these subeditors is the city editor, the person who directs reporters covering the city and, often, its environs. A few papers give this person the title of metro editor, because coverage of the metropolitan area is handled at the same desk. A second subeditor, the *state editor,* takes care of a broader area but rarely the whole state because few newspapers sell that widely. *Regional editor* or *country editor* might be a more accurate title than state editor, because such a person supervises the collection of news in the paper's circulation area outside the metropolitan district. State capital reports and most wire service copy usually belong in the wire editor's province, though technically they are part of the state news.

The *sports editor* cuts across area lines, collecting sports news from everywhere. The sports editor supervises writers, edits their copy, and selects news from the special sports wires of Associated Press and United Press International.

Like the sports editor, the *lifestyle editor* collects special news. Long ago the pages included reports on the social events of the elite, and the editor was called the society editor. Coverage was broadened, and the society editor became women's editor. Another broadening, which included appeal to men, and the title became family editor. Now lifestyle is applied, for the pages include the traditional weddings and engagements, plus stories on culture, child care, hobbies, social problems, food preparation, and fashions. Stories might be on such subjects as coping with divorce, handling a hyperactive child, or dealing with the problems of aging parents.

Some papers have a *suburban editor* as the fifth subeditor. Newspapers in larger cities without a suburban editor in name usually have one in fact, an assistant city editor assigned to the job. The task of covering the suburbs has become difficult, for often the area has a hundred little communities, each with its own city government, planning and zoning commission, and school board. Most big city papers include strong sections of suburban news because many people in suburbia are more interested in their own towns than in the center city. Increasingly, people live in suburbs and work there, causing a further decline in city news interest.

The suburban news almost always appears in *zoned editions,* with each edition tailored to readers in a section of the newspaper's circulation area. For example, Edition A will have news from towns north of the city. Edition B will throw out that news and insert stories from towns to the south. This way readers get the news they want, and space is not consumed with stories they don't want. Advertisers also can put their ads in one or two of the zoned editions, knowing that readers in other areas would not bother to come to their stores.

It would be ideal if every person had a year or more of experience on a desk before moving to a subeditor's chair. Preferably, the experience would be as assistant to a particular subeditor. But except on the biggest papers, this kind of background is usually impossible. Often a person will be told one day by the managing editor, "You're going to be the sports editor (or suburban editor or state editor)." The person may have had only sketchy editing experience and no steady experience in writing headlines or in design. No opportunity has existed to learn how to supervise the work of others. How can anyone make the jump gracefully and safely?

A new editor unfamiliar with the job should cram. Pumping other staffers, including predecessors, for information and tips, and even soliciting criticisms, without indicating a lack of confidence, can help the new editor overcome inexperience. Books, pamphlets, and magazine articles can be checked to broaden knowledge.

The subeditor, if possible, should delegate a certain amount of responsibility. By doing everything, an editor probably will do nothing well. Nor will there be time to do any planning or reflecting on how the job will be affected by changing times. Moreover, by delegating, the subeditor possibly becomes available to fill in for the news editor or even managing editor during sickness or vacations. Should the editor be promoted or leave the paper, the subeditor will be prepared to take over.

The subeditor whose staff can work without constant supervision can set aside a certain time to inspect the territory. The demands of the job can pressure subeditors into spending the whole work day bent over a desk, while they, especially the city editor, should be out checking community developments once in a while. Any editor should go occasionally to a meeting on a hot local issue to observe the debates and gain insight into public thinking. Such visits create empathy

The tasks of subeditors

with staffers, because they sense that their editor has become directly concerned with the events they cover.

Editors must direct the operations of reporters and copy editors, and that job is not simple. Some people cannot give orders without being abrasive. Others swing between joviality and gloom. Some editors demand quality one day and forget it the next.

Supervisors ought to be consistent and reasonable with the staff. When they were reporters or copy editors they certainly wanted congenial surroundings, a competent supervisor, and a chance to get an occasional laugh. Subeditors should at least try to fulfill their own requirements.

But an editor should beware of the tangles of doing favors for staffers. A day off given to one person may, because of circumstances, be denied to another. It must be made clear to these people that they couldn't get the holiday because of a scheduling problem, not a personal one. One solution is to give no favors that can't be given to everyone. Yet an editor creates a sense of well-being if occasionally a staffer can go home early or slip out during a quiet period to run a personal errand. When the subeditor is both flexible and impartial, staff morale goes up.

Praise and criticism

No editor should overlook the value of praise. Most journalists are immune to ostentatious flattery—they have seen so much that is phony—but they cherish a casual sentence of praise from a colleague. A simple "Good story, Charley," or "Nice headline, Liz!" will do more to spark professionalism than any scroll of merit.

Some papers, as mentioned earlier, put out a little sheet that gives credit for work well done. Others post good examples. Some subtle subeditors might be able to wangle a personal note from the publisher or editor-in-chief to commend the staffer. Discretion here is essential; the minute that an editor hands out laurels insincerely, the whole staff discounts any approval.

One of the best ways subeditors can improve morale is to get pay increases for deserving staff members. When requested raises come through, they can tell staffers quietly, "Your good work of the last several months means an extra thirty dollars a week from now on." Staffers so rewarded will be pleasantly surprised and grateful for a superior who works for the staff as well as the publisher.

But what happens when a staffer fails to measure up? In the old days, the editor probably would bellow, "You're fired!" Such abrupt dismissal is rare today because editors realize that it is cruel and that it often loses a potentially good employee. Furthermore, Newspaper Guild contracts bar dismissal without specific cause.

Instead of muttering deprecations about an inadequate staffer, an editor should aim to teach. A few minutes spent every day helping the new staffer correct shortcomings and speaking favorably about strong points will improve both the newcomer's morale and usefulness to the paper. Sometimes the editor assigns another person to go over a novice reporter's copy, sentence by sentence, to show how it can be improved. If all efforts fail in getting improvement, it would be better for the newspaper and the employees if the inadequate employees were urged to look elsewhere for work. Staffers who are not fired outright can more easily find another job that they may handle well. Any such conversation with a staffer, of course, should be private. The wise editor, under these circumstances, refrains from suggesting that a person get into another line of work. Many successful journalists, at one time or another, have had such advice and, fortunately, not taken it. But newspeople who recognize they have no journalistic talent should quit. They would be only tolerated on any newspaper and would be better off in another field.

Promising reporters and copy editors should be encouraged to attend the increasing number of workshops and study sessions being held throughout the country. They should be urged, also, to take courses at local colleges or universities. Some newspapers pay the tuitions if the person completes them satisfactorily. The courses need not be on journalism; almost any knowledge can be valuable to a journalist.

Sometimes even a good reporter or copy editor hits a slump, forcing an analysis of the problem in a talk with an editor. Perhaps some personal problem is causing worry, or the job itself has become dull. Talking it out may be just what the staffer needs to regain former enthusiasm and skill. Other times the subeditor can suggest or even provide solutions to the problem. For example, a person who has worked on the desk for a couple of years and basically likes the work may be getting a little tired of sitting all day. Couldn't a special reporting assignment be made once in a while for a change of pace?

Directing news collection

A subeditor soon discovers that the efficiency and morale of the staff depend partly on the flow of work. Everyone around a newsroom knows that news comes in spurts. News may be heavy for a week or more, and then for a few days nothing seems to happen. Some of these quiet periods can be predicted. Summer is the calmest season. Schools and legislatures are out of session, and most community action slacks off as workers prepare for vacations. The Christmas season repeats this lull in those civic affairs that produce most of the nonspectacular news.

In some places local news is heavy a couple of days a week and light on others. The city council may meet Mondays and the school board Tuesdays. Both normally provide several stories. The county board of supervisors, another good news source, also may meet on a Tuesday. If the city planning commission meets Monday night, and the zoning board Tuesday, then local government news may well pile up the first of the week. Unless the subeditor plans for peaks and slumps, many Thursday, Friday, and Saturday pages will be drab and insignificant — not worth reading — and the staff will suffer from being alternately swamped and idled.

During the dull periods the staff should be scratching for feature stories or digging for important information below the surface of events. If it is obvious that the city council will make news about building codes early one week, why not interview the city engineer the week before on new building techniques or talk to a leading architect on ideas for the city of the future? On the other hand, if the council makes a surprising or especially significant decision on Monday, the rest of the week provides time to follow up on the reasons for the decision and its implications.

The ability to create story ideas is one of an editor's greatest assets. The subeditor must develop this skill if the job requires more than a person who gives routine assignments, edits copy, writes headlines, lays out pages, and pats a reporter's back once in a while. An editor may do the routine well, but first-rate status will not come without imagination. And since imagination is always in short supply, an editor should encourage it among colleagues. The willingness to stimulate story ideas and the play of stories are characteristics that develop a spirited staff. People get excited on a newspaper where the editors listen to new ideas and where they are willing to experiment and reward enterprise. Every subeditor should have a drawer, box, or basket available for staffers' suggestions. But if suggestions are rejected the contributor ought to know why. An editor who repeatedly ignores ideas quickly freezes staff initiative. Every suggestion needs acknowledgment and at least a word of thanks.

The city editor

Journalists generally concede that the city editor's job is the most difficult of all the subeditor positions. The person with this task has to supervise the biggest staff of reporters, and fit the talents of these reporters to dozens of jobs. Throughout the workday alterations, suggestions, and specific directions must be given. The city editor gives assignments to reporters and photographers, sees that the copy is edited properly, and checks the fit of local copy to the available space.

On smaller papers the job may seem easier but often it is not. While the city editor on a small paper may have only a few reporters to supervise, the task also requires reading all their copy, writing all the headlines, and sometimes producing a few stories on the side. The city editor even must dart into the composing room occasionally to oversee makeup. Since many reporters on small papers are inexperienced, the city editor must try to make up for their deficiencies with editing and training. This training, because of a lack of time, often must consist of an over-the-shoulder comment from time to time or some brief instructions on how to get the information for a certain story.

City editors on medium-sized papers will have an assistant or two. One assistant may handle the assignment chore, with the city editor suggesting a special story, and another may edit local pictures. The editor and assistants all will edit some local copy and will mark headline size and story length before sending the copy to the universal desk. The city editor probably will lay out local news pages.

On the biggest papers the city editor has a half dozen aides, each with a specific job. The city editor checks the work of others, adding or subtracting copy and accepting or rejecting proposals.

This supervisory role gives the city editor the flexibility needed to handle the day's little or big emergencies. The gifted city editor manages to keep most emergencies in the newsroom from becoming severe. Adequate preparation allows the staff to move swiftly in any crisis. Preparation means anticipating major stories and having reporters and editors ready to handle all facets of the events. It also means the ability to alter plans swiftly when an unexpected event occurs.

Seeing beyond now

Preparedness is vital to the smooth operation of a city desk. For a coming election the inept editor fails to prepare for stories that anyone would expect to happen. The well-organized editor plans who will write the story or stories on state legislative races and who will handle city council contests. Someone is chosen to funnel returns from the central counting area to the paper, or someone may even have to plan collection of returns by the paper itself. This work may mean arranging for extra telephones or special lines. Preparation means the difference between a confused scramble to write stories and the provision of thorough, balanced coverage.

Though an election obviously needs planning if it is to be covered adequately, the demands of some events are more subtle. As an illustration, a newspaper in a city surrounded by prime farmland may become concerned by urban sprawl creeping over those rich and productive fields. The editors may worry about lower food production and the cost of new streets, sewer lines, and public transportation. Editors would need a careful but flexible plan if prospective stories on the subject were to be covered. The farm writer might discover how many acres have been taken out of agriculture in the last ten years. The county government reporter might examine zoning laws and how they have been enforced. Land use experts, developers, and farmers could be interviewed. Stories on the broad subject might run from time to time over a year. Every couple of months the paper might print a story summarizing in a few hundred words what had been discovered.

Almost no newspaper, of course, has the staff, the facilities, or the need to plan for a campaign that would take the energies of half a dozen staffers for six months. But every paper should look down the calendar a few months or even years to make sure that it does not muff a good story. For example, a school board issue may be brewing over whether to build a new school, and the town seems headed for a full-fledged dispute. The education writer should be on top of it, but some help may be required. The city hall reporter might note how the issue spills into city government; a general assignment reporter may visit a neighboring city to see how that town resolved a similar dispute. In another example, a prominent politician may be getting up in

154

years and just might announce his or her retirement an hour before deadline. Good planning would mean that when the announcement comes, stories are almost ready on that person's political life and the jostling by a dozen who will battle to take over the job. A sidebar may be ready on the politician's humble beginnings. These stories could be produced swiftly because reporters could flip through clippings they keep in their desks, check other information in the newspaper's library, and recall facts or anecdotes from their own memories. Editors could suggest calling people who have known the official for years.

Even when emergencies force city editors to make quick decisions, they should pause and ponder: "Are we getting the whole story? Are we missing anything? Are we overplaying? Have we got the right pictures? What's the best layout for all these stories? What must we cut or drop in order to print this hot news?"

To do the job properly, the city editor must be able to grasp instantly the value of news, coach the young reporters, juggle the staff to get the best coverage, and inspire respect, if not admiration.

The press of time

The city editor soon finds that the clock becomes the main obstacle to good coverage. How much time to deadline is the paramount question as to whether there is time to print any more than the bare facts of a story and get a picture or two to illustrate it.

To keep from being unduly harassed by the clock, the city editor strives to develop top efficiency. Aides are chosen who can move swiftly to solve the problems that develop. Editors learn the strengths and weaknesses of reporters and give the story needing the swiftest work to the fastest writer. City editors avoid answering the telephone, so they won't get tied up listening to some complaint that a copy aide or clerk could handle. They eliminate inefficient habits. Since memos, notes, and other newspapers usually surround city editors, they are tempted to set some aside to read later. An excellent city editor once remarked that no one should handle the same piece of paper twice. "Read it and decide what to do with it," was his motto. His desk was never a bottleneck for copy, memos, or letters. Now, of course, one task is to keep the computer from being jammed with outmoded stories.

The best city editors today keep tabs on more than the city room. In addition to getting around the city themselves, they read up on its history so they can guide their staffs to write stories that set the social and economic problems of the community in historical context. Tomorrow's newspapers will almost certainly require such emphasis. They will report such things as the changing political power base, local developments in mental health, the deep and often hidden frictions behind violence, or a real critique of the local educational system.

Gone are the days when reporters believed that news consisted of the acts of God and politicians. Stories of crimes, accidents, and fires are essential. A few speculative stories still are important, but they have been bypassed for stories that require digging and thorough interviewing to help the reader understand the world at least a little better.

The work of a state or regional editor often has a direct bearing on a paper's circulation. Many city dwellers will subscribe to a monopoly paper even if its city news coverage is poor. There is no other place to get local news. But often territory in rural or suburban areas can be contested by papers from other nearby cities. For example, eastern Iowa counties at one time were circulation battlegrounds for the *Des Moines Register* and *Chicago Tribune* as well as papers of such smaller cities as Davenport, Dubuque, and Cedar Rapids. The *Register* state desk has the same kind of circulation tussle with Omaha and Council Bluffs to the west. If a state editor slights the news from the outlying areas, readers there will switch to another paper or stop reading a newspaper.

The state editor's chief problem is that most of the staff never is in the newsroom. Communication with reporters is handled by telephone, Teletype, mail, and now the VDT. Frequently reporters work only part-time for a little extra money and status. Though they usually have serious journalistic limitations, no one else is available who can do the job as well.

Stringers and correspondents

A sizable number of papers have discovered that most part-time rural correspondents are not up to modern coverage. These stringers often write poorly, miss good stories under their noses, and find it almost impossible to meet deadlines. As an alternative, papers have tried to find professionals who are willing to work the smaller towns in bureaus. These are persons who not only can report well but also have the ability to cover the events of a good-sized region, perhaps a whole county. They can drive over the territory every few days, and, because they get to know the news sources, can do much spot checking by telephone. Some of these correspondents have Teletypes or VDTs in their homes or some little niche that serves as an office so they can communicate directly with the state desk. The state editor has less frustration keeping tabs on one efficient remote reporter than on half a dozen semicompetent stringers.

Some papers use staffers from smaller papers as stringers. A few regular staffers in the home office then provide all special coverage. These full-timers may tour their area a few days a week to get special feature stories and pictures that most stringers wouldn't be able to handle. The staffers then return to the home office, write their stories, and spend the rest of the work week on the desk. Each paper uses a system tailored to meet the particular paper's needs for covering a certain region.

Professionals willing to be correspondents in smaller communities usually are beginning their careers. The state editor should coach these beginners to write and report better. Editors can send them notes about their work and, in particular, urge them to read their copy in print to see how it has been edited.

Some state editors prefer to send beginners into the field after some specific training. They encourage the managing editor to keep the neophyte in the city for at least a month to work under the discipline of the city desk and to learn to cover events without much direction.

For example, the beginner should tag around with the courthouse reporter for at least a couple of days, soaking up information on the courts and county government. Some assignments could require a little coverage of business, police, labor unions, and city government with its main adjuncts: planning, zoning, sewage disposal, parks, revenue, and traffic.

While most such staff correspondents are young, occasionally a highly qualified older person wants to live in a little town. When a state editor has such a pearl, someone happy in one place and good at the job, everything reasonable should be done to meet the person's needs. A good salary, frequent bylines, and a note of praise once or twice a year from the editor-in-chief or the publisher are the least a good career correspondent deserves.

In the main, reporters work in the field for six months or a year and are ready to move. Sometimes there is an agreement that the person from the far reaches of the circulation district will get the first opening on the city staff. Such promises should not be made casually. A young person told that five or six months' hard work in Swampsville will earn a place on the city staff will, as the time drifts on to a year, feel betrayed. If this person becomes bitter and quits, suddenly the editor loses not only good coverage but a valuable staffer as well. Editors should be honest about future opportunities and keep correspondents informed of any changes in their status.

Of course not all correspondents are in the boondocks. Newspapers in major cities have bureaus in other metropolitan areas, and reporters there can live the city life. Sometimes their lives are easier than the city reporter's because they may have an easier commute.

The *Los Angeles Times,* for one, has staffs in Orange County, south of Los Angeles, and San Diego, as well as reporters in the sizable cities east and northeast of the city.

Planning state coverage

How thorough should the state coverage be? Obviously, if the state editor covers a sizable area with any kind of depth, many pages will be filled. If only the most important news is skimmed, circulation may dip. The solution is to set guidelines on coverage. They should be worked out in conference with the publisher, managing editor, city editor, and other subeditors. The circulation manager should be brought in, too, of course, to get the word on the law of diminishing returns. A town of a thousand with only twenty-two subscribers will not merit much coverage unless the circulation manager believes its circulation can be increased.

Bigger papers usually restrict news from outlying areas. They may have more than a hundred fairly substantial communities in their circulation area; they can't possibly cover each in detail. Smaller papers, of course, will provide quite thorough reports of the few villages under their circulation umbrella, and some papers even will print columns of personal items mailed in by a stringer. The trend, however, is to reduce trivia.

Once policy has been set on breadth and depth of coverage, the state editor has to struggle with personnel. Sometimes there is no alternative to stringers and possibly a few full-timers. Some papers send those staffers a pamphlet or news sheet that explains how to write news and features. These have to be short if the stringers are to read them, and even then the messages don't always get through.

A pamphlet to guide the stringer should be specific:

We do *not* want accident stories unless someone is killed or seriously hurt or unless there is an unusual angle.

We do *not* want more than three short paragraphs on weddings, unless the mayor is getting married.

We *do* want stories of some breadth, like the decline in school enrollment in your county or the plan to clean up Inky Stinky Creek.

We *do* want stories on politics, government, education, and social change.

We *do* want feature stories on funny or peculiar happenings.

The pamphlet can be supplemented by a monthly sheet that praises good work, naming the author, and that criticizes bad work anonymously. This sheet should be written entertainingly and without malice. It should educate, not persecute. Furthermore, if someone does a first-rate job on a difficult task, the state editor should take a few minutes to dash off a personal note. If the work is not so good, the editor should avoid fulminating. The writer must be called, asked to collect more information, and then told to rewrite the story. If state editors went into a frenzy every time they saw a miserable piece of copy, they would soon be palsied.

The sports editor

The sports editor has one advantage over the other subeditors: Almost all sports news is expected. The editor knows at the start of the workday that several games or sports events are scheduled, so plans for the section can be seriously altered only by such things as the cancellation of an event, the death of a famous athlete, the highly unexpected outcome of a contest, or the setting of some record.

To offset this advantage the sports editor does have some special problems. Because many people find sports and sports stars dramatic and spectacular, sports copy tends to be overly dramatic.

The sports editor has to guard against absurdly melodramatic stories. It must be kept in mind that victory for the home team really is not the greatest of glories, and defeat is not the greatest of tragedies. The pages should not treat athletes as super people, either, for sometimes off the field they are far from heroic. Fortunately, sportswriting has become far more objective and analytical than it was a generation ago.

Sportswriters, often weak in grammar and strong on clichés, need a watchful editor. Sometimes a writer attempts to be different and brings forth what amounts to an essay on a game. While this may be a fine piece of writing, too often the writer gets so wrapped up in unaccustomed rhetoric that the score is omitted. Hyperbole, a characteristic of sportswriting, should never replace accuracy. For years, sportswriters covering major baseball teams in spring training exaggerated the facts so greatly that a substantial number of fans became cynical. Today, these early reports are more restrained. A story from a Florida training camp may say, "The White Sox finished fourth last year, and if there is any change this season it will be for the worse."

Editors also must cool copy that heralds a forthcoming contest as the "Game of the Decade." If the game is disappointing, the misled fans will feel doubly cheated. A prediction of the "Game of the Century" is even more dangerous, since there have been several of these already in the twentieth century. Super Bowl hype has been so outrageous that even some eager sports fans almost gag.

Sports publicists, like politicians, constantly push reporters and editors to promote their pet topics. Editors have to be sure they are covering, not promoting, a sport. Long ago, sports pages ran all kinds of stories on professional wrestling, even though it was generally known that most matches were rigged. Finally, a number of editors, deciding not to promote fraud, quit printing stories and pictures about pro wrestlers. The rapid decline of the "sport" suggested that the wrestling promoters depended on free advertising disguised as news.

Minor league baseball is another sport where almost tearful requests for promotion must be resisted. In dozens of cities around the country, sports editors have been asked to boost the hometown team. If they decline, team supporters scorn them as disloyal. Yet most of the teams are owned by private businesses, the major league clubs. By excessive coverage the newspaper actually subsidizes private business. Such baseball teams often get more stories than any other group in town. No other public performance—movie, play, concert, or opera—receives the kind of coverage that is given a minor league team that may draw only a few hundred fans a night.

Sports editors today try to trim coverage of professional and top amateur athletes to make room for unorganized sports. More and more Americans are enjoying sport for its own sake. They sail, ski, surf, hike, camp, fly, shoot, and skin-dive. Because most of these sports, though vigorous, are not competitive, the modern sports editor seeks fresh ways to cover them. Usually this is done solely with feature stories and pictures.

The good editor always has to be attentive to pictures, not only

159

because photography plays an important part in sports, but because today's readers spend more time watching sports on TV, which means that only exceptional pictures are likely to capture their interest. Consistently good photographs are hard to find anywhere, and sports editors usually have the highest proportion of cliché shots. This means an abundance of photos showing someone sliding into second base or taking a basketball jump shot. Even the most attentive sports fan is going to ignore them.

The sports editor must demand truly extraordinary pictures, illustrating athletic grace, skill, and intensity. Any editor who demands good pictures, of course, must meet the demands of a good photographer—adequate time, excellent equipment, plenty of film, and the promise of seeing the best pictures in print.

Other subediting

In addition to the four or five subeditors of the typical newspaper are several workers who fall into a middle-range category under the managing editor. Some large papers have a *foreign editor* who directs, at a sophisticated level, a staff of foreign correspondents. Many papers have a *Sunday editor* in charge of the whole Sunday edition with its magazine and special pages or sections devoted to finance, real estate, books, entertainment, travel, hobbies, and television. This editor has a week-long job assembling articles, reviews, and photographs from regular staffers as well as special assistants and part-time writers. Some papers have editors who only handle features.

A few editors are really specialized reporters. They cover such areas as the arts, education, religion, business, or labor. The title editor is perhaps justified for reasons other than status or newspaper promotion, because such a person has more independence than the ordinary writer on general assignment. Science editors or music critics usually direct no staffs. They give themselves assignments. Some other editor, probably the city or features editor, is technically the boss, but one who usually defers to the specialized editor-writer's expert assessment of the news.

For many decades papers have divided editing responsibilities into subediting areas such as city desk and state desk, but better ways can still be found. For example, the *Des Moines Tribune,* before it was discontinued, established an effective subeditorship combining the jobs of city and state editor. This person came in very early every morning, surveyed the statewide news situation, and decided on the staff coverage for points outside the metropolitan area. Writers and photographers could be dispatched a hundred or more miles away, sometimes by plane.

For a time, the *Wilmington* (Delaware) *News-Journal* had a metropolitan desk responsible for coverage of its whole circulation area, which included the entire state and parts of four other states. The editor at the time said that social and economic problems crossed county and state lines, so there was no reason to divide news coverage between city and state desks. A later editor, however, decided that the new system put too much of a burden on one desk and switched back to state and metro desks.

The Wilmington experience should be noted by all newspapers as they adjust to changing conditions and changing readership. No one should assume that the organization chart should last forever. State or universal desks, if no longer useful, should be discarded. The growth of suburbs, the shift in public interest, and the increasing specialization of news all force the alert newspaper to examine its operations to see if there is a better way to get the news to its readers.

11

Picture editing: The art show

SOME JOURNALISTS DISPARAGE the use of pictures. "Television runs pictures all day," they say. "We see pictures of games, news conferences, and congressional hearings. How can print cope with that kind of competition?"

In many ways, of course, it can't. Yet some observers have noted that action photographs differ from still photos as the printed word differs from the spoken. The differences are subtle, but research shows that readers still look at printed pictures and that their eyes turn first to a picture as they look at a new page.

Television competition cannot be ignored, however. The public no longer accepts routine newspaper pictures, for much of what they see by the hour on TV is routine. Print must produce a stream of unusual, dramatic, clear, and informative pictures to attract more than a casual glance.

Good photos do not come easily. They must be taken by skilled individuals, using first-rate equipment. Photographers must have time to explore ways of getting outstanding pictures. Encouragement helps, as it does in any craft.

Photographers also need to work with editors, reporters, and artists to grasp how words and pictures blend to convey news. They must sense what makes news, for they are *news* photographers, not just photographers. Someone has said that a good photojournalist is an "informed talent," understanding the fundamentals of politics to photograph political figures, for example, or corporate world intricacies when photographing a tense stockholders' meeting.

The person in charge of photography, not surprisingly, is called the *chief photographer.* Picture editors decide which pictures to use and how they will appear in the paper. Only bigger papers have full-time picture editors. Subeditors on smaller papers all dabble with picture editing, often hastily and with little skill. These staff limitations too often mean that picture editing is treated carelessly or casually. Pictures are not selected thoughtfully, and photographers receive only sketchy direction about the purpose of the picture and its possible use. Pictures on such papers tend to be used as typographical devices to relieve the monotony of a page of print.

Even on papers where there is no picture editor, staffers can learn to reject ordinary pictures, to crop good ones to make them better, and to push photographers to do more than line up a few people and snap the shutter. After some practice and study, almost anyone with a good news sense can sort through a dozen pictures to choose the best two or three, rejecting the routine shots and picking those with originality. The staffer can learn to say, "Not one of these pictures is much good." In such cases photographers must be encouraged to seek different angles, to avoid contrivances like phony props, and to wait until a good picture is possible.

The full-time picture editor examines all available pictures for news pages and sometimes those for features and sports. Many photos arrive from Associated Press or United Press International. The photo editor seldom is a photographer, a fact that occasionally causes friction between photographers and subeditors. Photographers charge that "word people" have little appreciation of pictures and subeditors insist that photographers are so dazzled by their work that they see little need for words. Editors should realize that few photographers—and few writers—can take a detached view of their work.

Good photo chiefs and editors try to get each side to understand the other's needs. In the end, of course, the photo editor must decide which pictures get into the paper and in what form. Photo editors may have their decisions overruled by a higher editor from time to time but in general they have the final word.

All staffers working with pictures should spend some time conferring with city, state, business, sports, and feature editors to discover how photographs may help meet their needs.

At some newspapers, picture editors are little more than technicians and a liaison between other editors and photographers. They pass on assignments, decide a certain amount of policy, select, crop, and size pictures. This may lead to some organizational efficiency, and it is better than having no photo editor, but such a system usually produces uncreative photographs.

Harold Buell, director of photography for the Associated Press, insists that a good photo editor "must have a voice" in how the picture is used if photographers are inspired to do their best work. He means that the photo editor must be able to advise news editors to use one picture, instead of another, to crop in a certain way, and to make the picture five columns, perhaps, rather than three. Obviously, such an editor should be able to explain why the pictures need the recommended treatment. Otherwise, Buell says, the photo editor merely runs errands, handling pictures the way a news editor ordered.

A picture editor should "think pictures," always trying to find how a photograph may bolster a story. Cooperation with the photo chief is essential, for photographers do not take kindly to rejection of what they consider prize-winning pictures. The photo chief, in turn, must guide the staff with sensitivity, noting who needs special direction and who needs no help in getting outstanding pictures.

Tribune's methods

The *Chicago Tribune,* with a photo staff of fifty, has one of the nation's largest picture operations. It uses up to a hundred pictures a day in its three editions and many more on Sunday. The paper buys the latest equipment and even flies photographers in a *Tribune* plane to cover major events. Photographers are encouraged to take the time needed to get quality pictures.

Assignments take into account the special skills of each photographer. A few years ago a *Tribune* photographer, who had been raised on a farm, got assignments to cover all livestock shows and she always came back with dandies. Another, known for his patience, was sent to cover a Ku Klux Klan rally in Indiana. He took no pictures for several hours, moving through the crowd, chatting with attenders, getting them relaxed about his presence. Klan members hardly noticed when he pulled out his camera and started shooting. The results provided insight into the organization.

The chief photographer, William Kelly, aims to motivate the staff, praising good work and quietly criticizing the not-so-good. When necessary, he tells photographers exactly what he wants, but also encourages them to be innovative when they are ready to shoot.

Sports coverage requires the services of several photographers with special sports photography talent. Chicago has two major-league baseball teams, hockey, football, and basketball teams, plus university teams in the region. With wide interest in sports, mediocre pictures simply won't do.

Most pictures are funneled to a photo editor. William Parker, the *Tribune*'s photo editor, takes about ten of the best photos into a daily conference with top editors. He recommends two or three for page one and others for certain inside pages. Editors argue a little over his choices and sometimes reject his advice or propose minor alterations. This process is repeated for every edition, with some "old" pictures being replaced by new ones.

The *Tribune* crops pictures carefully to get rid of nonessentials and to provide more visual impact. A few pictures are retouched slightly by an artist, perhaps outlining a person's head or removing some distracting object. Nothing is done to distort the picture or to make the retouching obvious. Pictures usually are "made big," but the staff considers oversizing as bad as making them too small.

In nearly all cases the *Tribune* tries to get people in pictures because news usually concerns people. Photos omit people only when it would be ridiculous to put them in. A picture of a chemical plant whose fumes have killed trees, for example, probably would not include people.

Few newspapers can afford the *Tribune*'s operation. Medium-sized newspapers have fewer people working in the entire newsroom than the *Tribune* has in photo. Any paper, however, can borrow from the best. So even the small paper with one photographer can buy good equipment and lots of film and can give that person time enough to get more than the ordinary shot. The photographer can be sent to a short course at company expense. Pictures can be chosen with care, cropped with discretion, and made big enough so the reader does not have to squint.

The art of quality

Good picture editing starts with high-quality photos, which means technical excellence of the negative and superior visualization of the content. Every paper has to print some mediocre pictures and a few poor ones. A family brings in a tinted photograph on soft mat paper to go with an obituary or a reporter persuades the parents of an injured child to let the paper print a badly lighted snapshot of the victim. Such pictures fall short of photographic excellence in several respects, yet they will be published, perhaps even in large sizes. Sometimes the photo lab can make them better than the original by using special equipment. Most pictures, however, lose quality by going through the printing process. Newsprint is poor paper for photographic reproduction.

Newspaper photographs usually should be big and in sharp focus. They are printed in large sizes—typically 8 by 10 inches—on glossy paper. They are well lighted and show contrast between light and dark grays. The uniform grays of a flat black-and-white photo make it drab; good definition of tones is essential.

The routine photograph is often shot straight on at eye height. For a fresh approach, the photographer may crouch for a low angle—or go up a ladder for a high one—or walk around somewhere to the side to get an unusual viewpoint. "Photoletters," a booklet published by the newsphoto committee of the Associated Press Managing Editors Association, illustrates this point with the contrast of two pictures on a stock theme: one is the usual shot of a man giving a plaque to another, and the other, with a rather low angle, shows the winner grinning up at his framed certificate, which has been hoisted up to his shoulder. The first shot would be dreadful, the other at least passable.

When a president was on the White House lawn signing a bill for more parks, a photographer climbed a tree and shot the scene through the leaves. Both of these examples involve *record pictures,* and the photographers had to figure out ways to escape the monotony of the routine record shot.

News photographers sometimes strive for artistic patterns in their pictures. These may be rows of bleachers or bottles, lines of fence posts or windows. Highly patterned backgrounds that detract from the focal point should be avoided. Yet the best photo artist, seeking aesthetic results, sometimes violates tradition. Fuzziness, at least of some parts of a photo, may create a mood. Since stopping the action can mean a dull sports picture, there may be more drama in the blur

165

of a moving arm or leg, and racing cars with lines of motion may at once seem to whiz and be beautiful. It is difficult to do these well. If a blur picture is less than outstanding, it is better to use a conventional shot.

Besides a strong center of interest and a different camera angle, good photographers try for appropriate special effects. For example, the illusion of depth comes from using an angle that puts a pertinent subject in the foreground—shooting down a seminar table over the shoulder of a teacher, for example, or including a firefighter with hose at the edge of the picture of a building fire. This effort is similar to *framing,* another useful approach. Most commonly the frame is produced with the picture.

Good news pictures should tell a story and show action. A mug shot of a senator, for example, shows no action and tells readers only what the senator looks like. Action obviously is limited in most pictures; few news pictures show someone felling a tree or knocking down a circus tent. Most photographed action is more subdued: A secretary of state leaning forward to hear a question; a corporate trader looking warily at two investors. How dull they would look if they merely sat, smiling at the camera.

Almost all editors realize that news photos should include people. A picture of a lake at dawn may show great beauty, but interest soars if it includes a man gliding across the water in a canoe. Even the implication of life helps; a picture of a mountainside cabin with smoke rising from the chimney gives some human attachment. A few pictures, without people, will make the grade, however. Who could resist lingering over Ansel Adams' pictures, which rarely include people?

Great portrait photographers reveal character in their pictures. Portrait painters encourage us to spend a minute or two over their work, searching for insight into another human face. Meticulous news photographers sometimes can come close to such artistry.

As in the theater, props are valuable to the news photographer. A picture of a woman talking on the telephone is hackneyed, but probably better than a fast shot of her looking at the camera. Good photographers often wait until their subjects unconsciously grasp some prop, like a football, a trophy, or a paperweight before taking the best shot. Props let the subject relax and appear natural.

Fakery with props must be forbidden. One photographer dropped candy into a sousaphone and got a great shot of a little boy crawling into the horn. It was a fraud, however, for the child never would have crawled there without a rigged inducement. Other contrivances like a pointer, a funny hat, or the old hula hoop get labeled fake in most readers' minds.

Props already in use by the photographic subjects, however, can help produce excellent pictures. The feature shot of a little girl trying on hats before a mirror, for example, or the picture of an old man trudging home from the river carrying one fish can have great impact. The devices are not really props, and so their use looks natural.

The photographer, to turn out quality work, avoids gimmickry

166

and corn, such as a politician wearing a cowboy outfit or drinking milk from a huge bowl. The routine shot of a routine action, such as the signing of a bill, should be forsaken. So should clichés like handshaking (sometimes called "grin and grab") award presentations, ribbon cuttings, and gavel passings. Worst of all is the lineup, where three or four persons face the camera. The picture editor must take a pledge never to give assignments that result in corn, routine pictures, or clichés.

A picture editor learns to evaluate photographs as a news editor learns to judge stories, by experience and by observing how other journalists operate. Some pictures are obviously great, others blatantly dull. But the majority of pictures are in between, and only a fraction of them can be used. Those chosen will depend on the day's needs and the editor's personal tastes.

Judging pictures

Use of the artistic photograph has slowly grown in American newspapers. Some papers run color pictures of great art or even commendable painting by local artists. Surely pictures of boats resting at twilight in a marina or a cornfield covered in haze stop most readers. The *Washington Post* once ran a slender picture atop page one showing the wild ponies on Chincoteague Island galloping across the sand. The animals' rust color contrasted beautifully with the yellow sand and the distant blue water.

By reading newspaper studies, picture editors can determine what subjects interest readers. However, just as newspapers cannot finally be edited by polls, pictures cannot be selected by surveys. Ultimately, picture editors have to understand intuitively what will interest readers. What will interest editors probably will interest subscribers. If they exclaim, "Wow!" about a photo, it probably means that readers too will feel its impact. So photo editors must learn to understand themselves. Each editor will naturally have some enthusiasms, but they should not become hobby horses. Or an editor may temper dislike of a certain type of picture because experience has shown that readers react favorably to it. Editors give readers "what they want" if in good conscience they can, but they usually select what their judgment says is the best photographic journalism.

The tension between what readers want and what they should have suggests problems in ethics that the picture editor also confronts in making selections. Some readers may want the macabre or near-pornographic photo, yet may criticize the paper that uses photographs in bad taste. The picture editor must sometimes walk the hazy, wiggling line between the acceptable and unacceptable.

Ethics of illustration

Until the Vietnam War, pictures of bodies were generally forbidden and grisly shots were used sparingly. During the "first televised war," however, network news ran color pictures of slaughter and gore nearly every day. Since then newspapers, while cautious about bloody scenes, have been more willing to print pictures of brutality.

167

Some readers were angry a few years ago when pictures were printed of a woman and child falling from a Boston building. Firefighters had worked close to a fire escape and were about to take people down a ladder to safety. Seconds before the rescue, the fire escape collapsed. Stanley Forman, a *Boston Herald-American* photographer, took pictures of the falling people. The woman was killed and the child was hurt. The pictures, distributed by Associated Press, were used widely. Some readers were horrified and said so. Editors rechecked their judgment, decided it was a close decision but that they probably were correct in running such a dramatic picture. Harold Buell, AP's photo editor, said, "You're cursed if you do, and cursed for manipulating the news if you don't."

Nora Ephron, a media critic, noted that no one would have protested if the woman had survived. She maintained the pictures "deserved to be published because they are great pictures, breathtaking pictures, of something that happened. That they disturb readers is exactly as it should be. That's why photojournalism is often more powerful than written journalism."[1]

Television also has made the public more willing to accept other gruesome scenes. Reports of starvation in East Africa in 1985 included pictures of thousands of people, many of them babies, only days from death. These pictures so shocked the world that major relief efforts were started almost overnight by public and private groups.

Electronic camera

The electronic revolution has struck photography, too. The electronic camera takes pictures without film, merely recording light digitally in a computer within the camera. The photographer can transmit the digits over a telephone line to a newsroom computer, which produces a conventional picture. A photographer fifty miles from home could get pictures to the newspaper plant in several minutes. The advantages of such cameras are so obvious that editors are rushing to find how they can buy and use the new devices. As in most technical developments, problems still exist and manufacturers eagerly strive to make their products free of trouble.

Sources of photos

American newspapers get more of their photos from the wire services than any other source. Both AP and UPI send streams of pictures, usually of good quality, to their newspaper customers.

News pictures can be obtained also from more than two dozen picture agencies. Anyone wanting an AP picture, for example, can buy it from Wide World Photo Service. Religious News Service provides photos for the hundreds of religious publications in the nation.

---

1. Nora Ephron, *Scribble, Scribble: Notes on the Media* (New York: Alfred A. Knopf, 1978), 62.

Local sources

A close competitor of agency pictures, at least on the bigger papers, is the local photographic staff. Syndicated photographs cost less than ones made by the paper, but of course they can't include local events. With a single ambitious photographer and a miniature darkroom, a paper can have at least a few good local pictures for every issue.

Some newspapers use reporters as photographers, but the idea of the photo-reporter has never really caught on. A major reason is that many editors contend that a person can't report *and* photograph well. Many reporters and photographers will agree. Yet some picture editors feel that a reporter who is out on a story might as well have a camera along and shoot some pictures. A few small newspapers give their reporters "idiot cameras"—those with automatic focus—and let them take photographs as they cover their beats. Pictures taken by reporters may be adequate, but they rarely are a substitute for pictures taken by a full-fledged photographer using first-rate equipment. Papers seeking quality pictures and reporting will use specialists for each field.

Free-lance photographers place some pictures with newspapers, especially their magazine sections. Some of the most famous news photographs have been taken by amateurs who just happened to be on the spot. Though there would be headaches of organization, newspapers might buy more pictures from free-lancers and amateurs.

Some other local pictures are provided by news sources. Families may supply photographs for obituaries. Brides bring in their pictures for wedding announcements. Sometimes a reporter wangles a portrait from the family of a victim or a suspect. Some news subjects come into the paper's studio for a picture. While there is the ever-present danger of stilted photography, this plan works well for such things as awards and some feature pictures.

Public relations sources provide many more newspaper pictures than readers realize or most editors admit. Most of those glamour pictures come from press agents of screen and television celebrities. Photographs in the family section that feature new fashions, modern interiors, and luscious foods are usually from publicity sources. Local companies provide varied pictures for the business pages. And, as publicity workshops never tire of pointing out, the good photograph from the publicity chairman of even the P.T.A. or hobby groups may make the paper. Editors should accept such pictures, however, only if they show quality and genuine news value. Most public relations pictures are distributed for one purpose: advertising. In that case, public relations people should be directed to another newspaper department.

The daily newspaper has one other important source of pictures—its own library, the one-time "morgue." File folders should be established for many subjects and persons that reappear in the news. Many pictures used in the paper, and some that are not, should be saved, with careful identification. From its files of glossies the newspaper can rush into print photographs of newsworthy people when

169

they speak, win, lose, get into trouble, or die. (Only careless editors use pictures that are obviously ten or twenty years old; however, there are stories—such as the death of a once-prominent tycoon—when an old picture is better than none, but then the date of the photo should be indicated.)

Picture editors usually have two to twenty times as many photographs as they can use. The task is to pick the best without making some staffers feel unneeded. Photographers are a proud bunch and an editor must try to keep them alert and confident. So editors should ask for picture story ideas and encourage photographers to go out to get the story. From the dozens of prints available editors then must select, organize, and crop until the pictures tell the story.

Picture editors mark the photos for engravers. They *crop* pictures to eliminate useless material and *size* a picture to fit a desired space. The sizing problem changes with cropping, obviously, and vice versa. (See Fig. 11.1.)

Cropping and sizing

Cropping

Many pictures require little or no cropping, because the photographer has focused on the essentials. The experienced editor, however, may wish to crop severely, cutting out anything that seems to detract from the point of the picture. Perhaps only half or even a quarter of the picture will remain.

11.1. Don't touch it! Cropping this picture of a swimming pool paint job would ruin it. (*Champaign-Urbana News-Gazette;* photo by John Dixon)

Editors sometimes crop and size in relation to the makeup design, which may require a long one-column cut or a more horizontal picture three columns wide. Usually, the picture is cropped to attain the best photographic result and the makeup is adjusted accordingly. So editors cut out busy backgrounds, superfluous people and objects, and other distractions to bring the picture out of the photograph. Cropping should accentuate the focus of interest—the part of the picture that catches the eye.

Advice on cropping may sometimes seem inconsistent, but the wise editor follows the rules that will make the picture most effective. Editors crop ruthlessly, cutting off the backs of heads and bodies from the waist down, and letting imagination supply the missing portions. Yet they should try to retain the essential composition of a good picture. And they should crop only when it is necessary to improve the picture and to emphasize dominant points of interest. (See Figs. 11.2–11.5.) Sometimes cropping should be absolutely avoided as in Figures 11.1, 11.6, 11.7, and 11.8.

As they crop, editors should keep these other pointers in mind.

1. Look for other than the "obvious" crop, to get unusual results.

11.2. Not too tight. Only modest cropping is justified here. Readers must feel immersed in the snow. (*Champaign-Urbana News-Gazette;* photo by Brian Johnson)

11.3. Off goes the tail. This shot of a raccoon tussling with two hounds becomes more amusing when cropped. (*Roanoke Times and World-News;* photo by Gene Dalton)

11.4. Telling a simple story. Uncropped, this one merely shows a couple of women walking through the park. Cropping puts the focus on the women, without the distraction of tennis court and nearly a whole tree. (*Roanoke Times and World-News;* photo by Gene Dalton)

11.5. Attention, attention. Cropping puts full emphasis on the flutist trying to keep her hands warm. (*Roanoke Times and World-News;* photo by Gene Dalton)

11.6. Eye-stopper. Even non-basketball fans will linger over this one, trying to find what's going on. (*Champaign-Urbana News-Gazette;* photo by John Dixon)

11.7. Leave it alone. Cropping here would ruin the spacious effect. Captions are needed to tell readers that workers are spreading plastic over a football field. (*Champaign-Urbana News-Gazette;* photo by Brian Johnson)

11.8. Another puzzler. Readers will ask, "What's that?" It's a garbage barge, once towed from New York to the Caribbean and back. (AP/ World Wide Photos)

2. In head and shoulder shots, leave a bit of space on the side toward which a person faces.

3. Emphasize the action by leaving space before the thrust of an action, whether a racing car or jumping basketball player.

4. Avoid spoiling a hairstyle or cutting off legs at the ankle.

5. Keep vertical lines vertical.

6. Retain horizons for perspective, but be sure they are horizontal.

7. Avoid fancy and irregular shapes, unless there's a strong reason for them.

8. Experiment. Keep asking, "How can this be improved? Can I honestly dramatize the picture some way? Am I cropping out something essential?"

To visualize the picture when cropped, picture editors often frame different portions of the photograph with a rectangle formed between their extended thumbs and forefingers. The same framing can be done with greater precision if they cut *cropping Ls* from cardboard—two L-shaped tools they can place like an adjustable picture frame on the face of the photo.

There is no problem of sizing or scaling if the editor simply crops out of the picture an area exactly the size of the required *cut*. For example, it is no problem to mark an area a column wide and 3 inches deep. But rarely does the picture fit engraving needs so exactly.

Sizing

Most newspaper pictures are reduced in the engraving process, although from time to time a picture is enlarged. Both height and width are altered in the change, of course, just as television reduces both dimensions in shifting from a 21-inch to a 12-inch screen. The news desk needs to know the dimensions of the cut long before it is made, so the picture and stories can be dummied. It makes a lot of difference in dummying whether the cut is three columns by 8 inches or two columns by 5 inches. Since three of the four dimensions involved are known, it is fairly easy to figure out the fourth: the height or depth of the finished picture.

Assume that a picture is 4 inches wide and 3 inches deep. It is to be enlarged into a cut three columns wide, or 6 inches. The old depth, 3 inches, is compared to the depth of the cut, which is unknown. A simple equation gives the answer

$$\frac{\text{width of picture}}{\text{depth of picture}} = \frac{\text{width of art}}{\text{depth of cut}}$$

$$\frac{4}{3} = \frac{6}{x}$$

So $4x = 18$, and the cut will be 4½ inches deep.

Or let's assume we have a 10- by 8-inch horizontal photo we want to use, cropped full, and that we want to reduce it to a cut 5 inches wide. How high will the cut be? The mathematically oriented may see at once that the answer is 4 inches. But here is the method:

$$\frac{10}{8} = \frac{5}{x}$$

$$10x = 40$$

$$x = \frac{40}{10} = 4 \text{ inches}$$

Newspapers do not use arithmetic to calculate the unknown dimension. They use a device called a proportion wheel that quickly lets a person learn the dimension. (See Fig. 11.9.)

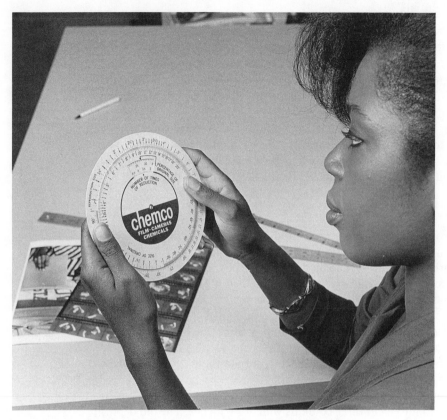

11.9. Simple arithmetic. A proportion wheel lets an editor quickly find the dimensions of an engraving. (Photo by Brian Johnson)

Marking

When editors decide just how they want the photo cropped, they put *crop marks* on its face with a grease pencil. The mark is simply a line a half-inch long or less at the edge of the picture—in the margin, if there is one, so as to mar the photo as little as possible. The grease pencil marks easily, rubs off with rag or finger, and ordinarily does no permanent damage to the surface of the print.

An overlay of tissue paper, folded over the photograph, may be used in the more precise world of advertising and magazines. In the faster processes of the daily newspaper, there is usually less precise instruction. The editor may put two crop marks on the side, to show top and bottom crops for the cut, put two at the bottom, to show the left and right edges, perhaps with an arrow between and a notation "2 col." Engravers then know they are to make a two-column cut, and the height will be worked out mechanically. (If there is only one mark, on the side or bottom, the engraver will simply cut from there to the margin.)

Editors write a slug (like the news story slug) on the back of the photo to identify it in a single word—"crash" or "vote." If the sizing has not been indicated on the face, it will be marked on the back (width first): "2 col. × 4," perhaps, or "7½ × 5½" (for a picture page). It may also be necessary to mark the edition or the section for which the cut is needed. Purists argue that no one should write on the back of a photo, and hard pencil lead can do damage. Some papers put an identification sticker on the back with all instructions listed.

At this point, retouch artists may work on the photograph. With a tiny paintbrush, they can heighten the contrast to get a better cut. Retouching can tone down busy backgrounds or even delete people. Excessive retouching, however, not only gives the final picture a painted look but raises ethical questions of distorting reality.

It is in cropping and sizing that picture editors have the opportunity to employ the real drama of modern newspaper photography. If the conventional method is to reduce everything to two or three columns, they will break away to put the best pictures into sizes five and even six columns wide, where they will leap out at the reader.

When a big English Channel ferry capsized in shallow water outside a Belgian port every paper made the picture at least five columns wide to show the vast bulk of the vessel.

The picture editor must see that every engraving has *cutlines* (sometimes called *captions* or just *lines*). Sometimes simply the name suffices for the picture with one person, such as the one-column head shot or a bride's portrait. Necessary explanation for a picture should be in short, clear sentences.

Writing cutlines

Pictures can be run through a copying machine so the copy can be used for caption writing while the picture is sent to the engraving department. The copy will be poor quality, but good enough to show what is going on in the photograph. Each person in the picture can be seen for proper identification.

Like headlines, cutlines are in the present tense: "Crewmen try to check flames . . . " or "Joe Doakes of Middle State hurls javelin . . . " Of the five Ws usually part of the news lead, the cutlines should include at least the *who* and *where*. *When* probably can be skipped, and most of the *what* is told by the picture itself.

Writers tend to worry too much about *what*. If the picture is good, an unmodified, simple verb is enough. It is amateurish to write "smilingly accepts" or "express delight about." The expressions "is shown" and "is pictured" waste space. However, if the reason for a smile or gesture is not self-evident, the reader deserves an explanation.

Editorializing is as dangerous in cutlines as in news stories. "Club-swinging policeman" may cast an onus on the officer, but "eyes blazing defiance, the looter" may shift prejudice in the opposite direction. Let the reader decide from the look of the clubs and eyes. Unless they misrepresent the full story, cutlines should be deadpan.

These other advices should be heeded by cutline writers:

1. Identify people, places, and things correctly. Identify people "from left," not "left to right."
2. If a story accompanies the picture, explain the picture, not the story.
3. Tell the reader what to look for in the picture.
4. Don't leave the reader baffled. Clear up any ambiguities.
5. Don't libel anyone.

True *captions*—copy above the pictures—have pretty well disappeared from newspapers. But some typographical device can well be used to lure the roving eye to the picture. Often this is two or three words of boldface caps that kick off the cutlines:

CANDIDATES GATHER—Democratic bigwigs of . . .

Or there may be a small headline in a larger type than the cutlines:

Candidates Gather
Democratic bigwigs from upstate counties barbecue . . .

Color pictures

Color printing technology is changing so fast that now it takes little more time to prepare a color picture for printing than it does for a black and white. Color transparencies (slides) can be used to make *separations* for printing.

Separation, as used here, refers to the process of using color filters to block out certain colors in an image. For example, if engravers use red and yellow filters (or an orange one) in shooting a color picture with blues of sky and sea, they will get an engraving with only those blues. With the appropriate blue ink, that engraving will then reproduce the blues in the original. Similarly they can make separations for the reds and yellows, and the resulting engravings will produce appropriate oranges, browns, lavenders, and so forth, when printed in combination with the blue plate. The screen is rotated slightly for each separation, so the dots of different colors are close together but not on top of each other. This is *three-color process*. A black-ink plate for gray tones is added for the more realistic *four-color process*.

Other artwork

Aside from photographs, line drawings—sketches in black ink on white paper—are the major editorial illustrations used in today's newspapers. Comics and cartoons are the most familiar line drawings, but imaginative editors also use graphs and charts, a division simply called *graphics*.

The addition of graphics has been a major recent change in

178

American newspapers. Elaborate charts and graphs can be produced on computers to accompany stories. Readers need not go over a half column of type to get information, for a chart gives the facts swiftly. Most of these graphics are used with economic and consumer stories dealing with such subjects as taxes, the gross national product, unemployment levels, and price comparisons of stomach remedies. Graphics no longer are expensive to produce, and some big papers cut their own costs somewhat by selling their graphics to other papers. The *Chicago Tribune* service has over a hundred customers. It is noteworthy that these graphics are not limited to newspapers. Television also is using them to explain complicated material. They're a good supplement to the reporter's words.

The picture production person on a large newspaper may have a staff of artists able to create drawings to illustrate all kinds of stories. These sketches may range from the humorous to the serious. They offer much variety and contrast nicely with print and standard photographs. Picture editors on more modest papers, however, handle only maps or charts that come from picture agencies. These reproduce best if made up as line cuts rather than halftones. The editor can even buy ready-made drawings that syndicates offer to brighten up the news columns.

The halftone process, which uses tiny dots to vary light and dark shades, allows the editor to vary illustration with wash drawings or watercolors. Fashion drawings, for example, are sometimes halftoned rather than harshly printed as black-white drawings. The artist may get the effect of an unusual halftone by putting lines close, as in cross-hatching, or with *shading sheets*. These sheets are ready-made patterns of dots or lines that can be cut to shade parts of a drawing.

Picture editors may have limited authority to suggest artwork other than photographs. On a well-edited paper, however, the staff takes a look at illustration as a whole, to help attain adequate variety and change of pace.

In the future, picture editors will have to keep up with technical developments and with changing styles in photography and art. Creative individuals will welcome the stimulation of such change. In it they will see the opportunity to make art more attractive and more capable of competing with magazines and TV.

12

Imagination in news editing

An editor must have his own profound vision of things. He cannot seek to fill his newspaper with what the reader wants for the simple reason that no editor *knows* what the reader wants. The editors I have admired have known, however, and quite clearly, what *they* wanted to put in their newspapers, what *they* thought belonged there. And they didn't get their ideas from readership surveys; they got their conception of the *good* newspaper from their own education and interests and understanding and instinct—in short, their own imagination.

—Tom Wicker, *New York Times*

ONE PAPER APPEARS TIRED, listless, routine; another impresses its readers as fresh, dynamic, and challenging. The difference often is imagination. An editorial team, given the freedom to use its creative powers, can generate new and improved newspapers in the same way as other professionals discover new methods to save hearts or make homes more livable.

Imagination is needed in many details of headlines, story structures, and display. But imagination is involved in three major aspects of newspaper operation: excellence of product, the progress and reform of the community, and the people's right to know.

180

Too often excellence is thought of merely in terms of preserving and imitating what is good. American editors never tire of asserting, somewhat chauvinistically, that they produce the best papers in the world. It may seem to them logical that all they have to do is keep doing the job they've been doing. The challenge, however, should be to make the newspaper each year at least slightly better than it was the year before.

True, if there is a better newspaper in a community down the freeway or in a city a thousand miles away, the editor can copy its superior features and, using imagination, learn and adapt from other editors. But the real challenge of editing is to create and test new journalistic concepts and forms.

Imaginative editing, by definition, can't be frozen into a textbook of rules, for it is impossible to anticipate the freshness and creativity that working editors must discover in themselves. Still some hints can be given for applying editorial imagination to problems of modern coverage and the use of specialized writers, editors, and critics.

Creative thinking

The key to creative newspaper work is the editor's ability to generate imaginative story assignments. It is easy to assign a reporter to cover a city council meeting, a school bond referendum, or an explosion at the popcorn factory. Editors can sharpen imagination in assignments by constantly asking as they read, hear, and see, "Is there a story in this for our paper?" In most cases there is not. But perhaps once in twenty or thirty times there is. Articles from magazines like *Harper's, Commonweal,* the *New Republic,* or *Nation's Cities* offer information and insights about problems of general interest, and creative editors always should consider how these articles could apply to home base.

The big-circulation magazines like *McCall's* and *Esquire* include solid reporting. The smaller magazines, however, are better sources of insight about trends in social change. Scholarly magazines, too, are filled with articles that may seem dry, but they sometimes contain fresh and even startling ideas. News assignments on politics, foreign policy, economics, sociology, and other topics spring from these articles to an alert editor's mind.

The same potential lies in current books. An editor need not read them completely to get practical ideas. First chapters, for example, often can be skipped or skimmed. Tables of contents usually give clues to important chapters, allowing an editor to pick and choose the material and thereby digest some books in an hour or two. Obviously, some volumes deserve careful attention, and a good editor identifies them quickly and gives them extra time.

Creative assignment

Having found an idea for a story, editors must ask themselves where the staff can obtain necessary information. Will a state official

181

have a few facts? Will someone in city hall be able to add a few details? Is there an expert in the community who could supply more information? Could that expert direct a reporter to other sources? Is there someone who knows the practical difficulties? Do staff reporters have clues about where to find information?

After editors clarify ideas on how to get the facts, they should make assignments to the reporter in detail. A mere "Get a little story on pollution of Hickory Creek" produces "a little story" with few facts. That article will bounce off the reader, and the next day concern for Hickory Creek's foul condition will evaporate. Rather, a note should describe the idea carefully, in such clear detail that the reporter can have no doubt that a thorough story is desired and that certain sources probably are most promising.

It is important, too, that the editor assign the story to a reporter who is interested in the subject. A writer who is unconcerned about an issue — and unable to get concerned — will do a poor job and may even consciously or unconsciously sabotage the idea. But the editor should not expect a reporter to signal an interest. Sometimes the quiet person sitting in the corner is itching to dig into a serious and important subject.

Creative encouragement

In a creative newsroom, ideas for stories will come from staff members as well as editors. Some city desks have a suggestion box where reporters, photographers, and copy editors can drop notes proposing stories. As mentioned before, this source will dry up in a hurry if the editor ignores the suggestions. When editors use a tip, they should thank the donor; when the tip can't be used, the editor should explain why. Some papers can even give a small bonus for an unusually good idea.

A word of praise for a professional piece of reporting also helps. So does posting a good story on the newsroom bulletin board. Mention of outstanding work in a staff publication stimulates more exceptional reporting, and so does a monetary bonus.

If editors take stories as they come, never suggesting changes or seeking more information, reporters' imaginations wilt. If editors lack enthusiasm, if they are as unconcerned about the discovery of a step toward a cancer cure as about the Cub Scout cookout, they drive away good reporters and encourage the mediocre.

Good papers today offer detailed coverage. The superior ones of the future will search for significance with even more imagination and care. They will seek to discover trends, strive for insight into complex issues, and explore ways to relate their findings to reader concern and interest. Consequently, leading editors will turn more and more to subjects that have not been covered and are not easily accessible. Recognizing the difference between imagination and imitation, they

Insightful coverage

will resist following fads. Few editors today are so perceptive. They think they are being imaginative when they run stories about a current social problem that has seized the general attention of the moment. As noted before, such subjects come and go, like clothing fashions, then fade into the background. A few years later they may take center stage again. Better editors go after subjects, not because everyone else does, but because of their own thoughtful judgment.

Television critics some years ago chastised network documentaries for dealing only with obvious issues, such as race relations, troubles with the space program, and the size of the federal bureaucracy. The same criticism could have been made against newspapers, for they often worked and reworked popular subjects. It's easy, of course, to think of stories on the national debt, the incidence of cancer, and the plight of farmers.

In the last decade journalists have delved into more unexpected issues: nutrition, soaring military costs, the drop in minority enrollment in colleges, and drug use by the upper middle class.

Perhaps television performed best when it graphically reported in the mideighties the widespread starvation in East Africa. The pictures of thousands close to death shocked the whole world, and millions of dollars worth of food sent quickly to the region apparently averted an even greater tragedy. In this case television reporters, like most journalists, ran the story for several days, then dropped it. Ideally, a review every six months would have provided complete information.

Journalists have become more aware that society changes, producing almost imperceptible changes in attitudes and activities. For example, over several years high salaries in business and finance motivated thousands of young people to prepare for business careers. Students often gave salary as their top consideration when choosing an occupation. This development continued for several years before journalists paid attention. Such trends and value changes should be picked up earlier and their effects evaluated.

Journalists are not the only ones to neglect changes and trends until they explode into spot news. Academic specialists as well sometimes fail to grasp what is happening under their noses, and often political leaders badly misread public moods and attitudes. Because of mankind's insensitivity to change, many problems are full-blown before they are recognized. To some extent this is inevitable. Humans seem almost incapable of paying attention to minor problems. Only when they become gigantic—and almost impossible to solve—are they tackled. Even then, it is tempting simply to reduce those problems rather than eliminate them.

Examples are everywhere. Air pollution was dismissed as an irritant until it killed many people. Nothing serious was done about water pollution until at least one of the Great Lakes became a cesspool. Mental health is little more than an unmentionable subject in a family until nearly every member realizes that one of them is in torment. Even when the ills of society are obvious, many people ignore them, apparently assuming that they will go away.

183

Fusing interest and importance

It is difficult under these circumstances for editors to print the news readers need if they are to act as responsible citizens. Criticize editors for not printing much of anything about Central Africa or South America, and they may reply sadly, "We printed stories about Africa, and a readership survey showed that only 6 percent paid any attention. The same thing happened to our South American articles. We can't fill up the paper with stories that only 6 percent will read."

Though the argument sounds irrefutable, there is a flaw in it. The editors are right in implying the paper must print what most readers want if it is to survive. But they are wrong in suggesting that everyone has to be interested in everything in the paper. Most items must appeal to large groups of readers, but this principle leaves room for some material that will be read by a minority, even a small one. Of the solid, important story, the editor should say, "The public needs to know this, even though many readers will not read it. So I am going to print it. If the majority of readers skip it, they will still find plenty of other items to interest them."

The editor has to keep in mind why people read newspaper stories. Wilbur Schramm, the communications researcher, argues that people read because they expect a reward. They find information satisfying even when it may be "bad news" because it provides a negative reward. College students avidly—and perhaps angrily—read about a tuition increase. Motorists read with satisfaction about the elimination of a dangerous stretch of highway, but they also read with concern about the closing of a shortcut. Young people read about the perils of AIDS. Older people carefully follow the obituaries. Probably none of these readers, however, will pay much attention to an election in Uruguay or a disease in Tanzania. Such subjects are too remote from their own concerns.

The task of the editor is to attempt to link these socially and politically important subjects to the legitimate interests and concerns of readers so that they anticipate and find some reward. This is not easy. The editor, working with the reporter, photographer, designer, and artist, must plan with care and imagination, striving for a compelling blend of copy and art. In some ways, the task is easier today than even a decade ago. More readers have attended college; more have traveled, read, and broadened their awareness through television news reports and documentaries. Also the political and economic involvement of the United States with the world has created a new global awareness.

It is easy, however, to exaggerate the increase of interest in peripheral subjects. College does not always educate. Almost everyone knows college graduates who are narrow, ignorant, and scornful of intellect. Many who have traveled extensively are less enlightened about foreign culture than the faithful reader of the *National Geographic*. So the alert editor must search for relevance, attempting to make the readers, through their self-interest, aware and concerned.

Presenting news imaginatively

Good reporting must be supported by imaginative presentation. To write a story and slap on a two-column head is not enough. Major pieces deserve major treatment. They require striking art, and they must jolt the reader's interest by presenting the drama of the facts.

Ideas for good visual presentation can be obtained from newspapers that consistently do a good job of combining words and art. Some Sunday magazines published by newspapers manage this effectively. Their small format helps, for if two facing pages offer type and artwork, the reader's eyes will have no distractions from the spread. The *Los Angeles Times,* the *Boston Globe,* the *Minneapolis Tribune,* the *Nashville Tennessean,* and the *St. Petersburg Times* are among the papers that cleverly present major stories. Magazines like *Fortune* and *Scientific American* consistently use dramatic layouts. Editors who actively examine their designs will discover ideas for exceptional visual presentations that can be adapted to the needs and character of their own paper.

Interpretative pieces need not be lengthy. It became fashionable several years ago to run "The Depth Story," in which a reporter wrote at length about every facet of one problem in a single report. By itself, the report may be outstanding. But an editor should worry that well-intentioned readers may become overwhelmed and put it aside, saying, "I'll have to read that when I get time." Others may go through the whole thing but forget the single impact after a few days. Because memory must be refreshed, continuing problems need big, medium, and small stories every week or so.

This kind of presentation is not cheap. It may take capable, well-paid reporters, photographers, and artists days or even weeks to do a short series. This sometimes means an expenditure of several thousand dollars, which only the wealthiest dailies can afford. But smaller papers can do excellent work a little less elaborately. The pictures can be good, if not superb. The writing can be colorful and thorough. The material can be put together in an attractive way, by using makeup devices mentioned in Chapter 6, such as boxes, color borders, white space, little sketches, copy set in wide measure, and a little extra space between columns.

All this takes additional time and money, but it is worth it if the reader lingers with the paper. It may even be financially profitable in the long run. Advertisers should prefer a paper on which people spend half an hour to one that is skimmed and tossed aside.

Trends to specialization

The specialized editor has come into prominence since World War II. Specialization probably will continue and spread beyond reporting. In the past, for example, most copyediting specialization was done helter-skelter. If a copy editor had a sailboat, he was given stories about the sea. If she had played a violin in the high school orchestra, she read the music critic's column. This has worked moderately well on some desks, but on better newspapers today it is inadequate. Most copy editors, as an illustration, usually do not try to work over science stories because they are afraid they will ruin them. This means that science stories often are not as lucid as they should be. Increasingly, however, copy editors who specialize in science and medicine, or in urban affairs, education, space technology, the arts, and dozens of other areas are appearing in major newspaper offices. The American newspaper is generating specialists on the desk as well as in the field.

The generalist

Though specialization is the trend, the generalist remains immensely valuable. Copy editors who can do a good job of editing copy about an uprising in Bucharest because they are fairly well-informed about Eastern Europe and who also can handle a story about heartburn because of considerable knowledge about medicine are good to have around. Besides, some specialists get into the bad habit of writing only for other specialists. They gradually take on the jargon of the specialty and sometimes become part of the specialty's establishment. Well-informed generalists can help the paper minimize such dangers of overspecialization.

A generalist, even a new reporter, may be able to spot a story that the expert overlooked because the expert was too close to the scene.

A nonsportswriter, for example, may examine with fresh eyes what many see as excesses in college football and basketball programs. Someone who normally does not write about education may look into teacher training or whether university administrations keep growing while faculty and the student body do not. The specialists not only may be too close to the subject but they also may depend too much on the opinions of their old sources.

Imaginative coverage of trends, however, usually requires specialists. Expert coverage has been long established in three journalistic fields: politics, sports, and business. For decades no editor would have dreamed of sending a football writer to cover the stock market or a society writer to cover the World Series. It is perhaps some kind of wry commentary on American culture that experts were ordinarily demanded only in these three areas. More and more, however, the educational level of our culture now demands expertise in science, health, labor, religion, education, and the arts.

It is no longer thinkable, as Scripps believed, that a diplomatic conference can be covered by a police reporter or a church editor—even though both may have expert knowledge of human nature. The foreign affairs expert who writes on international conflicts, the education editor who writes on changes in schools, and other such specialists are positioned to spot the vital trends of war, student unrest, medical breakthroughs, strike threats, aesthetic revolutions, and moral upheavals.

To many, critical writing about music, drama, and other arts is simply a form of news coverage. Some critics, however, see their work as another art, as comment upon a presentation that will guide ticket-buyers and help shape taste. But whether it is art or news, criticism is something that the imaginative editor has to ponder how to improve — or inaugurate.

Newspapers, except in the smaller cities, are doing a reasonably good job of covering the arts. Big city papers, of course, have full- or part-time critics for music, art, dance, and even architecture. Medium-sized papers, in recent years, have staffers who can judge the arts capably or they hire specialists on a free-lance basis.

The culture boom

"Culture" no longer is limited to big cities. Touring theater groups and orchestras come to cities of 150,000 people. Cities smaller than that have their own orchestra. Little theater groups are everywhere. Colleges and even high schools turn out quite good theater. Museums have sprouted in hundreds of cities and many are excellent. In any city of 50,000 or even fewer, one person could be kept busy most of the time covering cultural events, and even if the reviews are only moderately good, the growing number of educated readers will find the local paper more vital because of the coverage.

This observation especially pertains to the motion picture. If attendance is a criterion, the movie houses are the local institutions most deserving critical coverage. Traditionally, papers have printed puffs about movies in return for ads and perhaps "comp" tickets. The system is unfortunate, for the paper gives away valuable space and the film business encounters a generation of people who don't believe what they read about the pictures. It appears that there is a trend toward better cinema criticism in small and middle-sized as well as large communities. While honest and objective reviews may cause some turkeys to lose money, they may contribute to the success of good films. Sound criticism in newspapers around the country might improve the motion picture industry.

Newspapers hold the same potential for television, though syndicated criticism makes it more difficult for the local TV critic to contribute properly. By the time the television show is over, who cares about critical reactions? Some viewers, however, want to know what others thought, just as they do when they bring the subject up at the coffee break the next morning. Some spot criticism of bigger shows would be appropriate, just as some local editorializing on global issues is. Where local television shows do something out of the ordinary in documentaries or entertainment, the newspaper ought to take critical note, for other media will. Probably the greater opportunity for TV criticism in most cities, however, is to criticize, from a local perspective, what networks, producers, or certain shows are attempting to do over time.

Imagination should be used both in reforming the paper and in reforming the community. Traditionally the good journalist has served as messenger, watchdog, and crusader. As editorial emphasis moves from deadpan objectivity to depth reporting, it also advances leadership and guidance. What values are behind interpretative articles? What standards and goals are being suggested by the very fact of their appearance? The imaginative editor goes beyond the search for internal excellence to visualize, plan, and help build a better community.

Challenging power

Crusades seem to have gone out of fashion. It is true that many papers, fat and complacent, don't make waves. But the fact remains, as the annual Pulitzer Prize and other awards testify, that some newspapers still campaign for progress and reform.

Crusading often means bucking the powerful people in the community. Wealth means power, and more often than not political leadership is tied to that power. The newspaper publisher and the chief managers are probably close to the Establishment of the community—meeting on committees with them, golfing, dining, and drinking with them. It is not easy for a paper to break with and confront this aggregation of power, which provides much of the paper's own economic energy. Picking at the petty politicians may not be difficult, and may even be a pleasant sort of sport, but hitting at the real political, social, and economic power of the city takes more nerve.

A few observers, however, contend that journalists form a power bloc themselves. Journalists associate with bureaucrats, professors, other professionals, and other journalists. They rarely spend much time with high corporate executives, military officers, labor leaders, or police officers. The assumption is that journalists deal with people of new power, not the old, monied interests whose power once manipulated city councils, state legislatures, congresses, and even presidents.

Surely, some of the old power is gone, but it seems unlikely that much power has been spread to the professional classes. Now power comes from new money—money gained by inheritance, investments, and shrewd deals. It is new money that finances lobbying, political fund drives, and influence. Reporters, copy editors, editors, librarians, doctors, most lawyers, and professors simply are not in the same league. Editors, journalism educators, and journalism students should investigate and debate where power lies, watch for its misuse, seek progress and reform, and crusade where necessary.

Clark Mollenhoff, for many years an ace reporter of the Cowles newspapers and now a journalism professor, has argued that a reporter tracking down corruption "should follow the dollar." At times people engage in shady practices to gain power, to keep power, or to help their friends. But most often money is behind corruption. Editors, without becoming paranoid about the subject, should check routinely to see whose pocket might be lined as a result of an important proposal, act, or deal.

Editors must, at the same time, realize that there are altruistic people who work hard for changes that offer them no financial rewards. They toil only for what they consider will make a better world. Among these people are those who work for preservation of green space, recreation, family planning, safer highways, improved education, political reform, and dozens of other worthy goals—and even some goals the editor may consider mistaken. These people also make news—news of progress. One satisfaction of journalism is observing up close a spectrum of the human race, from scoundrel to saint. The editor should not assume, despite confirming evidence on certain days, that everyone is a scoundrel. Imaginative editing includes also the search for good news of change.

Campaigning against prejudice

Impressions, not necessarily accurate ones, are picked up by people from their papers. These impressions are the result of hasty reading, poor memories, and habits of noting only what bolsters their prejudices. A good newspaper should challenge such impressions by printing, from time to time, the cold facts of a situation. For example, every year or so it may be necessary to recap the concrete actions concerning school integration in a community or state. Not everyone will read such facts, of course, but some will, and perhaps by steady effort the myths, half-truths, and incorrect assumptions can be given a needed burial.

Political figures and others who frequently make public pronouncements often only repeat what is common prejudice. In some instances prejudices are studiously promoted by certain people or groups, and the newspaper must report the correct information. A sizable proportion of the public, for example, has accepted the idea that everyone on welfare is a loafer. It is commonly said that women on welfare have babies so they can get more money. The editor should check these common impressions. How much more does a woman on welfare get if she has another child? How much does a welfare family get? If a person on welfare got a job for one day, would the income be deducted from the welfare check—and thereby discourage looking for part-time work? The truth would make a story.

Even though the Supreme Court ruled on school prayers in the early sixties, many people assume that the court absolutely banned such prayer. Why not a review story, noting that *compulsory* prayers were abolished?

Or what about the impression that most college football players major in physical education? Why not a story examining the facts?

Dozens of other illustrations could be cited. While these are examples of national impressions, in most towns at least a few local misconceptions are bandied about without correction. Good editors will do their best to get at the truth, even though they may suspect that most subscribers would rather read editorials and stories that reinforce their incorrect impressions.

It helps also to consider whether a person making a proposal has a concealed axe to grind. This does not mean that editors must always suspect evil motives. But they should be skeptical. A senator once introduced legislation that would forbid imports of foreign firearms. This sounded like good news to those who supported gun control, but there was a joker in the proposal: The senator came from the state that produced most of the nation's firearms. A ban on foreign weapons presumably would endear him to home industry and the home work force.

Covering varied viewpoints

Good newspapers pride themselves on giving "both sides" — the pros and cons. William F. Buckley, Jr., is put to bed next to Anthony Lewis, amid columns that are pro-Democratic as well as pro-Republican. Better papers have their own strong editorial voice, but they open their letters column to replies that rebut and even insult them.

Actually, complex issues have more than just pro and con sides. There are various angles that a newspaper has an obligation to cover in both news and editorial pages. A major criticism of newspapers is that they present a narrow range of opinion. As presidential candidates and voters tend to cluster to the middle of the road on issues, so do newspapers. There have always been a number of right-wing columnists, from William Buckley to Patrick Buchanan, but columnists much to the left of center have been used sparingly. The late I. F. Stone occasionally had pieces printed in his last years, but for twenty years he was restricted to writing his own newsletter. A major challenge to imaginative editors today remains that of finding and developing columnists who can go beyond regurgitating the conventional wisdom and present fresh and stimulating ideas and viewpoints. They may infuriate hidebound readers, but even optimists agree that the country's survival requires creative thought that will jog us out of ruts. Many papers have found exceptional black columnists who do not limit themselves to comment on difficulties facing black people. Others have hired blue-collar columnists. Increasingly, papers seek Hispanic columnists to comment primarily on events that touch Americans with Hispanic backgrounds.

Imaginative editors also could turn up local writers who would present strong viewpoints. That happens, but, in a quite human way, editors too often print or reprint "a terrific piece" that is terrific only because it endorses their views. Alert editors should also go after articles from the sociologist who wants a much more basic attack on ghetto problems, the minister who opposes (or endorses) a war, and the teachers' union president who feels a strike may be necessary next fall.

Some dissenting comments will come automatically to the letters column, of course. Editors should take particular care to print those

190

which intelligently present views different from their own. Some editors try to print at least the nub of argument in every letter received. Others pride themselves—wrongly—in throwing away those from their opponents. Every paper receives a certain percentage of "nut letters" that deserve little space, but nothing angers the readership more than knowing that they have no chance to get their arguments into a paper, especially if it enjoys monopoly status.

In broadcasting, regulations supporting the right of reply are under review by the Federal Communications Commission (FCC) and the courts. As it has worked out, the equal-time doctrine for political news has hampered the best coverage; yet some important people would like to have such regulations applied also to newspapers. Court cases, as mentioned, have sought rulings that would require editors to print replies. Although these cases have failed, they raise important questions of press freedom. Do citizens' rights to present their views outweigh the right of editors to run their papers as they please? And what are society's rights? Taking a tip from this controversy, editors might improve the paper's handling of opinion (and forestall government regulation) by encouraging replies. Too often an editor is content to give a maligned figure a paragraph or two of denial deep in a news story. Some news personalities fear how the reporter may handle their words. Then why not give them some space to state their side? How about a "combat page" where those involved in controversy can slug it out?

In the early 1970s the nation, and the world for that matter, was buffeted with demonstrations, marches, strikes, and riots. That turmoil ended, possibly because the fury over the Vietnam War ended. But is the feeling of exasperation, anger, and helplessness that apparently triggered those disturbances still smoldering? Did those demonstrations come about because so many thought only dramatic protests could attract the media's attention? Perhaps editors should have examined news definitions to see if they incorrectly had given top news priorities to violence, unusual costumes, and bizarre happenings. Could editors be alert to the discontent around them and print some columns of dissent? Could they work harder to plumb the feelings of frustration and anger that plague so many ordinary people? The Establishment—white or military or university or labor or corporate—has ways of getting its messages out. The newspaper might provide space for "the little guy" as well as the powerful. People might stop saying that the newspaper is dull, that "there's nothing in it," if there were more real opportunity for a clash of ideas. Editors might, indeed, raise public controversy above the mindless level.

Imaginative editing, in short, must challenge every group—the Establishment, those once called "the silent majority," the radicals, conservatives, and moderates—and seek new ways to involve ordinary citizens in improving society. Waiting for a letter to the editor can't be considered an imaginative way to involve such people.

In their running battle with government, journalists for some time have emphasized the people's "right to know." Embedded in constitutional law is the idea that citizens must be fully informed to participate intelligently in government. Publishers and top editors like to boast how carefully they watch government, but the facts don't bear them out. Reporters dutifully show up at press conferences, ask some obvious questions, and run to their VDTs to report what the official said. Bob Woodward and Carl Bernstein, the chief journalistic probers of Watergate, have called such reporters "sophisticated stenographers." Some editors deserve the title of "sophisticated chief stenographer," for they print only what the powerful utter. Some readers understandably are curious why, for example, reporters hang on every presidential word but can't seem to walk two blocks to cover a hearing on why insurance rates differ so greatly. Instead of nit-picking with critics, good journalists should listen to the criticism and correct their own flaws. Editors even could hope that more readers would demand better journalism. Their demands might make it easier to get a better budget, hire more and better staffers, and put out an improved paper.

The reader's needs

In some ways the flaws of the newspaper are the flaws of the modern university. Students pick courses in history, political science, economics, and literature. Unless they are unusually sharp, they may not see how economics affects politics and how history affects literature. Some educators and some students would like to figure out how to mesh these subjects.

The newspaper provides a similar smorgasbord. There are stories about politics, economics, social movements, education, and conservation, but there is little effort to correlate them. Editors, if they think of it at all, apparently assume that the reader will put all these subjects into some loose order. It is quite an assumption, for most of the nation's editorial pages reveal that editors themselves are not gifted in catching the ties among all the subjects they cover.

Many editors, of course, are concerned about this fragmentation and try to relate one piece of news to another, so perhaps it is a safe prediction that more and more newspapers will try to help readers understand the relationships of events that pass before them. Today, we are limited to grouping of associated news events, an occasional news analysis, and a boldface insert directing the news reader to check an editorial on the subject. Good as this is, it is not good enough. Part of the solution may be in the blend of the visual and the written word.

How can the editor meet the demands of the better-educated and more skeptical reader? Many press observers think modern editors should function with these goals in mind:

1. To discover what the readers want to know and to sense what they need to know. The need can be met, in part, by careful reading, listening to intelligent critics, and diligently observing the community.

2. To keep alert to developing events, even though those events may not be worth a story for several days or weeks.

3. To report government and education in the community with thoroughness and care.

4. To explain how the reader can make a successful living, which would include money, job satisfaction, and the simple pleasures of life.

5. To assist consumers so they avoid buying, for example, shoddy merchandise and poor quality food.

6. To report the truth on economic conditions.

7. To examine events to see whether the traditions of news reporting should be altered to reflect changes in society and in the reading public's needs.

8. To be alert to assaults on human liberty and to educate the public about democratic principles.

9. To be as fair and honest as possible, for a newspaper's most precious asset is credibility.

The reader's nature

Perhaps the ideal editor would be one who is pushing constantly to get readers to attend to the serious events and trends of their time. Without such an editor, the newspaper is little more than an entertainment sheet. The job of prodding and luring the reader requires subtlety and patience. A reader will not get interested in Africa or even air pollution by reading one story. William Rockhill Nelson, founder of the *Kansas City Star,* talked about the need for patience by citing his paper's campaign for a new bridge across the Missouri River. For years, he said, his paper ran news stories, feature stories, editorials, pictures, and cartoons about how the bridge was needed, how it would be needed even more in the future, and how commerce would be assisted with a new bridge. The effort paid off. The bridge was built, but only after an editorial campaign that lasted ten years.

Such hammering at the public consciousness must be done if citizens are to grasp the significance of what is all around them. To accomplish this hammering, without boring or irritating the reader, requires imagination. The editor must be able to present this information in dozens of different ways and, in most instances, in ways the reader thinks offer a reward.

In some cases what would pass for imagination would only be alertness—an ability to capitalize on what was heard, seen, or read. For example, in the Great Depression, a neophyte pollster, George Gallup, told Columbia journalism students that newspapers were missing a bet by failing to give news about where job opportunities were. A half century later a few papers are following Gallup's advice.

The most obvious play of imagination comes in the selection of stories. Problems never will be acute to the reader unless they are brought close to home. Even a newspaper in Phoenix should report that Lake Erie, once so polluted, is regaining aquatic life. The public needs to know that. But a reader in Arizona is not going to be as concerned about Lake Erie as a resident of Ohio. The editor must take the shocking story of Lake Erie's pollution and tie it to conditions at home.

It takes no great imagination to do this. Water pollution in one's own area can be checked. How pure are the streams nearby? How about the lakes? Is the supply of pure water in any danger? What would happen to the water supply if the area's population doubled within twenty years? How can the present pollution be shown graphically, with words and pictures? What is the state water control board doing about polluters? Scolding them? Fining them only $500? Who is on that pollution board? Is anyone there a polluter? What toxic wastes are produced within a few miles of the town, by whom, and how are they disposed of? What could they do to you if they got into your groundwater?

Stories that result from investigation should not be pelted at the reader. A story today may be followed up in a couple of weeks. An editorial or a cartoon could be run from time to time. More ideas might be produced. Is there a conservation group? What does it propose? What is being suggested in other areas? Would those suggestions apply here? These local stories can be reinforced with national stories about water pollution. In so selecting and highlighting vital issues, the editor meets the readers' needs.

The paper's teaching role

The newspaper of tomorrow may set aside certain sections for unabashed teaching. Fifty years ago a few newspapers ran serialized novels each day. Some even published a short novel in the Sunday supplement. To this day, papers run crossword puzzles and bridge columns. Why not a learning column?

With the superior color printing available there could be a series on the history of art, with a text of perhaps a thousand words under a four-column picture of a famous painting. A little quiz could be printed, for self-grading, every few days. Readers probably would not immerse themselves in the subject the way they would if they were taking a formal course in art history. But perhaps they would learn something about art and so appreciate it more.

The art course might run a month and then there could be a shift to economics, or a study of the short story, geography, or transport. Perhaps even serious nonfiction could be serialized. Rachel Carson's *The Sea Around Us,* for example, would be an excellent book to serialize for a month. It would be possible that the "learning column" could always appear in a corner so the reader could clip each piece and put it into a folder.

Other instructional stories could be presented. The workings of the court system baffle many people, and yet news stories about the courts rattle off such words as *appellate, mandamus, stay,* and *tort,* as if anyone past the sixth grade were familiar with them. The series could tell the process of arrest, arraignment, the setting of bail, indictment, and trial. Another series could report on the history of the

Bill of Rights, explaining in detail why the grand jury system was implanted there or why a person could not be accused of the same crime twice.

Already newspapers sometimes republish a series of articles or special layouts, such as housing stories, in a booklet. Such booklets are sold or given away as newspaper promotion. This practice will probably spread even to medium-sized papers. The booklet preserves the reporting beyond the admittedly short-lived newspaper story, helps promote the paper, and, best of all, serves as a reference on the topic.

It is even possible that a newspaper might use the pictures and stories for a documentary film. This could be done inexpensively, with a stream of pictures (more than were used in the newspaper) serving as a backdrop to the words being spoken by a narrator. The film could be loaned or rented to interested schools and organizations. Again, the material would be excellent promotion for the paper.

The *Los Angeles Times* frequently publishes reprints of long articles or a series. One on prisons is used extensively in journalism classes as an example of careful and complete writing and research.

A few American newspapers publish books. Many of these are "instant books," in which several reporters each swiftly write three or four thousand words on some part of a big story. Copy editors quickly read copy and a printing firm does the rest at breakneck speed.

The *Wall Street Journal* has put out a dozen books, and the Associated Press published several on the major events of our time. The *Los Angeles Times* and the *New York Times* even own book publishing firms. Only a few big newspapers, however, have the staff and money to attempt book publishing, but probably a few more will make the effort in the next several years.

13

News crises and edition changes

TO MANY OUTSIDERS, the word newsroom evokes an image of excited people bellowing at each other, editors screaming at printers and printers screaming at editors, telephones ringing like fire alarms, and copy aides frantically darting from desk to desk. This picture may be great for dramatic presentations, but it would be a horrible way to put out a newspaper. If such turmoil were routine a newspaper could never be printed at all, let alone on time, and the staff would be ready for straitjackets in less than a month.

Newsrooms may not be as serene as libraries, but the noise level is almost always low and people seldom shout. Most sounds come from the barely audible clicking of VDTs. Staffs go methodically about getting the news in print, for the production of a newspaper is a major task, and orderly ways are required to get the job done.

On smaller papers the task is simpler because there is just one edition. Because most papers of less than 30,000 circulation put out only one edition a day, they avoid the emergencies of edition changes. Even so, the staffs of smaller papers are usually kept busy by the problems of a normal news day. In an emergency, they have trouble handling all the extra work. Bigger papers usually can take care of crises more easily because they have a large enough staff to cope with late-breaking stories.

Various emergencies can disrupt a newspaper. The press may break down, illness might keep three or four key people home, or telephone and power lines could be knocked out by heavy storms. In such times staffers may work by candlelight and hunt for a working telephone. The paper may have to be printed twenty miles away. Such emergencies are highly unusual. "Routine emergencies" come from unexpected news.

If the news is spectacular, as many as a dozen reporters and several copy editors drop what they are doing to concentrate on the big story. Some reporters handle the main part of the story while others get sidebar material. The editors remake page one, directing reporters and photographers at the same time, and struggle to pull together all the copy into a coherent picture for the reader. If the news breaks shortly before deadline, the reporters and editors will be able to print only sketchy details no matter how quickly they act.

The explosion of the *Challenger* spacecraft in 1986, killing all aboard, tested journalistic skills all over the world. The ship blew up at 10:59 A.M. as East Coast afternoon newspapers in the United States were locking up their first edition. Staffs in later time zones, of course, had more time, but they scrapped plans, ripped up front pages, redesigned new ones, tracked down any local angle, and scrambled to get pictures. All other news that day became secondary, for the explosion shocked and dismayed the whole nation. To tell the story in full, with its many ramifications, required initiative, quick judgment, and cooperation.

Fortunately, there are few such crises. Lesser emergencies, however, are frequent. For example, a major decision by the Supreme Court handed down minutes before deadline suddenly becomes the lead story of the day. Or the governor may take an unexpected step involving the city, and the staff must hustle to report the effects. Editors must adjust quickly. One way they adjust is to expect the unexpected. Each day first-rate editors ask themselves the question that they keep in the back of their heads: "What am I going to do if a big story breaks today?" By knowing the alternatives, they can come up quickly with emergency plans.

Preparation and routines

The well-ordered newspaper, of course, is prepared for all kinds of unexpected news. It has a good library, for one thing, where clippings and pictures of past events can be found quickly. Reference books are readily available. One or two reporters can gather new material and editors may juggle stories on page one.

Some papers have material in type or in the computer ready for a news break involving prominent persons. Using background supplied by wire services, a staff working in slack periods can prepare obituary material and pictures on famous persons who are ill or aged.

To newcomers, writing an obituary before the death may seem ghoulish. Nevertheless, it enables a paper to cover fully and swiftly the death of someone famous, without straining the staff. If two extra pages are necessary, the staff can "jump" the paper's size without difficulty, although few papers increase the number of pages except for a truly monumental event.

In a crisis, staffers should not get so excited that they make the news melodramatic. Editors should take pains to double-check their news judgment. The managing editor or news editor might even warn the staff to be certain of the accuracy of information gathered hastily from people whose judgment and powers of observation may be impaired in the excitement.

Editors should consider all the angles that need covering. Should the police be checked? Will comment from the mayor be appropriate or irrelevant? Should the governor be called? Are reporters available to cover not only the main event but also the subsidiary news? While decisions are made on coverage, at least one editor will have to decide what stories to change on page one, and even how to alter inside pages.

The front page almost always has something expendable: a routine picture, an entertaining but insignificant feature story, a news story that had barely made the front page in the first place. One or all of these pieces could go, or each story could be cut. Even two or three good but lengthy stories may be reduced to accommodate the late news. The news editor can sketch a fresh design as soon as it is clear what stories are being written. A truly big event displaces the lead story, and space may have to be opened for two or three sidebar stories. In an emergency the newsroom and the composing room have to cooperate more closely than ever, so printers should be alerted to expect new pictures, a surge of copy, and new dummies.

Everyone's productivity picks up astonishingly at these times. The excitement apparently pumps the adrenalin needed for printers to paste up pages more quickly, reporters to write more swiftly, and editors to handle copy at double-time. Everyone relishes the chance to get at least moderately excited, and the experience undoubtedly is a main attraction of newspaper work.

Lesser crises

In most lesser crises one reporter quickly writes the story. A single editor edits that story and writes the headline. Another editor will juggle something on page one, so the story—in type—slides neatly toward the presses. The change is almost routine.

The unexpected often results in the changing of a story already in type. In these instances the editor may put a new top on the story, add something to it, or insert some new paragraphs. Often the page is already pasted up, so someone has to make room for the new material. The editor usually first tries to throw out a few paragraphs of the original story to open space for the new parts. If every bit of the original story is important, the editor must decide on cutting or killing an adjoining story of less news value to make room for the fresh information.

Some newspapers, in such situations, would make the press plate, and start the presses rolling, to meet train or bus schedules or to load trucks headed for the suburbs. In perhaps fifteen minutes a new plate with the fresh information would be ready. The presses would be stopped momentarily, the new plate substituted, and the presses started again. This process means that a few thousand subscribers will not get the late development, but many more thousands will have a complete story and headline.

Readers nurtured on old movies may believe that when a spectacular news event occurs, the paper dashes out an extra. Unless they are up in years they probably have never seen a true extra.

A few extras have appeared in recent years, however. The *Kenosha* (Wisconsin) *News* in 1984 produced one when a suspect in a string of kidnappings and murders was arrested. The *Chicago Sun-Times* got out four extras the same year, all dealing with major events, but papers generally concede first reports of startling news to radio and television. Newspapers find that such broadcasts stimulate interest in the detail that print offers.

Emergencies of less critical importance require other kinds of handling. In years past, when a typographical error produced an obscene word, the presses might be stopped and the offending word chiseled off the plate or even smashed flat with a hammer. Those crude techniques never appealed to editors who cared about their papers' appearances. Besides, such brute force doesn't work with modern press plates. The good editor in such cases stretches circulation schedules a few minutes, stops the press, and makes the correction. The good editor also would rather delay the paper a little to get real news breaks than print stories that will be made obsolete within a few minutes by radio or TV. So if a good story breaks at deadline or a really important story already in type gets a shift of emphasis, the competent editor manages to get the latest news into the paper one way or another.

Changing the day's edition

All papers deal with changes, and the bigger papers deal with them constantly as every edition rolls on a different deadline. The number of changes, however, has been declining as most newspapers have reduced the number of editions. There had been little commercial reason for so many editions, because readers bought fewer papers on newsstands or from racks than they did a generation or more ago. Besides, the solid, detailed stories most papers print today do not need changing every hour or two. Big city papers stand ready, however, to *replate* if a story of real merit comes along. While the presses spin, they quickly get a story and headline in type, make modest changes in the dummy, produce a new plate or two, stop the presses briefly, and get the new plate locked onto the press. Today, papers are putting out zoned editions, as noted before, and these usually require altering a couple of inside pages for regional news but not the main news sections.

The Washington Post

The *Washington Post,* a morning paper with a circulation above 800,000, is an example of a big paper with only four editions. The first edition, called the *bulldog,* reaches the streets a few minutes after 10:00 P.M. and sells to people who work nights, to those coming out of theaters, to tourists, and to others seeking diversion downtown at night. It also is trucked to the far reaches of the paper's circulation area and mailed to subscribers all over the nation.

The second edition comes out about 11:30 P.M. with some fresh news and with some stories altered to take account of new developments. In the summer the results of some baseball games can be included. This edition circulates in areas a hundred miles or more from Washington.

The third edition, appearing about 1:00 A.M., is distributed to metropolitan Washington, which includes the District of Columbia and sizable chunks of Maryland and Virginia. This edition has late local and world news, several revamped stories, and final results of most baseball games.

The fourth edition, once called a replate, makes over page one with the latest information and few, if any, other pages. In the first three editions the *Post* uses either no banner or a restrained one (72-point type or less). The fourth edition occasionally has a moderately large banner that can be read at a distance, for this edition sells from newsstands and racks to people on the way to work in the morning.

Two Syracuse papers

A few papers continue to have many editions because they cover large geographic areas. The morning *Post-Standard* in Syracuse, for example, has six editions, but Syracuse is uniquely situated to justify them. It is the biggest city by far in a wide section of New York between Canada and Pennsylvania.

Years ago, when newspapers were beginning to expand their territories, the *Post-Standard* built circulation over an area of about 25,000 square miles. Habit is important to all readers, and thousands of people in the small towns in the area got the habit of buying the Syracuse paper. To keep these readers, the newspaper has run editions that include local news for each major region: north, east, the city of Auburn, south, west, and Syracuse itself. The edition changes are kept to a minimum as the paper adapts to readers more than to events.

The *Post-Standard,* except under unusual circumstances, alters page one only once during the evening. Only two inside pages, other than sports, are changed from one edition to another. The first edition has news from the area near Montreal and an area roughly a hundred miles north of Syracuse. The next edition scraps those pages for news from another section. The process is repeated until the sixth edition arrives. Local news then is put on those changing pages and alterations are made on page one.

The afternoon *Syracuse Herald-Journal* operates in a similar way with three editions, except that page one changes with every edition. News develops through the day, as governments make decisions and statements, business deals are announced, and university officials list building plans. Afternoon papers must make over pages to reflect such developments.

The trick in handling edition changes anywhere is to make as few alterations as possible while giving the reader late and significant news. Sometimes news may be fresh but not significant. For example, the wire services may give a string of new leads on one event. Each new lead tells the latest development, but the last scrap of information may have little significance for the story as a whole. The editor should look over the various leads and be willing to say firmly, "Forget that latest lead. It doesn't give the whole story as well as the one we've got."

All newspapers strive to get pages moving to the pressroom every few minutes during the work cycle. Some afternoon papers have two or three editors working through the night, editing wire or local stories and dummying a few inside pages. None of these stories is expected to change. This way several pages can be "closed"—ready for the pressroom—before the rest of the staff arrives.

Other pages, like editorial, opposite editorial (op-ed), and lifestyle, can be sent to the presses early. A sports page, the front page, and a key local page can be kept open until the last minute without causing any special rush at deadline.

Even if a paper strives to avoid change for the sake of change, there will be much juggling on most papers as the editions proceed. Just as some stories have to be lengthened because they have taken on a new importance, others must be shortened because they have lost significance. Some can be cast aside because they have been supplanted by better ones or because readers of the next edition would find the information irrelevant.

New headlines often have to be written to include new material or to fit a different size space caused by makeup shifts. A story worth a three-column head in the first edition may be dropped to a single-column head in the third, or a local story may require a bigger head in the home edition.

The developing story

While editing and headline writing are proceeding, someone—usually the news editor or slot person—will be preparing dummies. As editions change, the dummies have to change, obviously, but the new ones indicate only where new or altered stories are to be placed. After the first edition a complete dummy is unnecessary and actually may be confusing to the makeup person. If three stories are to be changed on page one, the dummy would have to refer only to the three places where something is to be altered. (See Figs. 13.1 and 13.2.)

While great efforts are made to avoid spoken instructions to printers and other staffers, the news editor and the makeup editor may occasionally have brief talks about changes in the dummy. If the paper is small, the various editors supervise makeup as well as a half dozen other operations. To make a last-minute change, they simply walk to the composing room a few feet away and give instructions to the printer about their particular pages. The composing room of big-

Revising dummies

13.1. Complete dummy. Most of the front page space of this paper has been filled with pictures and stories for the first run of the day.

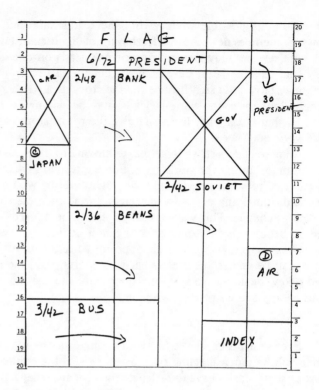

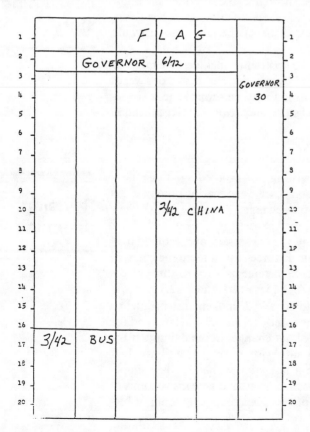

13.2. Revised dummy. The dummy of Figure 13.1 has been changed to bring it up to date. A new banner and a new "Bus" lead have been provided, and "China" has been substituted for "Soviet."

ger papers may be two or three floors removed from the newsroom, so conversations between a news editor and the makeup editor usually are over interoffice telephone.

Sometimes a story will be dummied in anticipation of getting the facts later, but sometimes the facts don't appear, and an editor has to find a substitute story. Many papers have a *bank* of *time copy* for use in emergencies. The staff adds to the bank in slack periods so the editor always will have a variety of stopgap material available.

Sometimes a person in the ad department will forget to dummy an ad or will dummy one twice. This means that when the error is discovered editors either will have to yank perhaps half a dozen stories to make room for the ad or insert as many to fill the void.

Some unexpected stories can be written in parts—even the last part first. There is a system for handling this kind of story, too. Assume that a gas main explodes at a busy downtown corner. One or two reporters and a photographer would be sent to the scene, another would check library clippings under "Explosions," and others would be telephoning the gas company, police, fire department headquarters, city morgue, and hospitals. Each reporter might gather bits of news that would be worth a couple of paragraphs. But in the confusion no one can be sure immediately whether anyone was killed, how many were injured, what caused the blast, or how much damage resulted.

Writing backwards

While attempts are made to find out all this information, it occasionally helps to get as much of the story written as possible. So the city editor directs reporters to write what material they have and slug each piece "BLAST." Reporters at the scene telephone rewrite people as soon as they have any information. Rewrite pounds out the facts as they dribble in, using the same slug. The top of the story will be written last, giving the fullest account of the who, what, when, where, and why. The lesser details, gathered earlier, can be resting in the computer or be sent on to the composing room well in advance of the top. This copy is called *A-matter*. The "A" stands for add; in effect, these pieces are adds to a story that as yet does not exist.

Editors mark the first one "10-add," the next one "11-add," etc. The figure 10 is the starter because the lead, which will be written last, may then have as many as nine adds without confusing the numbering system. Ten is safe because a lead almost never has more than nine adds. The adds for the body of the story, then, may look like this:

```
Blast   10-add

        One witness, Mrs. Carrie Blasingame, 1013 E. Arlington St.,

    said she had just stepped outside Heller's department store when

    she heard a terrific noise and saw a car flop over less than 75

    feet from her.  She said that the force of the blast pushed her
```

203

back against the store front, but that she was not hurt.

Blast 11-add

The explosion was the first eruption of a gas main in the city since 1927. That blast killed two persons at Kenwood and Main streets, three blocks south of today's accident.

A copy editor may go to the composing room as the story is pasted into position to make sure each graf naturally follows the one ahead of it. The whole newspaper staff, but the copy desk in particular, must keep searching for ways to squeeze big emergencies into small ones and to eliminate the small ones. Little things are important, such as having names and telephone numbers of key sources close at hand and maintaining a good library. Planning for emergencies is essential to avoid turmoil and to provide quality coverage.

Above all, journalists should strive to discover how to reduce trivia and how to improve newsroom efficiency. The new technology provides much more efficient news operations. It will pay young journalists to apply their own enterprise to make that technology even better.

14

The law and the copy editor

A COPY EDITOR CALLS UP A STORY about a trial. In the ninth paragraph is this sentence: "When Rogers finished his testimony against the sheriff, Judge Wilson launched into a bitter attack upon the sheriff, calling him a 'scoundrel,' a 'woman-chaser,' and a 'lewd, lascivious old man.' " The copy editor has to consider some important questions: Is it libelous? Will the sheriff sue? If it is libelous and the sheriff sues, how much could the newspaper lose?

What if a reviewer says this of a play: "Miss Smith did an adequate job of playing Ophelia, but she might have done better if she had laid off the sauce before curtain time." Is this caustic sentence going to get the newspaper into court?

Suppose a story about the mayor starts "Mayor Hector Adamson was convicted of stealing a car in 1932, and he served three months in jail for the offense, the *Post* discovered today." Is it safe to dredge up a story a half century old, even if it is true?

These examples are hardly typical of stories crossing a copy desk, but they show why a copy editor must be constantly alert to the possibility that, tucked away in an obscure story, is a sentence that will send someone running to a lawyer. That lawyer may decide to call on the newspaper's publisher to see about a tidy out-of-court settlement. He may even reinforce his efforts by stopping off at the courthouse to file a libel suit.

The lawyer may decide to sue the copy editor, too, since this staffer had a hand in the job. A suit also could be filed against the reporter who wrote the story. The working crew rarely gets sued, however. With only a house heavily mortgaged, a three-year-old car, two children free and clear, and $650 in the newspaper's credit union, the staffer would be too small a target. The newspaper is not. Most newspapers, if they had to, could borrow many thousands. In addition, nearly all newspapers have libel insurance, and lawyers know it.

The costs of libel

Back in 1927, Stanley Walker, in his book *City Editor,* advised editors to take an occasional risk on a libel suit, because at the worst the paper would lose only a couple of thousand dollars. That no longer is sound advice, if it ever was. While some libel judgments are for a few thousand, some these days are enormous. Imagine what the future would be for the copy editor whose error let the paper get socked for a million dollars. That award is still almost fantasy, but would any copy editor feel secure about the future if that blunder cost the paper even $5,000?

The cost of losing a libel suit is not only the judgment handed down by the court. The newspaper has to hire trial lawyers, and good ones do not come cheap. Defense attorneys have to be paid even if the newspaper wins the suit. CBS, in defending itself in one case, reportedly spent $250,000 a week, and the trial lasted ten weeks.

Libel judgments soared in the sixties and have been climbing since. One of the early big judgments involved Wally Butts, athletic director at the University of Georgia. The *Saturday Evening Post,* then a weekly, published a statement that a telephone conversation between Butts and Bear Bryant, football coach at the University of Alabama, revealed that Georgia was going to throw the football game with Alabama. The *Post* story quoted only one person, who said he overheard the conversation by accident. Both Butts and Bryant sued. At the trial in the Butts case, no one else could corroborate the statements of the sole witness. The witness also had changed his story somewhat and, besides, his reputation was attacked. Butts was awarded $3,060,000, although this was cut to $400,000 on appeal. Bryant settled out of court for $300,000. This catastrophe contributed to the death of the weekly *Post.*

Almost twenty years later, the entertainer Carol Burnett sued the *National Inquirer* because the paper had reported that she had been rowdy in a Washington restaurant. The original judgment was $1.6 million, later cut to $800,000, and then settled for an undisclosed amount. Miss Burnett gave the sum to the University of Hawaii for the study of journalism ethics.

A former Miss Wyoming won a $26.5 million award from *Penthouse* magazine, but a judge reduced the judgment to $14 million. Another judge, on appeal, threw out the judgment. He ruled that the magazine article would not reasonably be understood as describing the actual facts about her.

The *Alton* (Illinois) *Telegraph* lost a libel suit over a memo that never got into the paper. The judgment there was $9.2 million, and under Illinois law this sum had to be produced before an appeal could be filed. This case also was settled for less, but the amount was not announced.

Almost all whopping judgments are reduced sharply on appeal or even thrown out. Fewer than 10 percent of libel cases are won by the plaintiff (the one bringing the suit). Many suits are filed, partly to give the plaintiff a feeling of vengeance, and they are dropped after lingering for a couple of years in the courts. Nevertheless, libel today is serious, and anyone in the newsroom ought to have a good knowledge of libel law. The copy editor especially should be as informed about libel law as an average attorney. If such knowledge tells the rim person that something is libelous, the slot should be told, "This looks like dynamite to me." If the slot agrees, they can rephrase the offending words, remove the dangerous part of the story, or ask the newspaper's lawyer for advice. In most cases the lawyer is not consulted unless the editors, hoping to run the story pretty much as written, want to be as sure as anyone can be that the story will not cost the paper a suit.

Journalists should realize that civility provides one of the best protections against libel. A University of Iowa law school study found that many aggrieved persons call a newspaper to complain that their reputations have been sullied. Instead of getting a polite consideration of the complaint, the study found, some staffer responds harshly or the caller is given the runaround. The result is that the complainant, already irritated, becomes angry and gets a lawyer to file suit. The study has prompted warnings in many newsrooms to be courteous to such callers and to funnel complaints to one specific person, whose job is to placate the irate.

What is libelous?

It would be a relief to all journalists if someone could give them a flat yes or no answer every time something looks libelous, but a lot of cases are borderline. Besides, one never can tell for sure what a jury will decide. One woman sued a newspaper that reported she had given birth to a litter of pups. Almost any libel expert would have said she had a clear case. The jury, however, ruled that everyone knew that it was a biological impossibility for a woman to have puppies, so she lost.

Libel is usually defined as *written defamation* and it applies also to most radio and television programs on the ground that newscasters and performers are reading from a script. But someone is sure to look at the definition of libel and object, "Newspapers and broadcasts defame people all the time." Certainly a story about a man's embezzling $10,000 at the bank ruins his reputation. And a story about a woman's being convicted of running a con game will defame her and probably keep her from joining the Junior League. Obviously newspapers and newscasters defame people. They can do it legally because the law provides publishers with defenses that permit printing of certain defamations.

The law offers three main protections for publications printing defamatory information. In general, these legal defenses are the same in each of the fifty states and the District of Columbia. At the heart of the protection is the idea that the public has a right to know many things that are considered defamatory, so papers are given rights, or "defenses," to print such defamation. Theoretically, a person could still sue, but a lawyer would advise against a suit because the paper stands behind one of these three protections for the public interest:

Three defenses

1. Truth. In some states truthfulness alone is a protection. In others it has to be *truth with good motive.*
2. Privilege. This often is called *qualified* or *statutory* privilege because states let publications print *accurate* stories about the activities of the courts. Newspapers also may report what takes place in public bodies, like Congress or the state legislatures, and may take facts from various public records. Usually privilege does not cover juvenile courts, activities of grand juries, and lesser public bodies like school boards and village councils.
3. Fair Comment. A newspaper may criticize the activities of public officials and works or performances open to the public and publicly displayed, such as books, art shows, concerts, plays, athletic contests, and nightclub acts.

Truth

Truth, under law, is not simply what the newspaper editors believe is the truth or what someone told a reporter is true. From a legal standpoint truth is what can be proved in court to be true. Occasionally, therefore, a journalist will say, "I know the guy is a crook, but I can't prove it." So a story about him is not printed.

Sometimes a newspaper running an investigation will get someone's promise to testify to the truth of a charge in case the story ever comes to court. But suppose the trial date approaches and Mr. Witness is nowhere to be found? Because the truth cannot now be proved, a plaintiff perhaps collects a few thousand dollars and the newspaper collects experience. Instead of relying on a witness to appear in a case of libel, many papers take pains to have their sources give them affidavits to be used in case someone sues. The affidavits are sworn statements by the informants that certain assertions made by the paper are true. Newspapers even try to forestall the threat of suit by telling the readers, in effect, that they have the goods: "At least three police officers operate as bookmakers in their spare time, two former officers *declared in affidavits signed* today." Assuming that the three accused officers are named later in the story, they and their lawyers are forewarned that the newspaper has sworn statements for court proof.

Something true may still get the newspaper into difficulty. At the beginning of this chapter an example said that the mayor was a thief in 1932. Presumably, no reader had known this. If the story is true, one might say that the mayor could do nothing about it. But maybe he could. He could argue that although he had stolen a car when he was sixteen years old, he had led a respectable life since. The newspaper, he could charge, was being malicious in printing a story that old. (The legal meaning of *malice* is disregard for the rights of others without legal justification.) The newspaper, on the other hand, might argue that the public had a right to know that their mayor had been a thief. A Supreme Court ruling gives the edge to the newspaper, on the ground that the story was based on an open court record.

Privilege

Since the rights of privilege do not, in all states, apply to *all* courts and *all* deliberations of public bodies and *all* public records, copy editors should be familiar with the restrictions in their own states or the states in which the newspaper circulates.

They should be aware that accounts of committees of Congress and state legislatures are covered by privilege. The protection does not apply to closed legislative committee hearings. However, any publications issued by such committees are covered by privilege, even though the publications may be filled with material that would be libelous if printed by anyone else.

The question of privilege on the floor of the United States Senate got a workout in the early fifties, during the heyday of Senator Joseph McCarthy. The senator often declared in speeches about the country that the government, particularly the State Department, was honeycombed with Communists. On the lecture circuit he always was careful to speak in generalities and never called any government official a Communist by name. If he had, he might have been sued for *slander,* which is *oral defamation.*

On the floor of the Senate, where he was protected by law, McCarthy called various people Communists. The press was able to report what McCarthy said on the Senate floor without fear of a libel suit because what was said was privileged. Often the named people dared the senator to step outside the Capitol, where his speech would not be protected, and make the same charges. He never took them up on it.

Another situation involving privilege occurred when McCarthy held a Senate subcommittee hearing in New Jersey. The hearing was closed, but afterward McCarthy held a press conference and mentioned names. The papers printed the names and one man sued. The judge ruled that the press conference was an extension of the subcommittee hearing and therefore was privileged. While this was the decision in this one court, the press should be cautious about concluding that all such press conferences would be considered privileged by all judges or juries. In fact, the Supreme Court has ruled that a senator's press release is not privileged.

It is always advisable to remember that application and interpretation make the law flexible. The courts may rule at one time that such-and-such is the law. Within five or ten years, with a different political climate and with different evidence, fresh decisions may result in the opposite interpretation. As an illustration, many of the laws made in the forties and fifties to restrict radical political activity were invalidated by the Supreme Court within a decade or two.

Moreover, like the protection of privilege in many states on juvenile court proceedings, other laws are not clear. The police blotter, or record book, is a privileged document in some states, but in others either it is not or the law on the subject is fuzzy. It is clear, however, that once a lawsuit has been filed — is in the hands of the clerk of the courts — the contents of the charges are privileged.

An attorney, in launching a suit, may present *pleadings* to the judge. These are not privileged until they become part of the court record. If the case is dropped or settled in the judge's chambers, the pleadings never are opened to the public.

Any part of the trial that is removed from the court record is not privileged. If the judge rules that testimony is *stricken,* the protection is taken away. The same applies when the judge *clears the court,* for reporters either must leave the courtroom at such times or must not print anything that happens in the court after the judge has cleared it.

No story during or preceding a trial should provide any editorial evaluation of the guilt or innocence of the accused. Stories should stick to what has been said for court record. No story should refer to a person as a "killer" or a "burglar" until he has been convicted of such crimes. Obviously, this applies to the headline as well. A person can be called an "alleged burglar," for the word *alleged* is a synonym for *accused* and should be used accordingly.

Some people have the mistaken idea that if the word *alleged* is tossed into a story, the newspaper can avoid any libel suit. What if a reporter wrote, "It is alleged that the university president, almost immobile from drunkenness, shouted obscenities at the Student Council president yesterday"? There would be no protection unless someone had formally accused the official of this behavior or the newspaper could prove that the report was true.

Reporters often assume that what a police officer tells them is privileged. It is not, although quoting an officer may help prove lack of malice, so any damages assessed may be less. Some papers therefore take chances and tie the phrase "police said" to some defamations.

An arrest, however, is privileged. Nevertheless, it is worth being cautious about. Police may get a little overzealous and arrest people for insufficient cause. So an officer, in the midst of some excitement, may reach out and tell someone he is under arrest. The someone may be the vice president of a university. The newspaper might print a story of the arrest, only to find that while the presses were running the vice president had been taken to the police station and quickly released, with personal and profuse apologies from the desk sergeant, the chief of police, the mayor, and, of course, the arresting officer. The privilege might not hold up now, on the grounds that the vice president was not really considered arrested by the police.

Cautious editors print news of arrests only after an *information,* or preliminary charge, is written out at the police station. This precaution applies especially to mass arrests when police sometimes will shove a hundred people into paddy wagons, tell them they are under arrest, take them to a remote police station, and release them. Unless a reporter follows through to see that there is an official record of an arrest, police can deny later, after publication, that anyone had been arrested. A denial without a written *information* could leave the paper in a bad spot.

Fair comment

Sarcastic and sardonic play reviews flourished in the thirties and early forties. Reviewers struggled to have something snide or devastating to say about at least one performer, if not the whole cast. That approach to play reviewing spilled over into reviews of books, music, and art. The exaggeration and the strained efforts to be cleverly derogatory, fortunately, are less common today, but editors still must know where to draw the line.

It is legal to pan a play or performance in exaggerated language. The law provides that anything written about the performance, including how the person looked while performing, is protected by what is known as *fair comment and criticism*. The only qualification is that the writing not be malicious.

One case that has amused law and journalism students for decades concerned a 1901 newspaper review in Odebolt, Iowa. The reviewer covered the stage performance of a singing trio known as the Cherry Sisters. Since horses were common in 1901, the reviewer chose to use equine terms, knowing his audience would appreciate them:

> Effie is an old jade of 50 summers, Jessie a frisky filly of 40 and Addie, the flower of the family, a capering monstrosity of 35. Their long skinny arms, equipped with talons at the extremities, swung mechanically, and anon waved frantically at the suffering audience. The mouths of their rancid features opened like caverns and sounds like the wailings of damned souls issued therefrom. They pranced around the stage with a motion that suggested a cross between the danse du ventre and fox trot, strange creatures with painted faces and hideous mien. Effie is spavined, Addie is stringhalt, and Jessie, the only one who showed her stockings, has legs with calves as classic in their outlines as the curves of a broom handle.[1]

Effie brought suit and lost. She appealed, but the appellate court ruled against her: "Viewing the evidence in the light of the rules heretofore announced, and remembering that the trial court had the plaintiff before it and saw her repeat some of the performances given by her on stage, we are of the opinion that there was *no* error in directing a verdict for the defendants."

A copy editor must make sure, however, that a review does not deal derogatorily with the performer's private life, such as drinking

---

1. Robert H. Phelps and E. Douglas Hamilton, *Libel* (New York: Macmillan, 1966), 207.

habits, sex life, and political views. These are considered by law to be a person's own business, until the performer makes them public business by something like getting arrested for drunkenness.

It is almost taken for granted that the press can criticize public officials with impunity. But newspapers cannot report their private lives under the protection of fair comment, so any report on private activity would have to be defended by proof that the report was true. Some public officials, notably presidents, have virtually no private life, so criticism of practically anything they or their families do is allowed by custom, though ethics and taste restrain well-edited papers. Scandal sheets thrive on libel of famous persons and usually get away with it, for the famous often realize a suit would publicize the libel even more and that more people would believe it.

Fair comment is a common-law defense that varies from state to state. A constitutional protection for opinion seems to have replaced the fair comment defense to a large extent. Justice Powell in *Gertz v. Robert Welch, Inc.* wrote, "Under the First Amendment there is no such thing as a false idea. However pernicious an opinion may seem, we depend for its correction not on the conscience of judges or juries but on the competition of other ideas."

Although Powell was only referring to the libertarian roots of freedom of expression, lower courts have seized upon the statement as the genesis of a new defense. The rule that has evolved up to this point is that one potentially can be liable for expression of defamatory facts, but not for defamatory statements of opinion. The similarity to the fair comment defense is obvious, and the same problem occurs: What is fact and what is opinion? Is it opinion to call somebody a lousy agent? An incompetent judge? An amateurish performer?

One court said it was opinion to assert that a public official voted to "squander property tax funds for Tahoe airport." Another court ruled that it was not opinion to say a judge was "probably corrupt." Allegations of criminal activity are not considered opinion. Editorials and cartoons may contain more than opinion, and thus result in liability. Even if journalists cannot be liable for opinion, they can be liable for facts included with opinion or for undisclosed facts that were implied as the basis for the opinion. So, for practical purposes, the ambiguity of the opinion defense should deter editors from relying on it.

The columnists Rowland Evans and Robert Novak became involved in a case involving opinion. They had written that a professor's anonymous colleague had said the professor "had no status within the profession." The columnists lost in the original court, but an appeals court ruled that this expression of opinion could not form the basis of a libel suit.

In handling any possible libel story editors should ask a reporter the same questions that a plaintiff's attorney would ask that reporter on the stand: Do you have a source? Why do you trust that source? Are there other sources who would give a different version, and if so why is their version not included? Do you have your facts straight?

In recent years the courts have ruled that certain inaccuracies or falsehoods about *public figures* and *public officials* may be printed safely. The landmark decision on this subject was handed down in 1964 by the United States Supreme Court in *New York Times v. Sullivan*. Some three million dollars in judgments had been assessed against the *Times* in behalf of various Alabama figures, including Governor Patterson and four Montgomery city officials. One of the officials was L. B. Sullivan, commissioner of public affairs and thereby head of the police department. The judgments had been obtained because a full page advertisement, placed by a civil rights group, had appeared in the *Times*. The ad said that during a demonstration at Alabama State College police had "ringed" the campus, student leaders had been expelled, the "entire" student body had shown its protest by refusing to register for classes, and the campus dining hall had been padlocked.

A substantial number of these statements were not true. For example, nine students were expelled, but for demanding service at a downtown lunch counter. The dining hall never was padlocked, and the police did not "ring" the campus.

The Supreme Court ruled this way in favor of the *Times:*

> The constitutional guarantees require, we think, a Federal rule that prohibits a public official from recovering damages for a defamatory falsehood relating to his official conduct unless he proves that the statement was made with "actual malice"—that is, with the knowledge that it was false or with *reckless disregard* of whether it was false or not.[2]

The public figure rule has been decisive in other libel cases. The question that faces editors, however, is what constitutes a public figure. Obviously, the president, a senator, a famous football player, or a noted actor is a public figure. But what about a relatively well-known professor? What about a member of the school board? Are they well enough known to be considered public figures?

There are other tough questions. How incorrect must the news stories be for the public figure defense to be used? How reckless is reckless? Can a newspaper say that Senator Glotzenschlubber beats his wife every other Tuesday? Can a story say that Alderman Leddhedd goes out every Saturday night on a wild binge, when in truth he sticks to sarsaparilla?

No one knows for sure where the borderline is between a public figure and a nonpublic figure. No one knows how erroneous the stories may be before a newspaper gets in water so hot that the public figure plea won't cool it. Courts define individual, not general, cases.

One court, however, granted Senator Barry Goldwater $75,000 in a libel suit against Ralph Ginzburg and his magazine *Fact*. In 1964, when Goldwater ran for president, Ginzburg published a story based

---

2. The quote from a Supreme Court ruling on "actual malice" is from Robert M. Bliss, "Development of Fair Comment as a Defense to Libel," *Journalism Quarterly* (Winter, 1967), 627–37.

on the opinion of more than a dozen psychiatrists that Goldwater was not mentally stable. None of the psychiatrists had ever seen Goldwater. The senator was a public figure, all right, but the court ruled that Ginzburg had been guilty of malice and "reckless disregard" of the facts. So at least in that one case journalists learned the outer limits of the public figure doctrine.

Other court decisions have not clarified the issue much. In 1971 a ruling in *Rosenbloom v. MetroMedia* indicated that it would be most difficult for anyone to sue for libel. The court declared that even private persons would have to show *actual malice* or reckless disregard if the libel involved a matter of public interest.

A few years later, another decision showed that libel is not ready for burial. This ruling was given in the *Gertz* case, and legal scholars are confused about its effects. Gertz was a lawyer for a family whose son had been killed by a police officer. A magazine published by the John Birch Society said Gertz was a Leninist, a Communist Fronter, and part of a conspiracy to smear the police. All these claims were false, Gertz sued, and a jury ruled that the words were libelous per se and awarded damages. The appellate court, however, reversed the decision, citing *Rosenbloom* and claiming that the case was of public interest. The court held that Gertz had to prove actual malice on behalf of the magazine. Gertz had not made such a claim. The *Gertz* case went to the United States Supreme Court, which ruled that Gertz was a private plaintiff and that private plaintiffs, unlike public plaintiffs, do not have easy access to the media to counter false statements. Therefore, the court held, the *Times v. Sullivan* rule did not apply and Gertz lost that round.

Gertz means that a private individual, even when speaking on a public issue, can collect damages if he can prove negligence by the publisher. A mystery still remains: Who is a private individual? What is a public issue? What constitutes negligence?

The public figure defense was involved in a case brought against CBS in 1985 by General William Westmoreland, who had commanded U.S. forces in the Vietnam War. A CBS broadcast said that Westmoreland had misrepresented enemy troop strength in Vietnam to his superiors, including President Lyndon Johnson. The case was argued for weeks in court when Westmoreland suddenly announced that he was dropping out. Each side claimed victory, although CBS paid nothing. The network did agree not to sue the general for legal fees. CBS had used the public figure defense but mainly contended that the report was fair and accurate.

Another celebrated case hinged entirely on the public figure defense. Israeli General Ariel Sharon sued *Time,* claiming that the magazine libeled him in reporting that he had done nothing to stop a massacre in two Palestinian refugee camps near Beirut. Sharon was commander of Israeli troops in the area.

Sharon was handicapped at the trial in New York because the Israeli government would not allow certain witnesses to testify or certain evidence to be presented. The jury, after eleven hours of deliberation, ruled for *Time,* saying that it had been negligent and careless but had not stepped beyond the limits of press behavior protected by the First Amendment. In other words, Sharon was a public figure.

Again both sides claimed victory—as they struggled to pay their million-dollar legal bills.

The Supreme Court has given editors a little comfort by ruling that libel suits filed by public figures and public officials must be dismissed before trial unless evidence suggests that they can prove libel with "convincing clarity."

In a case known as *Time v. Firestone,* journalists learned to their surprise that those they might commonly consider public figures were not necessarily so in legal terms. Mrs. Firestone, wife of the tire manufacturing heir, frequently had her name and picture in the society pages. She was extremely prominent in the Palm Beach area, where she lived, and the Firestone name would bring recognition almost any place in the country. She even held press conferences after she filed a spectacular divorce suit. After the divorce was granted, *Time* magazine reported that the grounds for divorce were adultery, the reason cited when she filed for divorce. In the decree, however, the divorce was granted for "lack of domesticity." She sued, and the court rejected the public figure defense because she had not "thrust herself into the forefront of any particular controversy."

Strange rulings

Among others who have not been considered public figures are a research scientist using a $500,000 government grant, a criminal defense lawyer, and a man who pleaded guilty to contempt in 1954 for not appearing at a grand jury hearing on an espionage case. In this latter case, the Supreme Court rejected the argument "that any person who engages in criminal conduct automatically becomes a public figure. . . . To hold otherwise would create an 'open season' for all who sought to defame persons convicted of crime." It should be noted that every story crossing an editor's desk involving criminal charges against a named individual is a defamation. Any news medium that covers the police beat, in effect, has declared "open season" on those charged with crime. The narrowing of the public figure category has limited editors' resort to the actual malice privilege, the best general protection for journalists in libel suits.

The Court has expressed concern that the media can create public figures merely by giving them extensive coverage, thus creating a privilege to defame in the context of the defamation.

So the Court essentially has said that people who might generally be regarded as public figures are not necessarily public figures in the legal sense. An editor therefore should presume that *the subject of a story is not a public figure.* It always will be unclear whether a court will second-guess an editor's judgment, so it may be best to err on the side of prudence. The limitations on the actual malice privilege mean that it is more important now than it has been to rely on defenses such as accuracy and the use of information from the public record.

If copy editors set out to find just where the public figure borderline is, they may find their paper in court. Sticking to the provable

215

facts is the best way to stay out of trouble. The fact that something is legal is not cause for being sloppy with facts or careless with reputations. A loose newspaper is in no position to recommend virtue to anyone else. If a paper sticks to what the editors think is the truth and makes a mistake, it can use the public figure defense with ethical justification.

Per se *and* per quod

Libel comes under two main headings: *Per se* and *per quod*. Libel *per se* can be translated as "libel on the face of it." To be called a Communist when one is not a Communist has been considered libel *per se* for some years. The plaintiff would have to bring little into court except the offending newspaper clipping to prove the point. Libel *per quod* is the opposite. One must know the circumstances to determine the defamation. In other words, the plaintiff has to prove that a reputation was damaged. If the court decides that a person was defamed, it has to decide how much money the individual needs to soothe the damaged reputation.

In two historic cases, the plaintiffs did not want money. All they sought was a ruling by the court that they had been libeled. Theodore Roosevelt settled for a one-cent judgment. Henry Ford was less restrained. He took six times as much.

Civil and criminal

Libel is almost always a civil dispute. That is, it is a wrong being argued by two or more people. (Corporations are treated by law as persons.) No jail or prison terms are involved, unless of course the person adjudged guilty of libel does not pay the judgment.

Criminal libel does exist, but it is so rare it almost can be ignored. To get a criminal libel verdict the court would have to rule that a publication has committed a crime *against society*. In such instances, the newspaper story is held to have been so inflammatory that a segment of society riots, storms city hall, or tries to blow up the newspaper plant itself. In recent decades the idea that a newspaper could produce a riot was remote and the threat of this type of libel academic. Every few years some zealous prosecuting attorney files a criminal libel action, but nothing comes of it.

All journalists should be aware that the newspaper is responsible for *everything* it prints: news stories, headlines, features, comics, advertisements, editorials, letters to the editor, and pictures. Aside from the question of malice, quoting someone else on a defamation—such as the superintendent of schools or a policeman—does not enable a newspaper to avoid a charge of libel. It does not save the newspaper any responsibility if it is someone's signed letter in the paper that contains the defamation. Neither is there any help if the libel is in a

Classes of libel

Everything counts

216

paid advertisement. It is no relief, either, to have some letter writer say, "I will stand behind it." Don't bet on it. The paper may be assessed, say, $20,000 damages and run up a $20,000 legal bill defending itself, and may possibly lose reader confidence. Is the letter writer, who says he will be responsible, ready to cough up $30,000? Editors might cool off demands from hotheaded readers by saying, only somewhat facetiously, "Would you put up a $50,000 bond just in case we get sued for libel?" At the mere thought of such a sum most letter writers would throw their libelous prose into the wastebasket, or at least cross out the offending phrases.

Editors and reporters are often threatened with libel suits. A news source occasionally will shout, "If you print that, I'll sue you for libel!" Actually it is clear that the person doesn't have the slightest idea of what constitutes libel. So the journalist either ignores the threat or gives an ironic rejoinder. If the threats are based on ignorance, as most of them are, the journalist can take a few minutes to explain why the story is not actionable. If this isn't satisfactory, the journalist can suggest that the source consult a lawyer. A substantial number of people assume that they can tell a newspaper what to leave out, or to put in, and successfully sue if the paper disregards their orders.

In any case the journalist is smart to keep calm, although it is tempting to utter some scornful phrase. To maintain good public relations for the newspaper, staffers should be gentle in handling the irate people who dread exposure in print.

While truth, fair comment, privilege, and, to some extent, public figures are defenses against libel, there are several other ways that a libel suit can be voided:

Escape routes

1. Statute of limitations. The suit must be brought within a specified time after the offending material was printed. In most states this is one year. If the plaintiff brings suit 366 days after the story appeared, no case.

2. Out-of-court settlement. If a newspaper agrees out of court that it libeled someone and pays a certain sum of money, that act wipes out any chance of a suit.

3. Consent. This rarely occurs, but if a reporter showed a news source a story or recited the facts or charges that were going to be in the story and the source made no objection, the court assumes that the source "consented" to them.

Once a publication gets embroiled in a libel suit, its publisher, editors, and lawyers have to figure how to get out. In many instances there is no real way out. The publication then tries to show that it tried to mitigate the effects of the defamation as soon as it became aware of its error.

The best evidence of mitigation is a *retraction*. The most effective retractions appear in about as prominent a position in the paper as the libel did. If the libel appeared in a banner headline on page one, the retraction at least would have to be in a prominent position on the front page.

These other proofs of the newspaper's good faith may help:

1. The offending story was omitted or "cleaned up" in later editions.

2. An honest effort was made to retrieve the papers that included the libel. For example, if the libel was noticed ten minutes after the press run was started, the paper would have tried to call back the delivery trucks.

3. The libelous information had been copied by error.

4. The information came from a normally reliable source, such as a police chief or a judge.

5. The information was *common knowledge.* This claim refers to what "everyone knows." As an illustration, a gangster may never have been convicted of anything, but it is common knowledge that he is a gangster.

6. The newspaper had used normal precautions. This would require evidence that the paper had double-checked facts before printing them.

7. There were persistent and public rumors about the case.

8. The staffers were provoked into the publication, or they printed the statement in a campaign so intense that judgment was swayed.

9. The plaintiff can be proved to have a bad reputation.

10. There was a *prior article*—the story was printed before and the plaintiff had not complained.

Watchwords

Garrett Redmond, an official of a company selling libel insurance, has said that for years the main cause of suits has been careless crime reporting—of names, addresses, or size of crime. So the copy editor must particularly watch stories involving crime and the courts. As noted earlier, it is easy for a reporter to refer to "the killer" instead of "alleged killer"—he or she is not a killer, legally, until convicted. Sometimes police catch a person red-handed in a criminal act. To be on the safe side the story had better not say, "Joe Johnson was caught breaking into the McTavish warehouse." It would be better to write, "Police arrested Joe Johnson last night, accusing him of trying to break into the McTavish warehouse."

Picture cutlines or even placement of pictures can provide grounds for libel. If a sheriff and an alleged criminal are pictured together and the cutlines switch identification, one or both might sue. Also, if a picture runs next to a story so readers assume they go together, there may be grounds for action.

Implications and insinuations have to be watched with great care. The plaintiff can establish a good case by bringing only two or three people into court to testify that they inferred something defamatory from something the paper printed.

Not naming individuals in stories may be no protection. It is what readers believe is being said that counts. When a column in a college newspaper denounced a football player, but not by name, several readers, at least, thought the column referred to a certain player who had been accused of a serious crime. Actually, the columnist had meant someone else, but the person who some people thought was mentioned might have collected.

As a rule, a group cannot be libeled. It would be hard to convince a jury that something defamatory about a sizable group really applied to every member of the group. A rule of thumb is that the larger the group, the harder to libel. But this depends to some extent on how emotional the public is about the organization. A magazine once implied that University of Oklahoma football players came off the field and squirted dope into their noses. Some of the players sued, claiming that they had shot a peppermint solution into their mouths to relieve dryness. The Oklahoma Supreme Court agreed that the magazine should pay $75,000, which was distributed among some sixty players. The same implications might, perhaps, have been made safely about another large group, say, the Oklahoma marching band. Because band fans are fewer and less excitable than football fans, a court would probably be reluctant to see such an implication as doing an individual harm.

A few other points on libel should be considered. For instance, the dead cannot be libeled, for the simple reason that they can no longer suffer from slights to their reputations. A suit could be filed by the dead person's heirs, but they would have to prove specific injury to themselves, such as loss of income. It is possible, although unlikely, that criminal libel could occur over defamation of the dead, perhaps because a story on a dead person caused a riot.

The newspaper is safe to print charges once they are actually filed at the courthouse, as they have started through the judicial process. But a story had better not report the gist of written charges casually dropped by a lawyer on a desk in the county clerk's office. The lawyer might retrieve them twenty minutes later and throw them away.

A report on what people told a grand jury would not be considered grounds for a libel suit. But since the operations of the grand jury are secret, the presiding judge might decide the newspaper, or its reporters, are in contempt of court. For that, one can go to jail.

Executive acts are considered privileged, but it is safer to get them in writing than to quote them as given verbally. If the mayor tells a reporter that he fired the police chief "for moral turpitude," it would be helpful if the newspaper could get a copy of the letter dismissing the chief. The copy could be saved, in case the chief sues.

Copy editors should be suspicious of irony. A story that says, "George Zarfoss went to Boston to visit Mrs. Esmerelda Fisher, a 'friend,'" almost asks for a suit by Mr. Zarfoss or Mrs. Fisher, or both.

Once a plaintiff wins a libel suit, the court may award one, two, or three kinds of damages:

1. General. No proof of injury has to be submitted. These are simply presumed, without evidence, to have resulted from injured feelings or humiliation.

2. Special. The plaintiff proves specific injury. The actual pecuniary loss is assessed. Some statutes refer, in fact, to "actual damages."

3. Punitive. The court grants a cash award as punishment. Such damages may be quite high, to discourage the editors from libeling again. (Punitive awards, by the way, are taxable. The others are not.)

The First Amendment guarantees a free press and the Sixth Amendment guarantees a fair trial. The amendments clash from time to time, for what a newspaper publishes may jeopardize a fair trial, and some people, eager for fairness in court, seek to restrict the press. In a few cases, the courts have ruled that heavy publicity before trials has made it almost impossible for an accused person to receive fair treatment. The publicity may be so widespread in some cases that moving the site of the trial would not help the defendant much. For example, the President's Commission on the Assassination of President John F. Kennedy, chaired by Chief Justice Earl Warren, expressed grave doubts that Lee Harvey Oswald could have received a fair trial, given all the publicity surrounding the assassination. It is hard to believe, but a court in Washington, D.C., found twelve jurors who never had heard of the Watergate incident, and the trial of those involved in the cover-up proceeded without incident.

The ethical journalist will want to assure any accused person a fair trial and will try to inform the public about cases before the courts. Careful writing and judicious editing should eliminate nearly all conflicts between those goals. Reporters should be instructed to reject any editorial comment, to avoid inflammatory descriptions of crimes, to underplay grisly details, and to concentrate on a story tone that shows respect for the rights of the accused. It is the copy editor's job, if the reporter fails to follow these guidelines, to edit the copy so that it does.

The laws about privacy are fairly new and have not been widely tested in the courts. There has been growing concern, however, about invasions of privacy by the government, particularly with electronic snooping devices. The press has come in for its share of criticism, too, and some of it has been justified. Some reporters and photographers have the idea that anything they want to find or photograph is fair game, never considering if the picture or story could cause unnecessary anguish.

At one time it would have been enough for an editor to remind reporters and photographers to avoid the keyhole and the transom.

But today photographers and their employers may face a lawsuit over what appeared to be a good, newsworthy picture. The charge usually is invasion of privacy, and in a few cases the charges have stuck or have been an annoyance. As a result many papers have photographers get written permission from their subjects whenever a suit seems possible.

Where privacy may be involved, the newspaper editor is wise to focus on newsworthiness, not sensation. Invading privacy to get an entertaining or titillating story is dangerous as well as unethical. In court newsworthiness is a defense for invasion of privacy just as truth is for libel. News facts from the public record, for example, would be privileged, as would facts about a public figure. These and five similar guidelines are listed by Don R. Pember in "Privacy and the Press: the Defense of Newsworthiness,"[3] a discussion useful to the editor desiring more information about this developing body of law. "The press must remember," concludes Pember, "that when it is called into court in a privacy suit it is the judge or jury who will decide what is and what is not news."

As in several other legal problems involving the press, copy editors must become reasonably well acquainted with the privacy laws of their states. The state press association may have the material in booklet form, and a few minutes' reading may save the newspaper thousands of dollars.

Copyright

Any work published after January 1, 1978, can be copyrighted for fifty years after the author's death. Material copyrighted before that date is protected for twenty-eight years, with a twenty-eight year extension possible. Anything copyrighted, of course, is the property of the author or the author's heirs, and it is a violation of law to reproduce that work without permission of the publisher. The copy editor should be wary about reprinting such material to avoid getting the newspaper into an expensive and lengthy lawsuit. While nearly all books and magazines are copyrighted, few newspapers take the trouble and expense. The copy editor's concern with copyright is to avoid reprinting copyrighted material without permission from the publisher. Some newspapers, particularly small ones, often do reprint without permission material from copyrighted magazines, books, and other newspapers. In most cases the owner of the copyrighted material throws up his hands and says, "What can I do? It would cost me a thousand dollars of someone's time to get even an apology from the bum. So I'll let it go." Meanwhile, the unscrupulous editor steals editorials, articles, and cartoons without pushing any one source to legal action — and without having the courtesy to tell readers about the stolen goods.

It should be noted that relatively few papers indulge in this kind of thievery. Those that do usually pick on the small magazines, ones with no legal staff, time, or money to fight copyright violation.

---

3. Don R. Pember, "Privacy and the Press: the Defense of Newsworthiness," *Journalism Quarterly* (Spring, 1968), 14–24.

221

Thievery from a big magazine, like *Time* or *McCall's,* is a different matter. Those magazines are able to go to court for copyright violation and get a good-sized judgment, so their articles are rarely filched. Thieves also know that many people would have read the original article and would recognize that the material was stolen.

A newspaper occasionally will copyright a single story, usually something special like the result of some outstanding investigative work by the staff. The copyright also lets the paper print the story before the news is given to AP, if it is a member. AP or UPI may rewrite the story and, though quoting only a little of the original language, mention the source; then the originating newspaper enjoys the national publicity.

A few newspapers have copyrighted every issue to prevent radio stations from "reading the paper" over the air. It should be noted that the offending station would not have to read verbatim from the newspaper to violate the copyright law. A paraphrase of the stories would be a violation, too, although of course it would be harder to prove.

A rule of thumb on reprinting copyrighted material is that fifty words may be quoted directly without getting permission, as long as credit is given. This is arbitrary, to some extent. Obviously, a book publisher would be delighted if a newspaper quoted a much longer passage and contributed to sale of the book. Yet some author may object to the paper's use of twenty-seven words. The best principle is to quote copyrighted material sparingly and always with credit to the author.

Thoughtful people have studied how both the press and the public can obtain justice in libel cases. It is agreed that some people have been libeled and should be able to protect their reputations. It also is accepted that a newspaper, radio or television station, or magazine should not have to spend thousands if not millions of dollars defending themselves or paying outrageous judgments.

Reform proposed

One experimental solution has been launched at the University of Iowa. In this plan both sides in a libel case agree to forego litigation. Instead they submit their arguments to a third party in cooperation with the American Arbitration Association. After the facts have been established, a hearing is held to decide whether published material harmed a reputation and whether the material was false. The two parties will be encouraged to reach a settlement by themselves.

If the complaint against a publication is found valid, the publication would be required to print or broadcast a statement written by the arbitrator. There would be no appeal, but the publication would lose no money, legal costs would be low, and the libeled person would be assured of a correction.

The experiment and other proposed reforms may lead to simpler and less expensive ways to resolve libel disputes. All journalists, however, have had plenty of experience showing how slowly reforms are made, even when great need is obvious. It seems likely that for many more years the present unsatisfactory system will continue.

15

Ethics for journalists

THE SPORTS EDITOR of a university city newspaper talks earnestly with the managing editor. "We have evidence," the ME is told, "that two former football players at the university received gifts worth several thousand dollars when they were players. If such gifts were given to two it seems possible that others also got some. How do you think we should handle the story?"

The ME immediately senses danger. The players may be lying, seeking publicity. If they are truthful, how high does the corruption go? Are friends—coaches, university officials—involved? If the story is ignored, what might the reaction be? A full investigation could be conducted and perhaps dozens of hot stories could appear. What would happen then? Zealous fans would scream at the newspaper. Circulation would skid. A new ME might be hired.

Top editors must make an ethical decision in this case. The publisher, editor-in-chief, the ME, city editor, sports editor, and perhaps the paper's legal counsel will have to decide how to proceed. They know that they could tell the sports editor to forget any story, but their professionalism tells them that they should print news, not suppress it. They also realize that news of any suppression might leak and the paper would look cowardly.

In this fictional case, fortunately, no deadline faces editors. They have several days, at least, to make up their minds. In that time they may reach three alternatives: (1) dig for every possible angle to the story and, if the facts warrant, print the results fairly and calmly under big headlines on page one; (2) print the players' claims but nothing more, assuming that readers will discount the story; and (3) drop the whole thing, justifying the inaction by saying that the National Collegiate Athletic Association (NCAA) will discover the problem, if one exists, sooner or later.

Each alternative could exact a cost. If the first choice is followed, the paper probably will lose advertising and subscribers. The whole staff will be subject to scurrilous attacks.

The other choices will make staffers feel that they work for a spineless newspaper. Some may look elsewhere for work. If the NCAA cracks down a few months later, thoughtful readers may wonder why the paper had been so short of curiosity.

This kind of ethical problem, of course, does not erupt every week or so. Most papers set ethical rules as part of their policy. For example, they may require that a person accused of wrongdoing must have a right to reply. Or the paper will acknowledge that it has a financial stake in some newsworthy project.

Intelligent editors aim for a consistent policy, as noted in Chapter 16, to guide staffs through ethical thickets. They don't want a story today handled differently from how a similar story was handled yesterday. Most editors today try to play the news straight, so that readers will find the paper fair and believable.

One catchphrase of ethical coverage is "All the news that's fit to print." That slogan was introduced into a front page *ear* (upper corner) of the *New York Times* by Adolph S. Ochs, the publisher who brought the *Times* to greatness. It was 1897, when other New York City newspapers were vying in sensationalism, and Ochs used the phrase to emphasize the thoroughness and sobriety of ethical newspaper publishing.

The cynic may say that the slogan should be "All the news that fits," or that fits the editor's whims. Everyone knows that *all* the news can't be printed. But "all the news" implies a thoroughness that will not omit stories because of laziness or pressure. "Fit" implies that the editors will avoid sensationalism or pandering to low tastes. Yet they should find it fitting for the public to know what happens, however distasteful or terrifying, and regardless of pressures to leave out some events.

Freedom and responsibility

Some editors might say that what they print is their own business and not the province of philosophers. They would be right, in the sense that a free press is guaranteed by the Constitution, and that professional customs in the United States have evolved for handling these ethical questions. Custom probably controls more stories than editorial ethics. Yet there are philosophical bases for the rights of newspapers to operate as they do, and publishers ignore these at their peril. Society has given journalists wide latitude for their operations and decisions, but what society grants, society can take away. The number of flourishing totalitarian countries should remind everyone that press freedom is not automatic. Some nontotalitarian countries also restrict the press.

In the days of medieval kings and queens, there would have been no argument whether it was right or wrong to publish news of a scandal, even if there had been printing presses and editors. The monarch felt he or she had authority from God to make such decisions. A long trail of Star Chambers and jailed editors led from such dictatorship to a modern democratic system in which editors, within the framework of law, can print without license or censorship. People at first argued, as in the Declaration of Independence, that they had such inalienable rights from God. More recently, they are claimed as essential human rights.

John Milton provided the practical argument for press freedom. In the *Areopagitica* (1644) he argued for the "free marketplace of ideas." If all ideas were freely published, he said, the best ones would win out. It followed that people must have the right to know all the facts and arguments. So he rationalized the editor's freedom as one of the prerequisites for a working democracy. Thomas Jefferson argued for the citizen's right to the truth, being optimistic, like Milton, that a benevolent Providence allowed reasonable and moral people to run their own affairs. His idea of press freedom became one of the guarantees in the Bill of Rights.

But it is a truism that freedom implies responsibility. Those who get liberty must use it responsibly or risk losing it, whether in a developing nation or on a college campus. The grant of freedom to editors to purvey the news necessary to a democratic society carries the implied demand that they will print the news. When the press suppresses or distorts the news, it jeopardizes its claim to freedom. The unwritten expectation of American citizens is that the papers will give "all the news that's fit to print." This is the ethical imperative under which perhaps most editors work.

Recognizing these obligations, publishers sometimes proclaim idealistic platforms or policies. At conventions they are especially prone to speak in lofty phrases. A major statement of high principle became the "Canons of Journalism," adopted by the American Society of Newspaper Editors when it organized in 1923. This code states that the "opportunities [of journalism] as a chronicler are indissolubly linked [to] its obligations as teacher and interpreter." The canons speak of "sincerity, truthfulness, accuracy," of "clear distinction between news reports and expressions of opinion," of "fair play." But those canons had no teeth and, while mentioned in journalism histories, are now almost forgotten. Few working journalists could quote a single canon.

Watchwords for ethics

The difficulty is that, like democracy, freedom, and responsibility, principles of journalism must be stated as abstractions. Pessimists can readily dismiss pledges of public interest or high trust as pious hypocrisies. The problem is to relate high-sounding dictums to hard cases. Since no paper and no person is perfect, there are inevitably some tarnishes on the best papers, not to mention the corrosions on the worst.

Still, an effort must be made to set press standards. If such moral principles as love, compassion, and kindness are given lip service rather than devotion, they serve still as ideals or goals. Journalists need such abstractions to broaden their vision.

Truth is the word that summarizes many journalistic ideals. But what, philosophy has always asked, is Truth? Working newspaper

225

people know well enough what truth means on the job and don't worry too much about Truth. They check the truth of small details but also the truth of the big picture, so far as they can discover and portray it.

One important facet of truth therefore is *accuracy.* Newsrooms rightly develop a fixation on accuracy about names and addresses. But reporters must be at least as careful about accurate quotation, or about the accuracy of the impression that results from the way facts are put together.

Close to accuracy is *objectivity.* Reporters should keep themselves out of the story, and editors should see that they do. The profession's conventional wisdom dictates that editorializing will be confined to editorial pages, yet editorializing barbs in stories are always slipping by copy desks. Some reporters produce stories that are really editorials, and their editors, with sloppy ethics, byline them and print them in the news pages. The editor's job is to see that copy is accurate and free from editorial bias, whether it comes from a cub or a Washington correspondent.

The popular dichotomy of objectivity versus interpretation represents a misunderstanding of the journalist's problem with truth. The short deadpan news account, the so-called objective story, the feature story, and the interpretative piece are all on the side of objectivity. Opposite them is the subjective story by the reporter who, knowingly or unknowingly, distorts the news, whether of a minor accident or of international conflict. The sound interpretative story introduces the writer's evaluations (and these are admittedly subjective, with personal coloring), but as fairly and honestly — as objectively — as possible. The corrupt interpretation, by contrast, does not aim at truth but vents the writer's prejudices. (Editorials and editorial-page interpretations, of course, differ from news stories.)

Intertwined with accuracy and the objective search for it is the concept of *fairness.* Human limitations may prevent a paper's being really accurate and truly objective, but readers know whether the editors try to be fair. They treat everybody alike. Ideally, they are as gentle with the poor unknown as with the big shot, with the hated political party or enemy nation as with their own faction or country. Perceptive critics of the press see that it is the standard of fairness that is violated when papers over the years have blandly printed in their news columns accounts that refer to "welfare queens," "Commies," "bums," "peaceniks," and so on; the editor may protest that such highly connotative words describe accurately some social moods — but are they ever fair?

Keeping the watchwords

Editors often face pressures that may imperil accuracy and fairness. Pressure from government they understand and usually can combat, if they wish. But pressure from advertisers continues to plague journalists. Most of this pressure is subtle, for rarely does an advertiser roar, "You print that and I will yank all my ads from your paper." Instead, the advertisers may call the editor or publisher and express "concern" or "regret" that certain stories appeared. Business executives may lament the "tone" of the paper's coverage. Since the publisher often associates with business people it is hard to resist this almost constant pressure to bend to the business point of view. In many ways, this pressure is surprising, for most newspapers, being businesses, take a probusiness attitude that filters often into news, features, and pictures, as well as editorials.

Most business pages until recent years, as mentioned, were really puff sheets for the business community. They were filled with stories on financial reports, executive promotions, and new products. A story critical of business was rare, for much of the business page content was straight from the publicist's typewriter. The consumer movement has altered business coverage considerably. After all, if someone sues a major auto firm and collects a bundle, it is hard to ignore the story. If a hundred people jam city council chambers to protest poison wastes dumped by a local industry, that story can't be ignored either.

Perhaps the toughest pressure comes from the editor's or publisher's friends. What does the editor do when an old friend comes in and asks that news of his arrest for drunken driving be kept out of the paper? What happens to a letter to the editor that criticizes the pet project of the publisher's sister?

The whole newsroom usually learns quickly when the editor or publisher succumbs to such pressure. The result is a wave of cynicism, even though staffers may fail to resist similar pressure themselves. The opposite can happen, too, for the staff takes pride in learning that the boss gently showed someone his "Don't Yield" sign.

The ideals of accuracy, objectivity, and fairness are all contained in the larger ideal of truth. But are these really phony ideals, used to delude, as hypocrites use the flag and motherhood? Some hard-bitten cynics among newspaper editors would doubtless say "yes," and their shoddy papers reveal what happens when principle crumbles. Yet even the most ethical editors tend to be pragmatic about high journalistic principle. Pragmatism is an American philosophy that holds that the best way is the way that works best. Americans are idealistic, but they are also practical. Editors do not usually mount white chargers. They conform.

When the whole American society preaches that killing is wrong but sends its youth abroad to kill and be killed, when it preaches brotherhood but remains calloused about the hurt suffered by many black and brown families, it is not remarkable that this society generates publishers who preach the democratic canons but violate them in practice. They make practical compromises, as most people do.

The realistic goal for the ethical journalist is to compromise as little as possible, for being pragmatic is not the same as being venal or cowardly. The best editors aim high and therefore hit higher than those who aim low.

Much of the ethical problem for editors is one of balance. They must weigh the importance of pressures to distort or omit the news against the demands of their own conscience to be thorough and fair. At the same time they must counterbalance the frailty and limitation in their own freedom with the need to be socially responsible. They must put the individual's right of privacy in the balance against the public's right to know; and they must weigh a demand for compassion against the utilitarian requirement to do what is best for the most.

Editors, however, are not systematic philosophers who worry much about complete consistency. Pragmatically, and perhaps too hastily, they make a decision, and then another and another. This is journalistic life, and editors have to live with the results. Day to day editorial work focuses on three issues of press ethics. Each of them combines the tensions of different ethical problems, and editors must develop attitudes on each of the three that harmonize satisfactorily with their philosophies of journalism and life.

Taste in journalism as elsewhere is a subtle quality that must be learned. Still reacting against Victorianism, even cultivated editors hesitate to argue for good taste lest they be considered square. Frankness permeates our culture. As a result, the level of tasteful language in newspapers and in everyday speech has doubtless settled much lower than it was during the yellow journalism of the 1890s and the jazz journalism of the 1920s, which today's critics ridicule.

The popularity of bad taste

The pressures for bad taste in print have increased in the last dozen years. Perhaps it is healthy that readers and writers have been freed from some taboos on coarse words and profanity, when they are heard at every turn. Yet frequent use of these words cheapens language; for obscenities usually shock instead of communicate. Most editors have a rule of thumb on printing possibly shocking words and phrases: Use them only if essential to the story. That means using them rarely.

Editors face a special problem in medical reporting. If stories are thorough, it is necessary to use exact words to describe the human body and its functions. A few years back, those words rarely escaped medical textbooks. Circumstances, of course, forced changes. It is not possible to report on AIDS, for example, without being almost clinically exact on how the virus is transmitted.

Community standards

Newspapers of course must keep their standards somewhere near the levels of popular taste in their communities, and many factors have been pushing these down. Some put most of the blame on liberalized rulings by the Supreme Court. But the Court also tends to follow popular trends, and the many depressing influences on these include: the debauchery of several wars, the degeneration of plays and novels, the popularity of sexy paperbacks and sensational magazines, the proliferation of "adult" motion pictures, and the strains of living in a mass society.

The need to maintain standards in "a family newspaper" sometimes is cited to avoid the worst excesses in the press, but families already find it more and more difficult to prevent the erosion of taste in their children. One of the most important influences on family taste, of course, is television. Even more than the newspaper, TV brings into the family circle a vivid portrayal of what was once scandalous. Motion pictures exhibited with "adults only" signs a few years ago are now available to children in the living room. It takes a quick parent to keep ahead of society in "educating" a child, who may pick up on TV at age five what appropriately might be left until the teens. Many will not blame journalists if, like the tired parent, they give in.

The contexts of bad taste

While they have followed established positions on taste, many editors generally have been distressed by foul words in print but blasé about foul living conditions in town. The press—and society—have been indignant about an unmannerly act but casual about reports of people slaughtered, maimed, or scorched in a war. Press and society may be outraged by unconventional dress but only mildly distressed when commercial interests desecrate a place of beauty. Yet at this point we are discussing taste, not morals, and even if all the evil that people do were to be abolished, editors would still have problems with the good manners of print.

The problem of taste in newspapers is not, as many suppose, wholly one of restraint about vulgarity, profanity, and sex. There can be bad taste in political writing. In the partisan-press days of the early Republic, editors scurrilously attacked political enemies. During the depression of the thirties, newspapers indulged in calumny, and in recent years the issues of war, civil rights, and government scandal have triggered a barrage of bad taste.

Such issues bring up the difficulty of reporting violence with good taste. Riots and wartime killings must be reported to the public with the graphic aid of pictures where possible. Once newspapers avoided publishing pictures of dead persons. But if for comprehensive coverage present-day editors must use these pictures of the dead from riots and war, why not of the dead from disasters and accidents? Yet a line must be drawn to exclude the macabre and the gory. The grisly photograph and the lurid paragraph, in almost all cases, must be scratched.

As the chapter on picture editing indicates, the problem of taste is particularly acute in artwork. Restraint must be shown with photographs of cheesecake and gore, and what television may use cannot be the criterion. The fleeting quality of pictures on the screen may lessen

229

the objection to some material on television, but the permanence of the printed picture can make it more titillating or repelling, the factors in judgments of taste.

So editors must strike balances. They must satisfy the public's need for the facts, but they must also recall the high professional obligations of a free press in the area of taste as elsewhere. They will not let fears of the Nice Nellies keep them from portraying realistic aspects of the cruel and vulgar world as they are. But in an era when public taste has been cheapened and hardened, their greater concern will be to view the press as an instrument to maintain culture and even civilization itself.

The right to privacy

The right of privacy is a delicate thing. From the legal side, as noted, the newspaper can probably get by if its publication of personal matter is closely related to news events, but privacy is more than a question of law. Sometimes press ethics may halt an invasion of privacy that law would permit.

Since much of their most significant work is always close to invading someone's privacy, journalists may have to remind themselves not to be too hard-boiled on the question. Ordinary people, as distinguished from politicians and celebrities, have great sensitivity about "undue publicity." In an actual case a woman was incensed because the media printed and television carried the news that a teenager had shot her passing car with a BB gun. As a misdemeanor, the shooting became a public record, and an editor could see plenty of reasons for printing the news: The public could judge whether juveniles are delinquent, whether the neighborhood had gangs, whether the police were doing their job, and whether guns should be controlled. The mother could appreciate none of these arguments. She saw no reason why her age should be printed, and she feared that the teenager, knowing her name, would take reprisals against her or her children. Silly? From the editor's point of view, maybe yes. But from the point of view of privacy and her feeling about press invasions, it was her own business whether she was shot at. She wanted to be more than grist for "a couple of grafs." Some journalists have accepted this criticism and have stopped using names in some crime stories and have left out some victims' addresses, realizing that reprisals may be feared.

Mass labeling

Another level of respect for individuals is in news about whole masses of people, as in wars and urban violence. Communist newspapers for decades often stereotyped the Western world as "imperialistic warmongers." But our press easily slips into such dehumanizing labels too. In World War I we made the enemy inhuman with the word "Huns." Then in World War II it was "Japs." In more recent years those who vigorously disapproved of some United States policies were often labeled "Communist." It is much the same when reporters write loosely of "black rioters," leading white readers to react against a whole black community that may in fact be more than 99 percent peaceful.

By taking care of such issues as privacy and mass labeling, the press can be a good influence in maintaining respect for individuals. This is an area of the newspaper's greatest strength. When focusing on the individual because of honest human interest, journalism can repulse the dehumanizing forces of mass society.

The effects of news

Libertarian editors who say they print "without fear or favor" emphasize their objectivity. They override pressures to print or not to print. They learn to overlook the consequences of their decisions, for editorial action is paralyzed or biased if an editor worries about how an item is going to affect the coworker, mother, or friend of a person in the news.

There is a running debate whether newspapers have much effect anyway. Editorials have been discounted as political factors for decades. Communications researchers have been able to demonstrate few clear effects of simple reports and have drawn back from trying to analyze really complex but important problems such as how newspapers influence the vote for president.

Yet if the influence of newspapers cannot be pinpointed, can the effects of home or school or church be proved any more convincingly? Are they any less real even so? Would anyone seriously hypothesize that the media have less effect than parents or teachers? The person involved in the news does not doubt that the paper has an effect. The college football star knows that sports reporting influences his ability to get dates and a pro contract. The embezzler recognizes that at the very least news stories about his deeds can wreck his credit rating.

Editors also know that newspapers have an effect from the actions of publicity seekers asking space and acquaintances phoning to try to suppress news. They hope that the effect is good, and one of the strongest arguments for press freedom is that full reporting has a beneficial effect on the democratic process. They like to point to times when coverage has led to ouster of public chiselers and when crusades have brought civic improvements. The development of social responsibility theory urges them to be even more concerned about their paper's effect on society.

Chain reactions

As news of one suicide in a mental hospital gets around, other patients sometimes make suicide attempts. From that observation psychiatrists sometimes also conclude that news accounts of suicides tend to trigger other suicides. Some of them argue that accounts of dramatic, "mad" killings stimulate others to attempt such murders. The argument is plausible, since it is obvious that "good" ideas for

231

communities and business catch on because they get press notice. But can an editor start holding back "bad" news lest it stimulate readers to try the same misdeed?

Suicide is normally played down in papers, since usually the person who kills himself is not of great news importance. A celebrity's suicide can hardly be ignored. Except in narcotic-use deaths, many newspapers have followed the practice of giving few details on the method of suicide. They may omit the name of a poison, for example, on the theory that other depressed persons may want to take the same "out."

Other antisocial incidents are not so difficult to handle. The ordinary burglary hardly attracts others to the craft, nor does a speeding conviction encourage others to speed. In fact, news of frustrated or punished crimes is considered a deterrent.

The problem is touchier where mass emotion is involved. During an economic recession, milk-dumping reported in one agriculture center may set it off in another, and violence in one prison may touch off violence in another. News of violence and rioting seems to create a mass psychology that brings rioting elsewhere.

Newspapers can contribute to widespread panic. If the wire services carried news that an incurable flu had hit several West Coast cities, the whole nation could be panicked overnight. Similarly, the nation can become jittery if American troops are sent into a war zone. The jitters occur in most cases, however, because presidents, secretaries of state, and prominent senators make belligerent comments, often to impress the public with their bravery. The press could cool some of these eruptions by calmly reporting as many details as possible and putting them into some kind of perspective.

The editor's dilemma

Ethical editors have to consider the effects of their papers on the individual and on society. They must print, without malice or prurience, the necessary news of individuals. The truth will probably hurt less than wild rumors spread by word of mouth. The editor hates to print the news that bad conditions in the community lost it a government contract or to report news that might spread a riot. But they must be accurate and complete; otherwise they blunt their claim as defenders of the public's right to know. Practically, they will find that others disagree about their evaluation of what should be kept from the people and accuse them of venality. Editors weigh and balance personal values and may at times have to compromise a rigid application of personal principles when the public interest is at stake.

Underlying the discussion in this chapter is the assumption that the journalist will live up to the ethical standards of the community. As we assume that most cashiers will not dip into the till and that most government officials will not take bribes, we assume that editors should be honest. They will not accept gifts that will color their judgment; they will not take money to leave news out; and they will not promote a pet cause to win favors or preferment. Such general principles are easy to state but hard to practice. There are puzzling decisions to be made when journalists get down to concrete cases.

In instances of obvious pressure from advertisers or the subtle influence of the country club complex, it is usually assumed that the corrupted figure is the publisher or a top executive. Such convenient goats do not deserve all the criticism, however, for pressures to conform afflict the whole newspaper staff. A reporter may say, "I knew the druggists would be sore if I wrote that kind of a story, so I put the angle on something else." Or a desk person may say, "Man, if we printed that we would lose all the car dealers' advertising!"

Some common problems

Reporters, in particular, move among sources who may offer gifts. In most cases the gift is merely a token: a necktie or some handkerchiefs at Christmas, a lunch, or a ballpoint pen. But sometimes the gift is not a token, but a bribe. For example, reporters covering a professional football team some years ago were each given a quality portable electric typewriter at the end of the season. A reporter who accepts a $300 gift can easily slip into softening or eliminating any critical stories about the football team or its management. Wasn't that the purpose of the gift?

As mentioned earlier, gratuities to journalists are usually far more subtle. An invitation to a special cocktail party, a fancy dinner, or a plush weekend sometimes sways reporters into thinking that the merchant in trouble with the Federal Trade Commission is too charming to expose. The reporter's copy reflects this appraisal. Sometimes reporters have been flattered to the point of being obsequious when a president or a governor asks them for advice. Others can succumb to flattery coming from a much lower source.

Journalists, like everyone else, want to be liked, and it bothers some to play the role, even occasionally, of the curmudgeon. Perhaps the best advice is that the journalist should at these times ask, "Am I performing my professional obligations?"

Thoughtful reporters in Washington sometimes admit that an invitation to the home of the secretary of state for a "not for attribution" press conference causes them to crawl at least a little way into the secretary's pocket. After all, only about fifteen reporters are so honored. What reporters would not be a bit dazzled if they lunched at the White House? For weeks afterward the reporters could drop into all conversations, "When I was lunching with the president. . . . "

Personal favor

Public duty

Other governmental pressures have ethical overtones. A reporter or editor who criticizes the military is apt to be considered disloyal or at least "not on the team." A dissenter from American foreign policy may be reminded sternly, "dissent stops at the water's edge." In one case, a famous columnist critical of an administration was subjected to an organized whispering campaign to discredit him as senile. The critic of hometown business operations may be denounced in public as a "carping critic who is bringing scorn to our fair city." These pressures, often not expressed so bluntly, are hard to combat because they are subtle. In addition, the person who is pressured enjoys being praised by the rich and powerful as a person who "has helped our town a lot." What they probably mean is that the journalist has been a faithful puppet of the elite—a mouthpiece for a few rather than a person speaking for the many.

One of the toughest ethical problems facing journalists is when to be silent. All kinds of responsible people—police, industrialists, city officials—will ask the press to withhold information. The reasons are various, but at the highest levels the customary reason is *the national interest.* The best instance of silence in the national interest was President Kennedy's persuading the *New York Times* to soften a story that the United States was planning to invade Cuba. Later, when Clifton Daniel was managing editor of the *Times,* he said Kennedy had admitted that the paper should have printed the story and saved the nation the humiliation of the Bay of Pigs fiasco.

There are times, of course, when the press is quick to withhold information in the public interest. If the police are about to raid an unlicensed bar or are ready to make an unexpected arrest, the facts are withheld until after the police do their work. But the interest had better be clear; otherwise the press will not be serving the public but those who wish to operate in secrecy. Nothing so damages a newspaper's reputation and encourages rumor more than the public's realization that it omits news or favors the police, the mayor, or the manager of the town's biggest industry.

Political involvement

Another practical ethical consideration for an editor is whether to run for public office or to head a special committee. It inflates anyone's ego, of course, to be asked to run, but as a candidate or an elected official, the journalist puts the newspaper in a position either to be partisan or to be accused of partisanship. The decision becomes acute when journalists, being objective, believe that they are the best-qualified person for the office.

One newspaper editor became chairman of a civic committee to investigate new water sources for the city. It was an important job and a position he could fill capably. But the findings of his committee became controversial and the key issue in a mayoral campaign. Much of the public thought that the newspaper was acting as a mouthpiece for the editor's own views on water sources. The newspaper's standing in the community declined even though no bias was ever proved.

It would be unwise to suggest that no journalist ever take public office. Many editors have been good public officials and their papers good public servants as well. But no journalist should take such a position without thorough consideration of the perils and a couple of pledges that the newspaper never will sound like a press agent.

Ethical journalists, of course, work hard to be responsible. They do their best to set aside their prejudices and concern for professional acclaim. They strive to give readers and listeners the truth.

Using freedom responsibly

Experienced journalists know how difficult it is to get the truth. They interview widely, check their sources' claims with care, and examine records. They write and edit to produce stories that provide solid, pertinent information. Despite their care, they often discover that some important fact or set of facts has been overlooked. A source may have misled them; a record may be inaccurate; the evaluation of some fact could be invalid.

The journalist working on a deadline often no more than hours away obviously has special problems. It is tempting not to make one more telephone call, check another record, or reflect on the accuracy and completeness of the story at hand. The result occasionally is a story without specific error but one that has neglected certain facts or a breadth of opinion.

Too many journalists, who consider themselves ethical, unconsciously gravitate to mainstream reporting. They interview officials and private citizens with conventional views. They even have a list of such sources. Their basic sources may be a press secretary, a few in government, a think-tank expert, and a certain professor. Almost all of these people come close to sharing the same point of view. Sharply differing opinions or analyses are cited rarely.

Without thinking much about it, journalists often latch onto a current interpretation of events. They write story after story based on that interpretation until facts destroy the premise. An example can be seen in political reporting where for a few weeks journalists may declare that Candidate Smith hasn't a chance because of youthfulness, inexperience, and lack of key supporters. A month later these prophecies explode and a new interpretation is seized upon.

Ethical journalists should not flatter themselves by reciting, "I'm careful. I'm fair. I'm accurate. I'm as objective and ethical as I can be." Instead, they might ask themselves, "Am I missing anything? Am I getting tricked anywhere? Am I getting a wide range of viewpoints on crucial issues? Am I simply following the pack, writing stories that reflect the value judgments of my peers? Have I been charmed by a source?"

Such journalists, if they answer honestly, are more likely to produce fair, evocative, factual, and valuable information. They also will come closer to printing the whole truth.

16

Problems of policy

THE *ST. LOUIS POST-DISPATCH* carries this statement of policy by its founder each day in its masthead:

THE POST-DISPATCH PLATFORM

I know that my retirement will make no difference in its cardinal principles, that it will always fight for progress and reform, never tolerate injustice or corruption, always fight demagogues of all parties, never belong to any party, always oppose privileged classes and public plunderers, never lack sympathy with the poor, always remain devoted to the public welfare, never be satisfied with merely printing news, always be drastically independent, never be afraid to attack wrong, whether by predatory plutocracy or predatory poverty.

Joseph Pulitzer

April 10, 1907

Every newspaper should work out a clear and consistent concept of its aims and operations. The set of principles or guidelines for its procedures—the chart that sets its course—is called its policy. A newspaper policy may be Republican or Democratic, independent or nonpartisan. It may range from liberal to conservative on social and economic questions. Policy also has a good many other facets, including the paper's attitude on news, the community, and reform.

Much of the policy is unwritten, carried in the heads of editors. Some points may be vague, some may be inconsistent. But it does offer a kind of "common law" that governs the way decisions will be made.

The official policy of a newspaper is the publisher's responsibility. That is elementary, but there is so much obfuscation on the subject that the blunt statement of the object is necessary. Policy is not set by reporters, by the clerks in classified advertising, by advertisers, by professors at the local college, or by subscribers in the well-to-do part of town. All of them may be influential, but ultimately it is publishers who decide debatable policy issues.

In the American economy the publisher's power over policy rests on ownership. Our system does not give control of the press to the state or cooperatives, much less to any interest group. As the person paying the piper calls the tune, the person or corporation that puts up the capital for a paper decides what it will say and what it will not say.

One indication of confusion on this point is the perennial tendency of some college editors to claim greater power of policy than the colleges are willing to give them. In a private college, individuals put up the capital on which the student paper ultimately rests, and in a state institution, the taxpayers provided most of the original funds. The locus of real power is obscured by talk of campus democracy, by the fact that students may subsidize the paper, and by the efforts of wise administrators to give editors maximum freedom. But if there is a libel suit, the institution, not the editor, pays. When student journalists don't like it that way, they quit, perhaps to start their own off-campus paper. Then they meet the bills and pay for any libel suits, and they have a publisher's freedom to print and not to print, within the bounds of law and ethics. (Nor would they then, having put energy and money into their paper, probably be inclined to hand it over to others to run as they pleased, without strings! It's not the nature of publishing or ownership.) Though it would be nice to get something for nothing, there is no way to get the freedom to print as one pleases without paying in energy, money, and risk.

Because modern newspapers require substantial capital, only the prosperous or rich can own one that appeals to more than a small segment of the public. It is possible, of course, to rent a few rooms, buy a couple cheap word processors, and produce a good-looking newspaper that appeals to several thousand readers. A printing firm can handle the press work. Less handsome "alternative" papers were started in the sixties. Many failed but several survived in bigger cities and have become substantial and profitable publications.

Lest the publisher's power appear overwhelming, it should be noted that most publishers are more interested in checking balance sheets than in advancing policies. They infrequently hand down word on policy. More often, they turn day-to-day policy over to those who will formulate policies they approve. When Col. "Bertie" McCormick was chief of the *Chicago Tribune,* a Northwestern University professor often asked *Tribune* editors whether memos instructed them to be anti-British or antilabor. The teacher never found that the colonel gave such orders; the staff simply edited the paper on those lines because they thought he wanted it that way. Sometimes, indeed, the true policymaker of a paper is not so much the real-life publisher as a kind of newsroom phantom the editors see representing the publisher's wishes.

Though the publisher ultimately is responsible for policy and can change it, the top editors may have considerable influence in shaping it. Their first duty is to examine the phantoms for realities. They may find that the staff still worships sacred cows that the publisher slaughtered long ago. Changing conditions naturally demand new policies, which editors can either make or suggest in hope of approval from the top. At minimum, they can try to influence the publisher to adopt the best policy. As policies prove unworkable or unwise, editors also can encourage the publisher to change them. The editor has special professional competence, after all, and a smart publisher will consider any reasoned arguments. As an example, the managing editor of a paper in Rochester, New York, asked a copy editor how he thought their paper could be improved. He replied that the paper printed almost no news about neighboring Canada, just across Lake Ontario. The editor agreed, and it became policy to give more attention to Canadian events.

It is possible that strong and somewhat brash subeditors will, in effect, change policy by switching content. The publishers may not notice it, or they may even approve the change. They could grumble a little but not take the effort to order a reversal. They might be annoyed, of course, to the point of shifting the editor to a different job.

One troubling complication in this owner-policy situation is the ambiguity of absentee ownership, which today is widespread because so many papers are owned by chains. At its worst, the absentee system means that the owners are interested only in the money a paper makes. Management pinches pennies, lets editorial quality deteriorate, and adopts policies designed to save dollars rather than to better a community. At its best, however, absentee ownership may give dedicated professionals the authority to run a good paper.

William Randolph Hearst, Sr., personally sent editorials and orders through his whole chain of papers, and his editors everywhere reacted like bright puppets. But that is old-fashioned. Hearst papers under William Randolph Hearst, Jr., now have a much looser system. Gannett papers make such a point of autonomy that only recently has "chain" been used to describe them; they called themselves a "group" before. Looking back over his long career, the late president of Knight-Ridder Newspapers, John S. Knight, said he didn't believe in headquarters overseeing what his papers printed. He trusted his editors' judgment.

In looking at the publisher's role, it is also wise not to get too exalted a concept of what policy formation is. The publisher does not send down a code to some Moses. Such a code could no more cover all cases than the Ten Commandments, and, in any event, it would have to be interpreted by busy copy editors. The newspaper business is pragmatic. Let's say the publisher decrees the paper should be fair. Fine, but is it fairer to put in this news fact or leave it out? By repeatedly answering this question writers and editors form policy.

Or suppose a publisher orders that the paper support candidate A. Professionalism decides how far the editors can go with such a policy, and if it is pushed too crassly, the paper—and the publisher's bank account — will suffer. In short, policy is not like a statue, which is formed once and for all. It is more like a hedge, which editors can prune and nurture.

Goals and policy

Policies stem from a newspaper's objectives. Where the goal is full and fair coverage, editors can develop specific policies to reach it. But if the aim is simply to make as much money as possible, other policies are required. In his book *Responsibility in Mass Communications,* Wilbur Schramm lists six facets of the "emerging code of new responsibility." These are separation of editorials from news, accuracy, objectivity, balance, fairness, and reliability. Already, as ethical goals are envisioned, the outlines of a newspaper policy begin to emerge.[1]

Research on readers' ideals found that *accurate* and *fair* rank first and second. *Ethical* and *adequate* come next. These match those attributes listed by Schramm. Evaluative terms like *interesting, prompt, profitable,* and *conservative* scored poorly. One might be cautious on such findings, however, for almost anyone would guess before such a survey was taken that most people would vote for accurate and fair. They sound so respectable. One might suspect that readers may say they would put top priority on accurate, but in reality would choose interesting when it comes to pick a story to read. Nevertheless, professional journalists should establish accuracy and fairness as the leading demands they put upon themselves.

The editorial mix

Magazines operate with what editors, borrowing from chemistry, call a *formula.* The term refers to the combination of ingredients — articles, photos, stories, cartoons, and so on — that regularly go into the publication. The shifting nature of the news makes it more difficult to stabilize a newspaper's formula or recipe. A heavy mix of foreign news may be best on one day; several local stories may demand treatment on the next. Nevertheless, the concept of a formula helps show how editors develop practices that reach policy goals. The serious paper has one editorial mix, the frivolous another. Descending from the heights of press ideals, practicalities of policy are studied by considering three major ingredients — opinion, news, and entertainment.

Opinion

It is a truism that the American newspaper separates news and opinion, with the editors' views confined to the editorial page. Though the ideal may be violated, the policy remains sound. If editorial writers stay within the bounds of law and good taste, few ques-

---

1. See the chapter on "Truth and Fairness" in *Responsibility in Mass Communications* (New York: Harper & Bros., 1957; rev. ed. by William Rivers and Wilbur Schramm, Harper and Row, 1969) 217ff.

tions are raised about their right to support or oppose candidates or programs. Whether the publisher sets editorial policy or hands the task to the page's editors, decisions about the stands to be taken in these opinion columns are a keystone of the paper's overall policy.

Policy also has to be made for syndicated columns. Some editorial pages carry only columns that support the paper's own positions. A more common policy is to select columns that give "both sides." A vigorous, aggressive paper might, however, adopt a policy of selecting—even of finding and cultivating—columnists who will argue a wide variety of stimulating and nonconformist opinions.

Guidelines also must be established for letters to the editor. A sensible and common policy is to print as many letters as possible and to encourage contributions. If at least a little of every literate contribution is used, the policy wins wide reader support.

News

If accuracy and fairness are desirable goals, independence is a leading virtue in news policy. Selection of the news, as indicated already in discussions of news evaluation and journalism ethics, must be free from influence by editorial page policy, advertising pressures, or the biases of publisher or staffers.

Completeness and breadth of coverage are also important in news policy. Editors and publishers of papers outside the largest metropolitan centers sometimes complain when press critics hold up the thoroughness of the *New York Times* as an example. Though papers with smaller resources cannot offer such a wealth of news, the goal for even a paper of 50,000 should be coverage in breadth and depth of "all the news that's fit to print." By carefully selecting and editing news from local staffers and from the wires, editors can cover world news with at least moderate thoroughness and local news with completeness and enterprise.

As outlined before, newspapers should aim to cover constructive as well as destructive events and trends. The outstanding ethical example of one religious body's journalistic effort, the *Christian Science Monitor,* is enlightening on this point. The *Monitor* does not ordinarily print unpleasant items. Because Christian Science emphasizes the basic goodness in the universe, the paper developed from this faith plays up the wholesome and plays down the bad. Christian Science views evil, disease, and suffering as unreal. It follows that a newspaper founded on this view would print only news rooted in the real or true. So the *Monitor* usually does not print news of crimes or deaths or disasters. Evil is denied by its editors, and some newspaper readers wish that other journalists would follow the example.

No other newspaper, however, can ignore the reality of war and violence. Although trying to deal positively with such events, the *Monitor* makes the pragmatic compromise and does print news of these man-made disasters. This paper's general bias toward "good news," however, is wholly satisfactory only to members of this church and perhaps a few others, since most Americans probably do not want newspapers that ignore accounts of evil.

Newspapers, of course, print a great deal of good news. Stories on medical advances, tax cuts, or the arrest of a dangerous criminal are all examples of good news. But, as noted, what is good news to one person may be bad news to another. Democrats rejoice when papers print the good news of their party's victory. To Republicans the news is bad. A boost in the price of XYZ stock is good news to the stockholder but bad news to the person who sold the same stock yesterday.

A sizable number of people wish the press would play down the bad news. Business executives often want journalists to keep pretending that the economic picture blooms with roses when in fact business is down 8 percent over the previous year. Some sports fans go into rages if their heroes are described as anything less than magnificent. But faking, slanting, or distorting the news can be dangerous. People can be badly misled and take steps that cause considerable anguish. As an example, if a paper kept trumpeting how a city was growing, some builders might construct shopping centers or apartment houses that could not be rented, hurting the builders and the city.

A few papers for a time tried to promote the positive side of the community by printing lots of stories about civic accomplishments and saying little about crime, accidents, and job layoffs. Most of them gave it up after a few months. The efforts usually were strained. Editors were forsaking normal news judgment and the whole attempt smelled of "boosterism," not journalism.

Editors should deal almost daily with some specific policy as a guide. As an example, how should the paper handle the story of a crime allegedly committed by the thirty-two-year-old son of a United States senator? Should a big story be printed? Should the paper assume that the son has not been under the guidance of the senator for a dozen years and give the story little play or none at all? What about memoirs contending that thirty years ago the author and a famous person had a torrid romance? Is this item fact or fantasy? Even if it is fact, what play should the story receive? What is the policy on stories that sound as though the reporter was overzealous, reaching for a conclusion that was not buttressed by fact? How will the paper handle in-house conflict of interest, such as allowing a business writer to become a bank director? Too many papers let these policy questions go unanswered and the staff stumbles along until the paper unnecessarily hurts feelings and reputations or embarrasses itself.

Entertainment

It would be foolish for a newspaper to have a policy of *no* entertainment, though some observers apparently feel that should be the goal. It is true that certain papers strive for almost nothing else. On the other hand, in response to the disillusioning development of television largely as entertainment, some editors feel that seriousness is the best competing policy. The policy of a paper on this score, of course, must be tailored to its readership. But, along with opinion and news, entertainment has a legitimate place. It has been a part of newspapers almost since they emerged from flysheets, and it should continue in any editorial formula. The question is, how much of this leavening ingredient should be included?

Sometimes editors beg the question by contending that everything they print should be interesting, and therefore entertaining. That is neither possible nor desirable. Some important developments, such as crises in the gold market, are by their nature dull to ordinary readers. They can be explained clearly, and even interestingly, but it would be fatuous to twist these stories into entertainment.

Some people dismiss as entertainment only that which does not fit their own tastes. Some editors will rail against fluffy features, routine pictures, and agony columns as a waste of space. They will fight to keep the crossword puzzle, however, because they try to solve it every day.

An honest, objective look at newspaper policy would include an analysis of what is proper to the editorial page, what is real news, and all the rest—comics, advice columns, sports, feature photographs, and lifestyle sections. (Editors might differ as to whether cultural coverage—book reviews and music criticism, for example—is entertainment or a part of the news/opinion spectrum, but such features are part of a good mix.)

Sound policy would prescribe a balanced mixture of entertainment to keep the paper from dead seriousness or hopeless frivolity. (Since the *New York Times* is so often cited as quality journalism, it might be noted that its editors have consciously tried—and succeeded—in the last fifteen years or so to brighten its pages with material that must be categorized as entertainment, such as features on food, home decorating, and living styles. The *Times* carries no comics but the serious *Monitor* runs one occasionally.)

One guide to whether entertainment succeeds is to check the readership. One sometimes senses, as eyes wander over the two or three pages of comics, that half of them might be omitted with little loss of circulation. From time to time editors drop a comic and remark on how few complaints they get. A little survey ought to find whether certain features have any solid appeal. The results might be surprising. One editor of a paper with 13,000 circulation gave up *Little Orphan Annie* as she was descending to earth in a parachute and only four readers complained!

Witty or satiric comic strips came close to disappearance a few years back. One of the great ones, Walt Kelly's *Pogo,* dropped out about a year after Kelly's death. His widow said she could not continue to draw the strip in the smaller panels now used by newspapers. Charles Schultz' *Peanuts* survived, of course, and Garry Trudeau's irreverent *Doonesbury* has captured large and loyal readership. Some relatively new strips, *Frank & Earnest, Born Loser,* and *The Far Side,* have revived humor in the comics. These fit properly into the budget as entertainment.

Political cartoons have a hallowed place in world journalism, and editors both express opinion and win entertainment points by using good cartoons. These belong on the editorial page, although a few papers put them on page one, where readers sense that they really are editorials. The *Los Angeles Times,* however, shifted the brilliant work of Paul Conrad onto the op-ed page, saying that Conrad was free to express his own opinions, which did not necessarily always match those of the editorial page.

The newspaper as public utility

In the somewhat mixed economy of the United States, the newspaper today fits somewhere between the old libertarian theory of maximum editorial freedom and the emerging theory of social responsibility. And no matter how ardently Jeffersonians might wish it, they do not today have the freedom to be irascible and irresponsible, as did the editors when Jefferson was president. The role of the newspaper in the last years of the twentieth century must be thought out in new terms.

The image most appropriate for the modern American newspaper is probably that of public utility. The metaphor is imperfect but instructive. A telephone company or an electric corporation enjoys a monopoly that even free-enterprise enthusiasts rarely question. Though public commissions may control any aspects of the business, such as determining whether its rates are fair, the utility is relatively free to plan, purchase, and expand. Yet utility executives recognize that they must serve the whole community and cannot arbitrarily ignore any citizen, providing bills are paid. Similarly, the newspaper enjoys many protections under the Constitution and by informal tradition. It holds responsibilities both to the community and to individuals, no matter how odd their ideas may appear.

The public-utility concept may help publishers and editors form realistic policies for the times. The newspaper, as public utility, is a business but not just any business. It has a responsibility to convey essential information to a democratic society. Citizens have as much right to criticize how well it does this job as they have to criticize telephone service.

The newspaper is also a humanitarian enterprise, but not like the Red Cross. Rather, it is a business like the gas company, which serves people as it earns. Lumber companies may indicate in advertising that their sole interest is in planting trees, but ultimately they exist to produce profits for stockholders. The legitimate money needs of a newspaper should not be forgotten in fogs of humanistic discourse.

Publishers often sound hardheaded when they speak of their properties and profit and insincere when they carry on about their ideals. For their part, intellectual critics are inclined to be cynical about the business aspects of publishing and naive about the humanistic potential of our present newspaper system. Business people and intellectuals might find a common realistic ground if they recognize the modern newspaper as a public utility, requiring policies that produce profits and at the same time serve society well. Newspaper consumers, too, should examine their views with more care. Often lay critics of the press demand fuller coverage, more courageous reporting, and less advertising, yet they might be the first to complain if their demands were met. They most likely would not read the wider coverage, would howl if a courageous reporter raked a little muck in their own backyards, and would object to paying a dime more to help the paper reduce advertising.

Any editor, then, should not rush to accept the standards offered by critics. Human beings like to make lofty statements, but they often fail to match those statements with performance.

How does the concept of the public utility relate to policy aims? Such goals as accuracy and fairness, as noted, define the newspaper's stance toward information. But related aims emerge from its public utility role: Improving the community by reducing racial and sex stereotypes, trying to be sensitive to the feelings of all people, and campaigning to eliminate corrupt and tawdry conditions.

Three aims of policy

Community betterment

It would be difficult to find a publisher who would not say that his policy is to improve the community. That goal is minimal, but it is also a major challenge.

It will illustrate a paper's potential for community betterment if, in a seeming digression, light is focused on an issue where most papers have failed and where many are still failing: Their coverage of minority groups and, specifically, of the black, Puerto Rican, and Mexican-American communities. During the sixties, editors met severe problems in covering the so-called Black Revolution and the growing discontent of Hispanics. Those problems eased somewhat in the seventies and eighties, but no informed journalist would expect the solutions ever to be easy.

Basic to the problem is the fact that until about 1970 almost all newspapers were edited by whites for whites. Communities with "white schools" and "white churches" also have had "white newspapers," and blacks quite properly were bitter about a "white press." Blacks had been "the invisible men and women" to white society, including white editors and reporters. While there have been many gains, white journalists still don't see the world as a black reader does, and some continue to be blind to their blindness.

A traditional source of criticism has involved labeling: Mexican, Puerto Rican, Negro, colored, women. Part of the trouble is the general problem of identification. How can you make clear, sometimes, who people are without some label, such as student, Moslem leader, Klansman, feminist, veteran? Editors can reduce the problem if they do not use labels that reinforce stereotypes.

Journalists have made great strides in reducing stereotypes. It is somewhat rare to see racial references that have no bearing on the story. Sexist tones still creep into copy, of course, but the instances seem to get sparser every year. Journalists still tend to lump the young and the old as homogenous groups, as though all young and all old are almost exactly alike. Editors need to guard against these flaws.

One reason for progress is that women now make up a sizable part of news staffs and are rising often to top editorial positions. Blacks, Hispanics, and native Americans work as reporters, editors, and photographers. Some newspapers, notably the *Detroit Free Press* and the *Washington Post,* have a good many minority staffers, with several in management positions. All is not ideal, however, for some women and black staffers have won antidiscrimination lawsuits.

Some journalists have trouble grasping what is outside their experience. They may understand the major religious denominations, for example, but they get muddled on differences, say, between fundamentalists and evangelicals. Too often they don't take time to seek clarification. Sportswriters couldn't believe how a major basketball player, a vegetarian, could perform unless he ate meat. They apparently had never met a vegetarian.

Idealists puzzle some journalists, too, who find it difficult to believe that anyone would put ethics first, ahead of money and prestige. The idealist often is treated as a dreamer or a phony. At the same time, some saintly persons are lionized as flawless.

In the sixties and seventies many reporters and editors were chastised for concentrating on the spectacles in protests. Journalists were accused, often justly, of only reporting the statements and actions of the most militant groups. The lesson has not always been heeded. Journalists too often still respond hastily to the scathing statement, the exaggerated claim, or the rigged event, without bothering to seek reasoned and restrained comments. Many politicians have complained bitterly that their meticulous, cautious, and studious proposals get ignored by the press while a dramatic but shallow plan by someone else appears on page one.

Crusades

It may be the policy of the publisher and editor to pick evils to fight and to conduct what has long been called a "crusade." In news stories, pictures, cartoons, and editorials they hammer away to clean out gamblers, build a civic center, get the city manager plan adopted, or "run the crooks out of city hall."

Crusading easily slips into imbalance and unfairness, but it is exciting journalism. If crusading seems not so general or potent as it was a generation or two ago, the annual recognitions in the Pulitzer Prizes and the Polk and Sigma Delta Chi awards suggest that many papers still have crusading policies. To the crusader, merely giving the news is too slow a road to community betterment. Even when a paper is not seeking a crusade, important events are thrust upon it in such ways that honest journalists are forced to look for the hidden facts if the paper is to meet its responsibilities. Recent Pulitzer Prizes indicate that several papers have plunged into what often would be unpopular frays to correct abuses which involve people's lives or fortunes.

245

Some of the Pulitzer Prizes have been given in recent years to these papers or reporters:

John Woestendiek of the *Philadelphia Inquirer* for his stories that proved the innocence of a man convicted of murder.

Edna Buchanan of the *Miami Herald* for "versatile and consistently excellent police beat reporting."

Alex S. Jones of the *New York Times* for his specialized report on the sale of Louisville newspapers, owned by the Bingham family, to the Gannett chain.

Jeffrey R. Lyon and Peter Gorner of the *Chicago Tribune* for their series on the implications and promises of gene therapy.

Andrew Schneider and Matthew Brelis of the *Pittsburgh Press* for their stories of threats to airline passenger safety caused by inadequate medical screening of pilots. Schneider won a Pulitzer earlier for stories on the failure of kidney transplants.

Clark Hallas and Tobert B. Lowe of the *Arizona Daily Star* of Tucson won for their investigations into the University of Arizona's athletic department. The Arizona case brought angry responses from sports fans and team boosters. Advertising contracts were canceled and editors were vilified by the university president, business leaders, and alumni.

These stories probably did not make the newspapers an extra nickel from circulation or advertising. It is also probable that the papers spent thousands of dollars to get the information.

Community leadership

Policy also may concern the newspaper's role in community leadership. This leadership is continuing, perhaps less intensely than the crusading burst, but in a more vigorous and directed fashion than that necessary for general community betterment. For example, take the perennial issue of schools. A paper may work for community betterment simply by giving thorough coverage of what is happening in local education. A crusading paper may go after the hide of the superintendent or try to get its candidates elected to the school board. But a paper oriented toward leadership might search out the opinions of teachers and parents, discuss alternate possibilities on its editorial page, and develop interpretative stories showing how similar communities have tackled similar problems.

A paper may operate on all three levels at different times, or even at the same time. Most of its effort may go to straight coverage and editorials that help the citizens themselves better their community. The paper may crusade on the school drinking and drug problem, while, simultaneously, its editors may move in and out of leadership efforts on pollution, street violence, or international combats. A newspaper will be most effective, however, if the publisher and editors plan a coordinated policy small enough for the staff to handle yet big enough to make an impact. Too often the crusade starts out dramatically and then, like so many heralded grand jury or congressional investigations, it fizzles because of inadequate planning.

In one vital aspect of policy, a newspaper cannot avoid contributing to the community's betterment or, perhaps, to its decline. The paper's policies influence what the citizens think about. Television and radio, ministers, professors, and clubs all have some part in picking out the big issues for local discussion, but the influence of the newspaper probably outweighs all of them. Television has great influence on the perception of national issues and personalities, but little on state and local affairs. The paper establishes the agenda of concerns, as if it were chairman of a giant town meeting. If the paper prints a lot about muggings, the people worry about muggings. If it gives complete coverage to meetings that deal with school closings, the readers will be talking about the shrinking school system. Riots, pornography, peace activities, or drugs become public concerns or not as the paper covers or ignores them.

The community agenda

Especially through interpretative stories, the newspaper sets the agenda of public discussion and action. If it does not cover, say, the desires or demands of the black community, it is difficult for community leaders to generate public concern. If it does print such material the public becomes at least slightly aware. Sometimes unobtrusively, sometimes forcefully, the paper's policies change the community for better or worse. The changes came because readers got facts and analyses of those facts. With that information the public can decide whether to act.

17

Editorial management

ALL ORGANIZATIONS NEED MANAGERS to reach their goals. Newspapers, in particular, need a whole set of them to produce a daily product that informs readers of their community and world.

Publishers are the top newspaper managers, because they often are also the owners, and they select a range of people to run advertising, news, circulation, and production departments. Each department head chooses several assistants, often without consulting the publisher.

The head of the news department is the editor, who may also be the publisher. The editor, however, rarely deals with the day-to-day tasks of getting out the paper. An executive editor or managing editor, or both, manage the news operation. The executive editor usually fits into a niche between editor and managing editor. One or the other appoints the various subeditors: city, state, sports, wire, news, lifestyle, and business.

These subeditors may have considerable authority on what news to cover, how it is written, and how it is displayed. They confer with the managing editor only every few days, in some cases, although the city, state, wire, and news editors probably discuss the major news play with the ME once or twice a day. The aim is to inform the managing editor on what key editors are planning and, possibly, to let the ME veto or alter some plan.

Managing editors shuffle the staff to get the right people in the right jobs, solve personality conflicts, decide whether to launch some investigation, and strive to make efficient use of equipment and human talent.

The good ME deliberates a bit on how each task can be done. A bulletin board note or a memo to a subeditor or staffer might be the proper way. A short conference with the city editor and two or three reporters may be another. A blunt talk with a staffer may solve one problem while a pleasant lunch with someone else will settle another.

All editor-managers must be concerned with money, in some cases lots of money. They know that quality does not come cheap, so they probably plead with the publisher for a bigger budget to permit hiring more and better staffers, acquiring more modern equipment, and paying for special and costly reports.

They also must strive to make maximum use of the staff's talents. For example, it is foolish to let a $650-a-week reporter spend an hour typing figures into a computer when a $300-a-week clerk could do it. Managers might try also to stagger copy editors' work hours so they are likely to stay busy most of the day.

Management style

Every editor inevitably develops a style of administration and so puts a personal stamp on procedure. Some editors are authoritarian, barking orders and pulling rank. Others are more democratic, discussing rather than dictating.

Modern management stresses evaluation of people to understand how they can be motivated to work best for a common goal. Many publishers in recent years have grasped that fact and have sent some managers to conferences on learning how to handle their jobs better.

Too many editors, however, have taken key positions with no consideration of how to deal with people. As in other fields, a fair number of martinets or neurotics get into high editorial positions. A few others have tried the super-friendly approach, always forgiving blunders and incompetence. They can't, when needed, become firm and demanding. They stumble badly, too.

A newspaper manager ought to keep in mind that proud, educated, and talented reporters, editors, and photographers resent being treated like drones. They want to share in some decisions and want to be allowed to argue for specific change. The paper then becomes "our paper," not merely "the paper."

Editors should make an extra effort to fit young men and women and their talents into the operation, because they often have fresh ideas and can write or edit for a young audience. Young staffers probably have always complained that top management, usually middle-aged or older, is behind the times. Some of their criticism springs from youthful impatience, yet there is often a real lag as newspapers and other institutions cling to the old.

Newspaper executives must try to be open and flexible. They should take pains to review their policies frequently. Some rules perhaps never were wise or workable; now they hamstring and stultify. It is not unusual for a new staffer, hearing of a newsroom taboo, to mutter, "Who thought up that stupid rule?" If there is a good reason for the policy, it ought to be explained. Editors also must avoid defending outmoded standards with the cliché, "We've always done it that way."

Flexibility and imagination also help in the editorial managing of money. It is one thing to be economical and another to be parsimonious. Few things annoy a reporter or subeditor more than having the management pinch pennies on taxi fares or ordinary newsroom supplies. Fortunately, few mossback publishers remain, and most newsrooms are clean, attractive and comfortable, because the publisher was willing to pay for pleasant working conditions.

In newsrooms across the country money questions generate most of the headaches among managing editors. They are not trained as accountants, and their rise through the news ranks probably indicates that figuring budgets is one of their least favorite tasks.

If chief editors represent all the editorial underlings, they also represent management. Reporters and subeditors may feel such editors front for the publisher just as university deans are accused of fronting for administrations to hold down faculty salaries or throttle students. They have a delicate role to play as they interpret the realities of publishing to staffs no more enthusiastic about budgeting than top editors are. At the same time, the chief editors must convince everyone, above and below, that they are honest and fair.

Salaries and the Guild

The wicket is especially sticky in bargaining with the journalists' union, The Newspaper Guild. The Guild's job is to persuade all levels of management to give editors, reporters, and photographers a better break in pay and fringe benefits. Steps to organize this union were taken in 1933, in the depths of the Great Depression, by the newspaper columnist Heywood Broun. Since it is organized on industrial trade union principles, the Guild includes not only those employees in editorial but also those in advertising, business, circulation, maintenance, and promotion. Membership hovers around 33,000.

Union locals for papers in more than a hundred cities in the United States, Canada, and Puerto Rico now have agreements with publishers. Major magazines and both wire services also have Guild contracts. The Guild estimates its contracts cover more than half the newspaper circulation in the United States. Even though managing editors may have been members on their way up, they often have to take management's part in union negotiations.

The Guild is continuing pressure to raise the minimum pay for experienced reporters, photographers and copy editors, called journeymen. The so-called top minimum of $200 a week was first adopted at the *Washington Post* in 1964. That figure has at least quadrupled since, and it is not unusual these days for metro staffers below top management to make $45,000 to $50,000 a year.

Guild and non-Guild salaries on the biggest papers provide incomes that match pay for experienced professors, some lawyers, many dentists, and lesser business executives. Papers with 50,000–100,000 circulations usually pay about $5,000 less a year than the giants offer. On papers below 50,000 the salary picture is muddled, with some paying quite well while others start staffers at pay below those of public school teachers and keep them there. Many editors cry poor mouth, even when their papers are yielding 20 percent profits. Almost all newspapers could pay editorial staffers substantially more and still make profits better than almost any other business.

The Guild, of course, also aims for cost-of-living increases, medical insurance payments, more vacations and holidays, and a shorter work week. Most Guild members now work a 37½-hour week, with overtime payment for extra hours.

In the dickering—and sometimes bickering—with the Guild, managing editors can be crushed between the stones of management and staff. But if they are strong, and if they maintain good humor, they can often mediate differences. Editors of integrity will be trusted when the staff is told frankly about how far the publisher can go on salaries and fringe benefits. At the same time they can press management to remember that not only the newspaper's reputation but also its financial strength rests on quality, which in turn depends upon competitive salaries.

Managing editors may not fret if they cannot get the money they want for stenographers and copy aides. But they can bleed if they see their best staffers leave for higher pay at other papers. If they need two new reporters, and they persuade the publisher to give them $50,000 for salaries, they know they won't lure real talent with $25,000 apiece. If they can get $75,000, however, they might pay one $40,000 and another $35,000 and attract seasoned reporters, possibly even from bigger papers. More than money is required, however. Reportorial freedom, good assignments, and praise for good work are essential too. The editor with clear goals and drive can attract writers who admire sharp leadership, but in the end even that editor needs dollars in the budget.

The Guild also has tried in recent years to gain minor control over what once were thought to be the sole prerogatives of management. Some Guild contracts, for example, allow removal of a byline when the reporter requests. This may appear to be a minor point in the abstract, but in a concrete situation it can be extremely important. Sometimes reporters contend that their patched-up and altered stories are either unprofessional or erroneous, and they don't want their names connected with them. Tentative moves are being made to give the staff a chance to veto management's choice, say, of managing editor. Guild members argue that they know better than the publisher the kind of person they can work with and who meets professional standards. Many European newspaper staffs have such power. So far in the United States, however, only one contract says that the Guild shall be "consulted" when certain top editors will be hired.

The budgeting of news space, like the budgeting of money, is a source of cooperation—and friction—between business management and editorial chiefs. As indicated earlier, the news hole (the amount of space devoted to material other than advertising) varies from day to day. The reading public may not appreciate the need to expand or contract the amount of editorial material as advertising sales go up or down, but all managing editors recognize this fact of publishing life.

To be fair to readers, the managing editor wants some stability in news hole size. Publishers have cause to scream if the percentage of

Budgeting the space

advertising drops to, say, 50 percent. They will go bankrupt if the news hole widens. But it is the managing editor who should scream if advertising goes up to 75 or 80 percent. There is no set proportion suitable for all papers, but the managing editor should get nervous about quality when the news hole drops much below a third. It takes planning and discussion day in and day out to maintain a satisfactory balance.

Even though it does not cost much to set type electronically, it still wastes time and talent—and demoralizes staffers—to have many stories that never are printed. Managing editors can control space, and thereby newspaper income, by careful planning. They usually accomplish this by adjusting the news hole each day. For example, on Monday and Tuesday, when advertising is light, the news hole may be 110 columns. The space for news may jump to 140 on Wednesday and Thursday and drop to 120 on Friday. The new technology plays a role here, too, for it takes little time with modern typesetting to get 20 more columns into type. The extra columns require, of course, more local reports and more wire copy. Both of these take time to produce and process.

Proper use of the news hole demands consultation with subeditors to see whether a few columns in one department can be shifted on certain days to another section. For example, sports demand a lot of space on most weekends, while lifestyle might be able to give up a little space if it can be returned early in the week. Such consultations eventually must bring in the advertising manager so the ad dummy can reflect these planned adjustments each day. The good editor, naturally, will aim to fill the paper with quality news and features even when the space jumps 20 percent. Readers can become irritated if much of what is called news only fills space around all those ads.

A good example of this kind of filler appears in many papers on Wednesday or Thursday when the big grocery ads appear. A "food section," in elaborate color, goes on for twenty pages, sometimes with the news hole filled with pictures of gorgeous dishes, stories containing complicated recipes, and tales of how the well-to-do serve their food. Much of this material is filler to nearly all readers and in some cases is an advertising payoff. Some papers mix into those pages consumer information on how to get the best food buys that week and how to prepare those products into tasty and nutritious meals.

Food, of course, is a part of the editorial smorgasbord that includes national, state, and foreign news; local stories; and all kinds of features. The managing editor usually has the last word on those syndicated features that may range from the humor of Erma Bombeck to Jack Anderson's political column on the editorial page. Most papers buy more of those features than they need so they can take their pick of the lot each day.

More important for editors than allotment of dollars and white space is the budgeting of time, for both their staffs and themselves. It is best if, from the start, editors consider this budget question not in terms of hours and minutes, but of people who work for them. What are their wants and needs? What will satisfy and stimulate them as employees and as human beings working together?

Journalists believe they work on something important, and wise editors run their shops so employees keep sight of this. Their feelings of significance ultimately give them job satisfaction. Good feelings cannot replace good pay, but they do contribute to a quality paper. Editors find ways to help staffers express themselves, such as letting a photographer get that special art shot or a reporter dig into an exposé without fear of losing editorial support.

The good editor operates as democratically as possible, turning decisions over to groups or committees. Such procedure introduces all the well-known shortcomings of democracy—delays, circumventions, slowness. But it also sparks spirit and creativity. One newspaper editor, reminded that the newsroom was shabby, let the Guild unit form a committee to recommend plans for redecoration. The committee members, excited about the task, suggested inexpensive changes that made the place attractive and convenient. Reporters and subeditors alike felt that they had done well on a job normally considered management's baby.

Budgeting the people

Since managing editors are usually the major figures in the newsroom, it is necessary to look at supervision from their point of view. On the smallest papers managing editors do much of the copyediting themselves, lay out the pages, check makeup, and write an occasional editorial or news story. There rarely is enough time or staff quality to do anything first-rate, although a surprising number of little papers do good work.

On big papers the managing editor may have a half dozen assistant managing editors, each supervising a special department, such as foreign news or metro coverage. The managing editor then becomes the chief among subchiefs, examining the whole product critically and prodding top editors to keep looking for ways to improve writing and reporting. At critical times, of course, the chief may move into the middle of the newsroom to direct key editors and reporters.

Managing editors easily can be saddled with all kinds of pesky details, such as time cards, overtime slips, and expense accounts. Unless they are careful they will spend hours each day handling clerical duties. A competent secretary can handle most of these chores, plus writing most letters, and give the ME time to manage. All editors must set priorities so they can do the best with the abilities they have. This may mean giving away one task while taking on another, possibly shedding a job they aren't good at to allow time to do another task better.

The managing editor might find, for example, that hiring a clerk or a copy aide could relieve several staffers of routine work. The

Supervising the team

newsroom may be clumsily arranged so each staffer wastes several minutes each day dodging equipment. A minor shift of the furniture may smooth operations.

Perhaps the staffer writing features for the lifestyle page would bolster the city feature staff, or be ready to come onto the copy desk. Maybe a sportswriter has tired of the job and would like a crack at general assignment under the city editor. The managing editor must ponder such changes if the staff is to be kept alert and stimulated.

Many changes will result from conferences with subeditors. But not any kind of conference will do. A weekly meeting where no one has prepared criticisms or suggestions ends up in a long, tedious bull session, filled with gripes and half-baked ideas. A one-hour session, however, where each subeditor reports on plans for the next month or offers concrete suggestions for change, can yield all kinds of ideas and a sense of cooperative management.

The managing editor also will confer with the advertising manager so the two may gain an appreciation of each other's difficulties and perhaps solve at least some minor production problems. A talk with the circulation manager may result in a slightly earlier deadline for the first edition or a decision to trim coverage in Bogtown because there is no hope of increasing circulation there.

The managing editor must be wary of associating almost exclusively with six or eight subeditors and executives in the business department. Reporters are important, too, and a few chats with them can strengthen relationships and give the ME ideas from other staffers. The managing editor can contribute to staff enthusiasm in little ways, too, such as taking a reporter to lunch, financing a newsroom picnic, or having sandwiches and coffee brought in when much of the staff is on overtime to handle some major event, such as an election.

Most of all, perhaps, the managing editor needs to sense when to do nothing and when to keep still. Sometimes the best change is no change. Certainly an arrogant, all-knowing editor who constantly juggles and shifts will irritate and even enrage a staff, particularly those members who have spent months learning a part of the craft.

Commenting from the writer's viewpoint, Tom Wicker of the *New York Times* has said that the editor must rely on the eyes and ears of the reporters.

> He may point [reporters] where he thinks they should go. He may send them back if they miss the target. He may see, with the sharp eye of his own knowledge and understanding, room for improvement and demand it. But he may not, in the long run, override or ignore the reporter's primacy of knowledge, intimacy of contact, vital instinct of truth, and considered expression of meaning. . . .
>
> [The] editor often can be blind to significance, overcome by the limitations and conditions the newspaper process so copiously imposes on him, and callous of his prime asset—the reporter.

The managing editor should continually review the editorial operation for improvement. What new spot would excite and hold one of the better staffers? Which weak links need replacement? Is a basic reorganization needed?

Editorial hiring is still one of the soft spots of newspaper management. Too often is it hit-or-miss. An opening goes to a person who happens to drop into the office, or to one who persists, rather than to the best journalist available for the salary. Well-organized managing editors watch bylines on papers they can raid. They get acquainted with reporters at newspaper and professional meetings and on university campuses. When they lose a specialist in urban affairs or agriculture, they are able to pick knowledgeably from the best.

Some newspapers recruit in journalism schools, of course, but sometimes they only seek a list of people who might be considered for jobs in a couple of years, when the young reporters have gathered experience on smaller papers.

The editor may promote from within, and morale rises when staffers see that the editor looks around the newsroom to pick someone when a job opens. It may be that the would-be expert on education or the environment is now writing obituaries or society notes. If managing editors take the time to chat with their staff, they will know what their interests and talents are.

The *Dover State News,* a small Delaware paper, encourages staffers to follow their special interests whenever they can spare the time. Each person has an *enterprise beat* in addition to regular tasks. So one covers night life, another special sports, and someone else the *little people*—those who quietly do valuable and interesting things.

Home-grown specialists

Editors with tight budgets rarely can go scouting about the country to snap up one of the four or five best writers in a particular field. They need to develop their own skilled staffers. This can be done outright by asking staffers what they would like to cover if they had the chance. Then the staffer could be given a little time to read in that field, to attend a workshop, or to study at a local college at newspaper expense.

Almost no reporter starts out in a specialized field. Young people get out of college, take a general assignment reporting job or a desk spot, and sometimes by luck stumble into a specialty that fascinates them. They learn on and off the job until they are genuine experts. Young staffers, of course, can prepare for the break when it comes. They can study and observe—and tell the managing editor, for example, "If the courthouse beat is ever open, I'd like a crack at it."

In improving their editorial staffs, imaginative editors may want to particularly emphasize this development of specialists. Here they might take a tip from competing media in shaping goals and the staff to reach them. Recently, magazines devoted to specialized topics— travel, electronics, or boating, for example—have made the most

255

spectacular circulation gains. Public Broadcasting Service offers programs, not for a mass audience, but big segments of the population interested in special topics. Similarly, editors need not feel that every story must interest everyone. Some writers could well devote at least part of their time to cover medicine or psychology or other specialized topics of great interest to an important segment of readers.

Fundamental changes

Sometimes more than shifting and upgrading of staffers is necessary. Fundamental reorganization may be required after careful study. To grow in a changing environment, a newspaper has to change. If suburbs are growing and circulation broadening, the staff must be reshaped to provide different or wider coverage. Are the slums festering and threatening the city's life? Then a reporting team, not just a police reporter, must cover the problem. Are staff leaders so busy or so unimaginative or so locked into routines that coverage is bland and uninspired? Then basic changes have to be made to release new blood and imagination.

If encouraged, good reporters and editors can pinpoint organizational flaws and suggest remedies. Too often, however, innovative editors and reporters have been frustrated by superiors who insist on operating the way the jobs were handled a quarter century ago.

Fortunately, gradual changes are taking place. Traditionally, top reporters were moved into key editing positions. They had no experience or training for the jobs, and sometimes they had no aptitude for them. The result was semichaos until the job was learned, painfully, or some other inexperienced person got the assignment.

Alert publishers have taken steps to assure that middle management gets trained for specific jobs. Assistant city editors, as an illustration, may be sent to a two-week city editor training session at American Press Institute in Reston, Virginia. Or talented staffers may get training for a special job at the Poynter Institute in St. Petersburg, Florida. Northwestern University's Urban Journalism Center and the Knight-Ridder chain offer special instruction in all parts of newspaper management.

Other basic managerial problems have been noted by Norman E. Isaacs, former publisher of the *Wilmington News-Journal* and former editor of the *Louisville Courier-Journal.* He told a convention of the Associated Press Managing Editors' Association that managing editors take on too much work, crowding out time for imaginative thought or even for evaluating the day's paper. He urged managers to spend much of their time training key staff people.

To supervise and reorganize effectively, top editors must have the standards or goals of the paper clearly in mind, for they are not merely managing but managing *to a purpose*. If perfection is impossible, then their target can be at least improvement. The approach of the late Lester Markel, long-time Sunday editor of the *New York Times,* was not "Is it good?" but "What can I do to make it better?" Editors must know where they want the paper to go and have the courage to drive it there.

Gardner (Mike) Cowles, when he was president of the *Des Moines Register* and *Tribune* and editor-in-chief of Cowles Communications, Inc., complained that too many editors are "too careful, too cautious, too fearful of being controversial." Cowles advised young journalists to seek respect, not popularity.

Establishing priorities

These editors must establish priorities. No paper can be all they would like, or even close to it. Something has to give way, something has to be advanced. Editors must have the courage to focus on unpopular social issues but also to decide that no money or energy is available to ride out on this or that hobby horse, though important and influential and even highly moral forces press for it. Wicker has compared the editor's task to the reporter's:

> If the reporter is supposed to get into his story the right things in the right order, no more and no less, to make you hear, to make you feel, to make you see, what he has understood—then the editor has the equally sensitive job of getting the right things in the right order, no more and no less, in the newspaper.

How well editors succeed depends first on how clearly they see and enforce the priorities that will take the paper to its goal.

As they clarify those priorities, editors communicate, not only facts or instructions, but also the *feel* of policies and standards. Then they check how well the communications are heeded. At the end of the workday, many an editor sighs at simply seeing the miracle of getting the paper out again. That sigh is both a confession and a profound self-criticism. Executive editors or managing editors somehow have to organize themselves and their staffs so that they have the time to evaluate as well as marvel at the daily miracle. They must reflect and contemplate on what values are coming across. Only as they seriously ask such questions, day after day, and strive to get them answered right, are editors really dealing effectively with goals and standards. Perhaps the best title for top editorial administrators would not be executive or managing editors but evaluation editors.

18

Newspaper research

THE EDITORS of the *Boston Globe* thought their afternoon paper looked a little drab. The *Chicago Tribune* wanted to find out who read the paper and who might be persuaded to buy it. The *St. Petersburg* (Florida) *Times* decided to find what it is like to be black in its area. The *Dallas Morning News,* locked in a tight circulation battle with the *Dallas Times Herald,* wanted to satisfy readers' needs.

All four papers turned to researchers for answers. The research was not a simple nose count asking a few hundred people a question or two. Instead, the researchers probed deeply, taking time and phrasing questions with care. The results gave each paper solid information on which they made decisions.

At the *Globe,* researchers made up three flashy prototype editions, using big pictures and dramatic features. The three, plus the current *Globe* and the *Globe* of five years before, were shown to hundreds of people. The majority favored the design of the five-year-old paper. Why? Because it had *real news* on the front page. The *Globe* gave up plans to revamp its design.

The *Tribune* found that one in four suburbanites had a college degree. One in five city dwellers hadn't finished high school. Those with more education, as expected, were readers. It was not expected, however, that researchers would find that this group is reading more "with the passing years." It was only sensible that the *Tribune* would direct most of its news coverage toward this group.

The researchers also discovered that the most important single trend was *privatism*—people "are more concerned than before with self, home, and family. Newspapers have interpreted this to mean that people want more of themselves in the news. They need to know how major issues—breadbasket issues like inflation—affect them personally in terms of the costs of merchandise and services and where to find the best buys."

To get information on how blacks in the community lived, the *St. Petersburg Times* polled 884 residents. Twenty-four black and sixteen white pollsters talked to 459 blacks and 425 whites. Their questionnaires had been drafted with care by the paper's research director. The result was an excellent series that reported blacks were doing better than they had a decade ago but, as expected, they had not reached full equality. The series was put into a fifty-eight page booklet.

The *Dallas Morning News* asked readers which sections they read every day, which they read sometimes, and which they never read. The results caused the paper to trim some content and expand others.

These examples show research that can guide reporting, news selection, and newspaper design. Research staffs, which only exist on bigger papers, also collect information that helps other newspaper departments: display advertising, circulation, classified advertising, and promotion. Findings on demographics, car sales, family income, and so forth are shared with business places in their communities.

Papers in smaller cities often hire a researcher to spend a few weeks to a month to get certain information. These researchers may poll a hundred or more newspaper readers to find what the public wants to read, or at least what the public says it wants to read. It is important to remember that there is no one *public*. Readers fall into many categories of interest, and a sharp change in content may antagonize some of them. It is important to discover the *intensity* of reader interest, for a minority of readers may be so devoted to certain parts of the paper that they would quit subscribing if those parts were removed.

Many editors are skeptical of some findings. They realize how some people are fickle, wanting one kind of news one day and the opposite the next. Editors even point to auto companies' opinion sampling that led to the disastrous decisions in the early seventies to keep building big cars.

In addition, some readers will say they want to read things they don't read. They make these claims because it is socially desirable, for example, to indicate interest in foreign affairs or economic issues. Researchers carefully phrase questions to weed out such useless answers.

It probably is not wise to rush into major content or design changes because of one modest poll. On the other hand, shrewd editors do not ignore poll conclusions as they consider adjusting news content to meet changing tastes of readers. Careful and methodical research gives editors reasonably accurate and timely information they could not get by themselves through observation, calculated guesses, or unsystematic interviews.

Newspapers need not spend a lot of money, however, to give reporters, copy editors, and subeditors quick information. Simple polls can be taken by high school students, and adults may question several hundred people on the telephone. Questionnaires can be mailed to several hundred subscribers, but even this relatively simple way of gathering information has pitfalls. It's wise in all these modest polls to consult a researcher at an area university before plunging into such readership surveys.

Before any newspaper dashes off to sign an expensive contract

259

with a research firm, editors might look about to see what kind of information is available under their own roof or no more than a few blocks away.

The obvious place to start is the newspaper's library. If it is inadequate, staff members probably spend hours hunting for information. What they do find may be sketchy or even wrong. A good library, staffed by a competent librarian, can save a newspaper money by saving staff time, and it can greatly improve the paper's content.

The library

Libraries can concentrate on collecting local information, if the paper ties in by computer with super libraries, such as the service available from the *New York Times*. The super library can store all kinds of national and world events and it usually can be obtained by tapping a few keys on a special VDT.

All editors and reporters should have a few files of their own. Clips, magazine articles, book titles, pamphlets, and notes can be slipped into a few folders and pulled forth from time to time to get facts to bolster a story. If these can't be kept in a newsroom drawer, they can be stored in some filing cabinet in the library.

One source of information is the Census Bureau. Editors can find dozens of facts there to help them in their work, and almost all data are free. The Census Bureau, in the *City and County Data Book,* provides information on the average family income of a community, the proportion of people over the age of sixty, the number of people who are college graduates, the number who did not finish high school, the proportion who work in factories, the percentage of the population that is black, and other similar information. The Census Bureau has offices in most big cities, and an interview with a bureau official may provide special insights into the people who live and work in the community.

After reading bureau reports and talking to a bureau official, editors may decide to trim sports a little, add a few more stories of concern to the elderly, select a slightly wider range of foreign stories, and drop a couple of features.

But editors might make grave mistakes if, in making major changes, they add and subtract with only demographic information in mind. Their assumptions may be so wrong that circulation would skid. That's why it is prudent to hire a professional researcher to hunt for human perceptions of news desires, including perceptions that seem illogical, before making serious editorial adjustments.

In one study, *St. Petersburg Times* researchers examined the readership of a story headlined:

U.S. Autos Said Safer Than Foreign Compacts

A picture of colliding cars accompanied the story. The results of the study looked like this:

Readers	Noted (%)	Read (%)
Total	71	60
Men	83	63
Women	78	58
18–39 (age)	75	55
40–64	77	59
65 & over	83	64

It is noteworthy that the picture readership was four to ten percentage points *lower* than story readership.

These percentages may seem low, but of ten stories or pictures on page one, the auto safety story was the second-most read.

This kind of readership polling can offer surprises. One might think, as an illustration, that almost all readers in Florida, where many readers come from other parts of the country, would read listings of temperatures in cities all over the country and Canada. The information was placed conspicuously on page two of the *Times,* yet only 47 percent read it. The figures give other clues, however, for 68 percent of those over 65 read the temperatures. Presumably, older people were most concerned with weather far away, possibly because they did not live in Florida all year. Older people, of course, may have read the whole paper better than the average reader. In this case, also, it would have been essential to tell what time of year the poll was taken. In Florida, a July poll could differ mightily from one taken in January.

With readership facts, editors can make good decisions on news content. They *know* that certain features are read well or poorly. They *know* if letters to the editor are the best-read part of the paper. With this information they can decide, perhaps, to have more of one kind of a story and fewer of another. Editors may decide, however, that if editorials are poorly read it is the fault of the editorials, so the editors try to make them better. If world news gets light readership, perhaps it needs better display or improved editing.

For years the *Chicago Tribune* every six or eight weeks quizzed about two thousand readers on what they liked or disliked about the paper. The results were tabulated in an annual report. This survey revealed that young people desired news capsules; many others wanted a "warmer" paper dealing more with ordinary people; still others wanted more business information. One disturbing fact was uncovered: People are losing their daily reading habit. People will read the paper well for a few days, then barely look at it for a day or two. If this is a nationwide trend, it may have serious effects on the American newspaper.

The *Tribune* interviewed subscribers once a year when it wanted to look thoroughly into readership of a certain section. John Timberlake, the research director at the time, told the author in an interview:

> We probe for the more subtle nuances of attitudes and reactions which a self-administered questionnaire would miss. We have used this approach to uncover attitudes among young readers

261

toward the newspaper, among women to evaluate the family pages, and among all readers to evaluate the Sunday magazine.

Timberlake added significantly,

> We have found that the group research *works best when the editor concerned is involved from study inception to presentation.* In one case, an editor attended all group sessions and participated in the presentation of results to editorial management. Through this involvement, we feel that the editorial people see the research as theirs in a sense and are much more likely to feel comfortable with the results and, most importantly, *to act on the results.*

In recent years the *Tribune* dropped the survey, contending that by the time the findings were tabulated the results were dated. Now research aims to produce information every three months, not every year.

Tribune researchers put readers into four groups: loyal readers, potential readers (those who can be expected to become *Tribune* readers), average readers (those who read it but without zeal), and poor prospects. The paper aims to get the second and third groups into the loyal reader category. This will be accomplished, it is hoped, by altering content slightly and using promotion to appeal to the more casual readers. The paper assumes that there is little chance of luring the fourth bloc into buying the *Tribune*.

When the *Dallas Morning News* examined reader perceptions, researchers discovered that more people hungered for business news, so the daily business section was strengthened and a special section called *Business Tuesday* was inserted weekly. The demand for sports news became insatiable, with professional baseball, basketball, and football in town, so sports coverage was enlarged. Arts and entertainment stories were attracting readers, so that department became a full section and several staffers were hired, including an architecture critic. Dallas researchers also kept their eyes on youth by surveying teen interests and providing stories and sections of special interest for them.

The *Morning News* kept close tabs on readers' shifting concerns. For example, subscribers became distressed when oil prices skidded and became even more diligent readers of oil stories. The price decline produced other stories, mainly on state deficits, tax increases, and business failures. Editors quickly reacted to these changes and provided detailed information on the subjects that touched so many people's pocketbooks.

Nearly all research departments also provide information for stories. The *Times* calls this kind of research the Pinellas Poll, since St. Petersburg is in Pinellas County. The researchers, for example, tabulated data on the area's condominium housing: prices, number of units, number of empty units, and sales. The facts were given to a reporter who put them into a concise story that interested a sizable bloc of readers. Another Pinellas Poll disclosed that automobile sales were sagging. Full information on that story was tabulated, too. Reporters could gather such information, of course, but researchers usually are better at tallying and analyzing data.

The *Tribune* poll sticks closer to opinion polling and is careful to avoid nonscientific methods. For too long newspapers used man-in-the-street interviews or helter-skelter telephoning and tried to pass these off as opinion polling. Fortunately, these kinds of "research" bring so many derisive letters from readers nowadays that most editors have dropped them.

The computer can be of great help in sorting facts for stories. The human brain simply cannot absorb or pull together hundreds of scraps of information the way a computer can. A few papers, as a result, have been willing to let a reporter or a team of reporters meticulously gather facts and feed them into a computer. As an example, a reporter may want to find exactly what prison sentences have been given by area judges. Facts would be tallied on every case of robbery, burglary, assault, theft, and so on that had gone through the local courts for the last five years. The reporter then could give this kind of report: Judge A gave harsher sentences than Judge B. The average sentence for larceny was two years but terms ranged from six months to eight years. White collar crime brought modest sentences. Criminals represented by public defenders most often got severe sentences.

Such comprehensive fact-gathering serves the public well, for it gets the full story, and it takes the wind out of those who spout generalities based on impressions or fragments of information.

The editor without specialized training in communications research may do some simple but useful investigations. Serious opinion research should be left in the hands of professional pollsters, but there are some simple internal investigations where common sense suffices.

Ideally, editors would discuss research ideas with the research staff, but usually there is no such department. If a research department exists, it is often too busy to undertake all the questions an alert editor might raise. Most of the time, then, editors are on their own. As a first step they might take a course or two in research techniques at a nearby university. Certainly they would at least want to read a few books that provide elementary insights (see Bibliography). One does not have to be a statistician to know that five local columnists are too many or that 95 percent foreign news on a front page is too high. Minimal self-education may save an editor from a serious error, such as assuming that valid conclusions on readability can be drawn from calculating Flesch readability scores on two or three stories. Just as important, such research training will help editors interpret the media research findings that come to their attention, including the countless studies now reported on news flow.

What kind of rudimentary research can editors undertake? Front page news is a good place to start. Editors may want to check hunches—that there are not enough humorous stories on page one, for

Elementary behavioral research

example, or that there are too many stories from the state capital. It is no trick to set up a simple method to find out. The editors can establish categories such as local, area, state—or humorous, human interest, serious—depending on the focus. Then they can categorize, count, and record the stories on page one of every issue for a week or two, or every other front page for a month. When they strike a total, find an average, and discover trends and patterns, they have a reasonably accurate picture of the choices editors have been making for the front page. Perhaps emotions about the legislative correspondent, for example, pushed legislative stories to the front. Many questions remain, but at least the editors now have some data, rather than mere impressions, to inform them about future handling of front page news.

Clearly, editors would be foolish to decide that there is too much state government news if their count is made only when the legislature is in session. Editors should check pages throughout the year before generalizing. Common sense should keep them from making unwarranted conclusions.

Use of the news hole is also relatively easy to assess. What hunch—or hypothesis—does the editor want to check? Is too much or too little space going to pictures? Is the sports editor right to gripe that fewer columns are given to sports? Again categories can be set up, and this time the column inches of stories put into each slot are measured and added, perhaps by a copy aide or an eager young reporter. The editor may find, say, that the average daily use of photographs in the paper last month was 130 column inches, or about 10 percent of the paper's average news hole. Is that too much or too little? Did papers with 15 to 20 percent of the news hole given to pictures really look better? A simple ruler points the way for evaluations and decisions.

Or perhaps measurement shows that, because of an unnoticed shift in advertising, the lifestyle editor is actually getting a full column a day more than allowed by the space budget set up three years ago, and the sports editor averages 16 fewer column inches a day. The editor now has data for action.

Reading ease and human interest levels of writing can also be checked, according to the theories discussed in the chapter on writing. Here again it is wise to establish categories first. Perhaps it is useful to know the average score for 500 samples drawn at random from the paper during the last month. It is more useful, however, if 100 samples each are calculated from wire copy, local news, editorials, sports copy, and business writing. Then editors can make comparisons and suggest improvements. They may not be too bothered to discover that a college education is needed to understand some editorials. But they should be upset if readability testing shows that a tenth grader would find the sports reports too difficult.

Some basic studies

While editors probably will want professional researchers to undertake their audience studies, a staff can and should learn about its region through its own digging techniques. One journalism professor required students to research thoroughly the circulation area of some small daily. They wrote Chambers of Commerce, dug through U.S. Agriculture Department reports, and in other ways learned everything possible about their areas—the industries, employment levels, cultural activities, income, and so on. An editor might undertake this kind of research from time to time to check guesses and impressions about shifts in jobs, decline of dairying, rise in incomes, and the like. Such inquiry yields not only story ideas but also a better understanding of the community.

Academic research

It is unfortunate that antipathy exists between professional journalists and academic communications researchers. Practicing journalists often sneer at researchers as "the chi-squares" and researchers snap back that writers and editors can't see past their "green eye shades." Some of the sniping is deserved, even if it is juvenile. Too many journalists are content to keep doing things the way they have been done for thirty years, and too many researchers laboriously hunt the obvious or produce research of slight merit. Many good editors, reading *Journalism Quarterly,* where much of this research is published, sigh and ask, "Who cares?"

Yet once past the practical research done by newspaper staffs and a few others, how else but through academic research will editors find how human beings act or react? How else will they discover how messages are received or why they are ignored? How else but through research will editors grasp at least some understanding of psychological and societal pressures on readers—and staffers?

Journalists need concrete information to help them understand people and how those people can be served better by newspapers. To reach this goal, researchers need to abstain from trite and inconsequential findings and concentrate on shining a little light onto human conditions and journalistic problems.

Actually a number of academic researchers have produced work of direct value to journalists. The late Chilton Bush of Stanford, David Weaver of Indiana, Jack Haskins of Tennessee, and Galen Rarick of Oregon are among those who have turned out research directly helpful to editors. Maxwell McCombs of Texas directs research for the American Newspaper Publishers Association. Because of research, papers moved to the six-column format and 10-point body type. They concentrated on newsier pictures. They tightened writing and dumped outmoded features. Wise editors scan such findings in their quest for ways to make work easier or to help make reading easier. The "impractical" research should not be ignored either, despite frequent temptations, for among perhaps fifty pieces of pure research there may be one that will seriously alter an editor's perception of the world.

It should be noted that journalistic research is not limited to newspaper staffs or academics. The ANPA farms out content research from headquarters in Reston, Virginia, and conducts research of its own there, often seeking ways to reduce printing costs. Some firms handle research on a contract. The famous ones are George Gallup, Lou Harris, Carl J. Nelson Research, Opinion Research, and Market Opinion Research. The Gannett newspapers own the Harris firm.

All these various researchers, using scientific investigation, seek to discover how people act or behave. They try to find why people read one kind of story and not another, why they dislike or like certain papers, why one story is soothing or irritating. Mass communications theory and research are concerned with behavior that affects buying, reading, rejection, anger, pleasure, disgust, and dozens of other human responses. As a subdivision of the behavioral sciences, such as sociology and psychology, mass communications research focuses on people's attitudes and responses to newspapers and other media.

Typically, it is quantitative—it measures and counts, in pursuit of objective knowledge. Statistics help determine the significance of the calculations. If research generally is the careful investigation of a subject, then the researcher in mass communications scientifically studies the way humans act and react with the media—as journalists, decision makers, and readers. Even a study of news display or story content may be viewed as an effort to get at the way such communicators as editors act.

Several kinds of professional research are useful to newspaper editors, though many lack both the money and the time to use such help. Television executives, who depend on rating systems, are much more research oriented, and magazine editors have shown more concern than newspaper people for scientific studies. Still, many editors can find useful information in six areas of research: content, effects and influence, reader interest, audience, graphics, and gatekeeping.

Content analysis

Research on content is similar to the rudimentary studies of front page and news hole. Content analyses can determine accurately the percentages of material on various topics, the balance of news on politicians, the number of times certain concepts are repeated in the news columns, even the number of prejudicial color words in so-called objective accounts. Such analyses help editors ponder the quality of what is published.

Effects and influence

Attitude research is one of the most difficult kinds to conduct, although it probably is most often attempted. If the research succeeds, it can eliminate at least some of the guessing by psychiatrists, parents, business people, and editors. Journalists surely want to know whether editorials persuade and whether their news and feature stories generate much community discussion. An editor can ask family members, friends at lunch, and acquaintances at a party for their reactions, but such queries cannot carry the weight of objective research.

So far, researchers have found that people get a lot of information from the media and that newspapers, in particular, are important in telling people what to think about. Relatively few readers, however, follow editorial advice on what to think. Newspapers and magazines, by their content, do "set agendas" for public concerns. In particular, the agendas are set in areas where readers have no firsthand knowledge or experience with issues.

Reader interest

Finding out what people actually read and what interests them is obviously important, so newspapers frequently judge readership by *reader traffic surveys*. Researchers ask, "Did you happen" to read this or that, and they can come up with percentages of those who "began" or "read most" of a particular story or ad. This gives a rough indication of whether readers were interested.

Some more recent *uses and gratification research* works on the principle that what people read and watch — and their reactions — are functions of their motivation for watching and reading. This lets editors learn whether newspaper content is meeting readers' needs. The research also helps editors learn whether people read articles for unexpected reasons. For example, subscribers may read "people" columns as guides to changes in customs and mores, not out of idle curiosity.

Audience

Because advertisers want to know about readers and listeners, most corporate dollars for communications research go into surveys of the audience. Countless studies tell how many readers are college graduates, own two cars, or buy a major appliance once a year. Apart from commercial value, if a paper makes a good study of this kind for its advertising department, editors should use it to help understand their readers. It is important for them to know, for example, how readership is split among men, women, and teenagers.

Graphics

Studies have been made of which type face and what column widths are best for easy or rapid reading. Graphic arts research overlaps with studies of effects and interest as researchers look into what head type pleases most readers or what ink colors demand attention. Unfortunately, a great deal of typographic expertise is traditional, with experts suggesting only modest changes from what has been done for years. Much more research is needed to find how readers might react to substantial alterations of column width, headline sizes, page design, or use of color.

Gatekeepers

In focusing on the people involved in communication, research looks not only at the receivers but also at the communicators, the senders of messages. Reporters, copy editors, and subeditors all control gates that regulate what part of the news flow gets into the paper, and where. So their perceptions, goals, and prejudices are important. Editors will be wary of testing colleagues psychologically, but studies of gatekeepers in the media generally can give editors clues to the strengths and weaknesses in their own organization.

The research attitude

As research spreads among newspapers, it should influence editorial thinking at every level. The good researcher's emphasis on precision and thoroughness in fact finding matches the journalist's traditional emphasis on care and accuracy. The editor who applies the attitudes of research to the editorial job will think in fresh ways, whether in a story involving statistics or in planning for revolutionary change in the whole operation.

Great care must be used by editors in handling public opinion polls. Scientific polling by Gallup and others has replaced the pseudo-scientific "straw ballots" by individual papers, though some worthless newspaper polls survive as an anachronism. But when a politician or a party commissions scientific polls and releases only such results as they wish—and when they feel they will help most—newspapers have to be alert. Unfortunately, they are sometimes fooled.

Editors play close poll figures as if they revealed a difference, when in fact they do not. The margin of error that wipes out their relevance is ignored too often. In some campaigns candidates often are only one or two percentage points apart. Since margins of error always are three to four points in such polls, these are meaningless spreads. That is, if Candidate X has 39 percent and Candidate Y has 37 or 38, Candidate Y may actually be ahead. Yet newspapers headline the "fact" that X is ahead.

In other ways, polls have embarrassed editors; yet flimsy, contrived polls still get big news play. For example, at least a full year before presidential nominating conventions, pollsters are tallying support for potential candidates. So a headline proclaims:

McGillicuddy Out Front in Presidential Race

The story then lists the candidates and the percentage of support they have among the populace. It may run like this:

McGillicuddy	18
Gates	16
Fry	14
Carlson	12
Knight	10
Undecided	30

268

Such stories are ludicrous. Voters rarely have made up their minds on candidates a year ahead of the conventions. Experience shows that the person on top one month may be at the bottom next month. Often the best-known name goes to the top in early polling. Wouldn't it be much better to use the space to examine the voting record of just one potential candidate?

Or consider the question, "Do you favor the governor's proposed income tax?" The chances are good that only a bare majority is aware of the proposal and that no more than 10 percent really understand the issue. So all that is really found, if respondents are honest, is that people don't know much about public affairs. The *AP/UPI Stylebook* suggests that poll stories include when the survey was taken, the size of the sample, the sampling method, the error margin, and who conducted the poll.

Editors also should make it a point to move outside their own professional and social circles and their own neighborhoods to talk with a cross section of readers. "One of our top editors," says the research director of one large newspaper, "makes it a practice to make the rounds of the many neighborhood pubs to get the feel of the type of person who is a fairly large segment of his audience." Such down-to-earth research can supplement the best computerized study of audience profile.

An editor's starting point for research is a need for more information. There is little point in measuring, questioning, and analyzing just for fun. Research is a problem-solving tool. So what is the problem? Does the editor want to know which cartoons are read or what kind of story dominates the Metro Page? Perhaps the problem demands research beyond the capacity of anyone on the staff, but often a simple method will give a relatively accurate answer.

For example, one managing editor wanted to remodel the editorial page to increase readership. He wrote to some thirty editors in surrounding states for editorial page tearsheets. All but two responded. He checked the topics, the width of the columns, and the size of type. He then incorporated on his own editorial page the best of what he found. It is an example of elementary research that any other editor could profitably follow.

Editors whose papers have research departments should seek solutions to some problems from their own experts, just as they check possible libel with their attorneys. Sometimes they can consult communications researchers, sociologists, psychologists, or statisticians at a nearby university. But for the best handling of scientific research there is no substitute for skill on the editorial staff itself. Future editors will be interested and educated in research, and young staffers already are aware of its value.

In the early seventies, several consulting firms instructed broadcasters how to raise their ratings. A few years later they started advising newspapers on how to attract nonreaders and on how to satisfy more of the prosperous and well-educated readers. These researchers usually made specific suggestions on changing content, such as proposing more "soft" features, more sports, and more business news.

269

The editor, in dealing with these consultants, always must ask whether a particular suggestion is based on research results drawn from the paper's territory and whether the suggested changes will lead to a better paper or only a bigger one. The editor and researcher must work together, but the decision on changing the paper's content and appearance should be the editor's and publisher's, not the researchers'.

Good editors will use research as one of many tools in their kits. Research can give them facts to guide their judgment. Other tools will be experience, education, professionalism, and an ethical sense. Proper use of all these tools will produce an alert, timely, pertinent, and interesting newspaper.

19

The future of editing

CHANGES IN AMERICAN SOCIETY in the last generation are bound to have major effects on the American newspaper in coming years. While the newspaper almost certainly will survive, its influence may wane because fewer people seem interested in public affairs and other media divert attention. Circulation has not risen as fast as population, and many subscribers only skim their newspapers.

The changes thrust upon the press and other institutions can be seen all around us.

Television dominates the spare time of millions, leaving little time for reading. News messages bombard our eyes and ears from radio, TV, newspapers, and magazines until it is difficult to pay attention to anything or to reflect upon what we have seen or heard. Cable television, with its all-news channel, probably reduces newspaper readership.

More than half of the married women work outside the home. Both husband and wife often spend at least a few hours a day with household chores she once did by herself. These tasks cut into time for reading.

Millions of people are barely literate, and the number seems to be rising. The gulf widens between the educated, who read a lot, and those who read little. Editors struggle to try to satisfy both groups.

The American population is mobile, and people often are thirty before they settle long in one place. Late marriages and few children contribute to mobility. People moving from one town to another every few years rarely get interested in a community newspaper. Old people, once more or less ignored, now make up a growing and vocal bloc of the population and newspaper readers.

If it were not for immigration, the nation now would have zero population growth. No longer can publishers expect circulation to grow much, because there will be so few new potential subscribers.

Middle-class flight has caused cities to lose population. As people leave cities to live—and often work—in suburbs, they lose interest in city news. They read a suburban paper instead. The flight has left the city filled with low income, poorly-educated people. They often, as a result, are poor readers and many struggle with English.

Many people are angry at the press because it does not always tell them what they want to hear. In their wrath they tune out certain facts and even cancel newspaper subscriptions.

Television has conditioned us to quick solutions for everything. World problems, of course, drag on and on. The quarrels in Northern Ireland have boiled for decades. East-West frictions have ebbed and flowed since 1945, but they never have gone away. Readers often tire of the seeming repetition of stories about these events and quit paying attention.

Much news seems so complicated to many people. There are all these new countries with strange names. Several nations, so quiet a few years ago, now exercise great world power. Stories on trade, taxes, deficits, and debts sound confusing. The easy solution is to ignore the news.

In particular, these world events have endangered the big-city afternoon papers. Many of their former readers, now in suburbs, read only a morning paper, and city circulation skids. Because it is difficult to deliver papers through afternoon city traffic, some news seems old by the time people get to read the paper. Many workers get home in time for the evening television news and choose TV over a newspaper. Monthly collections make subscribing seem like a considerable expense for poorer people. They gradually look upon the newspaper as both expensive and redundant.

Many papers, often without adequate research, have shifted their content, hoping to adjust to changing readership. They run less government news and more lifestyle features, appealing mostly to those under forty. Even the mighty *New York Times* offers full pages on home decorations, food preparation, and fashion. Newspapers have been redesigned to get the modern, bright, sophisticated look. Columns appear to satisfy the interests of the investor, young women, older people, and travelers.

Greater attention is paid to economic problems, with stories explaining tax avoidance, pension plans, and investments. Many stories are aimed at particular age and interest groups, such as activities for the elderly, young business executives, or noncompetitive sports enthusiasts. Many of these stories appeal to the reasonably well educated and prosperous, for most editors and publishers see these "upscale" readers as their salvation.

Since afternoon papers, even in smaller communities, have had trouble in keeping circulation, about thirty newspapers in the country have shifted to morning publication. They have been satisfied with the switch, for their circulations usually have risen slightly. They are aware that the morning reader glances at the paper over breakfast, possibly steals a few minutes with the paper at work, and then reads it again a time or two in the evening. The afternoon reader looks only once, in late afternoon or evening.

As mentioned earlier, as people moved to the suburbs, many city papers have put out zoned editions, filling part of each edition with news from one locality. Perhaps 15,000 copies are run to satisfy the circulation in one area and another zone fills the needs of another region. These editions are tucked into the main newspaper, with its state, national, and world news.

Since so many people are interested in the arts—theater, books, dance, drama, sculpture, painting, films, and ceramics—most papers have expanded their arts coverage. They have found that these sections draw strong readership. They usually appeal, of course, to the well educated.

Papers also have moved to supply basic information that almost anyone can use at one time or another: movie listings, calendars of events, hotline telephone numbers for various social agencies, guides for tourists, lists of political office holders, and summaries of events that have occurred over many days or weeks.

Looking ahead

The next decade

Most editors probably would agree that newspapers will keep experimenting with content and design in the rest of the century, hoping to find or keep the right formula to maintain circulation and readership. After all, both editors and advertisers want readers who spend twenty-five or thirty minutes with the paper, not those who glance at the front page, run their eyes over the sports page, read the comics, and quit.

Those same editors may even wonder whether it is possible to keep some of those marginal readers. Editors might drop some stories and features designed to keep those subscribers who barely look at the paper. The wise editor will inspect the most successful papers and try to emulate them, assuming that if something works for one paper it may work for another. In general, these changes will take place:

1. Special effort will be made to have one or two front page stories that television will not have.

2. Front pages will have five or six stories and a picture or two. Few stories will be jumped.

3. Each inside page will contain at least one strong story. Readers will be directed to most of those good stories by front page references.

4. Editors will try to put out seven appealing issues a week, instead of perhaps four good and three mediocre ones.

5. Stories of little consequence, like minor crime and accidents, will either be ignored or limited to a couple of paragraphs by the metros. Smaller papers will run basic details of local crime because so many readers are concerned about neighborhood crime. Stories on crime statistics, prisons, criminal justice, and causes of crime will get much attention.

6. Editors will be skeptical of stories that offer easy solutions to

such problems as poverty, crime, pollution, and economic stagnation.

7. Less emphasis will be given to news of the last few hours, and more attention will be placed on summations and analyses of events of the last several weeks.

8. More space will be devoted to the arts, books, and travel. Many people travel throughout the world and are eager to learn more about faraway places.

9. A wider range of opinion will appear on editorial pages. The number of op-ed pages will increase. Most papers are monopolies and wish to show readers that they are willing to print a variety of political and economic views.

10. The popularity of Washington political columnists will continue but other columns, including home-based ones, will be used more.

11. Speculative political stories will be condemned by editors, but their use will continue, for journalists can't break the habit of guessing what will happen *if* certain things occur. Besides, plenty of readers eagerly search for such stories, hoping that the guesses can be used in their own speculations.

12. Government news will expand or shrink as governments become more or less active. Local government stories will emphasize pocketbook issues: taxes, services, and recycling.

13. Papers will use a few more graphics. Smaller papers will be able to make their own quite easily and inexpensively on computers, or they can have the metros transmit timely graphics over telephone lines.

14. The biggest papers also will enlarge their information retrieval sections. They will use computers to store facts and subscribers, mostly businesses, will be able to buy whatever is in the computer. Relatively little of this material will appear in the newspaper.

15. All but the small papers will have staffers who spend much of their workday covering the arts, business, youth culture, education, and labor. Big papers will continue to have specialists; medium-sized papers will have semispecialists.

16. Great effort will be made to keep stories short, but with adequate detail. This will help newspapers compete better with television news, which rarely provides details.

17. Circulation probably will decline slightly as interest in public affairs wanes and literacy programs fail to stimulate newspaper reading. Some papers will deliberately trim circulation, cutting out lower economic groups who have little appeal to advertisers.

18. Picture quality will improve and there will be fewer routine shots. The use of color will increase slightly.

19. Reporters and editors will be a bit more skeptical of what official sources say, but probably not skeptical enough.

20. More attention will be given to news about women, business, economics, minorities, science, nutrition, recreation, and medicine. More stories will deal with trends and economic projections, replacing some one-event stories.

21. Technological change, except for pagination and the electronic camera, will be modest. Most change will consist of refining present equipment.

More than content will change. More newspapers will belong to large chains. The home-owned newspaper will be considered an oddity, or even quaint. Big newspaper chains will continue to expand into other fields—or be bought up by expanding conglomerates.

Big newspapers will expand with satellite plants, possibly threatening circulations of smaller papers. With such plants, people a hundred miles from the big city will get editions at the same time they are available in the city. More papers will have more copy to choose from, for they will get high speed AP and UPI wires, plus several supplemental services.

These prophecies require a reasonably stable world to come true. Wars or other catastrophes could upset every prediction, of course. So could an economic crash, possibly brought on by public and private debt. Widespread feelings of exasperation or frustration might send the country into quarreling factions that would strain the economy and disrupt society. Some anger almost surely would erupt against the press, in those cases, because it is printing so much "bad" news. The recent past indicates that the world in the tail end of the twentieth century might be struck by the worst problems since the end of World War II.

Examining trends

In general, the most financially successful publications have emphasized thoroughness in reporting the news. As noted, papers like the *Washington Post, Philadelphia Inquirer, Boston Globe, Los Angeles Times, Wall Street Journal,* and *New York Times* have enjoyed steady circulation gains. Smaller papers have enlarged their coverage by subscribing to the wire service provided by the *New York Times* or to such supplementary information as the service offered by the *Washington Post* and the *Los Angeles Times.*

There will be exceptions, no doubt, but dull and listless papers and those guessing "what the public wants" will find circulation and readership declining. Several newspapers, once giants, will try to find a formula that will let them regain their prestige and profit.

One educational trend of the last decade is the shift by students from liberal arts to technical fields. Increasingly students direct their training toward a specific career. Some thoughtful editors fear that this trend may narrow interests in a way that could affect newspaper reading. Other editors see no particular threat from the educational shift, noting that college graduates usually are good readers, regardless of their majors. Perhaps another ten years will give editors and educators some solid conclusions.

Training to grow

Along with workshops, special courses, and training sessions, working journalists will be able to continue their education throughout their careers. The most prestigious of these educational opportunities is the Neiman Program at Harvard, which provides a year of study for some thirty journalists annually. No degree is given; students go to classes of their choice and take no examinations. More recently, special periods of study, less than a year, have been set up for experienced journalists at Northwestern and Stanford. The Washington Journalism Center was founded to give more training to young, relatively inexperienced journalists. Other opportunities exist for studies lasting a few weeks or a month. The American Press Institute at Reston, Virginia, offers several seminars a year for specialized groups of working journalists. Some grants allow a journalist to read at a major library for several weeks. Many papers expect their top reporters to read for a few hours a day on company time to keep their minds attuned and, perhaps, to dig up information for stories.

A few newspapers give staff members leaves of absence for study or travel. The academic sabbatical (a leave with pay) may be available occasionally. Perhaps union contracts some day will give journalists two or three months off every five years. For almost a generation union contracts in some other fields have granted such leaves. If this sort of vacation comes to newspapers, journalists would be wise to use the time to improve their knowledge by reading, discussion, and travel, plus the refreshment of mind and body that a change can provide.

True professionalism for tomorrow's newspaper, in short, rests in part on the encouragement of learning and fresh thought among professional journalists as well as journalism students.

Editors need a liberal education in history, philosophy, art, and other humanities. Though critics of journalism schools are sometimes unaware of it, students in such a school get a general education. They receive training in skills and liberal arts to apply to practical journalistic problems involving ethics, creativity, reform, and integrity. Edward W. Barrett, former dean of the Graduate School of Journalism at Columbia University, outlined succinctly, in his presidential address to the Association for Education in Journalism, the ideal education for journalists of the future.

> The primary aim of education for journalism is the development of disciplines, arts, and attitudes of mind.
> The discipline of giving attention to the distasteful as well as the appealing; the discipline of learning to gauge one's best effort to fit an allotted time span; the discipline of continuing self-education.
> The art of expression that is lean, direct, precise, and deft; the art of grappling with a complex new subject, extracting information from inarticulate specialists, and synthesizing the findings faithfully and coherently; the art of recognizing fine points of accuracy and subtle gradations of meaning.
> The attitude of profiting from criticism; and the attitude of

approaching new problems with the open-mindedness and imagination that make solutions possible.

Above all, one seeks the attitude of ruthless fairness, of reporting what he dislikes as honestly as what he likes — in short, true intellectual integrity.

In addition to having both liberal education and professional knowledge of techniques and traditions, the future editor needs to understand the new technology and what it can do for newspapers. The undergraduate journalism student must at least be aware of the trends, but many serious students will want the specialized knowledge that comes from a master's degree or even a doctorate.

Professional prospects

The closure of some newspapers has reduced the number of opportunities for newspaper jobs, even though surviving papers often have increased staffs. Still, experienced journalists are lured into business, government, and public relations jobs, creating openings for the neophyte. The shrinking number of metropolitan papers has meant that journalism graduates will have to start their careers on small or medium-sized dailies. The big-city giants hire almost no one straight out of school.

This situation disappoints some young journalists, who twenty years ago would have been snapped up by the biggest papers. The young should not succumb to dejection, however, for they may get their most valuable and varied experience on smaller papers. Their chances still are good that within six months to a year they will be able to move to a paper that suits them better.

Some young people may find that smaller papers provide interesting and satisfying work. Some of these newspapers give heavy responsibilities to people only a few months out of college. Sometimes these young staffers can see reforms brought about by their stories, pictures, or editorials. Few beginners in city newsrooms have such opportunities. Young journalists, by themselves, sometimes can change a fair paper in a small town into a good one.

Problems of pay

Publishers have long complained that the newspaper business is less profitable than other businesses. This means, they often say, that they cannot pay journalists decent salaries. But is this the truth? Certainly publishers never release their profit statements unless they have to. The big chains that sell stock publicly must announce their profits quarterly; and their profits, even during recessions, have been rising steadily.

While journalists, perhaps like almost everyone else, complain at length about their economic plight, they should realize that many of them are doing well. Even with a better-than-average income, many bright young professionals leave newspapers for much better paying jobs in public relations or television, although it should be noted that most beginning TV jobs pay less than newspaper positions.

To be better, both small and large newspapers will have to invest more in editorial talent. Unfortunately, it seems unlikely that this will occur on most papers. In times of recession, even though newspaper profits stay high, publishers are quick to institute hiring freezes. As people leave a paper, the rest of the staff has to take up the slack. In a matter of weeks a discerning reader can note that stories have been hastily written and some newsworthy events have not been covered.

New trends

Thoughtful editors and publishers often have pondered ways to have outside critics, of judicial mind, examine their newspapers to determine if journalists have been fair and accurate. The aim is to offer redress to those who complain that the press has committed errors and to prod journalists to get the facts straight. Some of the impetus for such a quasi-tribunal came from journalists themselves, for they often note inaccuracies in reports of their speeches and comments.

The British established a press council more than a generation ago and British law requires that all newspapers publish the council's findings. Since Britain is a small, generally cohesive country, it was fairly easy to set up such a board. The council, composed of prominent citizens, hears complaints against the media, weighs the evidence, and issues a report. If the report upholds the complainant, it is assumed that a public scolding will influence the media to be more accurate.

The press council idea was tested in a few communities in the United States, and one was set up statewide in Minnesota. The councils have not been great successes. One publisher noted that council members often sound off on their pet complaints, then have little to do, for so few complaints are filed.

The National News Council, however, in its ten-year life, had modest success, primarily because for a few years its cases were reported at length in the *Columbia Journalism Review*. Unlike the British Press Council, which is financed by the government, the American council got only private contributions, mostly from newspapers and broadcast networks. Council members were journalists from all media plus one or two nonjournalists. They functioned something like a court: hearing a complaint, getting comment from others involved, and reaching a conclusion. No one was required to publish the conclusion, and few newspapers carried the results. Most cases resulted in a finding of "unwarranted," since the complainant lacked enough evidence. In about 20 percent of the cases, the complaint was upheld. The council agreed with the complainant, for example, when it was charged that a columnist had not properly checked sources he was quoting. In another case, a magazine was ruled "guilty" of indicating that a university had not met certain standards that it did not even claim.

Also in the interest of accuracy, about thirty papers have decided to name ombudsmen, or media critics, to their staffs to investigate public complaints and to write a column every few days on their findings. These in-house critics must have real independence as they criticize the editor, stockholders, reporters, and copy editors. If they were under anyone's thumb their value would be eliminated, for readers would quickly spot that at least a few sacred cows were wandering around the newsroom.

Most ombudsmen operated in relative quiet for several years until the famous Janet Cooke case erupted in 1981 at the *Washington Post*. She had written a story about an eight-year-old heroin addict and the story won a Pulitzer Prize. Sadly, the story was a fake, and Cooke had faked her academic credentials as well. After the fraud was discovered and the prize returned, the *Post*'s ombudsman, Bill Green, was "invited" to examine the whole case. Green produced an account of the whole story, and the *Post* ate crow by running his report on page one and four inside pages of a Sunday paper. Green summarized his findings this way:

> Warning signals were ignored; senior editors were uninformed; competition for prizes clouded good judgment; a young talent was pushed too fast; a skilled news organization had a temporary lapse; the paper's most important asset—its credibility—was exposed to ridicule.

Since the *Post* made thousands angry seven years before with its Watergate investigations, the blunder caused the paper's enemies to sneer and jeer. *Post* editors must have expected that, but it was clear to them that they had to lay bare the whole story if the paper was to regain widespread respect. The independent ombudsman was the ideal person to investigate and report on the humiliating episode.

Alfred JaCoby, the *San Diego Union*'s first ombudsman, said that after several years on the job he found that most staffers were eager to see errors corrected. They realized that accuracy and fairness are the hallmarks of their craft. He also noted that the public appreciates the ombudsman concept, sensing that their complaints will get a fair hearing.

Frequently ombudsmen will defend staff actions, gently reporting that the criticisms are unfounded. At other times they may come up with something like this:

> I have examined the complaint of the mayor, who contends that a shortage of $125 in the city clerk's office was grossly overplayed by our paper. We printed fourteen news stories on this shortage, all of them with multicolumn headlines. The total of these stories was 212 column inches. In addition we ran four pictures and wrote one editorial. It seems clear that the staff exaggerated the news value of this relatively minor disclosure, and I would advise cooler analysis of news value in the future.

Publishers, editors, and staffers generally agree that when a newspaper has an ombudsman the paper is saying to the public, "We know we aren't perfect. So an experienced journalist will listen to your complaints. If those complaints are not valid, they will be rejected. If they are valid, the ombudsman will say so and we will print

279

his findings so everyone in town can read them. It is not pleasant to call attention to our flaws, but we can take it."

In years to come most papers can be expected to confess error by printing corrections even in somewhat prominent places. Some have cited flaws and complaints for years. As an example, one newspaper noted: One complainant objected to a story that told about two teenagers killed in a crash. The story said they were high school dropouts. The complaint said that the story implied that the people were "only" dropouts and not important to society. The reporter and copy editor probably never considered such an implication.

One public complaint is that some papers seem haughty, with their editorials, political cartoons, and interpretative stories. Apologies and corrections help relieve that impression and make staffers wary of finding their work mentioned in the "goof box."

There also may be new approaches to public discussion. Newspapers have long had letters-to-the-editor, interviews with the prominent, and statements by experts. With better-educated readers, could a more advanced and valuable kind of open forum be developed? Aside from the "combat page" previously discussed, a newspaper might, for example, pose important questions and then publish written contributions a certain day on a discussion page. The queries might range all the way from "What should the U.S. government do to reduce the deficit?" to "How can our schools be improved?" Perhaps the paper could first print essays by knowledgeable citizens to start the readers writing. Bonuses perhaps would help. One corner might be given to teenage replies. Editors should use their imaginations to stimulate fresher kinds of public discussion than those used for a generation or more.

As pointed out, what the newspaper prints becomes the subject of community argument, and what it ignores may be ignored by the public. To help establish trends instead of always bending with them, alert editors must provide news that focuses the citizens' attention. Do they make readers talk about TV stars? Or do they help them argue about new health hazards?

Newspapers already give serious attention to social and economic issues, so editors who choose to push on in that direction are furthering what appears to be a solid trend. Editors are squeezing the minor news to make room for detailed reports on pollution, education, poverty, military affairs, federal budgeting, economics, welfare, medicine, and urban problems. Lifestyle pages have stories that also appeal to people of all ages. As noted, arts and culture are being covered better than before.

These are healthy trends, and they should continue until 2000. Sharp editors with social consciences will find and print the important news in the future. Better technology and well-trained men and women will enable newspapers to provide stronger leadership to their communities and nation.

GLOSSARY

ABC. Audit Bureau of Circulations, which compiles statistics on *circulation*.

Add. The copy added to a story; also, one *take* or page of a story, such as "Add 1."

Ad side. The section of the business office where advertising is prepared.

Advance. The story written in advance of an event and held for *release;* also, a story written on a forthcoming event.

Agate. Five-and-a-half-*point* type, usually found only in classified advertising or lists.

Agate line. A measurement of advertising depth. Fourteen make one inch.

Air. See *white space.*

Alive. Usable copy or type.

All in hand. The situation when all the copy has been sent to the *composing room.* All pages for the *edition* are *closed* and "ready to roll."

All up. The situation when the *copy editor* or reporter has finished assigned work.

AM. A morning newspaper. The cycle sent by a wire service to morning newspapers.

A-matter. Copy set in advance of the *top* of a story, sometimes called *10-add* material because it is added to *lead* paragraphs of a story.

Angle. The emphasis of a story.

ANPA. American Newspaper Publishers Association.

AP. Associated Press, a cooperative newsgathering organization.

APME. Associated Press Managing Editors association. The editors represent AP member newspapers.

Area composition. Composing a page on a *VDT,* as in *pagination.*

Art. Any illustrative material, such as pictures, graphs, and sketches.

Ascender. The portion of a *lowercase* letter rising above average letter height; contrast to *descender.*

ASNE. American Society of Newspaper Editors.

Audience research. The study of newspaper readers—their education, wealth, etc.

Back room. The *composing room;* usually on smaller papers where it adjoins the newsroom. Also called *back shop.*

Back shop. See *back room.*

Bad break. An unattractive or confusing division of type in a story of more than one column. A column may end with a period, giving the impression that the story has ended, or there may be a prominent *widow.*

Balloon. A device used in comic strips to make words appear to come from a character.

Bank. A part of a headline, sometimes called a *deck* or, if the lower part, a *drop.* Also, a storage place for stories or ads set in type.

Banner. A headline running across, or nearly across, the top of a page; also called *streamer, line, ribbon.*

Bastard type. Type that differs from the standard *point* system.

Beat. The area assigned to a reporter for regular coverage; also, an exclusive story, or *scoop.*

Ben Day. An *engraving* process that provides shading effects in line engravings. Editors use Ben Day mostly for borders on key stories.

BF. The abbreviation for *boldface.*

Binder. A small *banner* across an inside page. It sometimes shelters several related stories; now rare.

Bit. An elementary unit of digital information. Several bits make a *byte,* which can describe one character.

Bite. To cut a story so it fits the space allotted to it. The part cut is called a biteoff or a bite.

Blanket. See *offset.*

Blanket head. A headline covering several stories, each with lesser headlines. See *binder.*

Bleed. To run a *cut* or *engraving* right off the edge of a page; also, the cut so run. Sometimes a cut run to the edge of the outside column is erroneously called a bleed.

Blind ad. A classified ad that gives a box number instead of the advertiser's name.

Blind interview. An interview story that does not reveal the name of the source, referring to him as "an informed official," "an unimpeachable source," etc.

Blow up. To enlarge printed or pictorial matter; the enlargement so made.

Body. The story itself, as distinguished from the headline and the illustration.

Body type. The type normally used for news stories. The size is usually 8-, 9-, or 10-*point.*

Boil or **boil down.** To reduce a story substantially.

Boiler plate. Editorial matter, usually *features* and pictures, once mailed to small papers in matrix or metallic form; a derisive term for poor, inconsequential stories.

Boldface. Dark or heavy type, as distinguished from *lightface;* sometimes called *fullface.* **This is boldface.**

Book. A group of several stories on the same general subject, usually from a wire service. See also *take.*

Border. Column rules surrounding an ad, story, or headline.

Box. To enclose a story or headline with four *rules* to give it more prominence; also, such an enclosure.

Box-all. The instruction to put the headline, *body,* and, possibly, picture of a story in a single *box.*

Break. The division of a story continued from one page to another or from one column to another. Compare *jump, bad break, break-over, wrap, carryover.* Also, a story breaks when an event occurs or when the news becomes available to reporters.

Break-over. The part of a story continued to another page. The page where break-overs are placed is called the break-over page, *carryover,* or *jump page.*

Brite. A short, amusing *feature* story; short for *page brightener.*

Budget. The listing of stories expected by a wire service or by another news-gathering group; also called *news digest.*

Bug. Any fancy typographic device used to break up areas of type, especially in headlines. Compare *dingbat.* Bugs are used with restraint by today's editors. The word also refers to the telegrapher's key and to the label of the International Typographical Union.

Bulldog. The newspaper's first *edition* of the day.

Bullet. A large black dot used for decoration, to separate sections of a story, or, at the left edge of a column, to mark each item in a series.

Bulletin. Important and often unexpected news. In wire service parlance only a *flash* is more important.

Bureau. A subsidiary news-gathering force placed in a smaller community, a state capital, or the national capital by a newspaper or wire service.

Business-office must. A story labeled "must" by the business office, which means the story cannot be omitted. Usually it is a page-one *box* promoting the paper itself.

Byline. The reporter's name atop the story.

C and lc. The abbreviation for "caps and lowercase," used to specify the conventional capitalizing used in ordinary writing; contrast to material marked "caps," which means every letter should be a capital.

C and sc. The abbreviation for "caps and small caps," used to set material all in capitals but with most letters smaller than those "capped."

Canned copy. Prepared news or editorials sent by a *syndicate* or publicity organization.

Caps. The abbreviation for "capitals"; also, *uppercase.* Every letter or a word so marked is capitalized. Compare *C and lc* and *C and sc.*

Caption. A headline appearing above a picture; now, through misuse, commonly a synonym for *cutline,* the words under a picture.

Carryover. See *break-over.*

Catchline. See *guideline.*

Cathode Ray Tube. An electronic device with a keyboard on which stories may be written and edited. The story appears on a screen. The devices, connected to computers, are used in setting type.

Chapel. A union local for printers or press operators.

283

Chi-square. A test of statistical validity; used in communications research.

Circulation. The number of copies a paper sells in a particular *edition;* the department in charge of distributing the paper.

Circus makeup. A now rare newspaper design that uses many large headlines scattered seemingly at random on a page.

City desk. The place where the *city editor* and assistants, if any, work.

City editor. The editor in charge of the reporters covering news within a city and its environs.

City room. The newsroom, where reporters and editors work.

Closed. A page ready to be made into a printing *plate.*

Col. The abbreviation for "column."

Cold type. Print produced photographically. Strips of paper so printed are pasted on a *dummy* and photographed, and a *plate* for a press is made from the negative.

Color. A story with human interest, often describing places and people in detail. But a "colored" story is a biased, or slanted, report.

Column inch. One inch of type one column wide; a standard measure of advertising space for smaller papers.

Column rule. A thin line separating columns.

Composing room. The mechanical department where type is pasted onto *dummies.*

Condensed type. Type narrower than the standard width of a particular type *face,* giving a squeezed appearance; contrast *extended type.*

Content analysis. A research method to analyze published material.

Copy aide. An errand runner in the newsroom.

Copydesk. A desk, frequently horseshoe-shaped, around which *copy editors* sit to edit copy. The *slot,* inside the horseshoe, is in charge.

Copy editor. A person who edits copy; a *copyreader.*

Copyreader. See *copy editor.*

Copy writer. A person who writes advertising copy.

Correspondent. A reporter who files stories from places outside the newspaper's city area. The person may be on salary or may receive a flat fee or a per-inch rate. See also *stringer.*

CQ. An abbreviation for "correct" in copy.

Crash. The computers have failed temporarily.

Credit line. A line acknowledging the source for a story or picture.

Crop. To cut away parts of a picture to eliminate unwanted material or to make it a particular size.

CRT. A *cathode ray tube,* also a *VDT.*

Cub. A beginning journalist.

Cut. To reduce a story's length; compare *bite.* As a noun, an *engraving* and therefore any *art.*

Cutline. Any explanatory material under a piece of *art.* Compare *caption.*

Cutoff rule. A horizontal line used to separate material.

Dateline. The words that give the story's origin and, sometimes, the date on which the story was written, e.g., CHICAGO, AUG. 25. (UPI)—.

Dayside. The shift of day workers in the newsroom.

Dead. Copy or type that will not be used.

Dead bank. A storage area for *dead* type.

Deck. See *bank*.

Descender. The portion of a *lowercase* letter going below the baseline; contrast *ascender*.

Desk chief. The head of a particular desk.

Dingbat. Any typographical device used for decoration. Compare *bug*.

Dinky dash. A short dash used to separate items in a series.

Directory. A listing of stories available in the computer. Sometimes called *menu*.

Diskette. A disk, resembling a phonograph record, on which news material can be stored in an electronic newsroom. See *floppy disk*.

Display ad. All advertising except classified and legal.

District man or **woman.** A reporter covering a particular district of a city or rural area.

Dog watch. See *lobster trick*.

Dope story. An interpretative story often based on background plus speculation.

Doublet. The repetition of some fact; also called *doubleton*.

Doubleton. See *doublet*.

Double-truck. A two-page layout, either news or advertising, that eliminates the margin, or *gutter,* between the pages.

Downstyle. A style with a minimum of capitalization. Contrast *upstyle*.

Drop. See *bank*.

Drop head. A headline with each line stepped (and so also called a *step head*):

**President Says
Budget Deficit
Above Estimate**

Drop line. See *drop head*.

Dummy. A diagram of a newspaper page used to show printers where stories, pictures, and ads are to be placed; occasionally called a *map*.

Dupe. A duplicate, usually a carbon copy; also, a story that appears twice in the same *edition*.

Ear. Upper corners of the front page, often containing a slogan or a weather report.

Edition. Each *run* of a newspaper *issue*. There may be marked editions, early editions, final editions, etc.

Editorial. Generally all the nonadvertising and nonbusiness material or operations of a newspaper; also, one of the opinion essays of the editorial page.

Editorialize. Putting opinion in a story or headline.

Em. The square of the type size. An em in 12-*point* type is 12 points high and 12 points wide. Sometimes erroneously used to mean ⅙ inch; see *pica*.

285

En. Half an *em*.

Engraving. A *plate* from which pictures and drawings may be printed; see *cut*.

Extended type. Type wider than the standard for a particular *face;* contrast *condensed type*.

Extra. A special, or extra, *edition* published because of spectacular news; now rare.

Eye camera. A camera specially arranged to record a reader's eye movements; used in research on design.

Face. A particular design of type; also, the printing surface of type.

Feature. A story emphasizing the human interest or entertainment aspects of a situation; usually in narrative form. Also, material such as columns and comics bought from a *syndicate*. As a verb, it means to give prominence to a story; to emphasize a part of a story.

FF or **ff.** The abbreviation for *fullface*. See *boldface*.

File. To transmit a story by telephone, telegraph, or cable. As a noun, it refers collectively to the back *issues* of a paper; also, one day's production by a wire service.

Filler. Short stories, usually *time copy,* used to fill small spaces in the paper.

First-day story. The first published account of an event.

Flag. The newspaper's *nameplate* or *logotype,* often erroneously called the *masthead*.

Flash. The highest priority of news sent by a wire service; used rarely.

Floppy disk. See *diskette*.

Fluff. Inconsequential material.

Flush. The instructions to set type even, or flush, with a margin; *flush left* means flush with the left margin, *flush right* with the right margin.

Flush head. A headline whose lines are even on the left:

**President Says
Budget Plan
'Unrealistic'**

Fold. The area where a full-sized newspaper is folded.

Folio. The line at the top of the page giving the page number, the name of the newspaper, the city of publication, and the date; also, a measure for legal advertising.

Follow. A story that *follows up* a *first-day story;* also a *second-day story;* also, a story *shirt-tailed* to a similar, but more important, story.

Follow up. A story that gives the latest news of an event reported earlier.

Folo. An abbreviation for "follow." Also see *folo copy*.

Folo copy. The order to set copy in type exactly as written.

Font. A set of particular size and style of type.

Format. The physical appearance of a page, section, or book.

Four-color process. A printing process using four different engraving *plates,* each printing one color — black, red, blue, or yellow — to make natural-looking color.

Fourth estate. The public press.

Front-end system. In the electronic newsroom, all the equipment used prior to platemaking.

Front office. The business office.

Fullface. See *boldface.*

Future. A reminder of a forthcoming event. Such notes are put in a "future book" to be used in making reporting assignments. "Futures" are stories to be used within a few days or weeks.

FYI. The wire service abbreviation for "for your information."

General assignment. A reporter without a beat; available for widely varied stories.

Ghost. A ghostwriter; a person who writes stories or books for others' signatures.

Glossy. A shiny surfaced photograph, best suited for *photoengraving.*

Graf. Short for "paragraph."

Graveyard shift. The work period that covers the early morning hours; also called *lobster trick* or *dog watch.* Staffers on this shift may write and edit, but they are there primarily to cover emergencies.

Gravure. A process for printing from an indented surface. See also *intaglio* and *rotogravure.*

Gray out. A section of a page that has no typographical contrast, giving a gray appearance.

Green eyeshade. A somewhat sentimental term for an old-time newspaper staffer; refers to a former custom among some journalists of wearing green eyeshades.

Guideline. The first word or two of a headline, written at the top of the copy to identify it; also called *catchline.* It is sometimes confused with *slugline.*

Gutter. The margin between facing pages.

Hairline. An extra-thin *rule.*

Halftone. An *engraving* using small dots of varying depth to produce shaded effects, as in photos; contrast to *line cut.*

Handout. A press release.

Hanging indent. A headline with first line set flush left and other lines slightly and equally indented:

**President Says
Budget Plan
'Unrealistic'**

Hard news. Stories based on specific, recent, important events.

Hardware. The physical equipment, such as computer and *VDTs,* in the electronic newsroom.

Head. Short for headline.

Head schedule. A sheet that displays headline types used by the newspaper; it includes the unit count for each type face. Popularly called the *hed sked*.

Head to come. The notice to the composing room that the headline will be sent after the story; abbreviated *HTK* or *HTC*. Now rare.

Head writer. A writer of headlines; usually a *copy editor*.

Hed sked. Short for *head schedule*.

Holdover. See *overset*.

Hole. See *news hole*.

Hot type. Type made from molten metal. Now rare.

House organ. A publication issued by a company primarily for its employees.

HTC or **HTK.** Abbreviations for *head to come*.

Human interest. The quality giving a story wide appeal. It often contains information on human foibles or oddities or heartwarming and sentimental matter.

Hyphenation and justification. The function of a computer that hyphenates words properly and provides space between words so each line is justified. Usually called simply *H and J*.

Indent. To leave extra space on either side of a column.

Index. The summary of the contents or highlights of a paper; usually on page one.

Initial. A large capital letter at the beginning of an article or paragraph, common in magazines but sometimes used for magazine-style matter in newspapers.

Input. Copy or directions put into a computer.

Insert. Copy or type to be inserted into a story.

Intaglio printing. The *gravure* process that prints ink from a depressed surface.

Interface. An electronic connection.

Inverted pyramid. A headline form with each line centered and shorter than the preceding one:

President Reports
Deficit Plan
Today

Also, a news story with facts arranged in descending order of importance.

Issue. One day's newspaper, which may have several *editions*.

Ital. or **itals.** Abbreviations for "italic."

Italic. Type with letters slanted to the right; used for cross references in this glossary. Contrast *roman* and *oblique*.

ITU. International Typographical Union, to which most printers (but not pressmen) belong; now part of Communications Workers of America.

Jim dash. A dash about three *picas* long, often used to separate a regular story and a *shirttail*.

Jump. See *break-over;* also, to continue a story. Compare *break.*

Jump head. The headline over the part of the story that was continued, or *jumped,* to another page.

Jump line. A line noting a story is continued (e.g., Continued on Page 6).

Jump page. See *break-over.*

Justify. To use white space between paragraphs to fill out a column; to space out a line of type so it is *flush* left and right.

K. A measure of computer memory. Stands for 1,000 characters.

Kicker. A few words, usually to the left and above a headline, to give it emphasis; sometimes it serves the same purpose as a *deck.*

Kill. To eliminate all or part of a story. Compare *mandatory kill.*

Label head. A headline, usually without a verb, that only labels the news (e.g., List of Graduates).

Laser. Beams used in newspaper platemaking or in photographic preparations.

Laserphoto. *AP's* picture machine, which uses *laser* beams.

Late watch. See *lobster trick.*

Layout. A planned arrangement of stories and pictures on one subject; also, the whole typographical arrangement of a newspaper.

LC or **lc.** Abbreviations for "lowercase."

Lead (pronounced "led"). The addition of white space to fill a column is called *leading.*

Lead ("leed") **editorial.** The first, and most important, *editorial.*

Leaders ("leeders"). Dots or dashes to take the eye across a column; often used in tables; in British papers, *editorials.*

Leftover. See *overset.*

Legibility. The quality of a type style that makes it easily and quickly comprehended or perceived; contrast *readability.*

Leg person. A reporter who gathers information and telephones it to a *rewrite person.*

Letterpress printing. The process by which ink is transferred to paper from a raised surface; the traditional method of printing.

Letter space. The insertion of thin spaces between letters to *justify* the line.

Library. A collection of clippings, newspaper files, and reference books; formerly called the *morgue.*

Ligature. One character of type that includes more than one letter (e.g., *fl* and *oe*). The initials of the wire services, such as *AP* and *UPI,* are also known as ligatures.

Lightface. The standard darkness of print; the opposite of *boldface.*

Linage. A measure of printed material based on the number of lines; also, the total amount of advertising over a given period of time.

Line. See *banner;* also, *agate line.*

Line cut. An *engraving* that prints only black and white; also called line engraving. Contrast *halftone.*

Line gauge. A printer's ruler.

Linotype. The brand name of a machine, no longer manufactured, which sets hot type one line at a time; also a loose term for all similar machines.

Lithography. The process of printing from ink impressed on a sheet; also called *photolithography.* See also *offset.*

Lobster trick. The shift on duty after the last *edition* of a morning paper has gone to press; the night shift of an afternoon paper. Sometimes called *lobster shift, late watch,* and *dog watch.* See also *graveyard shift* and *nightside.*

Local. A local news item; usually a *personal.*

Localize. To emphasize a local angle in a story.

Locked up. See *closed.*

Log or **logo.** Short for *logotype.*

Logotype. A one-piece line of type or a *plate* bearing a trademark, name, or frequently used phrase. A newspaper's *nameplate,* or *flag,* is a logotype.

Lowercase. The small letters of type.

Magazine style. See *upstyle;* also see *initial.*

Makeover. To make a new page *plate* to correct an error or to include late news; also called *replate.*

Makeup. To arrange type and pictures to produce a desired design. The noun refers to the resulting design.

Makeup editor. An editorial employee stationed in the *composing room* to supervise the *makeup* of the paper.

Mandatory kill. An order from a wire service to eliminate (*kill*) a story, probably because it has a serious error or is libelous.

Map. See *dummy.*

Markets. A section of the paper that includes news of livestock, commodity, and stock markets.

Masthead. A statement of the paper's name, ownership, subscription rate, etc., which usually appears on the editorial page; often confused with *nameplate* or *flag.*

Measure. The length of a line of type or the width of a column.

Menu. A *VDT* listing of available stories.

More. A word placed at the end of a sheet of copy to indicate that the story has not ended.

Morgue. See *library.*

Mortice. An opening, usually rectangular, for the insertion of material, such as an opening in an *engraving* for a heading.

Must. An order from a superior that a certain story must run in the paper that day. See also *business-office must.*

Nameplate. The *logotype* that carries the newspaper's name at the top of page one; also called *flag* and, wrongly, *masthead.*

New lead (pronounced "leed"). Also called *new top.* A fresh opening paragraph or two for a story.

News digest. See *budget.*

News hole. The space in a paper allotted to news reports and illustration, the rest being given to advertisements, comic strips, etc.

New top. See *new lead.*

Nightside. The night shift of a newspaper. See also *lobster trick*.

Nonpareil. Six-*point* type.

Obit. Short for *obituary*.

Obituary. A story reporting a person's death.

Oblique type. Slanted type, but without the handwritten appearance of *italic*. Contrast *roman*.

Offset. A photographic method of printing. Copy is photographed and a *plate* made by "burning" light through the negative onto a sensitized sheet of thin metal. The part exposed to light, or "burned," absorbs ink while the rest of the plate rejects it. The plate, wrapped around a roller, transfers, or offsets, the ink to a rubber roller called a blanket, which actually imprints the paper.

Op-ed or **opp page.** Abbreviations for "the page opposite"; usually the page devoted to columns and *features* and placed opposite the editorial page.

Overset. Set type that cannot be used because space is filled; called *holdover* or *leftover* if it can be used in the next issue.

Pad. To add useless words to stories or headlines.

Page proof. A *proof* of a full page. Such proofs often are taken of the front page, by running it through a copier, before it is made into a *plate*.

Pagination. The process of placing stories on a page by using a *VDT*.

Pasteup. Pasting *cold type* onto camera-copy preparatory to making a printing *plate*.

Personal. A one-paragraph item about minor family news; a kind of *local*.

Photocomposition. A photographic process to set *cold type*.

Photoengraving. See *engraving*.

Photolithography. See *lithography*.

Pica. Twelve-*point* type; also, a printer's measure—one-sixth of an inch. It is also called *pica em* or, wrongly, *em*.

Pica em. See *pica*.

Pick up. The instruction at the bottom of copy to tell the printer to pick up other type and add it to the story. In wire copy, it tells the editor where *adds, inserts,* etc., "pick up" into the story.

Pix. Short for "pictures."

Plate. A metal or plastic-coated sheet from which newspapers are printed.

Play. The typographical emphasis given a story, or the emphasis on a certain fact in a story. Facts or stories can be "played up" or "played down."

PM. An afternoon newspaper.

Point. A type measurement—$\frac{1}{72}$ inch. Hence, 72-point type is 1 inch high, 36-point ½ inch, etc.

Policy. The newspaper's position on how it handles news.

Policy story. A story that supports the newspaper *policy*.

PR. *Public relations*.

Precede. A *new lead* or story, taking precedence over a previous wire service transmission and usually intended to precede it.

Pre-date. An issue printed before its announced date of publication. (Metropolitan morning papers put out an *edition* in the evening with the next day's date on it.)

Preferred position. An advertising term that refers to an advertiser receiving a special place in the paper for his ads. Usually the advertiser pays extra for this preference.

Press agent. A person hired to get favorable publicity for an individual or organization.

Process color. A printing method that mixes primary colors optically to produce a full range of colors.

Proof. An impression taken from type. It allows errors to be spotted and corrections to be made before the paper goes to press.

Proofreader. A now rare employee in the *composing room* who reads and marks *proof* to make sure it conforms to copy.

Public relations. The craft of issuing news of and creating a good image for an individual, agency, or firm; more professional and comprehensive than work of a press agent. Often shortened to PR.

Puff, puffery. A publicity story or a story that contains unwarranted superlatives.

Pullout. A newspaper section, often a *tabloid,* easily pulled from the rest of the paper.

Purge. To erase many stories in computer.

Put to bed. See *all in hand.*

Q. and A. Copy including "question-and-answer" material, as in court testimony or a long interview.

Query. A question raised in a message to a wire service; also, a request by a free-lance writer to see if a newspaper or magazine would be interested in a particular article.

Railroad. To send copy to the *composing room* with little or no editing; to put type in the paper without *proofreading.*

Readability. The quality of copy that makes it easy to grasp; contrast *legibility.*

Readership. Research on the amount of newspaper copy that readers notice or read; also, the people actually reached by a publication, as distinguished from *circulation.*

Readout. A subsidiary headline that "reads out" (explains in more detail) from a *banner.*

Register. The correct placement or matching of *plates* in color printing so colors are exactly where they should be.

Release. The date and time that a news source says information may be released to the public; also, a publicity handout; also, authorization for the use of a photograph.

Replate. See *makeover.*

Reprint. Published material that came from a previous issue or from some other source, such as a magazine.

Retail advertising. Advertising placed by local merchants.

Retouch. To change a photograph, usually to improve it for *engraving,* by painting sections out (or in) with a small brush.

Revamp. To alter a story by shifting some of the paragraphs, but not by rewriting it. See also *rewrite.*

Reverse. Letters or *engravings* printed the opposite of normal, as white letters on a black background.

Reverse-6. The eye tends to scan the news page in a line resembling a reversed number 6.

Revise. A second, and presumably correct, *proof*—made after errors were noted on the first proof.

Rewrite. To write a story again, or to *revamp* a story from a wire service or from another newspaper; also, to write a story telephoned to the newsroom by another reporter. See also *rewrite person.*

Rewrite person. The reporter who takes facts from one or more reporters, usually by telephone, and writes the story; also, a reporter who revises stories written by other reporters.

Ribbon. See *banner.*

Rim. The outside edge of the *copydesk,* which traditionally is horseshoe-shaped.

Rim person. The *copy editor* who sits on the *rim.*

Roman type. The common vertical type that is popularly contrasted to *italic* and technically to *oblique.*

ROP. Short for *run of paper.*

Rule. A strip that prints a line dividing columns, stories, or sections of advertising; usually one or two *points* thick, but see also *hairline.*

Ruled insert. A story that accompanies another but is set off from it by *rules.*

Run. An *edition,* in the sense that the edition is "run"; also, a *beat.*

Running story. A story—actually many stories—continued for several days or more.

Run of paper. An order meaning that an ad, picture, or story could go almost anyplace in the paper. Also, color printed by regular newspaper presses.

Sacred cow. A person or institution unethically deferred to by being given special news treatment.

Sans serif. See *serif.*

SAP. Occasionally used in messages to mean "soon as possible." The superlative SAPPEST is used humorously.

Schedule. A record of stories assigned or already processed.

Scoop. See *beat.*

Screen. A mesh through which pictures are rephotographed in making *engravings* or *cuts.*

Second-day story. A story previously published but carrying a *new lead* or some other revision to make it news. Also see *follow.*

Second front page. Usually the front page of a second section; also called *split page*. Sometimes page two or page three gets the name because it carries important news with little or no advertising.

Sectional story. A story received in pieces or sent to the *composing room* in sections; also, a story that would be of interest only to readers in a certain area.

Send down or **send out.** The direction to send copy to the *composing room*.

Separate. A story related to another and displayed separately, but usually nearby.

Series. Related stories, usually run on consecutive days.

Serif. A tiny finishing stroke or squiggle at the ends of letters in most type faces. A face with simple, square corners is called *sans serif*.

Shirttail. Material added to a major story; also, a short *follow*.

Sidebar. A story that emphasizes one part of a main story and appears alongside it on the page.

Sidelight. A kind of *sidebar,* often dealing with a personality or one aspect of an event.

Side story. See *sidebar.*

Signature. An advertiser's name, often in distinctive type, in the ad; often printed from a *logotype*.

Sizing. Determining the size of an *engraving,* or *cut.*

Skyline. A line running above the *nameplate,* at the top of the page.

Slant. To emphasize a certain part of angle of a story; also, to distort the news. Compare *color*.

Slot. The inside of the horseshoe-shaped *copydesk;* occupied by the slot person, who directs the *copy editors* sitting around the *rim*. Arrangement irrelevant in electronic newsroom.

Slot person. See *slot.*

Slug or **slugline.** A mark on a story, usually one word like "blast" or "money," for identification as it passes through the newsroom and *composing room*.

Small caps. Capital letters smaller than the regular capitals of a particular typeface; used almost exclusively in magazines and books, and rarely there. See also *C and sc.*

Software. The "programming" in a computer.

Solid. Lines of type set without space, or *lead,* between them.

Space grabber. A publicity seeker.

Spike. To eliminate, or *kill,* a story.

Split page. See *second front page.*

Split run. The dividing of a publication *run* into two or more slightly different versions, sometimes for research. For example, to check the effectiveness of a new ad, one version would have the new ad and one would have the old.

Spot news. Information about a specific, recent occurrence, as contrasted to a story about a trend or continually developing situation.

Spread. A prominent display, usually with *art*. Sometimes the large, multicolumn head over the material is called a *spread head*.

Squib. A short news item.

Standing. Material kept in type because it is often needed, such as a column heading or the *nameplate*. A headline used repeatedly, such as the head over baseball standings, is called a standing head or *stet head*.

State editor. The person who edits the news from the newspaper's *circulation* area outside the metropolitan region.

Step head. See *drop head*.

Stet. The abbreviation for "let it stand," written above crossed-out words to indicate that they should be set in type after all.

Stet head. See *standing*.

Stick. A rough measurement meaning about 2 inches of type.

Straight matter. Regular editorial material set in *body type* without variations from convention.

Straight news. A story with only the bare facts, without *color* or interpretation.

Streamer. See *banner*.

String. Newspaper clippings to be added by or for *stringers* to see how much they should be paid. The term comes from saving the clips on a string; as a verb, to work as a stringer.

Stringer. A part-time reporter living outside the newspaper's central area. See also *correspondent*.

Style book or **style sheet.** A specific list of the conventions of spelling, abbreviation, punctuation, capitalization, etc., used by a particular newspaper or wire service.

Sub. A piece of copy that substitutes for something in a previous story.

Subhead. A headline, usually one line of *boldface,* that appears every few paragraphs. It should describe the news in the paragraph or two following.

Symmetry. Page design that balances elements on the page so neither the top nor the bottom, the left nor the right, dominates.

Syndicates. Firms that sell and distribute columns, comics, *features,* and pictures. A wire service technically is a syndicate but is rarely called that.

Tabloid. A newspaper half the size of a regular six-column, 21-inch newspaper. The dimensions usually are five columns by 16 inches. Though some "tabs" are sensational, the term is not a synonym for *yellow journalism*.

Take. A section of copy, usually a page long.

Tear sheet. A newspaper page sent to an advertiser as evidence that the ad was printed.

Telegraph editor. The person who supervises the editing of news from wire services; thus often called the *wire editor*.

Teletype. A machine that automatically types news from a wire service; also called *teleprinter* and *ticker*.

Ten-add. A method for sending details of a story to the *composing room* before sending the *lead*. The initial piece of copy (*take*) is labeled 10-add, the next 11-add, etc.

Think piece. An interpretative article.

Thirty. The end of a story; written –30–.

Thumbnail. A *cut* half a column wide.

Tie-back. A reference in a story to some previous event—to help the reader's memory.

Tie-in. A story or part of a story linked to some other event.

Tight. A situation of little or no room in the whole paper, in a particular story, or in a line. See also *tight line.*

Tight line. A line too crowded for proper spacing between words.

Time copy. Material current for days or weeks and therefore timeless; can be run whenever convenient.

Tombstone. To place similar headlines side by side so the reader tends to read from head to head rather than from head to story.

Top. The first few paragraphs of a story.

Top deck. The main part of a headline.

Trim. To reduce a story carefully.

Turn column. A few papers continue column six, page one, to column one, page two, and eliminate a *jump head.*

Typo. Short for "typographical error."

Undated story. A story with no specific geographical focus such as a war in the Near East, and therefore with no specific dateline. The source of the story is printed at the top, such as "United Press International."

Under-dash material. Prepared stories, principally *obituaries,* ready for publication. When an event makes the story timely, first come a few paragraphs about the event, then a *jim dash* or *dinky dash,* and then the prepared material (under, or following, a dash).

Universal desk. A desk that handles copy from several departments of the paper, usually city, wire, and state.

UPI. United Press International, a commercial newsgathering organization.

Uppercase. See *caps.*

Upstyle. A style that capitalizes more words than most papers do; also called *magazine style.* Contrast *downstyle.*

Urgent. A wire service designation for an important story, but less important than a *bulletin.*

Velox. A commercial product, used to reproduce art for camera-ready copy.

VDT. *Video display terminal.*

Video display terminal. The same as a *Cathode ray tube.*

White space. The blank space, also called *air,* around heads, ad copy, and stories; left blank to make the printed material stand out.

Widow. A one- or two-word line at the end of a paragraph; usually unsightly if the last line of *cutlines* or the first line in a column. See also *bad break.*

Wild. Copy that may run on nearly any inside page. See also *run of paper.*

Wire editor. See *telegraph editor*.

With story. A story or picture running with a bigger story.

Wrap. To place type in two or more columns under a multicolumn headline. See also *break*.

Wrapped up. See *all in hand*.

Wrong font. The designation for a letter of type different from the style used in the story.

Xerography. A process for printing with static electricity and without ink.

Yellow journalism. Sensational and often deliberately inaccurate reporting.

BIBLIOGRAPHY

Editing, general

Baskett, Floyd K., Jack Z. Sissors, and Brian S. Brooks. *The Art of Editing.* 4th ed. New York: Macmillan, 1985.

Berner, R. Thomas. *Editing.* New York: Holt, Rinehart and Winston, 1982.

Copperud, Roy H., and Roy Paul Nelson. *Editing the News.* Dubuque, Iowa: William C. Brown, 1983.

Gibson, Martin L. *Editing in the Electronic Era.* 2d ed. Ames: Iowa State University Press, 1984.

Riblet, Carl, Jr. *The Solid Gold Copy Editor.* Chicago: Aldine, 1972.

Rivers, William L. *News Editing in the '80s.* Belmont, Calif.: Wadsworth, 1983.

Westley, Bruce. *News Editing.* 3d ed. Boston: Houghton Mifflin, 1979.

Communication theory and research

Bogart, Leo. *Polls and the Awareness of Public Opinion.* 2d ed. New Brunswick, N.J.: Transaction Books, 1985.

DeFleur, Melvin L., and Everett E. Dennis. *Understanding Mass Communications.* 2d ed. Boston: Houghton Mifflin, 1985.

Emery, Michael, and Ted Curtis Smythe. *Readings in Mass Communications: Concepts and Issues in the Mass Media.* 6th ed. Dubuque, Iowa: William C. Brown, 1986.

Jamieson, Kathleen Hall, and Karlyn Kohrs Campbell. *The Interplay of Influence: Mass Media & Their Publics in News, Advertising, Politics.* Belmont, Calif.: Wadsworth, 1982.

Rucker, Bryce W. *The First Freedom.* Carbondale: Southern Illinois University Press, 1968.

Siebert, Fred S., Theodore Peterson, and Wilbur Schramm. *Four Theories of the Press.* Urbana: University of Illinois Press, 1963.

Wimmer, Roger D., and Joseph R. Dominick. *Mass Media Research: An Introduction.* Belmont, Calif.: Wadsworth, 1983.

Ethics and law

Aharoni, Dov. *General Sharon's War Against Time Magazine: His Trial and Vindication.* New York: Steimatsky/Shapolsky, 1985.

Braverman, Burt A., and Frances J. Chetwynd. *Information Law: Freedom of Information, Privacy, Open Meetings, Other Access Laws*. New York: Practising Law Institute, 1985.

Christians, Clifford G., Kim B. Rotzoll, and Mark Fackler. *Media Ethics: Cases and Moral Reasoning*. New York: Longman, 1983.

Dill, Barbara. *The Journalist's Handbook on Libel and Privacy*. New York: The Free Press, 1986.

Gillmor, Donald. *Mass Communications Law: Cases and Comment*. 3d ed. St. Paul: West, 1979.

Hulteng, John L. *Playing It Straight*. Chester, Conn.: Globe Pequot Press, 1983.

Overbeck, Wayne, and Rick D. Ullen. *Major Principles of Media Law*. 2d ed. New York: Holt, Rinehart and Winston, 1985.

Sanford, Bruce W. *Libel and Privacy: The Prevention and Defense of Litigation*. New York: Law and Business Inc./Harcourt Brace Jovanovich, 1985.

Writing and style

Baker, Sheridan. *The Practical Stylist*. New York: Thomas Y. Crowell, 1962.

Barzun, Jacque. *Simple and Direct: A Rhetoric for Writers*. New York: Harper & Row, 1975.

Bernstein, Theodore M. *The Careful Writer*. New York: Atheneum, 1965.

Bernstein, Theodore M. *Watch Your Language*. New York: Atheneum, 1965.

Bernstein, Theodore M. *Miss Thistlebottom's Hobgoblins*. New York: Straus and Giroux, 1971.

Bryant, Margaret M., ed. *Current American Usage*. New York: Funk & Wagnalls, 1962.

Callihan, E. L. *Grammar for Journalists*. New York: Ronald, 1957.

Copperud, Roy H. *American Usage*. New York: Van Nostrand Reinhold, 1970.

Flesch, Rudolph. *The Art of Readable Writing*. New York: Harper & Row, 1949.

Flesch, Rudolph. *The ABC of Style*. New York: Harper & Row, 1964.

Follett, Wilson. *Modern American Usage* (edited and completed by Jacques Barzun). New York: Hill & Wang, 1966.

Gowers, Sir Ernest. *Plain Words: Their ABC*. New York: Knopf, 1955.

Kilpatrick, James J. *The Writer's Art*. Kansas City: Andres, McMeel & Parker, 1984.

Newman, Edwin. *Strictly Speaking: Will America Be the Death of English?* Indianapolis: Bobbs-Merrill, 1974.

Safire, William. *I Stand Corrected*. New York: Times Books, 1984.

Strunk, William S., Jr., and E. B. White. *The Elements of Style*. New York: Macmillan, 1959.

Zinsser, William. *On Writing Well*. New York: Harper & Row, 1976.

The Press

Liebling, A. J. *The Press*. New York: Ballantine Books, 1961.

Mollenhoff, Clark R. *Investigative Reporting: From Courthouse to White House*. New York: Macmillan, 1981.

Patterson, Margaret Jones, and Robert H. Russell. *Behind the Lines: Case Studies in Investigative Reporting*. New York: Columbia University Press, 1986.

The People & the Press: A Times-Mirror Investigation of Public Attitudes

Toward the News Media, conducted by the Gallup Organization. Los
Angeles: Times-Mirror, 1986.

Sohn, Ardyth Broadrick, Christine L. Ogan, and John Polich. *Newspaper Leadership.* Englewood Cliffs, N.J.: Prentice-Hall, 1986.

Wolfson, Lewis W. *The Untapped Power of the Press: Explaining Government to the People.* New York: Praeger, 1985.

Typography

Crow, Wendell C. *Communications Graphics.* Englewood Cliffs, N.J.: Prentice-Hall, 1986.

Nelson, Roy Paul. *Publications Design.* 3d ed. Dubuque, Iowa: William C. Brown, 1983.

Society of Newspaper Design. *The Best of Newspaper Design,* 1984–85. 6th ed. Indianapolis: R. J. Berg, 1986.

Photography and picture editing

Benson, Harry, and Gigi Benson. *Harry Benson on Photojournalism.* New York: Harmony Books, 1982.

Evans, Harold. *Picture Editing.* London: Heinemann, 1972.

Feininger, Andreas. *Roots of Art.* New York: Viking, 1975.

Rothstein, Arthur. *Photojournalism.* Philadelphia: Chilton, 1965.

Miscellany

Blum, Eleanor. *Basic Books in the Mass Media.* 2d ed. Urbana: University of Illinois Press, 1980.

Clark, Roy Peter, and Donald Fry, eds. *Best Newspaper Writing 1985.* St. Petersburg, Fla.: Poynter Institute for Media Studies, 1985.

Cudlipp, Hugh. *The Prerogative of the Harlot: Press Barons and Power.* London: Bodley Head, 1980.

Emery, Edwin. *The Press and America.* 3d ed. Englewood Cliffs, N.J.: Prentice-Hall, 1972.

Eveslage, Thomas. *The First Amendment, Free Speech and a Free Press.* Philadelphia: T. Eveslage, 1985.

Heren, Louis. *The Power of the Press?* London: Orbis, 1985.

Hulteng, John L., and Roy Paul Nelson. *The Fourth Estate.* New York: Harper & Row, 1983.

Isaacs, Norman E. *Untended Gates: The Mismanaged Press.* New York: Columbia University Press, 1986.

301

INDEX

Alton Telegraph, 206
American Arbitration Association, 222
American Newspaper Guild, 14, 250–51
American Press Institute, 256, 276
Andropov, Yuri, 133
Areopagitica, 225
Associated Press (AP), 30, 138, 142–45, 163

Baker, Sheridan, 109–10
Banner, 56
Barrett, Edward W., 276–77
Benedict, Stewart, 62–63
Bernstein, Carl, 192
Bites, 102
Blum, Eleanor, 32
Boston Globe, 185, 258, 275
Boston Herald-American, 168
Boys Town, 106–7
Brace makeup, 79
Bryant, Bear, 206
Buchanan, Patrick, 190
Buckley, William F., Jr., 190
Buell, Harold, 163
Burnett, Carol, 206
Butts, Wally, 206

Camera copy, 44
Camera-ready copy, 46
"Canons of Journalism," 225
Carson, Rachel, 194
CBS, 214
Challenger spacecraft, 197
Chicago Sun-Times, 139, 199
Chicago Tribune, 79, 139, 156, 164–65, 179, 237, 258, 261–62
Christian Science Monitor, 125, 240, 242
Circus makeup, 79
City editor, 149
Cleveland Plain Dealer, 16

Color pictures, 178
Color printing, 52
Columbia Journalism Review, 278
Communications Workers of America, 45
Computer-to-plate, 45
Conrad, Paul, 243
Cooke, Janet, 279
Cowles, Gardner (Mike), 257
Cropping, 170–74
Cut, 50

Dallas Morning News, 258–59, 262
Dallas Times Herald, 258
Decks, 59
Desktop publishing, 47
Des Moines Register, 156
Des Moines Tribune, 160
Detroit Free Press, 245
Detroit News, 53
Dover State News, 255
Dry offset, 46
Dummying, 75, 94–103
Dynamic balance, 79

Editor and Publisher, 62
Engraving, 50
Ephron, Nora, 168
Evans, Rowland, 212

Fact, 213
Ferry, W. H., 7
Flesch, Rudolph, 118
Focus makeup, 79
Foreign editor, 160
Forman, Stanley, 168
Fortune, 185

Gallup, George, 193
Gieber, Walter, 8–9

Ginzburg, Ralph, 213
Globe and Mail, 134
Goldwater, Barry, 213–14
Good taste, 228–30
Graphics, 178–79
Green, Bill, 279

Halftone, 50
Hearst, William Randolph, Jr., 238
Hearst, William Randolph, Sr., 238
Horizontal makeup, 59, 77
Houston Chronicle, 109

International News Service, 138
International Typographical Union, 45
Isaacs, Norman E., 256

JaCoby, Alfred, 279
Jersey Journal, 62
Jump head, 73

Kennedy, John F., 3, 142–43
Kenosha News, 199
Keyline, 46
Kicker, 59, 72
Knight, John S., 238

Laserplate, 51
Layout, 75
Leading, 48
Letterpress, 46
Lewis, Anthony, 190
Libel
    classes, 216–17
    definition, 207
    law suits, 206–7, 211–15
    protections, 208–12, 217–18
Lifestyle editor, 149
Line, 56
Line cut, 50
Los Angeles Times, 53, 57, 127, 139,
    157, 185, 195, 243, 275
*Los Angeles Times–Washington Post
    News Service,* 125

McCormick, Colonel "Bertie," 237
McNeil-Lehrer News Hour, 4
Makeup, 75
Makeup editor, 102
Managing editor, 124
Map, 94
Markel, Lester, 257
Mechanical, 46
Milton, John, 225
Minneapolis Tribune, 93, 185

Modular design, 77
Mollenhoff, Clark, 188
Mott, Frank Luther, 112
Mountain Eagle, 5

Nader, Ralph, 131
Nashville Tennessean, 185
National News Council, 278
National Public Radio, 4
Nelson, William Rockhill, 193
Newhouse newspapers, 139
New London Day, 5
News digest, 94, 139–40
New York Daily News, 52, 58, 139
New York Post, 52
New York Times, 15, 16, 20, 25, 52–
    53, 59, 66, 93, 114, 115, 127, 138,
    195, 213, 234, 242, 257, 272, 275
North American Newspaper Alliance,
    139
Novak, Robert, 212

Ochs, Adolph S., 224
Offset, 46
Ombudsman, 278–80

Pagination, 45
Pember, Don R., 221
Penthouse magazine, 206
Philadelphia Inquirer, 127, 275
Picas, 47–48
Plateless printing, 45
Points, 47–48
Powell, Justice Lewis, 212
Poynter Institute, 256
Precedes, 112
Privacy, 230
Proportion wheel, 176
Public Broadcasting Service, 10, 256
Public figure doctrine, 213–16
Pulitzer, Joseph, 236
Pulitzer Prize, 106, 246, 279

Readout, 74
Redmond, Garrett, 218
Reference, 93
Reference books, 31–32
Religious News Service, 168
Reuters, 139
Reverse-6, 76

St. Louis Post-Dispatch, 30, 236
St. Petersburg Times, 15, 185, 258–61
San Diego Union, 279
Sans serif, 59
Saturday Evening Post, 206
Schramm, Wilbur, 184, 239

Scientific American, 185
Scripps-Howard, 139
Sharon, General Ariel, 214–15
Smith, Red, 25
Sports editor, 149
State editor, 149
Streamer, 56
Style, 112
Stylebook, 30
Suburban editor, 149
Sunday editor, 160
Sun Newspapers, 106
Syracuse Herald-Journal, 200
Syracuse Post-Standard, 200

Time, 214–15
Time copy, 102
Times of London, 134

United Press International (UPI), 30,
   138, 142–45, 163

Urban Journalism Center, 256
USA Today, 10, 77

Walker, Stanley, 206
Wall Street Journal, 10, 52–53, 58, 59,
   127, 195, 275
Washington Post, 58, 139, 167, 199–
   200, 245, 275, 279
Westmoreland, General William, 214
White, David Manning, 8
White, William Allen, 126
Wicker, Tom, 118–19, 180, 254
Wide World Photo Service, 168
Wilmington News-Journal, 16, 160
Window, 102
Winners & Sinners, 16, 19, 20, 115
Woodward, Bob, 192
World Almanac, 31
Wyoming, Miss, 206

Zoned editions, 150